To the memory of Meredith Kercher
and to her family members
who still seek justice

*"Do unto others
as you would have them
do unto you."*

Sermon on the Mount
(Matthew 7:12)

AS DONE
UNTO YOU
The Secret Confession of Amanda Knox

Andrew G. Hodges, M. D.

`

Also from Andrew G. Hodges

Jesus: An Interview Across Time
(A Psychiatrist Looks at His Humanity)

The Deeper Intelligence
(The Breakthrough to the Untapped Potential of Your Subconscious Mind)

A Mother Gone Bad
(The Hidden Confession of JonBenet's Killer)

Who Will Speak for JonBenet?
(A New Investigator Reads Between the Lines)

Into The Deep
(The Hidden Confession of Natalee's Killer)

The Obama Confession
(Secret Fear, Secret Fury)

Behind Nazi Lines
(My Father's Heroic Quest to Save 149 WW II POWs)
with Denise George/ release August 2015

Table of Contents

Preface

The forensic profile contained in this book is my expert, professional opinion based on extensive research and experience.

I developed this profile by using a new form of profiling, called "thoughtprint decoding." Thoughtprint decoding was developed as a result of extensive clinical research and experience with the unconscious mind and unconscious communication. It is applied to forensic documents and oral interrogations to identify the unconscious content "built-in" to such communications. I have produced several such profiles in prominent well-known cases utilizing key forensic documents as in this case.

I have reviewed the major forensic documents in this case which are all part of the court record. These include Amanda Knox's email on November 4, 2007, her written statements to the police and diary while in jail, and her court testimonies. In addition I have examined interviews with her and her public comments, researched various books and articles on the case, and reviewed her 2013 memoir.

Introduction

I am a motive specialist. Over decades of conducting therapy, I've developed a reliable method of accessing a person's "super intelligence," a part of the mind far below the surface which invariably speaks the whole truth and nothing but the truth. This is what I do in the world of therapeutic psychiatry, and now I do it in the world of criminal justice. This highly specialized cutting-edge psychoanalysis taps into the vastly superior genius that exists in our unconscious mind.

This super intelligence speaks in a clearly discernible symbolic language to communicate the darkest secrets of a patient or a perpetrator. The super intelligence picks up everything it can perceive--at such speed like a near-omniscient mind--and describes it in a hundred different ways unconsciously matching its story over and over, especially when it has something important to say.

When we apply our knowledge of the super intelligence to forensic profiling, the brilliance with which it speaks is breathtaking. From their methods to their motives, guilty parties always have something to tell you.

To put it simply, murderers *must* confess. They must free themselves from what police call "the prison of the mind." They replay the crime in their conversation and their written missives, but they do so in a coded, vividly symbolic language, but one which can be translated. I call these "thoughtprints."

A thoughtprint is unconscious communication hidden within verbal or written communication. Pay attention to the subject which a person introduces, the big idea not just the literal idea. He or she may link it to someone else: "Ralph was talking about seeing the sharks." The key image, "sharks," must be taken as an unconscious part of a person. Here the key thoughtprint "sharks" could suggest that the speaker is confessing he is the shark or had been deeply wounded by someone who behaved like a shark, or both on different levels of his mind. Both ideas would fit a murderer

> A thoughtprint is unconscious communication hidden within verbal or written communication.

("a shark") who was secretly controlled by a terrifying trauma some key person ("a shark") inflicted on him earlier in life.

In most cases, we find that a perpetrator's past contributed to the commission of a heinous murder. Many of them have been attacked—either emotionally or physically or both—nearly murdered, often more than once.

Funny thing about the mind—it never forgets. The only one way it can begin to forget and forgive is by bringing its secrets to the surface, recognizing its real motives and looking them straight in the eye. Missing motives lie at the center of the Amanda Knox case. Her super intelligence calls for a motive specialist trained in decoding her messages. In her 2013 memoir, *Waiting to be Heard*, Amanda unconsciously begs for her secret confession to be heard. That memoir spills over with her motives as corroborated by other crucial statements she made after the crime. Here is what we hear from Amanda.

A 'New Unconscious'—Waiting to Be Heard

When criminal investigators learn to utilize the most capable part of the human mind, solving major cases will become easier. We now have a new way of profiling that can lead police to perpetrators while explaining the criminal's motives. By decoding messages piece by piece, word by word, investigators can uncover the motives and hidden agendas of people who commit crimes.

Currently law enforcement partially recognizes the unconscious mind's abilities. Police have long utilized hypnosis on witnesses, for instance, to obtain additional information not gathered and retained by the witness's conscious mind. But the super intelligence is far beyond hypnosis and communicates its secret observations in its own unique thoughtprint language.

Police and prosecutors also recognize that killers communicate symbolically when they stage a crime scene. For example, a blanket found covering a deceased victim's body suggests the perpetrator was unconsciously protective and emotionally involved with victim. "Blanket" means caring. This is the killer's super intelligence prompting symbolic action. The next step for law enforcement will be to understand the *verbal* symbolic language—thoughtprint language—which perpetrators use unconsciously.

Now investigators have the capability of reading between the lines of documents in which the perpetrator secretly confesses and provides clues. The recent clinical discovery of a vastly superior unconscious intelligence allows investigators to obtain evidence unavailable from any other source. Investigators will be able to unravel crimes by understanding suspects' unconscious messages. First that means law enforcement personnel must know that a super intelligence exists. Then an investigator must understand the specific encoded thoughtprint language of the unconscious mind including how it continually communicates, how badly a perpetrator unconsciously wishes to tell his story, and how his conscious mind cannot prevent it. In short, a guilty perpetrator confesses to the police in code.

Speaking in Code

The super intelligence—*a strikingly new unconscious*—was discovered in psychotherapy when a brilliant psychoanalyst recognized his patients unknowingly understood themselves better than anyone. They demonstrated a super intelligence that was quick-reading themselves unconsciously in the blink of an eye and revealing to him what they saw in a unique symbolic language. In other words, every patient's super-intel was talking to him in code moment by moment revealing new truths about themselves.

For example, a patient might consciously think he wanted to stop therapy but his super intelligence picked up he still had more about himself to face. The patient would then unknowingly pattern a series of "unfinished business" messages to tell the therapist "I don't need to stop now." Seemingly casual messages such as, "my daughter wants to drop out of college but shouldn't," "I need to finish a major business project." These messages are all matching thoughtprints revealing the stunning clarity of unconscious super-intel thinking. As a result multiple therapists around the world have recognized that their patients were speaking to them in code providing far deeper insight.

Now as an investigator of the human mind, and a clinician trained in unconscious communication, I have applied my experience to a variety of forensic communications— ransom notes, letters, emails, threats, interrogations, phone calls, journals —in which people reveal their secrets between the lines. The super intelligence—which insists on total honesty—presents truths rarely available on a conscious level and clues that typical criminal investigators seldom, if ever, see.

Thoughtprints, like fingerprints, identify facts and point to the perpetrators. When written documents or verbatim oral communications are available, "reading between the lines" enables investigators to create a detailed impression of the perpetrator. Thoughtprint decoding has revealed that *perpetrators unconsciously profile themselves.*

Every single written or oral communication contains two separate trains of thought, and tells two separate stories, one literal and one symbolic. The surface story normally asserts innocence while the hidden story is far more accurate, detailed and truthful, vividly admitting guilt. Now investigators have a strong ally, a trustworthy eye-witness source, in the unconscious mind of a perpetrator who insists on telling the truth without realizing it and no matter how determined he or she is consciously to cover up the truth.

Besides the irresistible inclination to confess between the lines, perpetrators often unconsciously explain their hidden motives. They do this largely in an attempt to understand themselves and why they did what they did. In this book we will see Amanda Knox do just that. *Just as I saw other first time killers do in prominent cases* involving O.J. Simpson, JonBenet Ramsey, Natalee Holloway and Casey Anthony.

4

Put simply, the unconscious super-intel perceives reality in far more detail than the conscious mind and is an expert at analyzing deeper motives. A secret genius light years ahead of the conscious mind. Our super intelligence— the "other 90 percent of the human mind"— sees further, tells more, and remains unfailingly honest.

Chapter 1: Crime-Scene Payback

The Evening of November 1, 2007, Perugia, Italy

Amanda Knox and her new Italian boyfriend, Raffaele Sollecito, stood waiting and watching from a corner of the basketball courts at Piazza Grimana. It was 9:45 p.m., and they were trying to see into the house Amanda rented, a little cottage which sat below them tucked into the bottom of the hill.

They were looking to see if her roommate, Meredith Kercher, was home and alone. Amanda's other two roommates, both Italians, were out of town. They saw no movement in the apartment, but the lights were on which was good.

Meredith seemed to be alone, but they wanted to make sure. They didn't want anyone to see them together, or see either one of them. Which was also good.

It was a quiet night after the rowdy Halloween celebration had rocked all Perugia the night before. Now, the streets were empty just as they'd anticipated.

Nearby Rudy Guede hovered near the piazza, careful to remain out of sight. Amanda and Raffaele didn't want to be seen with him. Both Raffaele and Rudy carried knives. They kept remembering this was all just one big fantasy game, a vampire fantasy game. Amanda brought her Harry Potter look-a-like, Raffaele, to the party to take care of all the evil she had confronted last night at the hands of her stuffy British roommate.

Finally Amanda held up five fingers—signaling to Rudy five minutes—when she and Raffaele headed out to visit Meredith. Rudy was to follow them to the house. Clearly he had been invited to the party, a surprise party in honor of the unsuspecting Meredith. But Amanda and Raffaele wanted to go in together as if nothing were wrong. Her roommate might be a little surprised to see them but not alarmed.

Both Amanda and her boyfriend were high on drugs—but not so high that they didn't have their wits about them. The pot and the cocaine had only gotten them up and ready for their game. Rudy, as usual, was high himself.

Amanda was still steaming over last night and the growing rejection by her roommate. Meredith had crossed the Rubicon as far as Amanda was concerned. Nothing would ever be the same between them.

6

The Game Begins

Entering her house she and Raffaele acted as if nothing were wrong and spoke to Meredith through the open door of her bedroom. They wanted her relaxed. She was trying to study but was tired. Smoothly Amanda suggested she was going to close her door so they didn't bother her, Meredith nodding her assent. They wanted her totally surprised when they took the next step into the little charade they had planned. The fantasy game of all fantasy games, or so they thought. They'd be in and out like vampires, night people who disappear during the day.

Now, seeing Meredith at night exactly 24 hours after she had figuratively stabbed Amanda in the back the sight of her had enraged Amanda far more than she'd anticipated. While Meredith stayed in her room Amanda and Raffaele lingered, whispering in the kitchen.

Amanda was thinking how much she was going to enjoy this payback. Raffaele could still hear the simmering anger in her voice—and assured her that soon the books would be balanced. Meredith would get what was coming to her.

Before long they heard Rudy tap lightly on the door. Covering up the plan, Amanda said loudly to Raffaele, "I forgot something I left outside." Then she whispered to him under her breath, "Let the games begin" just before she let Rudy quietly into the house. He knew the drill. He would wait in the small foyer around the corner from the kitchen until he heard the magic word.

If by chance Meredith saw him he would say that's he was there to bring Amanda and Raffaele some drugs. But Rudy was anxious and moving fast he used the front bathroom where he left feces in the unflushed toilet.

Meredith was sitting in her room when Amanda then entered with Raffaele right behind her, announcing "Surprise. We have a surprise for you."

Amanda had intended to shock and control Meredith who started to stand. Instead Amanda's rage—combined with the adrenaline rush at the start of the game and the drugs—quickly got the best of her, and a one-sided catfight broke out. She pushed Meredith in the face with the palm of her hand against her chin, scratching her several times there before she finally punched her hard, knocking her head against the wall, stunning her, nearly knocking her unconscious.

While Amanda grabbed Meredith, Raffaele quickly flicked open his switchblade and placed it at her throat to control her. In the process Meredith fought back instinctively and the palms of her hands, especially her right hand, sustained a few cuts. Now panicking, Meredith cried out, "What are you doing?" The cat-and-mouse game had started.

Surprise After Surprise

Sarcastically Amanda informed her roommate, "Since you didn't include me with your group I wanted to include you with ours. We have a bigger surprise for you than you know." Forcefully, Amanda announced, "Surprise again! You know 'The Baron.'" On cue Rudy now enters.

After overwhelming Meredith, impulsively Amanda decided she needed a knife herself. While Rudy held her from behind with enough of a chokehold to keep her from screaming and Raffaele controlled her with his knife, Amanda left the room to get a weapon. She hadn't planned to go this far, but emotionally she was already further out on the limb than she had anticipated. She thought to herself, "No time to play around. I might as well take this game to another level. The little bitch deserves it."

> Amanda had intended to shock and control Meredith. Instead, as Meredith started to stand, Amanda's rage got the best of her, and a catfight broke out.

Amanda fumbled in the kitchen drawer to find a knife. She decided on the big one—a big knife would scare Meredith more. Raffaele and Rudy had knives and now she did too. Blood brothers all the way in the game. Still, no blood had really been shed, nor did she intend on shedding any.

Back in the room with Rudy holding Meredith's arms behind her back and Raffaele threatening her with his knife, they had now forced Meredith to the floor on her knees – and then on her back.

But Amanda now had another knife to her throat. Meredith became totally silent.

First Amanda—handing Meredith her purse—forced her to pull the 300 euros out of her wallet to pay her rent. She informed Meredith, "I need a loan. I'm short on cash because Patrick cut my best hours for getting tips on my job—all because of you sucking up to him."

Unexpectedly Amanda then pulled her roommate's blue jeans and panties down, leaving her T-shirt on. Looking at her now completely exposed Amanda commented, "You look like a slut." Pulling the pillow from Meredith's bed underneath the victim Amanda invites Rudy to come warm her up.

Quickly switching places with Rudy she controls Meredith with a chokehold from behind. During these tricky manueverings, with Raffaele holding the knife, Meredith sustains a few more cuts to her hand.

Rudy then pushes Meredith back on the pillow and spreads her legs. Amanda chimes in, "You know you really wanted Rudy all along when you'd seen him downstairs in Giacomo's apartment—you wanted them both, you slut!" At that moment, Rudy digitally penetrates Meredith briefly to prepare her for the action to come. Enjoying the moment—he acts like a teasing gynecologist carrying out a pelvic exam in front of onlookers exposing her as much as possible.

Then, to totally throw her off balance, while holding a knife to her throat, Rudy switched places with Raffaele. Increasingly shocked Meredith makes some effort to get up but can't—her big eyes were now fixated like a deer in the headlights.

With Amanda's gleeful encouragement Raffaele used a condom to rape Meredith—slowly, briefly, but like a vampire with a smile on his face. Just enough to see the terror on her face, long enough to enjoy it but not long enough to ejaculate. Not even close. That was the rule they had all set up. Meredith fought it to a point, getting bruised a bit on her legs, but with the ever-present knife in her face, Meredith is effectively immobilized. Amanda continues holding her arms back.

But almost as quickly as he started the sex, Raffaele stopped after a few minutes. As he got up Meredith really began to fight. During these moments her hands get cut numerous times—with Rudy trying to hold the knife to her throat and control her. Meredith periodically panics but they eventually control her, enough so that Raffaele and Rudy can change positions. The three armed musketeer vampires—in their minds—realize things have already gone too far. With Meredith's hands now bleeding, they realized they were in awfully deep.

Still they themselves remains free of wounds, no bruises really, just a minor cut on Rudy's finger and a long, vertical scratch on Amanda's throat.

Now Rudy assumed the position and opened his pants to begin the second slow dance. He was only going to rape Meredith for a short time—but menacingly—and that would seem like an eternity to her. He was going to make sure she was never really hurt vaginally, but absolutely horrified in her heart.

Just before he started, Amanda suddenly interrupted and made Meredith touch his erection. She commanded, "You prude. You didn't want to touch my vibrator, now touch Rudy."

Near Strangulation
Behind her victim, Amanda clasped both hands around Meredith's throat and alternately squeezed hard, then loosened in a frightful rhythm. Raffaele held Meredith's right arm while Rudy controlled her left.

While Rudy raped her, Meredith suffered Amanda's tireless taunts. "Say it, what did you call me? Say it. Say it...... slut, slut." For a second, Amanda slackened her grasp on her throat to allow Meredith to mumble, "slut."

As did Raffaele, Rudy made his dirty dancing with Meredith short and sweet. He left no obvious trauma, no vaginal bleeding, no definitive signs of rape. But he violated her long and forcefully enough that Meredith would never forget it. After his turn was over, Rudy again had his knife to Meredith's throat along with Raffaele.

Pushing away the blade, Amanda continued choking Meredith, then suddenly letting her breathe. Finally, Amanda goaded, "You won't open your mouth—like last night you wouldn't even speak to me. Speak to me now, you hear? You hear? Or you won't ever speak again!"

With Meredith now near asphyxiation—her red-face turning bluer by the moment, Raffaele yelled at Amanda to stop. She came to her senses, her enormous rage partially discharged. She had left a few red marks on Meredith's neck but nothing bad—besides nearly killing her with her bare hands.

Twin Vampires at Her Throat

Taking turns going after Meredith's neck like cats do, Raffaele continued holding his switchblade against the right side of her throat. Meanwhile Amanda grabbed her knife again holding it against the left side of Meredith's throat. Rudy now controlled their victim from behind.

Amidst her jeering, suddenly Amanda dropped her knife and, covering her finger with a condom, she began more aggressively than she intended sodomizing Meredith who reflexively twisted with the invasion. Toying with her sexually was another surprise attack. Amanda mocked her—"Don't you enjoy inviting strangers home to be your lovers?" She added coyly, "You were so worried about a little shit in the bathroom. Well, what do you think about this? You like it, don't you?"

But, like the rapes, the anal invasion was brutal but brief. Not enough to do any overt harm, just enough to make the point. Just enough to play with Meredith's mind. Cat and mouse—let her go, attack again, let her go, attack again. The three vampires cleverly created one death-like experience after another—their knives always at her neck.

Like a cat after its prey, quick as a fox and true to her name, and in honor of all the vampires Amanda took her large knife back again and held it to the left side of her roommate's neck. Joining her partner, Raffaele, with his trusty switchblade on the right side, they looked like twin vampires waiting to take a bite. Who would go first?

Amanda teased Meredith running the knife blade repeatedly across her throat, derisively whispering, "Remember the fake blood you had on your chin last night on Halloween? How would you like some more, Dracula?"

Waiting a few seconds for the terror to sink in deeper and deeper, wanting her roommate to feel fear she had never before known, Amanda continued, "Who are you going to call now Meredith? You're all alone. Remember last night when I was all alone? How does it feel, sister?"

Now they were at the edge. Meredith had her breath back, barely, but with triple terror. Would they let her go as they'd planned? Shove her back into her bed and be done with it? Would the cats simply drop their prey at the doorstep?

But things had gone on too long, the blades danced too close to Meredith's neck. They were all getting tired, and the terrified Meredith was on the verge of panic and wallowing in pain. As he shifted his weight a bit, Raffaele slipped and his switchblade nicked Meredith underneath her chin. Reflexively, Meredith jerked a way and started a super-human effort to get up. Excited by the blood and angry because his victim moved, Raffaele reacted without even thinking. He drove his blade deep down into the right side of Meredith's neck.

In the flash of an eye, Amanda knew the jig was up. Now their plan was really down the drain— blown to kingdom come, way past cover-up. Explosively, with a violence beyond belief, she plunged her large knife into the left side of Meredith's lower chin and neck with a vicious inward and upward thrust opening a gaping wound all the way into her mouth, exposing her oral cavity and the throat glands in her neck.

She created a wound the size of a mouth—as though Meredith now had two mouths, a new one on the side of her chin and neck. The cut was so deep Amanda severed the right thyroid artery on the other side of Meredith's throat. Amanda literally cut her roommate's throat. Bright, red blood splattered against the wall and poured onto the floor.

In unimaginable distress, Meredith erupts in a piercing scream, resounding through the night air so loudly that neighbors hear it blocks away. She sits up gasping for air but soon falls back against her bed.

Blood continued flowing like an unstoppable river. In shock, Rudy panicked and rushed to retrieve towels from the bathroom. Seeing what they'd done, Raffaele and Amanda decided to lift Meredith's shirt and expose her breasts. Eventually they cut her bra loose in the back after Raffaele failed to unhook it—and removed it. After all, they wanted it to look like a bizarre sadistic sexual attack by a voyeuristic half-crazed lunatic. They believed they'd covered their tracks sexually. At the scene, however, they knew what they saw. But how could they ever guess that Rudy's DNA would be found inside Meredith's vagina from the digital penetration?

Blood droplets from Meredith's wounds now dotted her freshly exposed chest which still heaved with her desperate gasps for air. Losing strength by the minute, Meredith choked on her own blood. She could no longer breathe. She died of asphyxiation before she could bleed out. All three of the fantasyland game-players stood there…and watched her die.

Both Raffaele and Amanda were covered in blood, but Raffaele was more seriously soaked because he'd been on Meredith's right side. And Rudy, who was behind Meredith, also had been splashed with blood that had spurted from the victim's face and neck.

The Cover-Up Begins

Quickly they cleaned up as much as they could. Somebody could've heard the scream, and police would soon be on their way. Amanda and Raffaele cleaned their knives in the bathroom, one in the sink, one in the bidet. Amanda changed clothes and Raffaele showered.

Rudy left to go his own way. Amanda warned him, "You had better keep the secret. Police will suspect a black man did it before us. " Amanda and Raffaele soon left together to return to his apartment, five minutes away. They took Meredith's two cell phones—one local, and one to call home in England. One of them attempted to throw the phones into a nearby valley of brush but failed—and the phones were left exposed.

Returning some time later, again they observed from afar. Since the police hadn't shown up the couple returned to sanitize the crime scene and hide all the evidence they could.

As they moved in and out of Meredith's room, they constantly saw her dead body oozing blood from the gaping wounds they'd caused. They saw the blood in her hair and her open eyes. Eerily the large mouth-like wound and the fixed look in her unseeing eyes reminded the couple of a dead fish. At one point Amanda couldn't endure it any longer. While standing on a towel reaching to get the comforter from Meredith's bed to cover her body, Amanda lost her balance and slipped. To stay standing, Amanda stepped on the pillow behind Meredith's body, leaving a blurry footprint.

The couple wiped down as much of the house as they could. (When evidence technicians later analyzed the scene, they found it strangely devoid of fingerprints. Other crime scene investigators used Luminol to identify several spots of blood the couple had mistakenly thought they had completely wiped away.)

Eventually they locked Meredith's door from the inside using some household trick—hinting the murder was an inside job. But they had no choice but to lock it in order to keep the body from being quickly discovered in case someone came in, even though Amanda knew Meredith never locked or rarely even closed her door when she was alone.

The cover-up continued as they desperately staged an amateurish break-in, making it look as if a burglary had taken place. But nothing was stolen except for Meredith's cell phones – in a non-burglary burglary. They left behind valuable computers and other items not wanting to be caught with them. They left clothes scattered about in one bedroom like a thief might going through things but then not in another. They had hoped police would buy the idea that a criminal threw a ten-pound rock through their roommate, Filomena's, window 13 feet above ground—and scaled a nine-foot wall to enter through the window.

Except they had broken the window from the inside after they had scattered Filomena's clothes about leaving the broken glass on top of the clothes instead of on bottom—as in a real break-in.

Amanda also happened to be at a local store that opened not long after daybreak at 7:45 a.m. to buy cleaning products. A little later that morning the discarded cell phones were discovered. Shortly that brought police to the villa to try to return them to a woman they didn't know was dead.

They found Amanda outside dumping a bucket of water into the gravel. She had obviously been cleaning inside the villa. The washing machine, which she claimed not to have used, was still warm. Eventually Meredith's body was discovered in her locked bedroom after police broke the door down.

There were spots of blood in the bathroom Amanda had not yet cleaned. Meredith's blood by itself and Amanda's blood mixed with Meredith's blood was found in places including Filomena's room where the alleged break-in occurred.

Now we look back to earlier in the day to better understand Amanda's growing rage.

Chapter 2: The Rage Builds

November 1, 2007 10 a.m. Perugia, Italy

The night of the Vampires—All Hallows Eve—had left Amanda Knox feeling abandoned, empty and upset. Boldly clad in monstrous masks and ghoulish costumes, thousands of college kids and townies alike had partied heartily for hours on end the night before across the ancient Umbrian town of Perugia. But not Amanda. Although she costumed herself as a cat complete with whiskers drawn on her cheeks, she spent much of Halloween night trying in vain to connect with her only English-speaking roommate, the vivacious Meredith Kercher, who was out there somewhere dressed as Dracula.

Meredith had failed to answer Amanda's phone calls and texts. Instead she continued to enjoy the company of her other friends and classmates as they drank and danced the night away. She didn't roll home until 5 a.m. Amanda, on the other hand, wandered the streets aimlessly for much of the evening, a cat on the prowl. Since Meredith ignored her messages, Amanda called it a night relatively early, at 2 a.m.

The following morning, Amanda sat brooding in the kitchen of the apartment she shared with three other young women on the upper floor of a cottage at 7 Via della Pergola.

Amanda had only returned to the villa two hours before, at 10 a.m., after staying overnight at Raffaele Sollecito's nearby apartment. It was the seventh night in a row that Amanda had slept in his bed—since the day they met at a Schubert recital.

After arriving at the villa, Amanda talked with one of her two Italian roommates, Filomena who was leaving for the weekend just as the other Italian, Laura, had done. Filomena was anxious to get out of town on this Thursday to visit her family. This was a long weekend which started Nov. 1, "All Saint's Day" also known as "the Day of the Dead," a national holiday in Italy. It was followed on November 2nd by "All Soul's Day" honoring deceased martyrs. A three-day feast celebrated the ritual remembrances.

Amanda had played it cool with Filomena. She gave her roommate no hint that inside she was seething over Meredith Kercher, the 21-year-old British girl who was still sleeping in her bedroom next to the kitchen.

14

Momentarily this Day of the Dead reminded Amanda of how far away she was from own family back in Seattle and of the birthday she had celebrated on July 8th before crossing the ocean to study abroad. For Amanda, November always symbolized the special family time of Thanksgiving which annually preceded the winter. On the other hand, November was always one of the worst two months of the year in Seattle, cold and rainy.

Here in Italy, Amanda was enduring a cold rainy season with her roommate, Meredith. They'd only met six weeks ago, but the relationship had faltered and fizzled. At least today, Amanda knew, she wouldn't have to put up with goody-goody Meredith again tonight. In fact Amanda was hung over emotionally on this All Saints Day. She was strung out and agitated. Halloween in Perugia had been one of the most stressful nights of her life.

She had finally had her fill of her roommate, Meredith, the snobby Brit she could see even more plainly now. She disdained her oh-so-refined English accent and her false smile. Tension between them had been simmering for weeks, and it reached its boiling point on Halloween when Amanda fully realized that Meredith was a completely two-faced hypocrite. While Meredith lay slumbering—after staying out so late on Halloween night with her friends—Amanda sat stewing at the kitchen table. She had been thinking about the night before, thinking about the good time Meredith had and Amanda didn't. Here Meredith was sleeping blissfully away, oblivious to the wounds she had inflicted upon Amanda. Meredith and her friends looked down upon Amanda. They saw her as a loud and obnoxious American.

Amanda thought about barging into the little queen's bedroom and waking up the little bitch. Since Amanda was so restless she considered denying Meredith any more rest.

Meredith had made such a big deal out of Halloween. The always rowdy college town of Perugia was abuzz with raucous excitement, and Meredith reveled in the ambiance of the eerie holiday. She was wild about her vampire costume. Meredith had bought a Count Dracula outfit and added plastic fangs and fake blood. On Halloween she had left their abode at 7 Via della Pergola in the early evening to eat dinner with friends followed by a night of partying.

Meredith was clearly elated about her Halloween plans, but she didn't bother to share her excitement with Amanda. Dressed as Dracula, she left for dinner without even showing Amanda her costume.

Halloween Night

For her part, Amanda decided to dress up like a black cat for Halloween—sweater and pants and face paint. Raffaele had come over to Via della Pergola and painted whiskers on Amanda's face. Amanda had repeatedly texted Meredith trying hard to meet up with her. Already an empty feeling gnawed at Amanda. She grew more frantic by the moment as Meredith ignored her texts—one after another.

But finally a little after 7 p.m. Meredith responded, *"I'm going to a friend's house for dinner. What are your plans?"*—signing off with *"xx love you."* That baker's dozen words had given Amanda hope. She finished dressing up and then headed out into the night. She now hoped that Meredith would continue to reply and invite her to go to a nightclub with them.

Quickly she told Raffaele that she would meet him later at the local gathering place Piazza IV Novembre, but now she had to drop by Le Chic—and wanted to be with Meredith and the other partiers.

Not wanting to appear too anxious, Amanda waited nearly an hour to reply to Meredith. Amanda put it off until just before 8 p.m., when she had just gone out among the partygoers and passed by the crowds at the popular Red Zone Club. So she finally texted Meredith, *"What are you doing this evening? Want to meet up? Got a costume?"*[1] The staccato questions came on the heels of repeated texts which reflected the urgency Amanda felt to be part of Meredith's party.

With no immediate response, Amanda texted again a few minutes later, *"I'm going to Le Chic and after who knows? Maybe we'll meet up? Call me."* Now the doubt had really started to set in—"who knows" and *"maybe* we'll meet up." Amanda was pleading.

She was so needy, desperate to hear Meredith's voice. Repeating "meet *up"* twice subtly suggested Amanda's mood was riding on the matter, she absolutely *needed* a pick-me-up text or call—and pronto. Although Meredith became keenly aware of Amanda's neediness, she never responded to either of Amanda's last texts. But Meredith expressed guilt to her friends for avoiding Amanda on that Halloween night. Obviously Amanda's persistence had affected her.[2]

Shocking Realization—Secret Withdrawal

Growing more frantic by the moment, Amanda suddenly realized that she had dressed up for nothing. Meredith had just dealt her a devastating blow. It was the last thing Amanda had expected, that she would do this to Amanda on such a big night as this—leave her totally alone. Meredith had signed off *"xx love you"*—blowing Amanda off with false affection.

No, what Meredith had shown Amanda was the exact opposite of love. She teased the annoying American by asking "what are your plans?" even though she actually had no interest whatsoever in Amanda's plans. Telling her in essence, "You're not included—oh, you might be—oh, I'm really just kidding." Meredith had answered Amanda's request, "who knows," with the silent message, "I don't know, and I don't care."

The longer it went on the more it was clear to Amanda that Meredith wasn't going to call her. She was going to leave Amanda out there, out on a limb, alone,

---

[1] Amanda Knox, *Waiting To Be Heard,* Harper Collins Publishers, New York, 2013, p. 59.
[2] John Follain, *A Death in Italy*, St. Martin's Press, New York, 2011, p. 51.

all by herself. That was the final straw.

Total rejection. Amanda had been feeling it in recent weeks and especially over the last two days. But this time the rejection was blatant. By not calling her name, not calling her home, Meredith was treating Amanda like an alley cat, like a vile, meaningless little creature who didn't belong anywhere.

After all, Meredith was the one who had gotten Amanda all excited about Halloween in the first place. It was Meredith's favorite night of the year to dress up and party. And it was, by far, the biggest party night of the year in party town Perugia. Then, as the bacchanal gets underway on the big night itself, Meredith pointedly disinvites her. It amounts to an in-your-face, "See what you're missing!"

> Amanda couldn't get past what Meredith had done to her. She went over it and over it in her mind. Even her black cat costume spoke volumes—that Meredith was treating her like a sign of bad luck to be avoided at all costs.

In her mind Amanda envisioned Meredith and all her British buddies at a club—laughing, dancing, and taking pictures of everybody. Everybody except Amanda. Meredith didn't want her in a single photograph. Meredith wanted no memory at all of Amanda on Halloween. Later, back home in South London, Meredith would look back at those pictures nostalgically, completely satisfied that Amanda's face was missing. She didn't want to take any part of Amanda back home.

And Amanda just knew that her British girlfriends were in on it. None of them liked her. None of them wanted her.

But Meredith was her roommate. Amanda couldn't believe that Meredith was treating her as though she didn't even exist. She had totally aborted their relationship—as though they never had one. What a snake!

Anticipating a big evening and then having the rug pulled out from underneath her, Amanda didn't know where to turn. She couldn't take the abuse any longer. These were the thoughts that plagued her on Halloween night. She had to get away and be alone.

Completely uncharacteristic of her, the center-of-attention Amanda was suddenly so distraught she was compelled to withdraw from everybody. Walking the streets by herself Amanda didn't know where she was going, but she headed off into a lonely corner of Perugia not too far from where she worked as a waitress at Le Chic. For several weeks, she had been serving cocktails at the small night club reggae bar owned by 44-year-old Congolese immigrant Patrick Diya Lumumba.

Amanda couldn't get past what Meredith had done to her. She went over it and over it in her mind. It seemed like an eternity. Even her black cat costume spoke volumes—that Meredith was treating her like a sign of bad luck to be avoided at all costs. Running from her.

At one point Amanda was close to tears. Way too close. Unexpectedly she felt the emotion rising, and she grew even more panicky. She rarely cried.

Her near-tears took her straight back to an incident years before when she'd been fighting with her sister as a young teen. Finally Amanda couldn't handle it and totally broke down—sobbing more deeply than she ever had in life. She whimpered and wept for nearly two hours straight. She thought she would ever stop.[3]

It was so frightening. She never wanted to be at that place emotionally, and here she was in Perugia almost there again. Now alone, rejected, unwanted by her surrogate sister Meredith—6,000 miles away from home and her friends in dark November surrounded by foreigners in dreary Perugia. It was altogether just too much.

Somehow Amanda gathered herself together—in spurts. Almost breaking down, then gaining control, then just as quickly almost losing it, pacing back and forth.

Finally she managed to pull herself barely together—enough to stumble off and head toward Le Chic—the one place where they knew her name. But with each step she was determined nobody there would ever see her pain. Never see her cry. Amanda was a master at concealing her real self.

Le Chic to the Merlin and Home

When she arrived at Le Chic two or three hours later, her boss, Patrick Lumumba, noticed right off that Amanda was sucking down the red wine he had opened for Halloween.

In her memoir Amanda told us between the lines all about her emotional devastation at the moment—how she still remembers the pain in the back of her mind, explaining her mood at the bar. Talking about Le Chic she's also talking about what Meredith had done to her that evening.

Amanda writes that she "hung out on the edge of the crowd for a while" at Le Chic, but for some reason she was "feeling a bit flat." Her very words suggested that she still remembers how Meredith had first left her on the edge of the group—then had unexpectedly flattened her, hanging Amanda out to dry. It had made the blow twice as bad.

Amanda went on to describe how she couldn't get into the party at Le Chic which usually had an "empty and desolate feeling," and that the "whole evening felt like a dud." Again implying she was also referring back to the whole downer evening starting beforehand with the enormous rejection by Meredith. Her continuous string of painful images points to the overwhelming effect of the pain Meredith had inflicted on her.

---

[3]Nina Burleigh, *The Fatal Gift of Beauty,* Broadway Paper Paperbacks, New York, 2011, p. 178.

She then alluded to the way the prosecutor had used Meredith's brief text as *"proof"* of their deteriorating relationship but stated, "I didn't expect to be included in everything she did."[4] Pay attention to her blatant denial.

Her dressing up, repeated texts, and marked withdrawal along with her numerous depressing words reveal Amanda indeed had high expectations for being included in Meredith's Halloween plans. If prosecutors wanted an immediate murder motive from Amanda's own words, here it was—and she even underscored the word *"proof"* for them. Certainly, Amanda's rage that eventually played out in the murder had to have been driven by tremendous pain. Amanda had shown us some of it.

Ironically, Amanda entitled her 2013 memoir, *Waiting To Be Heard,* in some way related to the trauma of waiting in vain for Meredith's Halloween-night responses.

Interestingly, Amanda said Le Chic's greeter, Juve, had questioned her about the black cat outfit she wore when she arrived. After Amanda had said, "I'm a kitty cat," and he replied, "You're supposed to be scarier."

Amanda didn't stay at Le Chic long before telling Patrick she was leaving at 12:30 a.m. Then she headed to the Merlin Pub to join her friend, Spyros dubbed "Internet Man," whom she had met at his job. She knew that she might run into Meredith there where the English hung out—but they had just taken their party elsewhere. Amanda never saw her that night but in her mind she could still see them all there earlier partying and taking pictures. A reminder she was not in a single one.

Just one phone call to say "here's where we'll be" was all Amanda needed from Meredith and her gang—but instead she got final abject rejection. It left a bitter taste in Amanda's mouth, a sickly sour feeling deep in the pit of her stomach. She hoped that one day Meredith would taste the same bitterness.

Amanda stayed at the pub a short hour but had no motivation to dance until dawn. All the fun was gone. And Amanda would never forget it—how the night had been stolen from her. She then went to meet Raffaele outside at the Piazza IV Novembre and they were back at his place by 2 a.m.

Setting off Amanda

The tell-tale sign that many have overlooked was that Amanda disappeared for more than two hours on Halloween after dressing up in a black cat costume. That was not at all like her. Something immediate had set her off. Even the prosecutor, Giuliano Mignini, was puzzled. Perceptively he commented that a happy girl didn't go out alone on Halloween in Perugia.

Amanda herself admitted that her sadness began just after she headed out. Clearly she had left her house at 8 p.m. and was only at Le Chic "for a while" before leaving there at 12:30 a.m. Unquestionably it was the most immediate

---

[4] Amanda Knox, *Waiting to Be Heard,* pp. 58-59.

trigger for Amanda's rage was Meredith's enormous rejection. But it had been building.

Six Short Weeks Together

On November 1st in her house as she waited for her roommate, Meredith, to wake up, Amanda continued to think over their relationship. It had only been only been six short weeks since they became roommates on Sept 20th. Meredith had arrived a couple weeks prior, and had already established a circle of friends among her British "home girls." Both foreign students studying abroad, both making the serendipitous choice to rent one of the two single rooms available in the small quaint Italian villa tucked away on the side of a hill minutes from the college. The town square, Piazza Grimana, was only a short walk away. After ending up as accidental roommates, the two women had seemingly hit it off immediately. Amanda thought it was a magical time, an engaging funny and fun-loving Brit and she a free spirit American—on their way to the greatest year of their lives.

Amanda had come to the University for Foreigners in Perugia for students from outside Italy and near the far larger University of Perugia mostly made up of Italians. The two schools combined made up a huge party school filled with Italian men and a melting pot of foreign students. The 40,000 students combined were the town's economic lifeblood.

Now the painful memory of the first time she had met Meredith and her British friends came flooding in—triggered by the fresh rejection Amanda had just experienced last night on Halloween. Amanda had tried to push it out of her mind, but now she could see the die was cast from the start.

It was clear that first night on September 20th, she didn't fit in with them. They had all visited a café for a pizza and wine. Free spiritedly Amanda had burst into song at the table in the café—as she had done before with her friends back in 'hang loose,' uninhibited Seattle. And if looks could have killed, Amanda would have perished on the spot.

The reserved Brits acted shocked and embarrassed, as if she'd just stolen the Queen's Jewels. The uptight Englishwomen had looked down their noses at Amanda—and were still doing it. Gradually they had pulled away from her. And Halloween night was one final rejection.

Meredith, the Sexual Prude

Amanda was put off by Meredith's prudishness. Several times she surmised that Meredith was talking to her friends about Amanda displaying a vibrator and condoms in her transparent beauty case in the bathroom they shared. The little Brit didn't dare want her friends to think it was hers. But she wasn't above borrowing a condom from Amanda one night when she needed one. Yet she simply could not handle Amanda's sexual liberation.

Amanda had also overheard comments Meredith made to her friends about Amanda bringing men home at night, basically calling her a slut.

Then a week before Halloween Amanda had tried to heal the relationship. She invited Meredith to a classical music concert. Meredith went with her but left at intermission to have dinner with friends and didn't invite her American roommate—another message that she was pulling away. Even though Amanda had reached out to her, Meredith couldn't return the favor.

Still that evening at the Schubert concert had worked out because that's when Raffaele, who also appreciated Schubert, asked if he could sit in the empty chair next to Amanda after Meredith left. That was October 25th and started a week of the most intense relationship in their lives. Amanda had become intimately involved with him spending every night with him in his apartment.

He had clearly chosen her over Meredith whose secret competitiveness was now clear in

Amanda's mind. And Meredith never had that kind of closeness with a guy in Perugia. Amanda could see how much Meredith envied her. No wonder she didn't want Amanda around on Halloween. She wanted all the guys to herself.

Meredith, the Jealous Competitor

Then there was their downstairs neighbor, Giacomo. He and Amanda had played guitars and smoked marijuana together. She could see that he really liked her, but Meredith starting competing for him. Amanda had let Meredith have him and casually told her that. Meredith ended up sleeping with him, but in public Giacomo never acted as if they were involved. Yet here was Raffaele publicly declaring his love for Amanda. She was sure that ate at Meredith's core.

It was the same story at Amanda's job where Meredith secretly competed with her. Amanda had been working as a waitress at Le Chic for owner Patrick Lumumba. One night Meredith breezed in and bragged about her drink concoction. She jumped behind Patrick's bar and mixed two rounds of her special little drink—a mojito—and charmed everybody.[5] Especially Patrick, who asked her to come back.

About the same time Patrick had cut Amanda's work back to the slow nights on Tuesday and Thursday nights and hired someone else who could better handle the busier nights.[6]

Amanda strongly suspected he was about to hire Meredith who she now believed coveted her job all along. Again, Meredith was trying to replace her. That demotion remained fresh on Amanda's mind. It had only occurred days before (very possibly one day before on Tuesday night October 30).[7]

---

[5]Paul Russell and Graham Johnson, *Descending Darkness*, Pocket Books, London, 2010, p. 156
[6]Knox, *Waiting to Be Heard,* p. 49
[7]Reports vary. Several authors have reported that around this time Patrick had fired Amanda or made it clear that he planned to do so.

Calling Amanda Names

Amanda thought about how fast and furious Meredith's increasing attacks had picked up. Meredith had pulled another stunt that really stuck in Amanda's craw the day before Halloween—on Tuesday afternoon, October 30th—less than two days ago. She had opened up to all three of her roommates that afternoon about feeling down and a little guilty over having such an intense sexual relationship with Raffaele. After all, Amanda still had a boyfriend back home. Both Filomena and Laura had comforted her, supporting her feminist freedom to enjoy herself, but not Meredith. She had come down upon Amanda with a hammer. Meredith pointedly declared that she herself would never stoop so low as to be unfaithful.

She was judging Amanda in front of others, trying to get them to gang up on her. Trying to convince them how bad she was. And this happened at a moment when Amanda was vulnerable and had exposed her private thoughts.

What a hypocrite Meredith seemed to Amanda. She was a two-faced British prude, sleeping with their downstairs neighbor and now she was pontificating on fidelity.

The Bathroom Brawl

On top of that she just couldn't stop judging Amanda. She had snapped at her again just a few days before about the bathroom. She jumped all over her because Amanda had forgotten to flush the toilet as she occasionally did—like sometimes they did back in Seattle to conserve water. Meredith was upset because Amanda hadn't scoured the bowl. Meredith fell apart over this little nothing. She had a toilet fixation.

She was so anal—a little anal prude. The little "shit!" Amanda just knew Meredith was talking to her friends about this too—implying she was trashy. Trashy!

Then Meredith ganged up with Amanda's other two roommates behind her back, and they formed a cleaning squad, assigning clean-up duties. What a back-stabber she was.

Meredith Risks Amanda's Life

Of course Meredith had forgotten all about what she had done to Amanda. Like the time she scared the American half to death. Amanda always had someone from work walk her home in the dark as she had to pass through a seedy part of town. No one was around to help, and Amanda had asked a guy named "Shakey" who knew Meredith. After Amanda jumped on his motor scooter, Shakey then refused to take her straight home and drove her to his apartment in a strange part of town. He ended up coercing her to wait inside and then into his bedroom trying to entice her into intercourse.

Finally Amanda convinced him to take her home. When she got there she was furious—and had been really scared. She burst into their house to tell

Meredith about it only to find out that Meredith had known the guy pulled this maneuver before on another female friend. But Meredith hadn't warned Amanda about that side of Shakey—and had instead set her up to be terrified. Lost, trapped, and betrayed all because of Meredith.

And Meredith knew about Amanda's terrifying experience her first day in Perugia when Amanda and her sister had gotten lost outside town and had to hitch a ride with a stranger. The man had kept trying to get Amanda and her sister to visit his place. She realized they were totally at his mercy. He could have pulled a gun or kidnapped them or killed them. The longer she had been in the car the more frightened she became. Finally he took them to her hotel. Amanda never wanted to feel that entrapped again. But Meredith had done the same thing to her.

Stealing

Meredith was taking everything she could from Amanda. Her reputation, a potential boyfriend, her boss and job, the other roommates and once—when Shakey totally tricked her—it felt as if Meredith nearly took her life.

Meredith was taking away her fun, her excitement over Perugia, and trying to take away her freedom. She was making life miserable for Amanda—always with some surprise.

Now she had undermined Amanda's employment. She had been "so charming," sucking up to Patrick, that Amanda would find her hours cut back. She felt on the verge of being fired. Amanda thought about stealing Meredith's money just to teach her a lesson. Let her feel the shock of somebody intruding into her private world. She deserved to lose the money after taking over Amanda's job.

And surely Amanda needed the money. Obviously she hadn't managed her money well and didn't have enough money to last her anywhere close to her remaining seven months in school.[8] And then she had been spending money on drugs, too.

Meredith Awakens

Back in her kitchen, as the past 18 hours continued reverberating through Amanda's mind, her roommate continued to doze, blissfully oblivious to the wounds she'd inflicted upon Amanda.

"Watch her, Meredith will come out with her smiley face on, acting as if nothing is wrong, acting like nothing happened," Amanda thought to herself.

Finally when Meredith awakened around 2 p.m. she came out of her bedroom with the fake blood of a vampire from the night before still on her face. She had fallen into her bed when she rolled home in the wee hours of that

---

[8]After paying her November rent Amanda had 3000 euros to last seven months or 425 euros/month. Her rent cost her 300 euros each month.

morning—too tired to take off her costume makeup.

Just as Amanda predicted, a still sleepy and hungover Meredith smiled and greeted her pleasantly. Amanda commented on the vampire blood still painted on Meredith's face, now running down her chin. How that chin stuck in her mind because she had not yet seen the Halloween costume Meredith bought.

Then Amanda couldn't wait any longer to bring up the previous night herself. She inquired, "What did you end up doing last night?" (We keep in mind Amanda's idea of where Meredith ended up.) Her roommate told her about the amazing dinner party with a frozen surgical glove filled with water to make an ice hand—so "cool floating in punch bowl."[9] She asked about Amanda's night. The American admitted, "My Halloween was lame—I was mostly bored." Amanda had reminded Meredith of how bad it was. She suggested the subtle message: I was crippled by your blow. I was bored, all alone with nothing to do.

But Meredith's striking image of a surgical glove, resembling an amputated hand floating in a pool of liquid, a strong suggestion of cutting and being cut by a knife. That image virtually shouted that intuitively she had unconsciously realized that Amanda was dangerous.

Really dangerous. Amputation suggests severe violence, bodily mutilation and also death—one step away from a body floating in a pool of water. Also Meredith told the story to Amanda, linking it to her. Consciously covering it over with a light story, Meredith unconsciously sensed she had a tiger by the tail. Meredith's super-intel informs us deep down she knew by now Amanda was capable of murder. Her guilt over not returning Amanda's phone call was also a warning sign. Yet not returning the call reflected Meredith's continued anger at Amanda—over her provocative disrespectful behavior—causing Meredith to discount her instincts.

At that point Meredith said she had plans for an early dinner with friends and went to take a shower. While Meredith was bathing, Amanda thought again about what a secret vampire her roommate was. How well the fake blood fit "Miss Fake" herself. She was sucking the blood out of Amanda with a little help from her friends—vampire friends.

She had the urge to go into the small bathroom and grab Meredith's head—hold it not only under the shower but underwater. Maybe stick her head in the toilet.

After her shower, Meredith left fairly quickly to go meet her friends. She had little idea if any Amanda was secretly steaming—as though she could chew nails. As Meredith walked out around 4 p.m. once again leaving Amanda, it was a vivid reminder of her casual sneaky two-faced departure the day before—and the ultimate in betrayal. She never once had apologized for failing to call Amanda back last night, just went on her way.

---

[9]Knox, *Waiting to Be Heard*, p. 60.

It would be the last time she would see Meredith that day. But maybe not, Amanda started thinking in the back of her mind.

Raffaele Arrives

In the meantime Raffaele had arrived while Meredith was preparing to go out. He too witnessed her leaving. He had no idea that Amanda had gone into payback overdrive, a plan starting to take shape in her mind.

Amanda and Raffaele immediately lit up some "marijuana pasta." (In her memoir Amanda reported that in her house in Perugia "marijuana was as common as pasta."[10]) Amanda knew about Raffaele losing his mother two short years ago—and knew today might be a hard day for him, an Italian steeped in the All Saint's holiday.

They began discussing their past and Raffaele was reminded of his deep guilt over his mother's death two years ago. He also recalled the effects of his father divorcing her. He felt responsible for her death—away at college when she needed him. But Amanda understood how he was betrayed in a way by his mother in her pain making him feel guilty and began to point this out to Raffaele. She empathized with his pain and how this left him a loner and withdrawn for a long time.

She spoke of her own betrayal in high school by friends who thought she was a lesbian. Smoothly she played on his deep betrayal to focus on how Meredith had betrayed Amanda at every turn.

With growing rage, Amanda disclosed to Raffaele just how badly she had been betrayed by Meredith. With enough betrayal baggage of his own, Raffaele listened intently. He felt Amanda's pain—her deep pain of separation and abandonment. He knew aloneness. Whatever she needed, Raffaele would be there for her. Amanda had thrown things out there… to simmer. They took a walk back to his apartment.

Raffaele's Apartment 5 p.m.

Lighting up more hash to escape and chill, the couple's inhibitions began to vanish behind a veil of smoke. Surely they both needed an upper. They decided to snort some cocaine as well.

Now Amanda would demonstrate why she described herself on her Facebook page as "without social inhibitions." In her fantasies a payback plan started to take shape. She knew Raffaele would buy in. The drugs only made their anger worsen.

Amanda then suggested to Raffaele the idea of playing a little sex game with her British roommate, show her what betrayal really felt like. She had seen Raffaele's extensive collection of eroticized "manga" comic books filled with violent, sexually stimulating female figures which consume one another—often

---

[10]*Ibid.*, p. 37.

in retribution. And she knew he loved his knives—how perfect.

How well his fantasy life matched Amanda's preoccupation with Harry Potter, the abandoned kid with magical powers who fought evil forces. In fact, she read the story incessantly.

The 'Games Plan' for Meredith

Amanda went over her plan with Raffaele—using knives to threaten Meredith, to taunt her. Not hurt her but just control her. Maybe if Raffaele started "a little" sexual activity, just enough to humiliate her. Shock her. Use the condoms about which she had ridiculed Amanda. How much more humiliating it would be if they sodomized her too—played the *anal prude game* with for the anal Meredith—payback for ridiculing Amanda. A game for a game.

They wanted Meredith to feel totally alone—unwanted in her own home, frightened in her own home with no one there she could trust. They wanted her to feel the terror that a vampire attack was imminent with their knives to her throat. On the other end of the *vampire tease game* exactly as she had teased Amanda with one measly text last night, never intending to tell her where she was.

Amanda wanted to deliver the message, "Gang up on me, we'll gang up on you." She reminded Raffaele about all those times people had ganged up on him—now with his trusty knife he could deliver payback.

Covering Their Tracks

Amanda and Raffaele tried to think it through—their sadism now taking full charge of them. Meredith would never forget their knives to her throat. And she'd be too shocked and ashamed to do anything. Meredith would be mad, but she would get over it soon enough. Just as people did after Amanda had staged a break-in with her five college roommates back at their house in Seattle last April Fools' Day.

As for the sexual games, it would be Meredith's word against theirs. Rape was hard enough to prove. And why would they do such a thing?

Need For Third Player

Now seriously immersed in their conspiracy, Amanda and Raffaele thought about their high-stakes game. They realized they needed one other man—to control Meredith while they all took turns taunting her. And he would maximize Meredith's terror. Give her a real Halloween night she would never forget.

One guy came to Amanda's mind. That shady Rudy Guede—a drug dealer who sometimes sold to them—a guy who was attracted to both Amanda and Meredith, a man who lived in the shadows. Not a student, unemployed, habitué of the nightclubs—a little older and street-hardened. They didn't call him "The Baron" for nothing. She had heard all about Rudy's self-made video announcing that he was Dracula. Amanda could easily see that Raffaele's manga fetish closely resembled Rudy's vampire ambitions.

Rudy only lived around the block, and they could walk over to his place and set up a meeting later at the basketball court near Amanda's house at Piazza Grimana. He would be perfect—a black guy to participate in the taunting, adding another dimension of unexpected terror, bringing strange men right into her room. Somebody from a different race, someone looked down upon in Italy as an immigrant.

How thrilling such a plan seemed. The scarier the roller coaster the better Amanda liked it. Raffaele declared on his webpage that he sought "thrilling new experiences."

Thursday 6:30 p.m.

Still early in the evening and dark, they found Rudy at his place by himself. He smelled of body odor and appeared a little down, but as they casually floated the plan to him he became more animated, even desperate for excitement.

They agreed to meet later around midnight at the basketball courts after Amanda got off work. If anything changed they would stop by and let him know. He, too, would load up on hash to calm his nerves. Maybe a little coke would heighten his anticipation, too.

The couple returned to Raffaele's apartment waiting for Amanda to go to work at 10 p.m. They decided to watch Amanda's favorite movie *Amelie* to let things settle down but the light-hearted movie had a dark side.

The central character is a young girl named Amelie who was roughly Amanda's age. She had grown up starved for love. Her father was cold and distant, and her mother had committed suicide. She lived a lonely life alone working as a waitress. Her life suddenly changes when she experiences the traumatic death of the British Princess Diana. From then on she finds happiness by getting others involved in finding their own happiness.

On this night, with her deep funk vacillating up and down, Amanda experienced the movie in an entirely different way. Unexpectedly, the movie reminded Amanda of how her own British princess roommate Meredith had died on her last night, had left her so alone. But Amelie had found a creative way of handling her pain of abandonment. Now so could Amanda and Raffaele—by taunting her rejecting roommate to the hilt.

At 8:30 p.m. Amanda received a text from Patrick alerting her that she didn't have to work that night. She wondered if this was another indication that he was getting rid of her. Nevertheless now the adventure could begin. Suddenly Amanda was excited again.

Around 9 p.m. both Amanda and Raffaele turned off their cell phones so their movements couldn't be traced. They had it planned. Maximum fear, maximum humiliation—without hurting Meredith. Just scaring the life out of her.

They snorted another line of coke and headed out to find Rudy. They wanted to get the show on the road. At the appointed time—the day after Halloween as All Saints' Day slowly gave way to All Souls' Day—Amanda and Raffaele headed out into the night to meet up with Rudy Guede. Later Rudy would sum it all up, "It was an explosive mix."[11] And comforted by their drugs, they made their way to No. 7 Via della Pergola.

Fantasy Revisited

All three players, deep into their own fantasy worlds, were now making their fantasy attack game become real. They would revisit power and abuse and create their own payback justice.

They were all high on drugs, they were all in another world, and they were all mad as hell.

Blind as a bat to inner machinations, Amanda couldn't see what she was doing and here she was joined by two other blind mice who thought they had all the bases covered and were primed to enact their fantasy game—secretly covering their rage.

So different these three seemed—an American college girl with little money, a wealthy Italian doctor's son and an Ivory Coast immigrant drop-out—yet it was no accident they got together. They had found each other by emotional radar.

Conscious Motives—Tip of the Iceberg

This hypothetical story does not purport to be an exact scenario of what unfolded the night of Meredith Kercher's murder. The evidence, however, makes it clear that something like this happened—a steady build-up of rage, understandable rage, simmering in Amanda Knox's mind that reached a boiling point and led to a gang assault.

It's important to remember that this story reflects how Amanda would have distorted her interaction with Meredith. Amanda revealed her tendency to misread Meredith as a secret monster when the monster secretly lurked within Amanda herself which will become even clearer. By all accounts Meredith was a kind person who often reached out to Amanda.

It would be a mistake to think the crime was simply all a drug-fueled black-out. Shortly after the murder, fully conscious Rudy Guede would end up in a nightclub dancing the night away until 5 a.m. All three later revealed that they remained aware of what was going on, however misguided and however impaired by drugs. We will also see that all three have confessed between the lines to *many of the details in the sexual assault.*

Likewise it would be a mistake to think that it's all unexplainable with no

---

[11] Paul Russell and Graham Johnson, *Descending Darkness*, Pocket Books, London, 2009, p 180. Guede confessed unconsciously when he reported, "This is a hand-written account of what happened. It was….an explosive mix…

real motive. Unquestionably there would have been two types of motives. Immediate trigger motives and far deeper time-bomb motives which caused such distorted thinking consciously.

First I have shown that if we put the pieces of the puzzle together there are known conscious reasons – immediate motives -- which made up part of the tapestry of this murder

While police theorized the three assailants met to carry out a drug deal at Amanda's house and a cat fight accidentally ensued, the motives point toward a planned attack. Reading between the lines of Rudy's own story suggests we can deduce he was invited to Meredith's house for sexual activity by Amanda and Raffaele. The conscious thoughts of all three pointed to ideas of a sexual assault.

We consider a few brief examples. Amanda at one point reported she witnessed Patrick Lumumba, her black boss, raping the victim.

Rudy also described seeing a white man—similar to Raffaele—who had raped and attacked the victim. He also reported mutual sexual activity just short of intercourse with Meredith. If he had had a condom he would have consummated the act. He specifically denied raping her.

All three murderers introduced spontaneously their own versions of rape—a central idea on all their minds. Additionally, Amanda described accusations she was a lesbian intimating sexual contact with a woman.

Can't Tell a Book by the Cover

These conscious immediate motives in the hypothetical story above are only the tip of the iceberg of the underlying motives controlled by 90 percent more *unfinished business* in the vast unconscious. That's the way of the mind—the hard cold facts.

Here is where seemingly puzzling aspects of the case get clarified, where all the pieces come truly together. These will become clear when we visit the forensic documents at the heart of this case produced by the communicator extraordinaire, Amanda Knox. Shortly in these documents we will hear Amanda tell the entire story of the crime. Eventually she will shoot a million more holes in her cover-up story—and provide the missing motives.

She will demonstrate the raw truth that you can't tell a book by its cover—unless you know how to look inside. Her parents, her friends, her lawyers, and her supportive public cannot do that. Yet Amanda will show us an entirely new way of reading the real book inside the protective covers of her mind.

But first we must look at the backgrounds of the three perpetrators to begin to grasp how they all came together on this particular night to carry out a vicious attack.

Chapter 3: Amanda Knox, the Raging Ringleader

Like most murderers, Amanda Knox can't wait to secretly confess. In the very first chapter of her 2013 memoir, she depicted a scene which explains a major source of her deeper rage, her unfinished-business rage, the primal rage that erupted in the bloody slaying of her roommate on November 1, 2007.

Before she can even begin to berate the Italian justice system for convicting her of murder in 2009, she takes us back to a warm spring night in Seattle, Washington, in April 2007.

Two things were weighing heavily on Amanda's mind—her future college plans and her parents' lingering break-up bitterness. That troubled parental relationship had negatively impacted Amanda's entire life. First she manages to get her divorced parents together for an evening to discuss her plans to spend her junior year studying at the University for Foreigners in Perugia, Italy, beginning in the fall. She was already studying linguistics at the University of Washington where she made the Dean's List. She reminded Curt and Edda that, when she was 15, she had traveled to Italy on a family holiday, and now she had an opportunity to further explore Italian culture. *As a sad and telling aside, she points out that April 2007 meeting with her parents was the first time in her life she sat down for a meal together with both parents.*

Amanda reports that her parents—Edda Huff and Curt Knox—first separated when she was only one year old and her mother was pregnant with her sister, Deanna. Notably, she fails to mention that when her parents married in 1987, Edda was already five months pregnant with Amanda herself.

How Perpetrators Tell Their Secret Story
When they start talking and writing, perpetrators of crimes don't realize how much information they're revealing about their deepest motivations, but now there's a way to read these statements between the lines. Here Amanda hints at important secrets.

First she's telling us to pay close attention to the immediate time frame—the roughly six-month period between her departure to Perugia and her roommate's death six weeks later. Then Amanda draws our attention to the short period of time in her life before her father left.

In her memoir she connects these key ideas: I am leaving for Italy in a short time. My father left me and the family after a short time when I was one and my sister was on the way. She implies that her trip far away across the ocean by herself for an extended ten-month period was certain to stir up memories of the divorce and a major separation issue in her life.

Indirectly she links these two ideas and suggests in no uncertain terms they had something to do with the murder—but she doesn't understand this consciously. Unknowingly Amanda continuously makes connections she doesn't see in an attempt to understand herself.

Early in her memoir, Amanda ponders the lasting effects of her parents' divorce and all that it entailed, admitting that she consciously failed to grasp its full impact on her. What kid can understand all the ramifications of such a divorce—even at age 20? In short she underscores the major traumas in her life—not only her father leaving but the circumstances of the marriage. She demonstrates her denial of the important matter that her parents married after she was five months in her mother's womb. She hints that this issue is even more traumatic because she can never mention it.

Unconsciously she has already promised to tell her story between the lines. Her key ideas, which she unknowingly links together, represent a major way she will craft her cohesive narrative. Follow her major ideas.

In summary we have:
- In six months leaving for faraway Europe for a year.
- My father left when I was one and my mother then pregnant with my sister.
- Can't talk about parents' wed after mother five months pregnant with me.
- Suggesting this background connected to why I murdered. (unfinished business)
- (Don't forget an Italian jury twice convicted her of murder. Overlooked in her desperate appeals to the public after the courts found her guilty was Amanda's statement right after her first trial, "Yes, the system was fair to me."[12])

As we have only recently learned, kids are far more perceptive and inquisitive than we ever imagined. They possess an extraordinary ability to look back and try to process what happened in their early lives. But certainly Amanda herself must tell us her story. Our role, if we wish to understand, is to listen.

There are invariably two types of motives in murder cases. Immediate motives function as triggers—the proverbial "straw that breaks the camel's

---

[12]Barbie Nadeau, *Angel Face,* Beast Books, New York, 2010, p. 189.

back." In turn these short-term events set off deep underlying rage—time-bomb motives, silently ticking away for years, unfinished-business motives.

Background on Murder and Conviction

At the time she wrote her memoir, Amanda had been convicted of murdering her British roommate, Meredith Kercher, on November 1, 2007—All Saints Day night—in Italy.

Meredith was a 21-year-old exchange student who was brutally murdered alone in her room in Perugia. Two of her three roommates were out of town that night except for Amanda, who claimed she spent the night at her boyfriend's apartment. The victim had suffered a horrific attack with two severe stab wounds to her neck from which she bled profusely. Her body had sustained a total of 23 cuts. She had also been beaten in the face, held down, choked, and likely raped and sodomized. Blood soaked her entire room.

The jury of six civilians and two judges found Amanda and her Italian boyfriend, Raffaele Sollecito, guilty on December 4, 2009. She spent nearly four years in Capanne Prison in Perugia before an Italian appeals court overturned the verdict and freed her and Sollecito in October 2011. In explaining their reasons for overturning the convictions a judge wrote there was a "material non-existence" of evidence to support the guilty verdicts. *The Daily Telegraph* reporter Nick Squires wrote that the judges decided that Amanda "was the victim of a miscarriage of justice following a chaotic Italian police investigation."

Prosecutors appealed that verdict to the Court of Cassation, Italy's supreme court, which overturned the appeal verdict on March 26, 2013, citing several judicial inadequacies. A new appeal trial began in Italy on September 30, 2013, while Amanda Knox remained free in the United States, this time tried in absentia.

On January 30, 2014, the same Italian Supreme Court denied Amanda and Raffaele's appeal and again sentenced them to prison.[13] Amanda received a sentence of 28 years while Raffaele's sentence was for 25 years. They have one final appeal left which will be heard by the Italian Supreme Court. Meanwhile Amanda has stated she will not return to jail if ordered to do so and will fight Italy's extradition efforts.

Motives Missing

Hanging ominously over this entire case is the question of motive. This has been the weakness in the prosecution's case all along. Not once in the three trials did the police allude to deep-seated motives. They also remained noticeably unsure about immediate motives. As a result, Amanda's defense attorneys harped on this, declaring, "no motive, no crime."

---

[13]Note the Court of Cassation and Italian Supreme Court are used interchangeably.

Experienced police detectives well know how guilty perpetrators who have dodged prosecution and punishment still live in a secret "prison of the mind." Their deeper moral compass eats at them daily. In her actions or words has Amanda reflected "prison of the mind" guilt, a prison from which she secretly wished to be freed? We keep this idea in mind as we observe her many writings, comments and her behavior both in and now out of jail. She provides many places where we can seek clues of her unconscious guilt. Even the Italian Supreme Court, as we will see, weighed in on this matter of specifically studying her memoir for clues.

Already in her memoir Amanda hints at what was behind the murder of her roommate. First she encourages us to examine her background. In the process we will return to the crucial discussion with her parents in April 2007 about going to Italy alone.

Amanda's Bio

Amanda Knox was born on July 9, 1987, in Seattle. Her parents, local department store executive Curt Knox and mathematics teacher Edda Mellas, were married on February 21, 1987. This meant Amanda was conceived around October 9, 1986. For some reason her parents waited nearly five months to wed. Later Amanda described her mother as a "free spirit," but Edda was also known as a devout Roman Catholic.

Amanda's father was 26 years old and worked at Macy's in Seattle, eventually becoming vice president of finance for the store there. A "shotgun divorce" soon followed Curt and Edda's marriage. It was a sudden and somewhat explosive separation. Her father left when Amanda was less than two years old and her mother was pregnant with Amanda's younger sister, Deanna. Curt left for another woman, Cassandra, who soon became his second wife. Importantly, it turns out that Curt Knox was adopted and never met his biological parents. According to some reports, Curt's mother willingly relinquished her custody of him.[14]

After Curt walked out, Edda became more serious about her maternal responsibilities and raised her two daughters in a single-parent home until Amanda was 14 years old. They lived in a lower-middle-class neighborhood. Money was always tight. For nearly a decade, Edda had to battle Curt to pry regular child support out of him. Records show she took him to court repeatedly. Did he have an anger-management problem specifically directed at his ex-wife? Public rumors suggest at least one judge thought so.

Amanda's mother had a strong work ethic and demanded a lot of her two daughters regarding their school work. She made sure they attended Mass and Bible classes.

---

[14]Nina Burleigh, *The Fatal Gift of Beauty*, p. 32.

Nickname 'Foxy Knoxy'

Amanda excelled in soccer and had a gift for reading the field. At the age of eight, the way she moved in and out of openings while controlling the ball earned her the moniker, Foxy Knoxy. (Just before going to Perugia she would use the nickname as her MySpace page signature.) As the oldest child, she could be feisty and was extremely protective of her younger sister, Deanna. Once when Amanda was seven, she had punched a guy in the nose after he threatened Deanna.

Stepfather

When Amanda was nine, her mother, then 35, was smitten by a young computer consultant at her job—23-year-old Chris Mellas. Despite the twelve-year age difference, Edda and Chris dated for four years and married when Amanda was 14. Chris was thirteen years older than Amanda—nearly as close in age to his stepdaughter as he was to his wife.

Later on his MySpace page, Chris would write, "I have two kids by marriage. They are both shitheads and I love them anyways."[15] In her 2008 prison diary Amanda reported that her stepfather apparently nicknamed her "obtuse retard." [16]

Amanda's biological father, Curt, had moved about two miles away in one of Seattle's more upscale middle-class neighborhoods. Meanwhile, he had fathered two more daughters with his second wife. Around age 14, Amanda quit visiting her father every other weekend after she and her sister Deanna were moved from a bedroom on their visits to a pull-out couch in the living room. Rather than put up with such slapdash accommodations, Amanda made up excuses for avoiding the visits. Although the demotion to the living room was apparently on behalf of her younger half-sisters, Amanda never expressed her hurt feelings or anger at her father.

All along Amanda excelled as a student and was eventually awarded a partial scholarship to a prestigious and expensive Catholic secondary school—Seattle Preparatory School. At one point when family financial difficulties arose for Amanda, the school waived fees and passed along used clothing.

She was socially awkward and even strange at times, clearly marching to the beat of her own drum. Her behavior was unpredictable. Often she seemed to seek attention. She often preferred males as friends, competing with the guys in rock climbing and was somewhat of a tomboy. She graduated from Seattle Prep in 2005.

---

[15] http://www.thedailybeast.com/articles/2009/03/13/behind-the-co-ed-murder-scandal.html
[16] http://truejustice.org/ee/index.php?/tjmk/comments/does_her_leaked_prison_diary_talk_to_knoxs_mental_condition/

College

She lived at home for part of her first year at the University of Washington. Eventually Amanda moved into the dormitory, but she felt restricted there. One dormitory friend said they all liked to smoke pot and "get trashed on the weekends," but Amanda *"really* used drink and drugs," not just to get high, but "It was like she wanted to get away from herself as if... she could only cope with by getting wasted." She began regularly smoking stronger 'skunk' cannabis.[17]

In 2006 she moved to an off-campus house with five girlfriends free from campus rules regarding alcohol use. The girls' house was surrounded by "fraternity row" and homes rented by football jocks.

As time progressed, one acquaintance said, "She just went wild... like the brakes were let off... smoking pot in the mornings before class and then partying at night. Even by student standards, she was wilder than hell."

One guy, a medical student who lived in her dormitory, implied she had casual sex far more often than she admitted. "She had what in polite terms you'd call a lot of close male friends."

Other acquaintances referred to her as a "maneater."[18] Reports of her sexual behavior vary. In his book, *Death in Italy*, author John Follain reports that, well into college, as compared to her female classmates, Amanda remained rather naive about intimate relationships. After the murder, her friends became naturally protective as did the American media. Many minimize her sexual behavior and drug use, but others admit that she was out of control.

For sure she was much more sexually experienced and "liberated" in Seattle than she later claimed. You don't get as out front as Amanda was in Italy about sex without having had significant prior sexual experience. And surrounded in college by jocks and fraternity guys at the University of Washington, she knew very well how to use her sexuality to her benefit. Certainly choosing to reclaim her nickname "Foxy Knoxy" at this point in her life suggests she was now "foxy" indeed and quite aware of the power of her sexuality. She could prey as a "maneater" in an entirely new way.

Sometimes a single event speaks volumes. An interesting incident occurred with her roommate, Meredith, in Perugia. Amanda would talk with her American boyfriend, D.J., on Skype, posing nude in front of the camera for lengthy periods of time. Not only did this shock Meredith, but it suggests that Amanda was physically comfortable with D.J. and equally comfortable with her sexuality. Later in her jail diary she listed her previous sexual partners and implied she had frequent sex with D.J. She also acknowledged using "condoms." Her list, however, turned out to be less than fully accurate. She had no absolute need to

---

[17]http://www.dailymail.co.uk/femail/article-498853/The-wild-raunchy-past-Foxy-Knoxy.html#ixzz2Uiq9pqHW
[18]Ibid.

tell the whole truth and, on some level, she knew police would eventually read her diary. As we will see, she blatantly left one name off her list, a young Italian she would later call "Cristiano."

Still while in college Amanda kept her grades up and worked three jobs to save money to study in Perugia. Some said she burned the candle at both ends. She confided in friends, they said, that she couldn't wait to escape Seattle, her free-wheeling style hampered by her inability to go to bars until she was 21, a birthday that loomed a full year away. A medical student in her dorm said, "I think she couldn't wait to get away."

On the Way to Italy

Without question Amanda carried heavy loads of emotional baggage with her to Perugia.

The conversation with her parents about studying abroad revealed major family dysfunction, according to Amanda's account in her memoir. She is telling us who she is and why. The most basic family gathering is at mealtime, and Amanda had never had a single one with her parents.

Learning Denial

Despite her father's move to a nearby neighborhood, Amanda never recalls her two parents talking except rarely on the phone. They would attend her athletic events, but when they did they always had a barrier of other people between them. At her school functions, Amanda's mother and father might sit a single row apart but never spoke. Amanda saw their attendance as proof of their love for her, but it was more, much more. They were modeling extreme bitterness—anger—toward each other constantly. It may have been carefully self-controlled, but it clearly communicated powerful emotions. Such emotions they couldn't discuss, but Amanda felt them keenly.

This was deeply embedded, unforgiving rage. Her parents' behavior had taught her: We don't speak and acknowledge each other. We do not even give each other a passing glance. And we do not look each other in the eye and speak. It was passive-aggressive anger at its finest.

The fact that Curt and Edda got married to each other before later settling into second marriages indicates that they believed in marriage as an institution. But they took their sweet time about marrying with Edda five months pregnant. What were they thinking? Were both reluctant to tie the knot? Or was only one of them reluctant? Did they consider another option? All sorts of family secrets are created at such moments.

And they didn't handle separation very well. Both Curt and Edda engaged in denial of separation anxiety including the grief—it hurts too much to discuss unresolved relationship issues and divorce. They continually expressed intense anger through behavior—"acting out." Behavioral communication is powerful, and it inevitably entails enormous denial.

It was a broken family steeped in denial of fierce emotions which were deftly covered with the agreement that they would both love and support their children. From her parents, Amanda learned denial about major emotional issues, especially denial of anger—and learned to disguise it in passive-aggressive ways. Again she learned to act out emotions instead of verbalize them. And above all she learned not to discuss separation issues but to simply carry grudges and allow anger to rule the day. Exactly as she did when, at age 14, she simply quit visiting her father on weekends without any real explanation.

Despite her parents' efforts to maintain support by living closely to each other, their silence toward each other communicated much more. Their silence effectively trumped their supportive stances. But Amanda did learn to put a good face forward regarding all these underlying passions. It was an angel face, but it was also an angry, bitter, wounded face like the ones her parents modeled.

This was the personality baggage Amanda was packing up to take to Perugia.

Projective Identification

One other thing about acting out—it often includes what psychiatrists call "projective identification." This is much more than simple "projection" in which someone talks about someone else seeing in the other person a secret part of themselves.

No, "projective identification" means a behavioral communication. Making someone else feel your buried emotions—feel that painful part of your secret identity. By their stone-walled silence, Amanda's parents communicated a ton of emotions through projective identification. Deep down she would have felt it all unknowingly as it became an intrinsic part of her coping style. So Amanda frequently resorted to "making others feel what she did unconsciously." Oblivious to her effect on others, she would routinely drop emotional bombs out of the blue. That was a primary way she revealed her baggage.

Warning Signs

An important sequence of events unfolded in the next six months as Amanda made her way to Perugia. In recalling her April 2007 conversation with her parents, Amanda reports her father was initially reluctant about the idea but she quickly convinced him. But in his book, *A Death in Italy,* author John Follain reports a different version. Initially Curt expressed concern, "Hey, how are we going to be able to help you if something happens? What happens if you get sick?"[19]

---

[19]John Follain, *A Death in Italy*, St. Martin's Press, New York, p. 19.

April Fools' Day 2007

Just before preparing for Perugia, Amanda's behavior was also a cause for concern. While her friends at the University of Washington knew about an important incident in 2007, Amanda never discussed it publicly until January 8, 2014. It involved an April Fools' Day joke in 2007 wherein Amanda and some friends staged a break-in and robbery at the house where she lived with her roommates. The house was trashed, and her roommates were frightened, feeling terrorized. Then, like a comedienne pleased that her punchline had its intended effect, Amanda proudly revealed that it was she who had pulled off the stunt and showed them where she had hidden their belongings.

On the surface it was a nasty over-the-top prank—but did it reveal something dark and deep? Clearly she evoked unexpected turmoil in others. It was another impetuous Amanda action—and she had remained blissfully unaware of its impact.

A Going-Away Party

Then in early July came the "separation party"—a going-away gathering—prior to Amanda's impending trip. She and the five roommates surrounded by the "wild guys"—University of Washington frat boys and jocks—threw the bye-bye bash. Before long, the party spiraled out of control. Neighbors complained when the boys started throwing empty beer bottles and rocks in the front yard—reportedly at windows in nearby houses and at passing cars. Some describe it as way beyond the pale of a typical college beer party deteriorating into unusual debauchery and violence. Uninhibited sexual activity was described as taking place all over their house.

Police came and cited Amanda for the disturbance. She ended up taking the fall and appeared before a Municipal Court judge. He fined her $270 and warned her that repeat behavior would result in much stiffer consequences.[20] Court records reveal Patrolman Bender—first at the scene—noted that Amanda offered the excuse that her behavior was due to her moving abroad. She clearly linked her wildness to her travel plans.

Typically Amanda minimized the party. Given her personality she suggests that the going-away party was highly symbolic—that the guys at the party were possibly a proxy for her with uninhibited drugs/alcohol, sex, violence, and even crime. She further suggests a strong tendency toward self-punishment.

To a discerning parent, the incident represented a huge red flag. It was Amanda's way of saying, "See? I can't handle the upcoming separation. This is how I will handle it. I'm not ready to go."

Her stepfather, Chris Mellas, got the message. He saw the out-of-control party as just another result of her immaturity. He had already expressed concern

---

[20]http://www.dailymail.co.uk/femail/article-498853/The-wild-raunchy-past-Foxy-Knoxy.html#ixzz2Uiq9pqHW Seattle Municipal Court —Crime No: 071830624.

about her lack of judgment, recalling the time she rode a bicycle home from school, a two-hour ride, at 1 a.m. Amanda was out on the road all alone in the dark riding a bike—a vulnerable female oblivious to danger and fear. So as her move to Perugia approached, Chris insisted, "Amanda, you're not ready for it, I'm scared you're going to go over there and something is going to happen to you. What if you're in an accident?" He added, "You're still immature."[21]

From past experience he knew that Amanda was a risk-taker, careless with her own life. Now again "Foxy Knoxy" was outfoxing herself, in denial—living out a family trait. In psychological terms she demonstrated "counter-phobic behavior" typical of fearless, immature adolescents. In daredevil fashion and in massive denial, they drive cars at 100 mph or rush into dangerous situations to prove they are invincible. It's false bravado.

Later her mother reflected on the same trait, "I hoped she would learn a bit of fear before she left... a little fear as far as self-preservation goes."[22]

Family Scapegoat?

Amanda had a baggage full of separation traumas all her own. Her parents waited to get married, were ambivalent about starting a home, and her father walked out on her and her sister-to-be. Curt left for another woman, blatantly rejecting Amanda and her mother. When Amanda was 12, Curt moved her out of "her bedroom" at his house—"to pullout couches in the playroom"—in favor of his two younger daughters from his second marriage. These were the preferred daughters, girls who Amanda called the "replacement children." Even the names of the two half-sisters—Ashley and Delaney—started with matching initials to Amanda and her sister Deanna, and were virtually the same length. This was when Amanda quit her weekend visits to her father.

Not only did Amanda lack the bonding that would normally come from shared family meals, whatever bonds she had with her father were seriously strained by her move to the couch.

Now her first long trip abroad when she found herself living with total strangers—only one of which spoke English well—would certainly stir her up, maybe more than just a "little bit."

Yet her parents left Amanda out there on her own. No one set limits. Didn't they miss her red-flag announcement, "First Major Behavioral Problem"—a behavioral message, her "criminal" behavior? The municipal court appearance and slap-on-the-wrist citation she received were not nearly as important as the symbolic message she was sending.

Curt, Chris and Edda failed to set limits for this 20-year-old woman who still needed guidance, limits she desperately needed. In the end, they let Amanda decide for herself, as they had long raised her to do. Denial piled upon denial.

---

[21]John Follain, *A Death in Italy*, St. Martin's Press, New York, p. 20.
[22]*Ibid.*, p. 21.

If Amanda was sending her parents a desperate, unconscious cry for help, it would be largely ignored. She would have read the ignored message as saying, "You're on your own, we're abandoning you as though you are unimportant—as though you don't exist, as though we don't care." Why would they do that? Amanda will eventually offer an answer.

As family therapists put it, the question is this: was she "the identified patient," the family member who unconsciously expresses the embedded secret emotions for the family? The trip to Italy was certain to trigger the powerful abandonment and separation anxiety enmeshed in the family dynamic, the secret pain and rage that haunted her parents. Her parents, including her step-father, suggest that as she headed toward Perugia they had realized—somewhere in the back of their minds—that Amanda was a walking time-bomb.

And in their blind spots, they had helped build the bomb.

Junior Year Abroad

On top of this, the junior year of college is itself a reminder of the imminent separation into the real world on the horizon. Finishing school remains one of the most anxious moments in a college student's life. Such a concern typically gets buried by parties and alcohol—but it's a major anxiety nonetheless.

Questions eventually emerged about the nature of Amanda's study-abroad program. It appears she was involved in a student exchange program less challenging than other, much more rigorous foreign-study programs. At the time, the University of Washington reportedly had two types of student exchange programs—supervised and unsupervised. The supervised plan—known as Departmental Exchange—had more built-in accountability where an advisor monitors the student's progress.[23] To help the student avoid problems, the advisor closely observed such matters as class attendance, living arrangements, behavioral problems, and signs of substance abuse.

The other exchange program was a completely independent process to studying abroad.[24] You picked your program, registered, and earned your credits. The foreign advisor and/or school simply served to account for the grades and transfer them back to the American university. Amanda was almost certainly in the latter program.

On top of this Perugia was known for its raucous partying and free-wheeling drug use among foreign students. Had Amanda selected the school for reasons other than learning?

Her parents seemed oblivious to the type of unstructured program in which she was actually enrolled. They blindly trusted her, or just didn't care. Her

---

[23] http://frenchitalian.washington.edu/study-abroad/nantes.html.

[24] http://truejustice.org/ee/index.php?/tjmk/comments/cutting_through_the_confusion_over_knoxs_status_in_p erugia/ Website describing "unsupervised" program has now been removed by the University of Washington. Did Knox cause them to revise their study-abroad programs with her lack of supervision and guidance?

surface persona, that of a smart, hard-working student earning her way through college, would quickly take a back seat to behavior better described as "loose cannon out of control."

So how would Amanda handle separation? How would the world handle it? Would the big bad world harm her as her parents had feared? She presented multiple signals which predicted her future there.

Sexual Behavior

In her diary Amanda included a "to do" list of tasks she needed to attend to before flying to Italy. This is the item that topped her list: "Number 1: sex store."[25] And indeed, before leaving Seattle, Amanda patronized a shop that specialized in intimate apparel and sex toys where she purchased condoms and other items.

With her priorities so clearly delineated, Amanda was in effect announcing *that sex was now going to be her "number one" concern.* She would use her attractiveness and her budding sexuality as a major defense against the challenges she would face in Perugia—academic, social and emotional challenges. Whatever her sexual appetite had been before, it was now going into overdrive. Again Amanda chose a behavioral defense—never a defense that necessitated putting into words what needed protection. Amanda would use pleasure to avoid pain, especially the pain of separation.

One of her two closest girlfriends, Brett, supposedly bought Amanda a vibrator as a going-away gag gift—and encouraged her to experiment sexually in casual relationships. The implied advice: when you go away, have a lot of sex so you won't be alone.

More Behavioral Messages

Body language can be interesting and informative. Strictly speaking we will rest the case on her words, but for starters let's see how her body language reveals important clues and tendencies.

Photographs serve as vivid markers for crucial verbal language which is at the heart of this case. They can provide an opportunity for a person to portray themselves in certain ways reflecting how they unconsciously see themselves and how they interact with others. With this in mind, we'll examine three such pictures of Amanda Knox.

---

[25] John Follain, *A Death in Italy*, St. Martin's Press, New York, p. 20.

Photo One—Party Animal Amanda

Symbolic Language

Keep in mind that body language is a symbolic language. Unconsciously a person arranges the body in various poses to communicate deeper messages, disguised messages. With that in mind we must pay attention *to the other symbols in a picture*—how a person dresses, whom they interact with and what else they are doing (drinking, holding a red cup, wearing a hat, etc.). Constantly we keep in mind the images—either from body language or other objects including people.

We look for patterns, striking powerful patterns to her symbolic language, looking so see if it's true that—at a key moment—a picture can actually be worth a thousand words. We look to see if each of these photos contains a key moment, a super-intel clue to her makeup. And it's important to remember that the super intelligence can stage or arrange a picture in a heartbeat, just as it can instantly stage a crime scene.

Remember, too, art experts spend hours decoding paintings and sculptures in galleries, searching the images for the artists' deeper meanings, even unconscious meanings. The super-intel potentially brings an entirely new level of decoding to a specific moment in time as captured in a photo, which Amanda Knox will demonstrate. But art analysts instinctively see the deeper meanings. If we apply the same expertise, we can see how much certain photographs have to teach us.

Following her November 2007 arrest in Perugia, a picture of a drunk Amanda emerged on a YouTube video. Around the same time a color photograph of Amanda partying in Seattle surrounded by five guys made its way quickly around the Internet after the Kercher murder. Amanda's unusual white outfit and everyone's creative costuming suggest the picture was snapped at a masquerade party—which provides a revealing view of Amanda's unconscious role in life.

In the picture Amanda's mouth is wide open with her tongue clearly visible while she gives a nearly horizontal "V" sign with the fingers of her right hand—reminiscent of the "V" rabbit ears symbol that Playboy bunnies wear atop their head. Especially since she's dressed in what appears to be a strapless white bodice—a "matching" short "Playboy bunnyish" top visible only from the just above the waist—and wearing long white, satiny gloves.

Amanda's bright white top contrasts strikingly with the guys' darker garb, and her glowing appearance seems unusual at first glance.

On the one hand we have just another typical college party picture, but we always ask what did it mean uniquely to Amanda and for the young men with whom she interacts? *So we read the picture symbolically, paying special attention to body language.*

The super intelligence has much to teach us about body language and how it fits with the symbolic verbal language of the great unconscious mind.

In the photo, Amanda sits on the far left facing the camera with the five guys to her left. She leans left slightly into the picture. Our eyes naturally read from left to right with Amanda at the center of the action. This matches the most obvious matter—Amanda, the center of attention, surrounded by five men. Four of them are standing behind or to the side while she appears seated, three with drinks plainly in hand.

The guy standing directly behind Amanda, the first one of five to her left, reaches out with his left hand and appears to nearly touch her left arm. He may hold a drink in that hand. He has leaned away from her to get in the picture with the other guys, but his left hand makes plain he was standing closer to her.

He appears to wear a red hunting cap and suspenders suggesting a northwestern logger or hunter. The hunter has found Amanda but apparently pulls back a bit for the moment.

The only seated man appearing in the photo sits across from Amanda, the closest to her. He's the only one wearing (wire-framed) glasses and has light brown hair, much lighter than the others. (Does she have a secret affinity for light-headed men with glasses similar to her hero Harry Potter and later Raffaele Sollecito?)

Amanda's strapless top is shaped in a three-part sharp triangular fashion across the top of her bust—revealing a hint of cleavage. In her left hand she holds an uplifted drink in a red cup which contrasts harshly with her gleaming white top. Her drink is perfectly in line with her cleavage and the cups of her dress. Unconsciously she draws attention to her breasts. She frames them with her lower right finger pointing to the red cup grasped in her left hand—and with her left arm bent at the elbow. Symbolically she suggests exposing her 'white and red' breasts and even further offers them up to be grabbed. She suggests an intense need to be grabbed and to grab sexually. The open cup and her open mouth likewise suggest, "I'm open, take a drink of my seductive milk." And her seductiveness doesn't stop there.

We find a plethora of "V" signs. Her left arm—bent at the elbow with drink in hand close to her body—forms a distinct "V." *Closest to the camera on the right side of her body the first two fingers of her right hand—higher than her left hand—are widely spread in a prominent "V" sign and perfectly frame the front and back of the right side of her neck, pointing straight to it.* The sharp angular edges of the top of her dress—"V" symbols in themselves—point upward to her neck in front. Upon close inspection the first two fingers of her left hand holding the drink also display a subtle "V" sign.

First the "V" reminds us of the universal "peace" symbol. Peace and love for the entire world. But she suggests far more than this.

The "V" alludes not only to a peace sign, but also to the *popular crude "V" for vagina sign* often seen in sexually oriented videos, rap performances, and in informal social photos (especially of young women) on the Internet.[26]

Her hand signal also has an exhibitionistic side, "See, I have a vagina!"— and matches Amanda's continual sexually aggressive persona which was increasingly on display in Perugia and prior to her departure from America. In this photo, she strongly implies a seductive invitation. A desperate sexual invitation, so desperate so preoccupied she suggests a sexual addiction, an insatiable need to grab, both sexually and any other way she can.

The second guy to Amanda's left is further behind the others and has his only visible (left) hand extended far out, his fingers widely splayed, palm up, underneath all the drinks held high. He mirrors the first guy whose left hand also reaches out toward Amanda. He suggests he's unconsciously ready to receive Amanda's offer. His open palm suggests he desires to touch and caress, perhaps

---

[26] "The V-sign in the last five years [from 2001] or so has become very common on the Internet, particularly in informal social photos and videos of young females similar...to the Black Power clenched fist.... [one] reason seems to be a ...declaration...of 'woman power,' These typically are given with the palm inwards, and the closer the hand is to the face, the more emphatic...meaning; such as the... similar...'Vagina Power' concept. The letter "V" is... often associated with "vagina" in these issues. All of these represent a[n]... exclamation...of proud female-ness: 'I am Woman!' and... the 'V with tongue' gesture signifies cunnilingus... even without the tongue out, but with the mouth near the crotch of the fingers...[means] the same thing or extremist 'Vagina Power.' In these cases, the V of the fingers seems to symbolize spread legs in a sexual context as well as: V for Vagina. Most often, Lesbian acts are implied." http://en.wikipedia.org/wiki/Talk%3AV_sign

The satirical all-female punk rock group "V for Vagina" in Glasgow, Scotland, signifies the same messages. https://vforvagina.bandcamp.com/

The V-sign has been adapted by some women to proclaim a global "V-day" protesting violence against women. Symbolic spin-offs include the Vulva Choir. A picture of Jane Fonda flashing a Vulva V sign on V-day in 2001 made its way around the Internet. http://ratconference.com/blog/?p=45

grab. It is exactly at the same level of Amanda's breasts. But his head leans down and, despite his closed eyes, suggests symbolically he wanted to look lower toward her genital area. His closed eyes perhaps suggest he knows he really shouldn't look there.

In the background the third guy to Amanda's left wearing beads around his neck holds a drink in his right hand with his first two fingers also clearly signaling an obvious "V" in tandem with Amanda. His mouth is wide open with perhaps a protruding tongue. His left hand at waist level grabs his long beads which taper to a single strand hanging down. It's as if he answers her, "I'm with you. I hear you." The overall message implies uninhibited partying and unbridled sex.

Amanda's "V" finger symbol also perfectly frames her extremely wide open mouth—far more than anyone else in the picture.

She suggests exuberance, wildness, severe neediness, consuming, feed me, pleading—and I'm about to bite you, yelling "Ahhhh." Her far-apart lips form no meaningful word, except perhaps, "Oh" for oral or out of control.

Her protruding tongue and wide mouth dominate her smile with her upper teeth showing. The image suggests an oral orientation and a desperate sexuality—that she's ready to consume whatever pleasures life has to offer her and suggests that deep inside she's starving emotionally. This seemingly matches her intense primitive need to grab a breast implying a frantic desire for basic nurture, maternal (and even paternal) nurture. Her wide open mouth suggests that need was frustrated and as a result she could bite. She points to a deep early wound in her life.

She also suggests again that her sexual invitation contains a warning that she's dangerous, that she's capable of inflicting a terrible, biting vampire wound on a man. *She provides a vivid example of why one classmate in college described her as a "maneater."* Two of the other guys besides the hunter have ropes or long, chain-like beads around their neck, and another has a belt across his chest. Are they secretly her slaves who also wish to enslave *her*?

Amanda's apparently seated in the picture as the five men gather around her, four of them standing, as though she is a queen holding court. Three of the guys hold their glasses high as if to toast Queen Amanda. Her long white gloves even suggest royalty. Later her roommate, Meredith, and others in Perugia will describe Amanda's constant need to be the center of attention, whether costumed as a Playboy bunny or a sexy, young American princess.

In the context of this photograph's rather blatant hedonism, Amanda's gloves also suggest that at some point she might take them off so that her naked arms would seductively complement the skin already revealed by her strapless top.

For the moment the gloves also imply that she doesn't want her fingerprints on the scene, a cover-up in a way, a denial of who she really is. And the message, "Look but don't touch." But "the gloves coming off" also suggests a secret fury, an aggressive Amanda who might punch you or puncture you.

Yet her seductive appeal shouts at all the guys. Surely she appeared extremely comfortable around men, and we can imagine her hanging out with the wilder guys with whom the subject of sex came up frequently.

Scissors

Strikingly, Amanda's two fingers forming the "V" also suggest scissors—perfectly arranged symbolically—scissors which could cut her head off at the neck. In effect she suggests cutting her own throat and further suggests that earlier in her life someone had "cut her throat"—traumatized her severely. She leans her neck toward the scissors' "V" further suggesting vulnerability and exposure when the wound occurred—early in life. Turning her head while keeping her left ear mostly hidden suggests the wound was a secret she should not have heard (known). It's a secret she keeps from herself consciously, a secret that leads to self-punishment as she leans into the wound.

As a result she implies she has the capacity to inflict such harm on someone else. In the picture, going even higher with the "scissors" would also decapitate the immediate two guys to her left.

Likewise the "scissors V" is perfectly angled simultaneously with her widely open mouth just above her neck with her prominent tongue slightly out of her mouth. She suggests it would cut her tongue off if it continued upward. She again implies a deep secret connected to her extreme neediness about which she cannot speak.

It's something she cannot allow into consciousness. She suggests she has a dangerous secret leading to massive guilt and self-punishment for such knowledge. Something terrible she should not know. Again framing her wide mouth with her two fingers suggests she herself had suffered a terrible vampire bite emotionally but could never face the fact of who did it.

In addition the two-finger "V" also connects exactly with her delicate necklace, *highlighting her neck again.* She implies something or someone was choking her, inflicting an all-engulfing 'vampire' bite of sorts. The barely visible delicate necklace suggests both a secret and a chain, as she's enslaved and possessed by the overpowering secret trauma. The necklace also symbolizes femininity—it's possible it was a woman who caused her primary wound.

The pendant hanging down from the necklace points to her cleavage. Again she suggests her wound involved a major trauma in her basic nurture symbolized by her breasts. She also points again to her defensive seductiveness, "Look at my cleavage." She keeps her mind off her secrets by using her sexuality as a primary defense.

In this photo she wears no earrings, and her only jewelry is the necklace. In the other two photos below she selects a single piece of jewelry, earrings, strong symbols of femininity which also draw attention to her neck.

The picture here invites these deeper messages since, in the not too distant future, Amanda will be charged with the heinous murder of her roommate in Perugia. It seems more than ironic that her roommate will be partially strangled and her throat cut as Amanda later described in the crudest terms at the police station. The crime scene highlighed the victim's neck. And it was a woman-on-woman crime.

All in all she conveys a mixture of unbridled primitive sexuality and aggression and a secret desperate need. Her red plastic cup suggests that alcohol and/or drugs will fuel her passions. Ironically the one guy with the ropes around his neck also drinks his potion from a red cup.

We will continue to see how intuitively in a split second each person in the picture could read the scene and unconsciously arrange his or her body language (and symbolic items)—strike a pose—to communicate many of the suggested messages.

Could the super-intel mind that shapes the body language really be this bright? Such revealing capability prepares us for a far more stunning verbal "mind language." Indeed the unconscious has inordinate ability to "show" and "tell." The "tells" come later.

Photo Two—'Addicted to Love'

A photograph Amanda posted on her MySpace site before leaving for Italy is a self-portrait, almost certainly set to singer Robert Palmer's popular 1985 video, "Addicted to Love," the song title itself a telling behavioral communication. The snapshot was taken by her sister, Deanna, a year or so before Perugia.

Dressed in a tight black outfit of sweater and pants, Amanda's seated provocatively on the front edge of a piano bench separated from its piano. Her right foot, wearing a spike-heeled shoe is up on the bench, her right arm straight out resting seductively over the knee at the elbow with her open palm hanging down. Her left hip is turned slightly open facing the camera, suggesting action, suggesting she's about to move. She leans back on her left hand behind her on the bench displaying her prominent athletic thighs, her legs about to open up further.

With her one foot up "in the air" on the bench in a spike heel, Amanda suggests she's sexually preoccupied.[27] She's sexually ready. At first glance her body language oozes seductiveness.

Yet there's more. Her right arm resting on her right knee across from the right side of her body forms a triangular opening "window"—with a sharp angle at the base pointing toward her crotch. Look closely and we find a picture full of angles, and embedded "V" signs everywhere we look. Block her face out, and the image leaps out. Two bent knees in alignment, bent wrist, and her right elbow on her knee angle all create a "V" effect. Her left leg—cropped at the knee in the photo—presents a particularly striking image.

Her right hand hangs down pointing to the spike heel with her thumb and aligned fingers forming yet another (inverted) "V" matching the angular inverted "V" of her shoe.

In perfect alignment, the spike of the heel itself points to her crotch, specifically suggesting "the V of her crotch"—further imploring "spike me."

As in the party picture, Amanda repeatedly flashes a "V for vagina" sign—not only pointing directly to it in multiple symbolic ways but her overall body language emphasizes the centrality of her "available exhibitionistic" crotch. In addition the words to the song "Addicted to love—can't get enough" imply a central identity: 'Addicted to sex—can't get enough.'

---

[27] "...both the foot and the shoe have been imbued with powerful phallic and fertility symbols as evidenced in the contemporary practice of tying shoes to a newlywed couple's car. No other shoe, however, has gestured toward...sexuality, and sophistication as much as the high-heeled shoe. First mentioned in London's *Daily Telegram* on September 10, 1953, the exaggeratedly slender heel and narrowing of the toe equated sheer height with chic and strongly suggested phallic-erectile symbolism and sexual maturation. For many feminists, high heels indicated subservience and sexual stereotyping by men...Critics, particularly feminists in the 1980s, argued that fashion...challenges cultural meaning. This change of heart about high heels...was provoked...by feminist debates about pleasure and female desire...Western women now claimed they were wearing high heels for themselves and that heels gave them not only height but also power and authority. Perhaps influenced in part by successful TV...hits as *Sex in the City* and *The Devil Wears Prada*, some women are even going under the knife to shorten their toes or inject padding into the balls of their feet... to fit more comfortably into a pair of stilettos." http://www.randomhistory.com/1-50/036heels.html

Addiction

Yet she's not happy. Like the notably unemotional brunettes who dance to a harsh staccato rhythm behind singer Robert Palmer in the famous video, Amanda's hair is pulled tightly back. Like Palmer's stoic dancers, she sports dark eye shadow and does not smile—no teeth showing, her mouth closed as a distant look in her eyes is offset with a hint of innocence.

She suggests a delicate balance, her body ready for action, her face in another world. She's mechanical and alive all at the same time. She's a princess but not a happy one. She's a princess robot, a cold statue which moves as if alive.

Remember she chose—unconsciously for sure—this pose to match the song and video. She chose the words "sex" and "addiction," and paired them up. In a strange but subtle way "addiction" certainly fits the picture.

Dynamic but stilted. Entrapped. Looking alive and dead at the same time. Beautiful and sad. Out of it. In another world.

She points us more strikingly to the video. The song's all about being lost in oblivion ("all you crave"), escaping personal responsibility ("your will is not your own"), giving up total control to another person ("another kiss and you'll be mine"). But an addiction is what it is. A one-track mind that consumes you ("you're addicted to love...can't get enough").

Amanda suggests she is secretly consumed by control, by being controlled herself and by controlling others. She can't be a separate individual. She's addicted to sex as a means of escape, a way to lose herself. But the song mentions the entrapping denial of addiction ("you think you're immune to the stuff...truth is you can't get enough").

Pointing Out Danger

The more we look the more the spiked heel comes into play, cold and haunting, a hard, sharp edge (like the music), the single object to which her fingers point. In so doing, she also underscores danger and damage, specifically first the spiked heel grinding into the piano bench fabric. She points to a spike. She's a "spiker"—heel up on the bench for emphasis—eerily recalling her soccer days when the role of a "striker" came into play—the most advanced player on the team whose primary role is to score goals.

Right off she's announcing that she's a rule breaker, a character trait which she boldly brags about. In this photo, she visually flaunts one of the fundamental rules of the home, "Don't put your feet on the furniture."

Already noted, her V-shaped spiked heel specifically aligns with her crotch and by implication all the other "V"/vampire images.

She points to her sexual addiction but more. Her imagery suggests that her sexuality carries a spike in her cold come-hither stare. A spiked heel close to a stiletto heel—a symbolic stiletto knife, a bite even.

Her imagery implies she is a vagina vampire who will addict her victims sexually. This is her unique "vagina monologue"[28]—her body language in all its symbolism combined with the Robert Palmer video.

Her closed mouth suggests a secret: she has vicious teeth, as vicious as an enticing addiction that secretly destroys. Not by chance, the sharp spike of her heel matches the sharp scissors "V" embedded in the party photo. But why is she so vicious?

Peeling the onion of her psyche she provides the subtle but distinct answer—those who damage have themselves been damaged. The spike on her heel grinding into the padded bench now suggests she herself has been spiked in some crucial way—perhaps by another wounded woman herself. Amanda offers up the idea unconsciously that the padding that protected her in life has been damaged.

Then we have the bench that holds her up—a symbol of security, of stability, of home. It doesn't secure her very well and she's about to slip off. At the same time she can lean back and rest on it. She suggests leaning back into a fetal position if she can keep from falling off. Her left hand grabs the bench fingers wrapped around the edge. The palm of her right hand faces down empty, not ready to receive but in defeat as if her needs were refused. As if some key person(s) didn't hold her—a deep pain frozen like a statue inside suggesting a picture of the deepest trauma on display. Turned down, turned out. Her two fingers not connected, no oneness here but clear separation—another marker of her alienation that explains her left hand that grabs? Her two hands telling the story. At the same time her right hand was not letting her left hand know what was going on. Perhaps reminiscent unconsciously of the Scripture from her Catholic-school days, "But when you give to the poor, do not let your left hand know what your right hand is doing, so that your giving will be in secret."[29] Amanda suggests she has a deep dark secret about just how needy and poor she is.

One mixed message after another. The piano bench suggests the music of home, singing to a child, an idyllic scene that was sorely lacking in Amanda's early life. Somehow she was about to slip out of the home. And the home was far too small, unavailable to hold her. She further implies a fall, more damage. For a small child, it's a long fall off a bench to the floor. The younger the child, the more precarious it is, and her potential fetal position further implies that her emotional wound occurred very early in life.

With her left buttock half-way off the bench, she appears not only about to fall but also ready to leap off the bench toward the camera in an "in-your-face"

---

[28] *The Vagina Monologues* is a 1996 stage play by Eve Ensler made up of a varying number of monologues read by a varying number of women. Each of the monologues deals with an aspect of the feminine experience, touching on matters such as sex, love, rape, menstruation, female genital mutilation, masturbation, birth and orgasm. A recurring theme throughout the piece is the vagina as a tool of female empowerment, and the ultimate embodiment of individuality.

[29] Matthew 6:3-4, New American Standard.

move. Amanda suggests her impulsiveness, her constant leaping into the action, was motivated by her impending sense of a fall—damage—unless she took action. Her spiked heel also suggests that her sexuality will cause her fall—ultimately fail her as a primary defense. Subtly, the missing lower left leg and foot in the cropped image also suggest she's missing something—both damaged and destabilized.

Pierced Flesh

Amanda presents another major clue that she has been severely traumatized emotionally. Note the earring, the only overt image of pierced flesh, suggesting another sharp object that pierces (like the spike, like the scissors).

It's also the thinnest image in picture. Earrings make a woman beautiful, lovely and enticing. But earrings can fall off—all the way to the ground. *She will use the key image of earrings over and over in her verbal communications.*

Here they subtly suggest 'hanging by a thread' with her neck turned away from camera—exposed. The earring dangles to subtly align with her chin and neck. We can't see fully the other side of her face—her left ear remains hidden. One message—"listen for my secrets that I'm whispering to you."

For some reason deep down Amanda's violent imagery suggests she saw herself as almost physically damaged, her flesh almost pierced by a sharp object. In the end she suggests she viewed her life as hanging by a thread likely due to a deeply buried powerful near-death emotional experience.

This explains the angular theme running through the photo. Her body all bent up. She implies she's broken, majorly so—into numerous pieces and angles. She's clearly traumatized and this photo is a haunting self-portrait from her mental gallery, a powerful dark moment frozen in time in her mind as though she's a statue.

Ironically or not, there's a red mark on her skin at the bend in Amanda's right wrist. It certainly suggests an abrasion, a tattoo, or some type of flaw, possibly an artifact, something that doesn't belong. The idea fits with Amanda's impaired psyche.

Her super-intel quietly makes its presence known, its rich imagery silently shouting, keeping time to the beat of the "Addicted to Love" video. Suggesting she's really "addicted to sex" because she never got enough love. She hints again at deeper motives.

In this stark self-portrait she bends over backwards to show us the mindset and the needs that controlled her. She's trying to tell us just how mentally disturbed she was underneath. She points unmistakably to the video to explain who she is, a child who was never shown the love she deserved and needed.

Through the song's lyrics, Amanda paints a picture of her own desperate needs, so deep she's consumed by them.

Throat so tight she can't breathe, and can't eat—nearly starving, barely surviving but trying to deny it at the same time. But there's the cure—"Another kiss is all you need."

She's got to have that fatal, addictive kiss from the one who controls her. Again, she's alive but she's dead.

Yet she has found a way out—her seductiveness enables her to shift roles. Instead of being choked, she will become the choker. She will deliver the controlling kiss, and then she'll possess her victim for the moment, a victim who can't be saved. It all comes down to whoever has the power of the kiss.

Again Amanda compels us toward the defining image of a "vampire." Just as she had been fatally kissed, she would, in turn, kiss her victims. But it was still an addiction.

This picture was taken about a year before Amanda brutally spiked her roommate, Meredith, on the night of November 1, 2007. The self-portrait snapshot of Amanda's psyche suggests that when she dressed in all-black—as she did on Halloween, the day before the murder in Perugia—she prowled the night attempting to feed her addiction to love. After what happened to Meredith, this picture takes a decidedly darker turn. Her unique "V for vampire" stamp appears in both photos so far and will occur in the last photo pictured below.

Photo three—'Amanda get your gun' (drawing substituted)

The photo of Amanda related to this drawing circulated worldwide on the Internet after her murder charge.[30] In it she kneels on the ground behind an antique World War I Vickers machine gun mounted on a tripod base in the military Museum of the Castle Garrison in Graz, Austria. The picture was taken in late August 2007 by her sister, Deanna, when they toured Germany and Austria together after visiting their German relatives. At this time the two of them were on their way to Perugia where Amanda hoped to find a room before college classes began in late September. They had stopped by the museum in Graz because their mother had lived there as a young child as well as in Germany. Significantly, Amanda's Prussian-born grandmother, Oma, had lost her own mother at age eight when she was killed in an Allied bombing raid. Unresolved violence surrounded the family. Oma (to whom Amanda was closely attached) later lived nearby in Seattle with her ex-U.S. Army husband.

Spotting the gun, Amanda had spontaneously dropped to her knees and grabbed it—compelled to act out the scene reflecting her desperate need to "grab." It's all strikingly immature but strikingly revealing perhaps suggesting she suffered an early wound when she was immature/young and violently grabbed. She suggests that the setting resonated with something deep inside of her. Remember, her unconscious constantly communicates in response to immediate situations and must tell deeper truths. *Those things said or done in jest can secretly speak volumes.*

We read the scene symbolically as a serious message adopting a basic principle of forensic profiling: take everything from the mind of a suspect as a revealing super-intel communication no matter how it appears on the surface. This photograph has to do with violence. It puts Amanda in possession of a long murderous weapon. Coincidence? We will see as we continue to decode the picture.

She grimaces in pain, her mouth wide open as she appears to be screaming "Ah…" in agony, pretending as though she's firing away. Her closed eyes suggest she's been wounded perhaps fatally and also screaming in retaliation, her rage enormous. The pose reminds us of movie scenes in which a wounded soldier grabs a machine gun to fire back at the advancing enemy.

The photo tells several stories. The vintage weapon suggests that she's secretly furious after having sustained severe deep-seated wounds early in her life—her closed eyes at the same time reflecting her denial. The gun rests on its large tripod suggesting an inverted "V" which is another reason she was attracted to this particular gun. Just as the other two photos we examined were replete with "V" symbolism, so is this one.

Both of her arms are bent holding the massive weapon, her knees are bent up under her and her distinct closed thighs apparent slightly exposed and her

---

30 http://www.dailymail.co.uk/news/article-1233399/Amanda-Knox-Behind-Hollywood-smile-liar-narcissist-killer.html#ixzz2odOWCyDu

dress opened above the knees emphasizes her lap/crotch—in a series of "V" images. Her body merged next to the huge gun with no space between them suggests the weapon represents an extension of her—as does its large V-shaped tripod. Her familiar "V" code suggests again "V" is for vampire. She implies she is the "Vampire—Machine Gun Amanda"—and can inflict unimaginable damage in a burst of secret rage. She's prepared to erupt at any moment.

Her open mouth—her teeth showing as the bullets are biting her target—confirm the message, "See how bad my vampire bite can be. See how big a hole I leave in my victims." Once more she reflects on how dangerously seductive she is.

Like the dark photo with her spiked heel on the piano bench, here she reveals how quickly she will violate boundaries. For instance, she shows no regard whatsoever for the exhibits in the museum. Whatever and whenever she wants to touch or possess she will do so in a heartbeat.

But we must not miss that she prominently exposes her neck again, pulling her head to the left. She grimaces, and at the same time she suggests a possible neck wound on the right side—or one about to occur. The massive gun is also on the same side of the neck suggesting that she suffered a brutal emotional trauma, her open mouth itself suggesting a severe vampire bite at this exact moment. It's show and tell time.

Her head turned revealing only one ear repeats the message that she has a terribly dangerous secret which she cannot face. Again, the exposed ear is pierced. She suggests again she experienced a sharp, penetrating physical wound and/or an emotional trauma so severe it was the same thing in her mind. She wears a huge but narrow circular earring suggesting femininity but also it's as if someone invisibly grabbed her from behind with it, jerking her head back, exposing her neck. The circular metal earring suggests entrapment. Was she telling us that her injury took place in the family circle, reminded of it here in her mother's home town?

Her body also suggests a fetal position and an early emotional wound. Was her body language hinting again at that secret which she could never admit to herself? Was her super-intel predicting that she would end up behind entrapping metal bars because of her reactionary rage?

Other Visual Clues

Don't overlook the rest of her pose—Amanda dropped her large purse in the background, temporarily left behind. Shortly we will review a key forensic document Amanda wrote right after the crime in which she uses the key image of a purse (her bag) to portray her identity.

A container that safeguards her private things including her identification suggests another picture-message—that Amanda herself was left behind, neglected, in some major way. She wasn't sure who she was or where she belonged. This went on behind her back pointing to an early event that she also doesn't want to consciously recognize, but it's there in the back of her mind.

Even more frightening, another powerful gun also on a tripod points directly at her purse or handbag, a feminine symbol. Unconsciously, she has that gun aimed at herself. For some powerful reason she envisions herself as on the verge of being blasted to smithereens at any moment by another vampire. Some major event in her life implies the message, "See how badly I was bitten previously, wounded, virtually destroyed." She reminds us in another way that she constantly saw her life as hanging by a thread, precisely matching the self-portrait snapshot linked to the Palmer video.

And she is furious about it—and deeply needs to retaliate. Dropping to her knees Amanda also suggests how suddenly she can get lowdown and deliver unexpectedly violent blows. Fatal blows delivered while wallowing on the floor. We remember the morning before the murder Amanda conversed pleasantly with her roommates including Meredith whom she would brutally kill within the next 10 hours. Strangely enough, she suggests a roller-coaster ride as well—one second she's up, and in the blink of an eye she's down.

Ironically, Amanda's grimace also suggests a hint of a smile. Again she points to a primary way of coping—laugh it all off. Consciously this picture was just another lark for Amanda, another strange move on her part. She burst into laughter when her sister took the picture, again implying how she covers up her rage. Her closed eyes suggest massive denial of her rage. Yet Amanda wrote "The Nazi" on back of picture.[31] She buries her pain and rage but one symbolic word gives it away, Nazi. Somebody—some key figure in Amanda's life—was a Nazi. Was Amanda suggesting she was angry with her parents, specifically her German mother? She strongly suggests that her mother's German relatives would have reminded Amanda of being far from home and her mother. They would remind her again of being abandoned by her family in America—the real targets of her rage. But don't miss the fact that Amanda declares that she was a "Nazi" headed to Perugia.

Her super-intel chooses this key moment to speak symbolically in the language of "jest"—both in action (dropping to the floor and grabbing a gun) and word ("Nazi"). To verify the message she ties unconscious body language to unconscious verbal language. In this way, she demonstrates how the deeper mind works.

She uses this combined deeper language to speak on "another channel" simultaneous with her conscious mind message, "this is just a joke." Think of the familiar Separate Audio Program option on today's digital TV sets. A person is watching TV in English, and with a click of the button he can hear the same program in another language (e.g. Spanish). The human unconscious mind communicates in another language if we want to hear and see it.

---

[31] John Follain, *A Death in Italy*, St. Martin's Press, New York, p. 22.

Decoding pictures with vivid symbolic images prepares us for decoding the verbal "word pictures" of the super-intel. The three photos of Amanda Knox prior to her murdering her roommate present astounding body language and associated symbols—offering a working hypothesis.

The reader will find time and time again how the photos highlight the written forensic profile--making the images behind her words come even more alive.

We must not overlook that her extremely impulsive behavior in the museum represents the deepest of urges, her primitive painful need to grab, to touch, to be touched and nurtured. She suggests a continuing saga in body language, that when she couldn't grab a breast, get the nurture she needed, she grabbed a symbolic gun. In Freudian terms she grabbed a phallic symbol substituting sex for nurture. But she was still the secret one in power. And when that failed in all its secret destructiveness and all her secret fury she then grabbed a real 'gun,' a real weapon. One more photo, one more reckless grab.

Amanda came by her masculine side honestly. She tried to be the son her father never had. She was the only one of his four daughters who could maintain emotional control by never crying, just as men were never supposed to weep. But it was all a cover. She could never be still and would constantly shock people with her sudden shifts from stoicism to impulsive behavior. She was always directing her joking, passive-aggressive behavior at her father by doing thiongs such as jerking a pillow from behind his head as he drank a beer on the sofa often raising his ire. It was exactly as she experienced him disrupting the soft comforts of home. She would have the last word, "She would just do 'and deal with it later.'"[32]

Amanda crouching behind the machine gun provides a vivid show-and-tell picture of just how wounded she was and the severity of her rage—like nowhere else except the crime scene.

The picture foreshadows that scene and soon she will provide the words that match.

They will confirm the photographic image represents a secret confession of just how big and bad a murderer she could be. And this image was created immediately before she arrived in Perugia.

All three photos contain violent images: scissors, spikes, piercings, and machine guns.

But unconscious body language only serves as an introduction to a vastly superior unconscious "mind language." It is that language which holds the key to the case and it will begin to unfold in Chapter Five.

---

[32] Burleigh, pp. 33-34.

56

Passive-Aggressive Behavior
Roller-Coaster Rides

Around the time she was leaving for Italy, Amanda reflected on her Facebook page that a lot of her friends thought of her as a hippie, *"but I am... just weird. I don't get socially embarrassed and...have very few social inhibitions...I love new situations...The bigger and scarier the roller coaster the better."* In truth, "roller coasters" scared Amanda. One time you're up, one time you're down, always going real fast. Was there more to her image?[33]

Surely these words reflected her major way of coping—her counter-phobic swagger. Charging head-on into fearful situations like roller coasters thinking they are really fun in a momentary conscious dose of invincibility. There's no better way of describing such false bravado. It reflects major denial, but exceptionally thin denial. It was the same "roller-coaster denial" she demonstrated in the military museum when she suddenly dropped to her knees.

Upon reflection, describing herself as having "few social inhibitions" was Amanda's way of saying, "I am a rule-breaker. I do anything I want to do, act anyway." Subtle in-your-face passive-aggressive anger, "get over it." This becomes clear soon enough with her roommates in Perugia.

In any case, she raises the question—had she been on a scary emotional roller coaster in her life and denied it?

Hair-Raising Parents

Her life with her parents was a roller coaster of sorts. Her parents offered her a home and family but stalled and took their time about it. Her father offered her love and nurture, but then he left so quickly, down a chute. Her father loved her, but balked at providing child support. Her parents loved their kids, but remained constantly angry with one another. Her parents offered her wisdom but too much freedom. They expressed serious concern about her going far away to Italy but then let her go to ride a sky-high roller coaster all on her own.

Amanda secretly implies that deep down she was a very scared person—and she was especially vulnerable when she was "up." The higher she went, the greater the potential fall.

She implies that there was something deeply disturbing about her life.

And she suggests that she was taking her roller coaster personality to Europe—planning on taking others for a ride.

Her behavior prior to her departure from the U.S., amidst her European travels before settling in Perugia, and immediately upon landing in Italy suggest that she had come to take the most hair-raising roller coaster ride of her life. It would be a thrill a minute until she and those around her quickly ran out of thrills.

---

[33]Follain, p. 20.

The 'No-Show' Job

The minute she disembarked in Europe, Amanda manifested signs of passive-aggressive behavior. Before classes started in Italy, she had gone to Germany in early-September 2007 to take an ideal short-term internship job for several weeks with the Berlin government at the Bundestag. Her uncle in Hamburg had used his political connections to obtain the hard-to-get position for her. Amanda lasted less than two days on the job.

She's quickly frustrated with the work and the language difficulties. She reportedly feigned illness on her second day on the job and impulsively left work. She reported there was nothing for her to do—suggesting Amanda had to be on the move, and got bored easily but secretly very anxious. (She would never slow down until she was arrested two months later.) Amanda recovered quickly but she never resigned her job, just didn't show up. She then spent her time touring and drinking wine in cafes—seeking pleasure, avoiding the pain of responsibility. She much preferred sight-seeing, calling it "fantastic."

Amanda had taken all her uncle's hard work and thrown it away—claiming it was all a misunderstanding. And she apparently lied about matters as well. Her impulsiveness invariably leads to destructiveness.

In leaving her job Amanda expressed passive-aggressive anger at her uncle, but that displaced anger was actually meant for her parents who had neglected her. Looking closer at leaving work she described on her MySpace page on September 15, 2007, *"I was in the way and they didn't need me there anyway."*[34] We must not miss how this might fit her deep down feeling when her father left—how she saw it looking back. Walking out on the job repeating how he had walked out on her.

An absent worker also suggests absent supervision by her parents. That "no-show" on the job reflects "no-show" parents who let her travel halfway around the world even though they realized she wasn't ready tackle life's complexities. By walking off the job in Berlin, she was announcing, "I cannot handle this trip—I am overwhelmed."

Her dramatic behavior reflected a change from her work habits in Seattle signaling again a separation problem. Her "addiction" to pleasure also quickly emerged. Typically, it included personal indulgence and avoidance of responsibility undergirded by her typical denial.

Keep in mind that Amanda had just turned 20 on July 8th before leaving for Perugia. Of course, every birthday vividly reminds her of the circumstances surrounding her birth.

Secret Anger

Amanda used promiscuous sex as a behavioral defense—she hid her vulnerability behind it. As an example, she had sex with the first guy she was

---

[34]Nadeau, p. 16.

attracted to in Italy. On August 30, 2007, shortly after arriving in Italy, she and her sister, Deanna, traveled by rail from Milan to spend one night in Florence before heading to Perugia the next morning to find Amanda a place to live.

On the train Amanda appeared to be on the prowl. She made eye contact with a handsome young Italian man whom she called Cristiano. Although she described him as barely able to speak any English, they flirted and ended up sharing a café meal in Florence that night—and very soon thereafter Amanda shared his hotel bed.

Boldly she claims in her memoir, *"This was my first bona fide one-night stand."* Understand this was not about sex. It was about separation.

> As she lived out her "addiction to love," Amanda demonstrated that addiction is just another word for abuse—self-abuse and invariably abuse of others. It's just another word for anger.

Having just arrived in Italy, she visited Perugia the following day, the college town where she planned to spend the next year. She was living out the "Addicted to Love" video. Her promiscuity reflected major separation anxiety—fear. She desperately needed to quickly undo the individuality of separation.

Promiscuous sex serves to cover a million anxieties. It's pleasure versus pain. Those free-spirited authors, those "Friends of Amanda" who endorse her "freed-up feminism," totally overlook her intense, long-standing pain.

Even Amanda later implies that the one-night stand with Cristiano was foolish and left her with a permanent case of oral herpes. It left her with an open wound, one visible and one deep inside, which reoccurred from time to time. It haunted her throughout her trial when she appeared in court with prominent cold sore on her lips.

In short six weeks in Italy, Amanda slept with numerous guys. Besides Cristiano from the train, she got together with a Greek guy, an Albanian, an Argentinian, an Italian (Daniel de Luna on two different occasions including the night they met), in addition to her Italian boyfriend, Raffaele, whom she also slept with on the night of their first date and continued to do so for seven passionate days, one of the six weeks.

Much later in the summer of 2014 news emerged that there was even more to "Cristiano," the man she met on the train. An Italian crime magazine, Giallo, reported the police had linked him to a drug ring in Perugia. Police allegedly got his name—they referred to him as "F"—from Amanda's phone after the murder, which led to his trial for dealing cocaine in Perugia. She had phone contact with him in the days before and after the murder. Police suspected that she bought drugs from him, and he continued an occasional sexual relationship with Amanda. It appears she now had a source for cannabis and possibly other drugs. Her admission that they had smoked a joint together easily could have been an unconscious confession she obtained drugs from him.

This also fits with a possible denial confession in her memoir when Amanda admitted lying to police initially about smoking pot but wrote, "I never bought any pot; we didn't know any drug dealers."[35] The fact Amanda mentioned that she contracted oral herpes from him could reflect an ongoing poisonous relationship whereby he continued to supply her with toxic illegal drugs.

Ironically her suspected drug dealer friend, "F," was reportedly connected to man named Luciano who had previously been arrested for trying to murder his own brother with a kitchen knife, inflicting 16 wounds during a fight over money and drug dealing in July 2006.[36]

The closer we look at Knox's life in Perugia, the more dark corners emerge.

Sex and Anger

Her promiscuous sexual behavior offered her another cover, another shield against an especially unacceptable emotion—her anger. Her sexual carelessness reflected her need to degrade herself, her need to abuse herself. She used it as a defense mechanism which distracted her from recognizing how she turned her anger on herself. It's just another display of passive-aggressive anger.

Two incidents reveal what guys thought of her easy availability. One young man described that Amanda was not the kind of girl you would bring home to your mother. That was after she performed oral sex upon him shortly after their meeting.

Word got out about her sleeping with Daniel, a friend of her downstairs neighbor, Giacomo Silenzi.[37] Meredith's friends also heard from the guys downstairs that Amanda was earning a reputation as a slut.

As she lived out her "addiction to love," Amanda demonstrated that addiction is just another word for abuse—self-abuse and invariably abuse of others. It's just another word for anger.

In her book, *Angel Face*, author Barbie Nadeau writes, "Consensual sex is not a crime. So Amanda's promiscuity has little bearing on the murder itself."[38] But if we read her promiscuity as symbolic of disguised anger, then that's another matter altogether.

Roommates in Perugia

In *Angel Face,* Nadeau picks up on Amanda's disguised aggression. The author detected Amanda's escalating passive-aggressive anger—often expressed through her sexuality. It was becoming her most familiar cover.

For Amanda, sexuality always entailed exhibitionism. In a transparent

---

[35] Knox, p. 109.
[36] http://www.telegraph.co.uk/news/worldnews/europe/italy/11000907/Amanda-Knox-drug-dealer-associate-arrested-for-attempted-knife-murder.html
[37] Nadeau, p. 23.
[38] Ibid., p. 29.

beauty case she kept in the bathroom she shared with Meredith, Amanda brazenly displayed her pink "Rampant Rabbit" vibrator along with condoms. That vibrator, which Amanda described so innocently as a "gag gift," shocked the British roommate. Indeed it gagged Meredith. She felt embarrassed when friends visited. Meredith was compelled to deny that the vibrator was hers. She explained it as an example of her American roommate's outrageous behavior.

Nadeau observed, "It seemed as if Amanda was brandishing it as a symbol of her sexual power over Meredith."[39] In reality it was another hostile act on Amanda's part. It symbolically said to Meredith, "I want to shock you and overwhelm you." It also implied the put-down, "I'm experienced, and you're not. I am sexually uninhibited, and you're not." Such braggadocio is childish but by engaging in such, even symbolically, Amanda emphasized that she still suffered from childhood wounds and resulting feelings of inadequacy. Her audacious sexuality, ostensibly "adult" activity, covered up for a severely wounded inner child.

Amanda abused all of her roommates in a similar fashion, startling them with her sexual behavior. She would bring strange men home at night, not always to have sex with them apparently. Nevertheless, this caused her roommates to fear being robbed or raped by these strangers. Thus they viewed Amanda as careless and endangering. This was yet another powerful projective identification.

Amanda's extreme disrespect and passive-aggressive tendencies reared their ugly heads.

She continued taking all the people she met on her personal roller coaster ride of unpredictability, constantly jerking them around. The only question was where next.

Alienating Antics

Amanda's immaturity revealed itself on September 20, 2007, her first day in Perugia at her new abode, No. 7 Via della Pergola. It was her very first meeting with Meredith who had overcome obstacles to gain entry into the University of Perugia, much larger and more prestigious than the University for Foreigners in which Amanda was enrolled. Right off Amanda felt Meredith had researched the opportunity better than she had and wished that she "hadn't been so laser-focused on her own program."[40] Amanda discovered her new roommate "had been crushed when her British university turned her down for the program abroad but she fought the decision and won."[41] Meredith, who had already been in Perugia for a few weeks, invited Amanda out to meet her newly made British friends. It did not go well.

---

[39] Ibid., p.30.
[40] Ibid., p. 27
[41] *Knox*, p. 25

In her memoir Amanda reports that, "Meredith's friends fit the reserved British profile. I'm sure I struck them as a…loud American. I was energetic and outspoken, even by nonconformist Seattle standards…probably louder than I meant to be." Next she reprised an outburst she'd been infamous for in Seattle. Amanda suddenly erupted boisterously into song while her new acquaintances were in the middle of a conversation, sipping wine and eating pizza at a local restaurant. The reaction of everyone at the table spoke volumes as Amanda tells us, "…what drew laughs in Seattle got embarrassed looks in Perugia…the same quirks my friends at home found endearing could offend people…who were less accepting of differences. A person more attune to social norms would have realized that immature antics didn't play well here."

She added, "It was my first day here and reality had punctured my expectations." Not only had Meredith and her friends pierced her dreams, Amanda herself had punctured her own balloon of expectations, self-sabotaging her reputation. It would not be the last time. Again, Amanda had demonstrated that she would embarrass others at the drop of a hat. She admitted only later that she violated social norms to the extreme. Her words, "didn't play well here" reveal that she knew she was difficult and didn't interact well with others.

That particular dinner apparently took place on the third day in a row that Meredith had invited Amanda out with her friends. By now, Meredith's friend, Sophie, was turned off by this brash American woman. In addition to her bizarre singing in public, Amanda also annoyed Sophie by lapsing into monologues exclusively about Amanda herself.

Right off Sophie sensed that Amanda was jealous of her. Pisco, the owner of the Merlin pub, was fond of Sophie, and Amanda was not used to sharing the spotlight. Amanda was about competition and power—clearly a cover for her pain.[42]

Increasingly Erratic

In the six short weeks Amanda lived in Perugia before Meredith's murder she became increasingly erratic. Her actions didn't play well at home. She was slovenly, leaving her things scattered around the house and neglecting to wash her dishes—to the point that her older Italian roommates, Filomena and Laura, set up a cleaning schedule for everyone. Predictably, Amanda failed to abide by the rules. Again her actions communicated disrespect and disguised anger.

But it was Meredith who bore the brunt of Amanda's disrespect and passive-aggressive anger. Amanda would often leave the toilet unflushed or failed to scour it. Even when menstruating she wouldn't flush the toilet. At one point not long before she was slain, Meredith told her friend, Robyn, that she had quarreled with Amanda over the flushing issue. Their roommate, Filomena, was aware of tension in the house and observed that Amanda could be "mildly

---

[42] John Follain, *A Death in Italy*, St. Martin's Press, New York, p. 28.

anti-social." Filomena's mother also thought Amanda "was always cold and distracted. She seemed to be in a different world." In contrast she saw Meredith as "always very sociable."

Again Amanda had secured a job working at a new local bar, Le Chic, owned by African Patrick Lumumba. She worked there for about a month. But soon she began slacking off at her job. She proved flirtatious to the extreme, constantly seeking attention from men, not taking orders, not cleaning tables.

"Every time I looked around she was flirting with a different guy," Lumumba noted. He couldn't believe how she would even two-time her boyfriend, Raffaele, right before his eyes whenever he visited. "She was on the lookout for men all the time," the tavern-keeper said.[43]

Lumumba's wife, who normally trusted him, felt that Amanda was cold-hearted and deceitful. She believed that Amanda would push her aside in flash if she could get her claws into Patrick.

Later Patrick minimized this story but again suggests that he just wanted out of the media spotlight. In other ways he confirmed Amanda's viciousness. The story's believable because it was so consistent with Amanda's enormously competitive nature over guys.

Around her enough to know, Patrick Lumumba observed that Amanda didn't sleep much. And he knew she was smoking a lot of pot, drinking more, and becoming more irritable. At times she flew into rages and then apologized. Was it possible Amanda was also dabbling in cocaine? Lack of sleep, irritability and increased tolerance to alcohol are all indicators of cocaine abuse.

Finally Patrick told the same writer he had informed Amanda that he was also hiring Meredith part-time. The British girl had occasionally dropped into Le Chic, and Lumumba liked Meredith's friendly, winsome demeanor. Amanda said, "Fine," but Lumumba knew how jealous she was of Meredith.[44] Such behavior by Patrick seems consistent with his easy-going nature—first to demote Amanda, then have Meredith start up for a few hours a week to let Amanda down as easy as possible. He had noted the two roommates had drifted apart.

Later during her police interrogation while seemingly trapped without an alibi, Amanda actually blamed the murder on Patrick Lumumba. That was an absolute lie. He would be jailed for two horrendous weeks, but then freed after Amanda's story proved false. Her behavior suggests she was secretly furious with Patrick over her demotion and knew she was on the verge of being fired.

From the beginning to the end of their employee-employer relationship, Amanda had taken Patrick Lumumba on the most terrifying roller-coaster ride of his life.

---

[43]Paul Russell and Graham Johnson, *Descending Darkness: The Murder of Meredith Kercher*, Pocket Books, London, pp. 155-56.
[44]Ibid., p. 157.

Non-Stop Sex and Drugs

Seven days before Meredith's murder, Amanda met Raffaele Sollecito at a classical music concert. Amanda had gone to the concert with Meredith almost certainly in an effort to undo all the other damage she was doing to the roommate relationship. But Meredith left at intermission to go have dinner with friends, not inviting Amanda. Her leaving was a picture itself that their relationship was taking a break, and now Amanda would be moving into the next part of their lives together increasingly by herself. She would make her own music if she could.

That's when Amanda met Raffaele. They hit it off immediately. They tuned into each other's secret needs like heat-seeking radar. The couple began an unhealthy symbiotic relationship. Amanda spent every waking moment at Raffaele's apartment except to shower at home or to work.

The shy and inexperienced Raffaele announced to his friends that he was having non-stop sex with Amanda—accompanied by smoking pot or even stronger hashish. Raffaele had a longstanding history of abusing drugs, and now he was off and running again. Amanda had characterized Raffaele to friends as "having had a serious drug problem." Meanwhile, Amanda was taking her own drug use and sexual activity to a new level.

She was so sex-obsessed that—behind Raffaele's back—she even made love again with her former one-night stand, Daniel de Luna. It was passive-aggression on top of passive-aggression, this time betraying Raffaele. Her own carefree betrayal strongly suggests that, in her earlier life, someone, in a similarly carefree manner, had seriously betrayed *her*.

Like Patrick Lumumba and like her roommates, especially Meredith, now Raffaele was on the roller-coaster ride of his life, totally oblivious to it, unaware that it was picking up speed. And Amanda rode that roller coaster with him, going higher and higher—literally (with drugs) and figuratively. Police who delayed drug testing on both Amanda and Raffaele later found traces of narcotics in both of them. Her self-abuse was increasing exponentially.

Amanda's Guilt

And her betrayal behavior ate at her. In the incident on October 30th sitting around her cottage she had told her three roommates that she was depressed for deceiving her American boyfriend, D.J., by sleeping with Raffaele.[45] Again her two Italian roommates assured her it was normal to see someone else when she was away. Meredith was the only one who stood firm, declaring unequivocally she would never cheat on a boyfriend.

Amanda then declared, "But I don't really feel guilty because with Raffaele I'm happy—he treats me well." Yet she had even betrayed him with Daniel.

---

[45]Follain, p. 48.

Her passive-aggressive betrayal anger level now rose higher than ever, making her lower than she ever expected, low-down guilty—and, as usual, she remained in denial about it.

In the same conversation with her roommates, Filomena and Laura reminded both Meredith and Amanda the rent would be due the following week. Meredith offered to pay the 300 euros early, but Filomena told her to wait.

Amanda's Prophetic Announcement

Looking back we can see that Amanda was sensing Meredith pulling away—rapidly. By late October the rift was ever widening as their two Italian roommates had also noticed. When Meredith left the concert with Amanda at intermission the week before on October 25th it was another acute separation moment for Amanda—symbolizing far more than she realized on the surface. Once again Meredith was leaving to go with her friends and Amanda was alone— staring dead-on at the future of increasing alienation in her own home. Her two Italian roommates were getting tired of her act, too. Deep down Amanda knew how her behavior continually distanced others.

Despite having set up the entire rejection herself completely outside her conscious awareness, still her antennae were on high alert. How would she handle the awful terrifying moment?

Predictably, she handled it the same way she had been especially for the last six months. She would cling. She would have sex as soon as she could. She needed an out from the suffocating separation that unconsciously engulfed her at that time.

Magically, Raffaele appears and asks to sit beside her—although Amanda had already been protecting herself by eyeing him as a substitute. Now her hero Harry Potter was in the house and sitting beside her as his look-alike Raffaele. In her memoir, Amanda described, "he came along at the moment I needed a tether."[46]

She had no idea if he was as needy as she was but she was hoping. Her dreams came true beyond her wildest imagination and his. That is they came true before they turned into a living nightmare for both of them and Meredith, a nightmare that hasn't ended yet.

Raffaele was a clear substitute for Meredith. And he offered sex and drugs immediately—two wonderful escapes. But he offered one more dangerous escape—fantasy. He was into make believe like she was and together they could conquer anything.

But deep inside Amanda was secretly in a panic and coming to a not-so-slow boil. She would never spend another night in bed at No. 7 Via della Pergola. She would never spend another night in her bed there as Meredith's roommate. In fact Amanda would never spend another night there period, except

---

[46]Knox, p. 52.

on clean-up duty when—out of sheer terror of the police—she would finally clean the place up, after Meredith was gone.

Seething Rage

Two months before leaving America for Italy, Amanda had posted on her MySpace page a short story she wrote back in 2006. Proudly she reported that this short piece of fiction had won an award.

The story had its origins in her creative-writing class when the teacher assigned the task of producing a dark short story. Amanda's mind could go any direction it wanted. The assignment was similar to a psychologist's Thematic Apperception Test (TAT) in which a person is shown a picture of a scene and asked to make up a story about it.

Her story was entitled, "Baby Brother." It centered around two brothers who live together—Edgar, 8 years older than his younger brother, Kyle. They shared a room together growing up. In the story Kyle is 21 and supported by the older Edgar. The action begins as Edgar anxiously confronts his younger brother about recently drugging and raping a girl.

Kyle maintains that it really wasn't rape. *"A thing you have to know about chicks,"* he explains to Edgar, *"is that they don't know what they want. You have to show it to them."*

Edgar becomes furious with Kyle and asks him, *Did you know her name?"* Immediately Kyle viciously attacks Edgar, hitting him in the face. At that point Edgar orders Kyle to leave but a soon realizes that when Kyle returns the next day he will take him back. He can't really separate himself from Kyle.[47]

Violence was preying on Amanda's mind. In her short story, she argued that sex was really about power and dominance, not intimacy. She depicted sex as disguised rage.

Was Amanda cultivating a dominant role to cover her vulnerability? Was she painting a picture of herself? Was she secretly all about violence instead of sex? Surely, she had allowed us a brief glimpse deep into her mind.

She also invokes her usual "denial code"—that her "no means yes"—a recurring pattern of denial which will come into play during her interrogations and trials.

In her book on the case, author Nina Burleigh commented that Amanda's short story (and one other) had "provided the world a glimpse into the inner working, *maybe the subconscious*, of the sunny girl. It was not at all as pretty as she was. Like everything else she posted, *no one knows why she chose those stories*. They deal with rapes, self-cutting, voyeurism, and domestic violence, but their most striking aspect is an intense detailed description of the physical sensation of *suppressed rage*."[48]

---

[47]Ibid., p. 18.
[48] Burleigh, p. 60.

But Burleigh unknowingly picked up on the key to Amanda's story and the one party that does know why she chose those stories, that knows the secret rage behind those stories and knows all her secrets. That would be Amanda's own unconscious which tells the entire story. To be correct, for every ounce of suppressed (conscious) rage— Amanda had a thousand ounces of repressed (unconscious) rage. Suppression is conscious and known. Repression is unconscious and known only to the all-seeing unconscious super intelligence.

Attorney's Trick Backfired

The picture of Amanda painted by her parents is awash in soft pastels and wispy watercolors.

Their daughter was an honor student, a totally honest person who had no behavioral problems other than "brief" promiscuity. That air-brushed picture of Amanda suggests idealization, parents' nature inclination to see their children in a positive light.

Early in Amanda's memoir she tells of conversing with Spyros, a Greek guy in his late-twenties who worked at an Internet café and had inquired about her soccer talents. She told him, "I prefer to play soccer rather than watch it. I was a defender on a premier team." She wanted him to know how good she was and volunteered that she was *"'sly like a fox'...that's what I was—fast and reliable for finding an opening and stealing the ball. My teammates nicknamed me 'Foxy Knoxy.'"*[49]

Once again sometimes people confess without realizing it. Here Amanda presents the image of a crafty animal, not all that big or muscular, but one who hides out, catching his victims completely off guard with a sudden, lightning-quick move and a vicious, fatal bite. An animal which constantly seeks an opening—a way to steal its victim's life—while the prey has no clue about what is to come. In describing her soccer talents, Amanda suggests who she really is deep inside while she's simultaneously hiding that true personality. Also note her reference to stealing. She had reportedly stolen money from Meredith which certainly would have aggravated their conflicts.

Remember that "Foxy Knoxy" was the title of her MySpace page, a title she had chosen herself. At her first trial, her attorneys had stated that "Foxy Knoxy" was an old nickname from childhood. That clumsy effort to mislead the jury may have backfired. That jury—which found her guilty—understood that this defendant was "foxy" indeed. She even killed like one.

---

[49] Knox, p. 31.

Chapter 4: Rafe and Rudy, her Blood Brothers

Raffaele Sollecito

Raffaele Sollecito was born March 26, 1984 in southern Italy. Both his mother and father came from well-established, well-to-do families. His mother had given up a career as an accountant to raise her two children. Raffaele was the youngest, his sister seven years older.

At the time of his birth a marital crisis between his parents loomed large. His father Francesco was a successful surgeon who spent long hours at the hospital.

Raffaele's comments about his early life and later behavior suggest that he had faced major obstacles. He described both parents as loving, "I was always the darling of my mother and father, but above all of my mother. My mother's world revolved around the family, and especially around me."[50]

His comment suggests he may have been *too* special. The danger in an overly symbiotic relationship is that his mother might make him too dependent on her, too needy, and usurped both his identity and his masculinity. She may have made him "addicted to her."

His mother also had a family history of depression. We can imagine she was depressed at times over her circumstances. *Naturally this mother—dealing with the constant threat of separation from his father—might well cling to her baby boy.*

When his mother had such increased neediness, Raffaele would have perceived it deep down. The unconscious mind reads situations in depths we never before imagined. In such a case Raffaele would have felt not only loved but simultaneously attacked by her—consumed. He would be aware that his mother needed to cling to him. Likewise he would feel his father encouraged the attack and thus exposed Raffaele's own weakness. Surely the son, the youngest child, would be wholly unprepared for separation—as was his mother. His behavior will suggest that was the case—that from early on Raffaele had a separation problem.

---

[50]Follain, p. 44.

Lastly he would feel deep abiding anger about the whole rotten deal—rage even. But how do you express anger at such a loving mother? So you bury it in that huge emotional closet we call the unconscious. You carry on, and if you're naturally shy as Raffaele surely was, you keep that rage at bay. It gets totally submerged. On top of this he had an older sister who would also take charge letting him retreat further. (She took a job in law enforcement as a police officer in Perugia, and before the Italian Postal Police arrived, he would call her the morning Meredith's body was discovered.)

All this can go on with only a few overt clues. Certain key ideas would have formed very early in his mind. His view of women would be shaped by this experience. He idealizes the strong dominant woman who takes care of your every need, who protects you. And the woman who hurts you, and the father who permits it. But—as much as you hate it—you like it, too.

Don't think for a minute such powerful emotions aren't concealed behind a wall of denial. Raffaele would describe his childhood as "idyllic."[51] Obvious denial because it was far from that behind the scenes. We know how important the first three years in a child's life are. The major emotional task in these years is to "separate and individuate" from his mother—move toward a secure sense of himself, his own identity. Raffaele suggests he never fully individuated which will become more apparent.

Tension, Terror and Separation

Marital tensions continued over the next eight years and Raffaele would have picked up on it in a heartbeat. He would experience deep abiding impending separation every single day. Kids know what's going on. He would have immediately buried such fear as deeply as possible. But it loomed there waiting to erupt at any moment. As the marriage disintegrated, Raffaele's mother likely clung to him ever more tightly.

When Raffaele was age 8, his parents separated and eventually divorced. With it came the hurricane of emotions Raffaele had long dreaded. He described his father as the one who sought the divorce—his mother always loved his father but it wasn't reciprocated. He saw his father as unable to settle down—apparently seeing several women. In the end, Raffaele lived with his mother. Now his separation issue became more massive than ever.

Inevitably he would have experienced a multitude of confusing emotions. He would particularly grab onto his mother more—making him even weaker. He might even feel a desperate need to consume her—to cope with the enormous separation anxiety. For example, patients undergoing in-depth therapy who have experienced such significant early loss often reveal engulfing cannibalistic impulses buried deep in their unconscious. It's as though they then have the

---

[51]Ibid.

person permanently inside them, never lose them—a very primitive variant of the familiar Christian communion. It fulfills a need for maximum oneness in order to stave off the terror of being alone.[52]

Guilt—Raffaele the Nuisance

Raffaele felt guilt over his parents' breakup. He described his childhood shyness which made him afraid of people because "I didn't want to be a nuisance or say something stupid."[53] Invariably kids see life's traumas through the lens of "my fault." Notice he implies that deep down he even blamed himself for the divorce—*he was a nuisance.* Somewhere the thought surfaced that if he hadn't come along he wouldn't have taken his mother's attention from his father.

On top of this, he had lost his masculine role model in the home on a daily basis—his father. It would have been a very confusing time for Raffaele. Now wounded, feeling abandoned, lost, guilty, fearful and confused—all the myriad of emotions that go through a vulnerable child's mind—he would have been quietly very angry about it all. No matter how furious he felt, however, Raffaele would not feel safe about expressing it.

All his experiences would center around the loss of the home as he knew it: the loss of his father, the loss of a mother who couldn't give him his space, and the loss of his self—his individuality—being unprepared by his mother and father to handle it.

Of course some people handle trauma better than others, but as we will see, Raffaele folded under its pressure. Now he carried the scars along with a boatload of unfinished business. In the years ahead his pain quickly made its appearance. On the surface, such people can appear as though all is good with the world but as the years pass we can see that something devastating was controlling and guiding him. To understand his behavior we must appreciate the intense emotions behind them, emotions which he would have buried.

Obsessive Hobbies & Habits
The Knives

Now comes the fixation on knives. During his early childhood Raffaele started collecting knives as a hobby. Knives and swords—big knives. Don't think it's by accident. Read the tea leaves amidst the storm. He desperately needs the sharp and shiny objects for some powerful underlying reason. He starts carrying one wherever he goes. While he wouldn't let his friends use his knives fearing they would cut themselves, but he would casually carve designs on trees.

His obsession with knives suggests a strong need for protection in the face of an imminent attack. He also hints that he would like to hurt others, maybe

---

[52]These are revealed in their dreams, stories and images.
[53]Follain, p. 44.

wound someone the way he had been wounded. But he fears hurting them as well, and maybe himself. His knives suggest that he's locked in a struggle pitting his violent impulses against his fear of violence. He keeps his knives closed, but he really likes switchblades that he can flick open in a second. He needs quick protection. Under stress he could attack with the flick of a wrist.

Manga Cartoons

As a young teenager, Raffaele developed another fixation, this time with violent Japanese manga cartoon characters. In the *Pretty Soldier Sailor Moon* series, the comic's heroines are teenage females with magical powers who battle evil forces attacking earth. His schoolmates ridicule his manga mania, and he's an outcast.

Raffaele's preoccupation with evil forces suggests that he's afraid of being attacked but also afraid of attacking. It's also a projection of his extreme rage. These powerful forces in his mind explain why friends later described him as detached. Unconsciously he was constantly in overload.

In his mind who might be the evil forces? Likely the family situation, with its intense mixture of love-hate relationships—way beyond the norm—would have produced fierce emotions, feelings that, on a deeper level, all seemed downright evil to him. He had been consumed and lost his identity, never really had it and all, and the process was all covered over with love and good intentions.

Then his father, whom he feared, became the epitome of evil—loving on the one hand but emasculating him on the other, while in total denial about his shadow side and effects on Raffaele. But there's a deeper issue. Like all sons, Raffaele surely competed with his father.

Subliminally, and at times consciously, a young child wants to be his mother's favorite, and wants her all to himself. Raffaele had crossed the danger point for a young male child. He had grown too close to his mother. In his mind, he had taken his father's woman away. He had stabbed his father in the back.

Remember, too, his father was a surgeon who made a career out of using a knife. Raffaele would have been well familiar with the surgical idea of "going under the knife."

No wonder Raffaele constantly needed a knife. In one important side of his paternal "love-hate" relationship, he implies a deep fear of his father. Strong and domineering, this was the one person from whom he needed to be protected because Raffaele had witnessed his father's hostility—his long-running quiet or not-so-quiet neglect of his mother.

This may well explain Raffaele's excessively withdrawn, non-assertive demeanor. It further explains his need to discharge his emotions in a fantasy world. It was too unsafe in the real world. The intensity of his emotions led him inexorably to fantasyland, where he was safely in control.

His particular fantasy of the strong woman who protects the vulnerable world, males included, is a recurrent theme in his life. Perhaps this hints at his "angry" feminine side—safer to disguise himself in a woman's role. Or better yet let an aggressive woman act it out for him.

His potential for explosive rage is initially expressed in the form of outlandish fashions. During this time Raffaele cut designs in his hair, dyed it yellow and—mimicking the manga cartoon characters—wears earrings.

Violent Pornography

At age 18, Raffaele enrolled at the University of Perugia, a long distance from his hometown on the coast of southern Italy. He needed to get away from the continual bickering of his divorced parents. His father insisted he enroll in small men-only college of 350 students, a private school within the larger university.[54]

But Raffaele couldn't get away from his secret violent tendencies. Before long he began watching explicitly violent pornography on DVDs. His fascination with porn was so conspicuous that a classmate actually complained about it to the administration. One official investigated and discovered Raffaele watching a bestiality video depicting an animal having sex with a woman. In this way, he vicariously experience increasingly violent impulses toward women—impulses intrinsically merged with sexual excitement. At times, Raffele became morbidly fixated on sex.

He immersed himself in fantasy. His fellow students noted, for instance, that he masturbated constantly. His exhibitionism drew ridicule from classmates concerned about his unchecked sexuality.[55]

Drugs

Before Raffaele left for Perugia along with two friends, police charged him with possession of hashish. Drugs provided a new momentary escape. He continually lost himself in the false comfort of substance abuse.

Again he has another obsession—drugs. Raffaele repeatedly filled his web page with drug-centered content often posting pictures in a drug haze. He wrote about always staying high. Unquestionably he had a major drug problem.

Drugs have another advantage. They allowed Raffaele to express major passive-aggressive anger through his use of mind-altering substances. His attraction to illegal drugs gets a huge reaction from his father whom he can now control. Feeling helpless, his father talked to his son daily reminding him to stay away from drugs. In addition his father kept Raffaele further dependent upon him to maintain his affluent lifestyle, with his well-appointed apartment, fine clothes and a sporty Audi. A surgeon and not a psychiatrist, Raffaele's father in

---

[54]Ibid., p. 45.
[55]Nadeau, p. 33.

his desperation failed to realize that indulgent financial support providing him plenty of money for drugs and the constant telephone efforts at control usurped his son's autonomy. Instead, it all encouraged his son's dependent personality. Those phone calls—during which his father could tell if his son was high and would berate him—were still a daily occurrence when Raffaele met Amanda Knox. Yet from his side Raffaele invited emotional abuse with his drugs.

Mother's Death 2005

After ongoing health problems, Raffaele's mother died in 2005 when he was 21 years old. Her death occurred at the same time his father was finally settling down and close to marriage. Raffaele's father remarried in September 2007 only months after the death of his first wife. Some think Raffaele's mother committed suicide, but there was no real evidence. Raffaele thinks she died of a broken heart—figuratively and literally. In fact, she died of heart failure. His wound and accompanying anger at his father over leaving his mother years ago had been freshly reopened.

He has now experienced the maximum separation event in his life—the final separation from the mother he loved so. She died when he was off to school. She died after she had informed him she had nothing to live for. Here he had finally separated and individuated, he had his own life to some degree, and now his mother was gone. His guilt would have been overwhelming, as he later confessed to Amanda.

Castrated By His College

A thread of violence continued to run through Raffaele's life. After his mother died in 2005 he wrote a blog attacking his college for what he had experienced there his first three years. He revisited the time he wasn't allowed to have women in his room, which actually suggested unconsciously that he was now alone without his mother. He complained that the college "castrated" the male students trying "to keep everyone's instincts in check."[56] It's his own self-description—his masculinity was deeply wounded. He had experienced *significant violence: castration.* Who really inflicted the wound?

By implication, he significantly blames his father the "knife man." Remember, his father was a urological surgeon who often operated on male genitals. At times, he would also carry out necessary castrations. Such a reality would have played with Raffaele's mind, and now his father seemed even more dangerous—propelling Raffaele even deeper into a fantasy world. The men-only college was also his father's idea, confirming Raffaele's belief his father wanted him to stay away from women.

Raffaele made the connection between "knives" and his father after the murder. *He bragged to his father that he had carried his ever-present*

---

[56] Follain, p. 45.

switchblade with him to the police station during questioning.[57] Such behavior expresses a need for protection around authority figures such as his father and the police.

But Raffaele also realized that his mother wounded him, undermining his masculinity by keeping him weak and dependent—a status exacerbated by her death. On top of this he had effected a self-castration by his own choice to avoid intimate relationships with women.

Yet he has displaced all of his enormous anger onto the university. Compelled to express it publicly, he could not contain himself. And with his mother gone—the strong, loving woman who protected him against the dangerous world—he felt extremely vulnerable.

He remained shy with girls and continued to act out his sexual impulses in fantasy. He had had few sexual experiences with girls until he met Amanda.

Manga Takes a Violent Turn

Raffaele continues with his preoccupation with illustrated stories depicting brute violence. But now his manga fascination shifted to more vicious images with vampire-like characters couched in erotic scenes. He was attracted to a volatile mixture of violence and sex.

When he got involved with Amanda he was reading *Blood: The Last Vampire 2002*. The police used it to build their case against him. Again the heroine is a young girl, nude throughout much of the book, who violently rids the world of evil forces, the vampiric Chiropterans. The sexy slayer commits extreme violence including beheadings and total bodily destruction of her enemies. Yet she herself is controlled by the government until she breaks its spell. *Blood*'s central theme celebrates the idea of violent payback, raging revenge.

Raffaele saw himself as the secret feminine vampire who must deliver payback revenge and simultaneously punish himself for being the aggressive male. He would also be very vulnerable to a woman enacting such violence on his behalf.

Violent Internet Photo

On his Facebook page, Raffaele posted different photographs of himself spaced out on drugs. One particular picture stood out. In it he was wrapped like a mummy in white surgical bandages all the way to the top of his head with his eyes peering out. In his partially free right hand he displayed a meat cleaver, ready to cut. He also held a jug of pink alcohol.

The image suggests first that he's both severely wounded and imprisoned, almost in a straightjacket. Surgical bandages say that he was wounded by his father, the surgeon—cut over his entire body including his head and neck. It was

---

[57] Nadeau, p. 33.

so severe it was a near-death wound, that's how destructive his early pain really was.

The pink drink subtly suggests a blood-tinged liquid and indicates that he has been consumed in a vampire-type attack and now wants to strike as a vampire in turn. Somebody sucked the life out of him, and now he wished to suck the life out of others. His vampire manga preoccupation underscores this continued theme in his mind. He realizes that drugs are consuming him and others, and that drugs could potentially fuel a loss of control.

Accompanying his Facebook pictures, Raffaele wrote about being stoned for an entire day and asserted that he enjoyed indulging in risky behavior. "Sometimes I am completely crazy," he wrote.[58]

One Step from Graduation

Bright and still capable despite his ongoing drug use and his fantasy obsessions, Raffaele managed to get through college. It was often a struggle, but he did it. He kept his head above water. Still his frequent daily use of marijuana and hash kept his fears at bay while fueling his fantasies. Surely Raffaele experimented with harder drugs, too—even up to the crime.

On the verge of one of his few accomplishments—his graduation from the university— Raffaele's life took a turn toward rage and ruin when he met Amanda Knox. In October 2007 Raffaele stood on the verge of personal success—graduating in December and moving to Milan with a promising future in computer technology. His stepmother had spent months preparing a big family celebration in Milan for his graduation. But he has a problem—it is an acute separation-individuation moment. Deep down, he's terrified of trying to make it in the world by himself. He is extremely vulnerable and at that propitious moment unconsciously Amanda is looking for him—and Raffaele is looking for her.

A Fusion of Forces

Once again Raffaele met Amanda at a classical music concert on October 25th, 2007. She had arrived at the concert with Meredith who as we know left Amanda at intermission.

Meanwhile, Amanda and Raffaele had been eyeing each other at the concert, and he asked if might take Meredith's empty seat. Amanda agreed. And only eight days from then Meredith will have no place in her Via della Pergola home either. Raffaele will help remove her from it.

Meeting Amanda offered Raffaele an escape and an opportunity to break out of his shell. But the break-out will end up breaking him. It was a broken relationship from the beginning.

---

[58]Ibid., p. 33.

He immediately finds himself hopelessly lost in this American beauty. That night, after their first few hours together, he invited Amanda to his apartment where they had sexual intercourse. For Raffaele it was a particularly momentous occasion. That night he lost his virginity at age 23. After years of masturbating to images of pubescent cartoon characters and porn movies, he had actually become intimate with a real woman. On the one hand now he was enacting his buried self—previously discharged in fantasy and escape. Before long, he and Amanda started having sex three and four times a day with her—in real life. No wonder he bragged about it to his friends – his instincts finally unleashed. But he immediately retreated into drugs, routinely smoking pot and hash before and after sex. It's possible he was also using cocaine or even heroin over those seven intensive days in October when Amanda was with him constantly. He can't stand being an individual. Nor can she.

Secret Violence

Such an intense situation entails subtly disguised violence. They were breaking all the rules of a real relationship. They had too much connection, too much closeness, before each one even knew the other person. Their unconscious destruction of the boundaries of individuality was heightened by constant use of pot and hashish. The immediate fusion, replete with the soaring joy of sexual ecstasy, felt so right to Raffaele, so good at the moment but underneath it was secretly producing a fusion bomb of nuclear proportions.

Unconsciously Amanda recognized the devastation as she started to feel guilty for betraying her American boyfriend, D.J., for getting so extensively involved with Raffaele. She is also betraying the naïve Raffaele and herself with the illusion of "caring." They don't know each other well enough to really care yet. It's mutual betrayal, mutual deception—shared self-deception.

Briefly recognizing her guilt she then buries it, saying, "I really don't feel guilty. Raffaele treats me well." Deep down she knows neither one of them are treating the other one well. In any case, during their concentrated "romance," Amanda overtly betrayed Raffaele by sleeping with another guy. Maybe Raffaele looked the other way. He certainly did when Amanda was at work openly flirting with customers in his presence.

She and Raffaele are feeding their "addicted to love" sides, at a fast speed. Their high-speed relationship severely damaged their judgment and self-esteem, as they rolled faster and faster into no-man's land of fantasy. Turns out, they were not far from taking one more giant step.

Raffaele told his father about it and how he treated Amanda like a little girl, but he was talking about both of them really. Two wounded children.

Quickly the question becomes can these two severely wounded people— who are now wounding each other and others—stay in their own world and leave the rest of the world alone? Raffaele's answer is a blatant "No!" Now he's addicted to Amanda, using her to escape and guide. But secretly he's waiting to explode like she is—furious at all those who have wounded him so. He's furious over his vulnerability, furious over his evil but blaming it on others.

Harry Potter

While Raffaele preferred manga, Amanda was fixated on Harry Potter books. J.K. Rowling's hero was an orphan who had magical powers to overcome evil people. In certain ways Harry Potter was similar to Raffaele's manga female hero who conquered evil.

The way Raffaele looked, with his glasses and innocent demeanor, even reminded Amanda of Harry Potter. So now she had a willing Harry Potter under her own control. Raffaele later made the connection himself noting the similarity of Amanda's Harry Potter obsession to his manga mindset, "What we have in common is the love for fantasy, dreams, imagination."[59]

These two abandoned orphans, each harboring secret violent tendencies, became a team and Amanda called the plays. Amanda loaned him her cynical view of the world feeding into his. They're in a battle with evil, and consciously they're the good guys. That's always the way it is with the conscious mind with its infinite ability to rationalize—a tendency tripled when drugs are involved.

And Amanda whispers in his ear that now he can enact his fantasy. Now he can unleash his payback revenge. All he has to do is pull out his knife.

When Amanda connected her world of hurt with his world of hurt they truly became one, more than one. *The whole is greater than the sum of the parts.* Their rage combined registers off the charts. When Amanda offered him the opportunity to enact his fantasy life by conquering someone and teasing someone as he was teased—especially when that someone had hurt his newly beloved Amanda—the offer is too appealing. Now he can enact the cruel game of life played on him, blind to how he played it on himself too. Now they can make faces at the world whose face had been so cruel to them.

Now they could play their little knife/sex/ridicule game on Amanda's roommate, Meredith,

What they never counted on was that the intense emotional baggage they both carried would be detonated when their teasing game suddenly spiraled out of control.

And they planned to employ the help of one other person who had as many emotional wounds as they did, Rudy Guede, a fellow escape artist who dabbled in his own manga world of fantasy and drugs. And comforted by their drugs, on that fateful night they made their way to Via della Pergola 7.

When all was said and done they carried a lifetime of explosive emotions times three. Yes, this hash-fueled trio secretly carried matching baggage. And it was heavy as hell.

---

[59]Burleigh, p. 118.

Rudy Guede

Rudy Guede's origins are littered with dysfunction. He was born to one of his father's girlfriends, Agnes, on Christmas Eve 1985 in Agou, Ivory Coast—a poor country and a former French colony. His father, Roger Guede, never married his mother. A few months before Rudy was born, Roger impregnated another woman who gave birth to another son.

Because of tough economic times in the Ivory Coast, Roger immigrated to Italy in 1987 to find work. Roger never attained actual Italian citizenship, as Italy only issued registration certificates for most foreigners. Roger did manage to learn a trade as a bricklayer, and found that he could find plentiful work. He mostly lived in Perugia, the Umbrian college town, but his construction jobs took him all over Italy as he labored long hours at each jobsite. As a result, he was often gone for weeks at a time.

When Rudy was five years old, his mother announced she could no longer look after him, and

Roger ended up taking Rudy back to Perugia to live. Like his father he would become a registered foreigner and it was those official fingerprints which the police found on file years later. Those fingerprints would identify Rudy Guede as one of Meredith Kercher's killers.

At first Rudy spoke to his mother on frequent telephone calls to Africa. Those long-distance chats soon stopped. He would see his mother only once more in his life during his only trip back to Africa at age 12. After that, Rudy refused to visit there again.

After arriving in Italy with 5-year-old Rudy, Roger quickly abdicated his parental responsibilities. He became an absent father in too many ways. Rudy would roam the streets. Occasionally, he was underfed and was always poorly clothed. After his wanderings, if Rudy arrived home too late his father would lock him out of the house. Young Rudy would have to sleep outside or in the attic.

Rudy's first teacher, Mrs. Tiberi who was also a neighbor, observed much of this and learned more from Rudy. She was struck by how alone he was. He had little communication with his father, and lacked any maternal figure, a significant loss, she thought, for such a young child. But Rudy never complained and kept his secret pain to himself. Mrs. Tiberi described his father as "very young, disoriented, and not prepared to take care of a child."[60]

The teacher arranged for neighbors to feed Rudy after school and make sure he was clothed and did his homework before sending him home to his father at night. Mrs. Tiberi was the closest surrogate mother he ever had and remained involved in his life all through high school. Like a good Italian, she made sure he became a church member and introduced him to the priest along with coaches and teachers who became surrogate father figures.

---

[60]Ibid., p. 93.

Rudy's Personality

Mrs. Tiberi's son, Gabriele Mancini, who was 10 years older than Rudy, described him as extremely likeable, polite and someone who elicited the help of others spontaneously. It's likely Gabriele sensed Rudy's deep needs. "He never showed anger," Gabriele said. "He would stay quiet if he was upset, he was melancholic, not violent."[61] Friendly Rudy played it close to the vest about his pain. He kept it all locked up inside so it's no wonder that it would sometimes send him plummeting into depression.

His repeated losses and abandonments were so threatening and frightful they amounted to near-death experiences. A child in a foreign country roaming the streets, lacking food and clothing as well as emotional nurture, he would know deep down, "I could die." Instantaneously he would bury the thought, shifting into his familiar oblivion: "Don't talk about it, don't even think about it." That was his reflexive escape response, going off into his own world. But a deep abiding fear continued to haunt him. Beyond his coping mechanisms, at his core he remained deeply wounded, extremely afraid, extremely angry and guilty which would transform him into a classic self-punisher.

Later the local priest connected him to the local semipro basketball team. Rudy was a talented athlete and also focused on basketball for a while. At age 16, he began exhibiting signs of trouble. He dropped out of school after his father was gone for an extended period and Rudy had argued with his father's common-law wife. Rudy was again wandering the streets, basically parentless.

Mrs. Tiberi, still in contact, intervened with social services, and Rudy seemed to have struck a gold mine. Overnight, he went from street person to first-class foster child. He was brought to live in the home of one of the wealthiest families in Perugia. Paolo Caporali owned and operated a successful vending company and also owned the Perugian semiprofessional basketball team. Rudy had played basketball with Caporali's son who asked his father to take Rudy in, and the family agreed.

Truly they treated him like one of the family. He lived in their palatial home and ate three meals a day with the family. He vacationed with them at the beach in the summer and in the mountains when they went skiing in the winter.

Before long, Rudy opened up to the Caporalis. He told them about times when his father had abused him by locking him up all day in a bathroom while he went off to work. Later Rudy would write about another instance when his father had broken a stick over Rudy's head and he bled "like a fountain."[62]

Self-Sabotage

But eventually Rudy couldn't handle success. He could not handle being the poorest kid in town who suddenly lived with the wealthiest family.

---

[61]Ibid., p. 94.
[62]Ibid., p. 95.

After being with them for more than a year, the Caporalis had enrolled him in a prominent mathematics school. But Rudy soon quit going to classes and lied about it. Even after they hired a tutor Rudy continued to avoid his lessons and kept lying. He failed all his courses.

Everybody in the family became angry with Rudy for breaking their trust, and Mr. Caporali insisted that if he wasn't going to school, Rudy had to get a job. The family even provided him a job as a gardener at a villa they owned outside Perugia, and he lived there. But he continually missed work or was late showing up, always making excuses. His pattern of dysfunction and lying continued.

So the Caporali family cut ties with Rudy in the fall of 2006. His adopted sister, Ilaria Caporali, saw him as charming but unscrupulous. "He was a good guy," she said, "but he lied. He didn't know the difference between good and bad. He had no values." The father later commented that they knew Rudy was a liar and had been in trouble, but they gave him every opportunity as a son. When it became clear that he wasn't interested in work, Mr. Caporali said, "In the end we asked him to leave our home because we couldn't take it any longer."[63]

This well-meaning family couldn't take Rudy's extreme passive-aggressive anger expressed through lying. He continually let them down after making big promises. After he'd earned their trust, his blatant disregard for their work-ethic values made their pain that much greater. All he was doing was letting others feel what he'd felt deep down all his life while blocking it all out of his mind. And he directed his extreme disguised anger at himself in a violent self-sabotage. Indeed, the loss of his Caporali family status was an enormous self-imposed abandonment. One more home he had lost. *Rudy also suggests that massive guilt drove him.* He didn't think he was worthy of anything good. And he surely would have felt guilt over his abuse of the Caporalis.

Down the Slippery Slope

During the winter and spring of 2007 Rudy went to live with his father's sister and her husband in northern Italy near Milan. His Aunt Georgette had immigrated to Italy from Ivory Coast years before and had taken care of Rudy briefly off and on. Once again they provided a home and helped him get a job working in a café. Once again Rudy started out with promise but soon lost the job when the café closed. In the late spring of 2007, he moved back to those familiar streets in Perugia.

He had little money, no job prospects, nor any real future. But Mrs. Caporali came to his aide and provided a reference which allowed him to rent a small apartment in Perugia *centro*. Rudy now lived just a stone's throw from Raffaele's apartment.

---

[63]Ibid., p. 96.

Perugia Party Scene

Rudy again hung around the fringes of Perugia's college environment which merged with the local nightclub party scene. He smoked pot, was a small-time drug dealer and played basketball at the Piazza Grimana courts right next to Via della Pergola 7 where Amanda and Meredith lived. These courts were on the shady side of town and near the center of the local drug trade if not the center.[64] Rudy had become known as "The Baron" when his intended nickname "Bryon"—for the American basketball player Bryon Scott—morphed into "Baron." But he was a hanger-on, and barely hanging on.

In July 2007 he met Victor, a 19-year-old American college student coincidentally from Seattle's University of Washington (Victor, however, was not familiar with Amanda Knox). Rudy and Victor met at a nightclub and shortly began playing basketball together.

Victor noticed some unusual things about Rudy. At one point Rudy had bought some cocaine prior to going out to a club. Not much later Rudy became phobic about the drug dealers, refusing to go near them. Victor surmised that Rudy was avoiding the dealers because he owed them money. Clearly self-destructive behavior. Rudy also made comments about feeling threatened *because drug dealers and robbers frequented his neighborhood.* His paranoia became so pronounced that Rudy began spending nights at Victor's place, sleeping on the floor. He didn't feel safe at home. And he was telling bizarre stories about watching a guy follow a girl home and how Rudy had come to the rescue and fought him off. *Violence dominated Rudy's mind increasingly.*

Rudy operated below the radar, hanging out with lots of free time and his reference to numerous drug dealers and robbers in the neighborhood suggest he was actually one of them. He was surrounded by cocaine and heroin dealers. He could easily obtain drugs for others as he did for the four guys who were Amanda's downstairs neighbors. At times he would pass out in friends' homes because of excessive marijuana use or other drug use, even falling asleep on the toilet. His paranoia, preoccupation with violence and his allusions to drug dealers and thieves suggest not only a downhill slide but a preoccupation with drugs and stealing to get them. That surely included stealing from drug dealers by not paying. He implies, as does his behavior, that he was using more drugs—contributing to more depression. Or he stood on the verge of it. Habitual stealing, if not already in place, appears to have been just around the corner. Rudy's judgment was poor and getting worse. He was extremely vulnerable and desperate.

He also seemed to be lying more than ever. At one point he told his friends that his father was a computer programmer in Florence who gave him an allowance. Remember, lying is passive-aggressive behavior—deception. And he was lying about money.

---

[64] Russell and Johnson, p. 152.

Soon Victor and his roommate deduced that Rudy didn't like to sleep alone at his house because he had a severe sleep-walking disorder. This reflected a possible dissociative state often connected to major childhood traumas. While clearly still asleep, Rudy would get up and act out scenes: lecturing to Victor and his roommate like a teacher or even crawling on the floor like a dog barking. The problem got so bad that Victor asked Rudy to move back to his own place— only weeks before Victor returned to the United States in late-September 2007. Those were two more abandonments for Rudy to absorb—"go home" and "I'm leaving."

Friends Concerned

Rudy had been depressed and withdrawn in late-2006 after losing his golden opportunity with the Caporalis. In September and October 2007 longstanding friends reported he was depressed and really lost. One said that Rudy "had lost his bearings," and his situation was "unstable" partly because he was running out of money. The friend noted how Rudy escaped temporarily by meeting new people, especially foreigners, but noted, "I think he was very down."[65]

In October Rudy ran into Mrs. Tiberi and her son, Gabriele, who knew Rudy had no job. They were extremely concerned, but Rudy brushed it off in his typical denial, mentioning he had been lucky to have had so many families helping him in Italy when he was young. But Mrs. Tiberi said Rudy's response to their concern led him to reflect on unresolved familial issues. "He didn't have a true family, a blood family, but he had a lot of families." He didn't have a true blood family—no blood because it had been sucked out of him by those blood kin who wounded him.

Rudy Meets Amanda

In late-September as Rudy slipped further and further downhill, he met Amanda Knox. He knew her four downstairs neighbors—the guys—from the basketball courts. One night he drifted into their house and one of the guys, Stefano, recalled waking up to see Amanda, Meredith and Rudy in their kitchen. No one knew for sure, but many suspected Amanda had invited Rudy. She had met him some time earlier at a nightclub—and had seen him on the streets enough to speak to him.

Rudy also described visiting her downstairs neighbors one night, smoking pot when Amanda came down. Her neighbors reported that Amanda smoked a lot of marijuana and hash, and Rudy watched her repeatedly smoke joint after joint. Rudy was strongly attracted to her and wanted to bed her. When Meredith also came in, she appealed to him, too. But neither girl was sexually involved with him—until Meredith's last night.

---

[65]Burleigh, p. 125.

Break-Ins and Robberies

In late-September and October Rudy's behavior appeared to take another major turn. He was increasingly linked all too coincidentally to thefts and break-ins with unusual matching features.

On Monday, October 8[th,] the owner of a nursery school in Milan (which is several hundred miles north of Perugia) discovered a break-in had occurred over the weekend. The intruder had made himself at home cooking large meals leaving the kitchen in a mess and also robbed the cash drawer. The nursery had never before been robbed. Was the perpetrator announcing that he or she had been robbed emotionally by a lack of nurture signified by the kitchen? He left a mess reflecting passive-aggressive anger over the neglect. *Two weeks later Rudy was caught in the same nursery school after spending the night there in a questionable break-in.*

Back in Perugia on Saturday October 13th, a thief had broken into the office of lawyers Brocchi and Palazzoli, smashing a window and disabling an alarm. The burglar stole Palazzoli's laptop and Brochhi's cellphone *which police would soon find in Rudy's possession.* In addition he consumed a Fanta from the refrigerator and randomly rummaged through the office scattering many things about but also arranging certain items in neat piles or aligned in a puzzling, possiblky ritual, fashion. He had left two jackets—one from each attorney— spread out on the floor covering the broken glass window.

Strangely the perpetrator had turned up the heat when the weather was still mild leaving the office stiflingly hot when Palazzoli discovered the break-in. Was the perpetrator confessing through the crime scene that he lacked nurture and warmth, and that he was under pressure—that the heat was turned up on him and in turn he was getting heated up himself?

Ten days later, on October 23rd, the house of Rudy's next-door neighbor, Mrs. Madu Diaz, was severely burned while she was away. The fire had been apparently been accidentally caused by a thief or thieves. They had broken in, cooked up a feast pulling food stuffs out on the floor, and had started the fire by leaving a scarf over a lamp in the bedroom. Mrs. Diaz's cat died in the fire, and her mother's gold watch was stolen. This resembles Rudy's increasingly bizarre behavior. The discarded scarf matches how the Caporalis observed that Rudy was always losing his jacket when he lived with them.[66]

Leaving discarded clothing suggests being unclothed and unnurtured especially in a bedroom which also symbolizes rest, comfort and home. A lost scarf suggests lack of warmth particularly around the neck which itself signifies extreme vulnerability. Was this another announcement by the perpetrator vis-à-vis unconscious staging that he was neglected to the extreme—especially by a woman since he burned a woman's house? Carelessly leaving a scarf over a light suggests blocking out light, symbolically covering the light of life and putting it

---

[66] Ibid., p. 127.

out. *We keep in mind that shortly Rudy would participate in a specific attack on Meredith Kercher's neck where her life was snuffed out.* In so doing Rudy again suggests extreme rage at a female, certainly an announcement of rage aimed at his abandoning mother—the most basic warmth or lack thereof a human being ever experiences.

Did this crime involving his next-door neighbor prefigure Rudy's intentions deep down reflecting his overwhelming pain—reflecting where his vampire rage originated? It has all the earmarks of Rudy's self-neglect and his passive-aggressive fire to go with it, and another sign that he was escalating.

Only four days later, on Saturday, October 27th back in Milan, Rudy was caught after an apparent Sunday night break-in by the owner of the nursery school where the previous robbery had occurred on October 8th. Rudy had obviously spent the night there and the owner testified at the Knox trial she thought he had broken in when she arrived on Monday morning, and called police.[67] He appeared unruffled and kept saying, "I didn't take anything." (Later she conceded that one of her staff workers may have given Rudy a key to the school.) But when police came they found a knife he had just stolen from the nursery school kitchen in his knapsack along with the stolen laptop and cellphone from the Perugian lawyers' office two weeks prior.

Rudy would later be charged with possession of stolen property and his eventual sentence in the murder would be extended 16 months. He was never charged with breaking and entering. But the coincidence that his "break-in" at the same nursery school where a previous break-in and robbery had occurred only weeks before along with simultaneously possessing stolen property from the recent break-in at the lawyers' office seems too much to bear.

Two days after his encounter with the police at the nursery school, on October 29th Guede bizarrely shows up back in Perugia at Brocchi's office. He wore a basketball tank top despite the cold weather insisting he didn't take the cell phone or laptop. He claimed to have bought it from someone at the train station in Milan. Rudy suggests that massive guilt over his violations also controlled him.

Vampire Violence

People always described Rudy as gentle and non-violent, but even a cursory examination of his life reveals an active and angry dark side. In a video he made long before Halloween 2007, Rudy posed with his eyes rolled-back, teeth bared and declared in English, "I'm Count Dracula. I'm going to suck your blood." The video was posted on YouTube by friends. Rudy additionally wrote on his MySpace page that he was a vampire and loved drinking blood. Think— what was he trying to tell us, then and now?

---

[67] http://truejustice.org/ee/index.php .

After he was arrested, Rudy made up a story about meeting Meredith at a club Halloween night and asking her, "Wanna suck up my blood because you lost the Cup?"[68] In fact, nobody recalled seeing Rudy there. His comment suggests an unconscious confession that he was involved in Meredith's bloody death where indeed she lost to him in a huge way—her life.

He then extrapolated this lie by claiming to have watched the rugby final with Meredith when England lost to South Africa a few weeks before at the downstairs neighbors' apartment —which is uncertain. The bigger picture remains of a contest in which Meredith herself played and lost.

> All three had overwhelming personal pain, similarly coped with denial, spoke through actions and demonstrated enormous passive-aggressive anger— inflicting their pain on others and making them feel it.

Rudy had also enjoyed violent manga and American comic books which fused murder and sex. His Internet sign-on name was Trigon—a sadistic, cruel and powerful demon character from the American comic *New Teen Titans*. Like Raffaele, in a number of ways he signaled his penchant for violence existed. It may have been submerged, but it had sudden submarine torpedo potential. And—given the many attacks he experienced in his short life—why wouldn't he? Despite the praiseworthy rescue attempts by kind Italians, Rudy's torpedos had already been locked and loaded, waiting for the "fire" command. Rudy was that close to the edge, closer than he ever consciously imagined.

To say Rudy was vulnerable to acting out in an explosive way seems like an understatement now with knives and arson coming into the picture. Looking back at his behavior, we see plenty of disguised aggression—lying, skipping school, missing work, breaking all the rules, dealing drugs, stealing and now carrying a knife. He was circumstantially linked with break-ins in recent weeks. Like Amanda's and Raffaele's lives, Rudy's life was swiftly spiraling out of control.

Secretly, Rudy was furious. And he spoke through actions—like his abusive mother and father. His early foundation with all its holes had come back to haunt him and others. He was on the verge of major violence as his fingerprints and DNA all over the crime scene would testify. And for the record he was secretly furious with his father. *After he was jailed, Rudy specifically requested that his father not contact him.*

Two days before Meredith's murder, Rudy was seriously short of cash and asked to borrow 10 euros from a student acquaintance. His rent was likely coming due on the first of the month.

In desperation, Rudy was about to become a real-life Dracula and suck the

---

[68]Burleigh, pp. 134-5.

life out of someone else, repeating what had happened to him. All the forces were aligned.

Rudy was ready to drop another bomb just as he did on the Caporalis. His behavior had said to them, "Do you think you can save me? I am destruction itself—Dracula—watch my rage and guilt go to a new level." He had hurt the Caporalis—"the haves." He would find another way to hurt one of the "haves"—Meredith Kercher, who unlike Rudy had a promising future.

Crime was how he eventually coped with his pain. He derived temporary power from committing crimes and threatening others and taking from them what he needed. (Later his DNA would be found on the zipper of Meredith's purse where she kept her money.)

We can see the similarity of his baggage to that of Amanda and Raffaele. All three had overwhelming personal pain, similarly coped with denial, spoke through actions and demonstrated enormous passive-aggressive anger—inflicting their pain on others and making them feel it. And all three made extensive use of fantasy for escape. Meredith's murder started out as a fantasy game and ended up as a symbolic act of payback revenge misplaced onto their victim.

All three possessed a striking ability to detach themselves. They were a trio of footloose roamers who wouldn't talk or complain, who couldn't express pain. Consider this: immediately after Meredith's murder Rudy went dancing for two hours at the Domus club. Then he fled the country to hide out way up in Germany.

The following email contains Amanda's secret confession explored in Chapters 5—15.
Email   November 4, 2007   2:45 a.m.

To: My close friends
From: Amanda Knox, Perugia
This is an email for everyone, because id like to get it all out and not have to repeat myself a hundred times like ive been having to do at the police station. some of you already know some things, some of you know nothing. what im about to say i cant say to journalists or newspapers, and i require that of anone receiving this information as well. this is m account of how i found my roommate murdered the morning of friday, november 2nd. The last time i saw meredith, 22, english, beautiful, funny, was when i came home from spending the night at a friends house. It was the day
after halloween, thursday. I got home and she was still asleep, bu
after i had taken a shower and was fumbling around the kitchen she emerged from her room with the blood of her costume (vampire) still dripping down her chin. We talked for a while in the kitchen, how the

night went, what our plans were for the day. Nothing out of the
ordinary. then she went to take a shower and i began to start eating a
little while i waited for my friend (Raffaele-at whose house i stayed
over) to arrive at my house. He came right after i started eating and
he made himself some pasta. as we were eating together meredith came
out of the shower and grabbed some laundry or put some laundry in, one
or the other and returned into her room after saying hi to raffael
i began to play guitar with raffael and meredith came out

p 2

of her room and went to the door. she said bye and left for the day.
it was the last time i saw her alive.
after a little while of playing guitar me and raffael went to his
house to watch movies and after to eat dinner and generally spend the
evening and night indoors. we didnt go out. the next morning i woke up
around 1030 and after grabbing my few things i left raffael's
apartment and walked the five minute walk back to my house to once
again take a shower and grab a chane of clothes. i also needed to grab
a mop because after dinner raffael had spilled a lot of water on the
floor of his kitchen by accident and didnt have a mop to clean it up.
so i arrived home and the first abnormal thing i noticed was the door
was wide open. here's the thingabout the door to our house: its
broken, in such a way that you have to use the keys to keep it closed.
if we dont have the door locked, it is really easy for the wond to
blow the door open, and so, my roommates and i always have the door
locked unless we are running really quickley to bring the garbage out
or to get something from the neighbors who live below us. (another
important piece of imformation: for those who dont know, i inhabit a
house of two stories, of which my three roommates and i share the
second story appartment. there are four italian guys of our age
between 22 and 26 who live below us. we are all wuite good friends and
we talk often. giacomo is especially welcome because he plays guitar
with me and laura, one of my roommates, and is, or was dating
meredith. the other three are marco, stefano, and ricardo.) anyway, so
the door was wide open. strange, yes, but not so strange that i really
thought anything about it. i assumed someone in the house was doing
exactly what i just said, taking out the trash or talking really
uickley to the neighbors downstairs. so i closed the door behind me
but i didnt lock it, assuming that the person who left the door open
would like to come back in. when i entered i called out if anyone was
there, but no one responded and i assumed that if anyone was there,
they were still asleep. lauras door was open which meant she wasnt

home, and filomenas door was also closed. my door was open like always
and meredith door was closed, which to me weant she was sleeping. i
undressed in my room and took a quick shower in one of the two
bathrooms in my house, the one that is right next to meredith and my
bedrooms (situated right next to one another). it was after i stepped
out of the shower and onto the mat that i noticed the blood in the
bathroom. it was on the mat i was using to dry my feet and there were
drops of blood in the sink. at first i thought the blood might have
come from my ears which i had pierced extrensively not too long ago,
but then immediately i know it wasnt mine becaus the stains on the mat
were too big for just droplets form my ear, and when i touched the
blood in the sink it was caked on already. there was also blood
smeered on the faucet. again, however, i thought it was strange,
because my roommates and i are very clean and we wouldnt leave blood
int he bathroom, but i assumed that perhaps meredith was having
menstral issues and hadnt cleaned up yet. ew, but nothing to worry
about. i left the bathroom and got dressed in my room. after i got
dressed i went to the other bathroom in my house, the one that
filomena dn laura use, and used their hairdryer to obviously dry my
hair and it was after i was putting back the dryer that i noticed the

p 3

shit that was left in the toilet, something that definately no one in
out house would do. i started feeling a little uncomfortable and so i
grabbed the mop from out closet and lef the house, closing and locking
the door that no one had come back through while i was in the shower,
and i returned to raffael's place. after we had used the mop to cleanup the
kitchen i told raffael about what i had seen in the house over breakfast. the
strange blood in the bathroom, the door wide open, the
shit left in the toilet. he suggested i call one of my roommates, so i
called filomena. filomena had been at a party the night before with
her boyfriend marco (not the same marco who lives downstairs but we'll
call him marco-f as in filomena and the other can be marco-n as in
neighbor). she also told me that laura wasnt at home and hadnt been
because she was on business in rome. which meant the only one who had
spent the night at our house last night was meredith, and she was as
of yet unaccounted for. filomena seemed really worried, so i told her
id call meredith and then call her back. i called both of merediths
phones the english one first and last and the italian one between. the
first time i called the english phone is rang and then sounded as of
there was disturbance, but no one answered. i then calle the italian
phone and it just kept ringing, no answer. i called her english phone
again and this time an english voice told me her phone was out of

service. raffael and i gathered our things and went back to my house. i unlocked the door and im going to tell this really slowly to get everything right so just have patience with me. the living room/kitchen was fine. looked perfectly normal. i was checking for signs of our things missing, should there have been a burglar in our house the night before. filomenas room was closed, but when i opned the door her room and a mess and her window was open and completely broken, but her computer was still sitting on her desk like it always was and this confused me. convinced that we had been robbed i went to lauras room and looked quickley in, but it was spottless, like it hadnt even been touced. this too, i thought was odd. i then went into the part of the house that meredith and i share and checked my room for things missing, which there werent. then i knocked on merediths room. at first i thought she was alseep so i knocked gently, but when she didnt respond i knocked louder and louder until i was really banging on her door and shouting her name. no response. panicing, i ran out onto our terrace to see if maybe i could see over the ledge into her room from the window, but i couldnt see in. bad angle. i then went into the bathroom where i had dried my hair and looked really quickley into the toilet. in my panic i thought i hadnt seen anything there, which to me meant whoever was in my house had been there when i had been there. as it turns out the police told me later that the toilet was full and that the shit had just fallen to the bottom of the toilet, so i didnt see it. i ran outside and down to our neighbors door. the lights were out but i banged ont he door anyway. i wanted to ask them if they had heard anything the night before, but no one was home. i ran back into the house. in the living room raffael told me he wanted to see if he could break down merediths door. he tried, and cracked the door, but we couldnt open it. it was then that we decided to call the cops. there are two types of cops in italy, carbanieri

p 4

(local, dealing with traffic and domestic calls) and the police investigaters. he first called his sister for advice and then called the carbanieri. i then called filomna who said she would be on her way home immediately. while we were waiting, two ununiformed police investigaters came to our house. i showed them what i could and told them what i knew. gave them ohone numbers and explained a bit in broken italian, and then filomena arrived with her boyfriend marco-f and two other friends of hers. all together we checked the houe out, talked to the polie,a nd in a big they all opened merediths door.

i was in the kitchen stadning aside, having really done my part for
the situation. but when they opened merediths door and i heard
filomena scream "a foot! a foot!" in italian i immedaitely tried to
get to merediths room but raffael grabbed me and took me out of the
house. the police told everyone to get out and not long afterward the
carabinieri arrived and then soon afterward, more police
investigators. they took all of our informaton and asked us the same
questions over and over. at the time i had only what i was wearing and
my badg, which thankfully had my passport in it and my wallet. no
jacket though, and i was freezing. after sticking around at the housr
for a bit, the police told us to go to the station to give testimony,
which i did. i was in a room for six hours straight after that without
seeing anyone else, answering questions in italian for the first hour
and then they brought in an interpreter and he helped my out with the
details that i didnt know the words for. they asked me of course about
the the morning, the last time i saw her, and because i was the
closest to her, questions about her habits and her relationships.
afterward, when they were taking my fingerprints, i met two of
merediths english friends, two girls she goes out with, including the
lat one who saw her alive that night she was murdered. they also had
their prints taken. after that, this was around 9 at night by this
time, i was taken into the waiting room where there was various other
people who i all knew from varous places who all knew meredith. her
friends from england, my roommates, even the owner of the pub she most
frequented. after a while my neighbors were taken in too, having just
arived home from a weeklong vacation in their home town, which
eplained why they werent home when i banged on their door. later than
that another guy showed up and was taken in for questioning, a guy i
dont like but who both meredith and i knew from different occasions, a
morracan guy that i only know by his nickname amongst the girls
"shaky". then i sat around in this waiting room wthout having the
chance to leave or eat anything besides vending maschine food (whcih
gave me a hell of a stomache ache) until 530 in the morning. during
this time i received calls from a lot of different people, family
mostly of course, and i also talked with the rest. especially to find
out what exactly was in merediths room whent hey opened it. apparently
her body was laying under a sheet, and with her foot sticking out and
there was a lot of blood. whoever had did this had slit her throat.
they told me to be back in at 11am. i went home to raffael's place and
ate something substantial, and passed out.
in the morning raffael drove me bck to the police station but had to
leave me when they said they wantrd to take me back to the house for
quesioning. before i go on, id like to ssay that i was strictly told

p 5

not to speak about this, but im speaking with you people who are not
involved and who cant do anything bad except talk to journalists,
which i hope you wont do. i have to get this off my chest because its
pressing down on me and it helps to know that someone besides me knows
something, and that im not the one who knows the most out of everyone.
at the house they asked me very personal questions about meredith's
life and also about the personalities of our neighbors. how well did i
know them? pretty well, we are friends. was meredith sexually active?
yeah, she borrowed a few of my condoms. does she like anal? wtf? i
dont know. does she use vaseline? for her lips? what kind of person is
stefano? nice guy, has a really pretty girlfriend. hmmm…very
interesting….weìd like to how you something, and tell us if this is
out of normal.
tehy took me into the nieghbors house. the had breaken the door open
to get in, but they told me to ingonore that. the rooms were all open.
giacomo and marco-n's room was spotless which made since becaus the
guys had thoroughly cleaned the whole house before they left on
vacation. stefano's room however, well, his bed was strpped of linens,
which was odd, and the comfoter he used was shoved up at the top of
his bed, with blood on it. i obviously told then that the blood was
definatley out of normal and also that he usually has his bed made.
they took note of it and ussred me out. when i left the house to go
back to the police station they told me to put my jacket over my head
and duck down below the window so the reporters wouldnt try to talk to
me. at the station i just had to repeat the answers that i had givne
at the house do they could type them up and after a good 5 and a half
hour day with the police again raffael picked me up and took me out
for some well-deserved pizza. i was starving. i then bought some
underwear because as it turns out i wont be able to leave italy for a
while as well as enter my house. i only had the clothes i was wearing
the day it bagan, so i bought some underwear and borrwed a pair of
pants from raffael.
Spoke with my remaining roommates that night (last night) and it was a
hurricane of emotions and stress but we needed it anyway. What we have
been discussing is bascially what to do next. We are trying to keep
our heads on straight. First things first though, my roommates both
work for lawyers, and they are going to try to send a request through
on monday to retrieve important documents of ours that are still in
the house. Secondly, we are going to talk to the agency that we used
to find our house and obviously request to move out. It kind of sucks
that we have to pay the next months rent, but the owner has protection

within the contract. After that, I guess I'll go back to class on monday, although im not sure what im going to do about people asking me questions, because i really dont want to talk again about what happened. Ive been talking an awful lot lately and im pretty tired of it. After that, Its like im trying to remember what i was doing before all this happened. I still need to figure out who i need to talk to and what i need to do to continue studying in perugia, because its what i want to do.

Anyway, thats the update, feeling okay, hope you all are well,
Amanda

Chapter 5: The beginning

Thirty-six hours after police found 21-year-old Meredith Kercher brutally murdered in the four-bedroom ground-floor flat they shared in a house in Perugia, Italy, *Amanda Knox writes a five-page email.* She hits the send button at 2:45 a.m. November 4, 2007. Suspected of being involved in the killing of her "college-abroad" roommate, Amanda has something she needs to get off her chest. Meredith's lifeless body had been discovered in the early afternoon of November 2, and Amanda had been questioned by Italian investigators over the next two days stating her innocence.

Her email—overlooked by prosecutors—is the freshest most spontaneous communication after the crime and the second version of her story. Pay close attention whenever a criminal suspect insists on putting something in writing.

In the next three days from November 5th to November 7th, 2007, Amanda will present four more versions. Following Raffaele Sollecito's retraction of her alibi on November 5th (stating she was not with him the entire night of November 1st), *Amanda will provide three different stories and signed statements on November 6th alone.* In her first two stories that day (one at 1:45 a.m. and the other at 5:45 a.m.—both recorded by interrogators) she now reports that she was with her black boss, Patrick Lumumba, when he killed Meredith at their house. She blames a sketchy memory on smoking pot and thinks possibly Raffaele was also there during the murder.

Around noon, however, she delivers a hand-written statement in English to police, her third version of the day. Now she claims her memory was questionable and doubts whether Patrick really did kill Meredith although she has untrustworthy flashbacks that he did. She elaborates in the long letter that now she does remember much of the night providing specific details: how she and Raffaele had in fact spent the entire night together at his apartment without going out. Once again she clearly proclaims her innocence. (In Chapter Ten we will review the letter in more detail.)

In light of her confessions, Amanda was arrested later that afternoon of November 6th. Alone in her cell, Amanda wrote one last version of her story the next day on November 7th when she reports her memory had spontaneously completely returned. (We review that story in Chapter 16.)

Judge Matteini, the investigative magistrate, ruled on November 9th that Amanda's three confessions on November 6th could not be used against her but could be used in court against others. The statements were never ruled to have been obtained illegally. Neither the judge nor the prosecutors later saw any real importance to her last two hand-written letters. Everyone focused on the contradictions in her stories, contradictions over which her supporters and prosecutors have battled.[69]

Amanda later claimed she was pressured by police interrogators into a false confession. Outside experts including former FBI agents and profilers will support her claims. The various stories create an atmosphere of confusion which has puzzled many observers. Overlooked in the matter are the three lengthy hand-written documents: the November 4th email, and the November 6th and 7th statements. But nothing compares to the fresh email, unencumbered by investigators, which serves as the template for explaining this crime and how her mind really communicates.

> Although her deeper mind secretly spoke to the police on multiple occasions in detailed, coded messages, the investigators still disregarded its import.

In this amazing email Amanda's super-intelligence, *a hidden unconscious intelligence*—truly a super-mind—speaks between the lines. We wonder whether this inner voice will point toward her innocence or guilt. We know that Amanda's conscious mind will present herself in the best possible light. But we will listen instead to the voice of Amanda's super intelligence, the voice that explains the *real* meaning of her email.

And as we will see here she tells the whole secret story of what really happened the night her roommate was murdered. She solves all the dilemmas raised early on by her additional four versions of the night of the crime.

Through her email, Amanda's super intelligence will teach investigators all about how it communicates and how it can't help but confess. Amanda's super-intel truly knows everything about Meredith's murder, down to every dark detail.

But first we consider some introductory comments made by her super intelligence, messages gleaned from another communication—her 2013 memoir—which help us tune in to her unconscious voice. This hidden mind is a special kind of expert, one which fully understands itself—how it observes and how it communicates.

---

[69] On November 8th Raffaele, in his third version of the night in question, retracted his indictment of Amanda and mainly restored Amanda's alibi. He declared they were together at his apartment the entire night although Amanda possibly left for a short while.

New Witness

In reality there is one wild card in the murder case involving the brutal death of Amanda Knox's roommate, one key fact everyone has overlooked. There was a secret witness constantly on the scene, a witness who basically saw everything, a witness who knows if Amanda Knox or Raffaele Sollecito were really involved in this crime. That witness possesses an unbelievably perceptive mind, observing details police missed, observing deeper motives investigators couldn't comprehend. And now this witness comes forward. This witness previously communicated extensive details about the crime, but it did so in secret. Now this completely trustworthy witness makes public that confidential information.

That special witness is Amanda's own super intelligence. Although her deeper mind secretly spoke to the police on multiple occasions in detailed, coded messages, the investigators still disregarded its import. Unfortunately police do not know the super intelligence even exists—and have missed the crucial discovery of this special *unconscious* intelligence.[70] Police must learn how desperately a guilty person must confess despite consciously avoiding it, how desperate they are to speak to them. In case after case, guilty suspects confess in a unique, disguised, symbolic language. Basically, they tell a secret story, a hidden narrative that exists between the lines.

Memoir Clue

In Amanda's 2013 published memoir, *Waiting to be Heard*—which she wrote following her release from jail while her case was on appeal—she unknowingly provided another key communication for understanding what happened to her roommate. She failed to account for her unconscious mind totally unaware of the existence of her super-intel and its phenomenal abilities to speak, and speak clearly. On the surface she had no idea she was also speaking to the police on a deeper level, with her super-intel secretly in total control of her memoir.

Unconsciously she hinted at the key method police could use to hear her secret confession now as she described her initial interrogation back in November of 2007. Then she had difficulty explaining herself in Italian, and she had requested an English-speaking detective. "*Anything* might be a clue for the investigators," he said. "Don't hold back—even if it seems trivial. The smallest detail is important. You never know what the key will be to finding the person who did this."[71]

---

[70]The existence of a newly discovered unconscious super intelligence has been well documented in a popular best-seller on the unconscious mind, *Blink* by Malcolm Gladwell. My book, *The Deeper Intelligence,* goes a step past Gladwell—determining that the super-intel speaks in its own language.

[71] Knox, p. 77.

While dealing on the surface with a past interrogation, she was cluing the police in on how to conduct a new investigation now. The lesson still applies.

In recalling that story, Amanda was informing investigators that above all she was speaking to them "in code" through her memoir and elsewhere as a secret detective herself. This code had to be translated as revealed in her hint, *ask for an interpreter who speaks her super-intel language.* She goes on informing them in code this is the secret to breaking the case—they must "know what the key will be." Her images give them further hints. Pay attention to her encoded symbolic language, "anything [any word] can be a clue"—"even if it seems trivial." And of course such messages initially seem trivial to the detectives' conscious minds.

Then comes the payoff of the new investigative method: now you "know the key…to finding the person who did this." She gives them the key to the case on a silver platter—if they can hear it. And she hints that she was one of the killers.

The Grid for Decoding All Her Messages

Read the symbolic messages again one-by-one to see the secret grid Amanda provides for decoding all her messages. If we string the major messages together, her thoughtprints tell a more comprehensive and cohesive story.

- need English-speaking detective (the super-intel is saying, "I constantly speak in code/get an interpreter for my symbolic messages—just as you would get a translator to interpret a foreign language.")
- anything can be a clue (each word contains a new clue, a deeper symbolic meaning, so learn how to read the "figuratively speaking" language.)
- even if it seems trivial (to the conscious mind, a word spoken in code almost always appears trivial.)
- don't hold back (and thus fail to investigate the symbolic messages.)
- smallest detail is important ("small" symbolic messages—words— are most important.)
- details contain important secrets (key to secret motives/confession: details of crime in word-by-word symbolic messages.)
- the more words used, the more secret details are revealed.
- you never know what the key will be (so you need to learn to listen in code.)
- the key to finding the person who did this (the super-intel's symbolic code will identify killer.)
- She also points toward decoding her previous communications—starting with her email.

If investigators think "speaking figuratively," they'll be able to decode her story. In fact the very title she chose for her book, *Waiting to be Heard*, suggests that her secret story lies concealed within its pages like a secret spy letter begging to be decoded, waiting to be heard.[72] No question about it—her super-intel spies on her, insisting on the truth.

To doubly emphasize her point, Amanda adds a special "author's note" at the very end of her lengthy memoir—the crucial wrap-up point. She tells us, "so much has been said of the case and of me, in so many different languages" but now she was "about setting the record straight." Set it straight indeed. Pay attention to her big idea—*a different language.* She headed straight to her unconscious and its special symbolic language. There she delivered on her promise. Two languages—her literal cover-up conscious story *and* the true story in her unconscious figurative language.[73]

Intuitively, the Italian Supreme Court understood the mind's ability to communicate between the lines. In January 2013, by rejecting the appellate court's verdict which had allowed Amanda to be released from jail in October 2011, the Supreme Court wisely recommended authorities review her memoir due to be published in April 2013. The Supreme Court justices instinctively knew that clues to Amanda's guilt would be found there.

Although they are not psychologists, these wise judges instinctively know that perpetrators are invariably guilty and prone to confess. A "tell-all" memoir—with its rambling autobiographical narratives and countless self-serving denials—is the perfect place to seek clues from the suspect's unconscious.

And once we look, we find from the outset that her memoir subtly, unconsciously, points the way to possible motives—both immediate and time-bomb. We will review the memoir's numerous revelations in more detail in a later chapter.

Unconsciously the super-intel quick-reads situations and analyzes the self in the blink of an eye before telling all about it. The super intelligence is vastly brighter than the surface mind. In fact, there's really no comparison. It speaks as "the other 90 percent" of the mind versus the conscious "10 percent." Deep down it knows everything and must tell the truth which Amanda will do in her November 4, 2007 email.

How do we know what the super-intel wants to communicate? It all comes down to how we listen. It inevitably speaks symbolically in its own unique language. It's figurative, just as is Amanda's instruction to "pay attention to the smallest detail" when she was indirectly and symbolically addressing the police.

---

[72]Don't be concerned that Amanda also had a ghostwriter for her book, Linda Kulman. No matter, Kulman's super intelligence would have the same need tell the truth and she would do so from her interviews trying to stick as closely as possible to Amanda's voice. She succeeded beyond her wildest imagination.
[73] Ibid., p. 459.

Of course her conscious mind speaks literally, very plainly, and always tries to paint a favorable self-portrait, even if it must resort to lying. On the other hand, her super-intel voice is ultimately *incapable* of lying. It may speak symbolically, but it speaks the truth, the whole truth and nothing but the truth.

In Amanda's email she alerts investigators that her mind has two parts—conscious and unconscious—and far beyond the obvious conscious communication, she is speaking to them in a deeper, subliminal way which must be translated. Once we learn how to interpret that symbolic language—decode her messages—we will learn why Amanda did what she did.

Parents Speak in Code in Front of Kids

The super-intel speaks to investigators in code just as parents do in front of children in order to convey hidden messages. The seemingly casual conscious messages carry great import underneath. The literal conscious message contains a deeper symbolic message.

In the same way we bypass our conscious minds—by analogy, the kids—by speaking an encoded language. The deeper mind constantly instructs investigators to bypass their conscious ways of listening just as the super-intel itself bypasses the conscious mind in speaking. Police must develop their understanding of the super intelligence in order to pick up on the symbolic messages it imparts. Amanda's deeper mind tells them this over and over in her email.

Beyond Crime Scene Codes: New Way of Listening

Investigators deal in codes all the time. They "listen" to unconscious body language, and they try very hard to discern messages left at crime scenes in the form of carefully arranged objects.

Profilers observe such scenes to detect staging—a perpetrator's effort to throw them off in certain ways. And they read the scenes for messages and clues, often looking for an unconscious signature, a unique characteristic of the perpetrator.

At Meredith's murder scene in the house she shared with Amanda, investigators immediately saw the supposed break-in as a staged situation, a phony attempt to portray an intruder who came in through a broken window. And investigators interpreted the comforter over Meredith's lifeless body as indicating a nurturing "female killer involved." In a word, they attempted to break the crime-scene code.

Now they must take the next step and break Amanda's super-intel communication code by continuing to think symbolically—and then listen symbolically. Investigators need to read her verbal communications symbolically exactly as they do crime scenes or body language. If our minds can arrange an unconscious symbolic "body language," they can arrange an unconscious symbolic "mind language."

Of course police are only trained to listen with their conscious minds to the conscious minds of those they interrogate—but they do utilize their instincts, a minimal use of their own super-intel. Later we will see how prosecutor Guiliano Mignini's instincts led him to elicit Amanda's unconscious behavioral confession of murder.

Secret Details, Secret Guides

Police want to know the details of the crime. Notice that Amanda wrote this detailed, five-page email soon after the murder. In it, her super-intel speaks between the lines in details—symbolic details. Realize these small details contain her super-mind's keys to the true story. Exactly as she told investigators in her memoir, the clues are in the "smaller," less obvious details, meaning those details found in her hidden symbolic language. Once I decode her email starting in the next chapter, the details of the crime will be clear.

She has secretly arranged this email in intricate detail. A pioneering forensic document examiner once recommended that examiners pay attention to *every* detail—commas, semi-colons, apostrophes, and beyond.[74] And this preceded the discovery of the super intelligence. As we will see, Amanda makes clear that her email is indeed a forensic document. In that light I would add to the forensic wisdom: pay attention to every word, every image, every story, every denial, every link from one word or idea to the next—the order of her ideas, and every slip of the pen or tongue. The super-intel puts ideas in a certain order to secretly tell a cohesive story. All between the lines—the only way the super-intel can get its messages in and fool the conscious mind's plans to cover up the truth.

'Tells'—Message Markers, Slips, and Denial

As her super-intel begins explaining its hidden messages to the police in Amanda's email, it underscores primary guidelines advising how to listen. It points out how it uses "message markers" to signal an important message-to-come, a crucial detail. This includes communication references such as: "talking, told, giving testimony, information, documents, fingerprints and the like. In a word these are "tells"—likely admissions that the deeper mind is confessing, revealing hidden guilt and pointing the way to the details of the crime. She's playing mental poker with the police, and—if they learn her tells—they can determine if she or they hold the winning hand.

The super-intel will also show how Amanda's frequent surface denials—"I didn't do this," etc.—represent secret tells, secret key markers. And it will

---

[74]Osborn and Osborn, *Questioned Document Problems,* Patterson Smith series in Criminology, Law Enforcement and Social Problems, 1991.

demonstrate how to read them, how to see past them, to enable investigators to develop a working hypothesis—to be attuned to a possible hidden confession.

The super-intel also speaks purely at moments in "slips." The unconscious mind simply takes over and writes or speaks what it must say. Amanda Knox will reveal crucial slips to highlight her secret confession and overtly bypass her cover-up.

Amanda Knox's email is two emails in one. On the surface, we can read it literally. Looking deeper, we must read it symbolically and we will hear her truer self, her larger self, her "brighter self" telling us the entire story. Two emails, two voices. On the surface she uses her conscious mind voice, but looking deeper, she uses her unconscious, super intelligence voice. If you overlook her talking in code, you'll entirely miss the message.

Now that we have unlocked the secret code, however, we wonder exactly what will Amanda reveal to us next—in her November 4th email.

Trigger Decoding

Here's what we're looking for in Amanda's email. A guilty perpetrator typically reveals four central issues in a thoughtprint profile: confession to murder and method, the immediate motive, the deeper motive, and addressing the police in code.

Her brilliant super-intel quick-reads each reality—who, how, why, and the police. Each reality triggers a set of unconscious thoughtprints, hidden messages. This means the same words can have different meanings depending on the trigger.

One set of thoughtprints can conceal another. Each trigger then becomes a separate lens through which we can decode her thoughtprints. If we read one way, she's looking at her guilt. If we read it another way, she's examining her motives either immediate motives or deep-seated, time-bomb motives. When we read it one last way, she's talking to the police. In any case, it becomes a cohesive story told one set of thoughtprints at a time.

The bottom line: the unconscious mind speaks on several levels simultaneously. The forensic process in essence is "trigger thoughtprint decoding."

The forensic profiler must focus on one trigger at a time but always shifting lenses as the messages lead. He must always be prepared for an overlooked set of thoughtprints which present an overlooked trigger motive. Other thoughtprints may reveal an overlooked detail of the crime such as a confession to staging or an identifying an unknown co-conspirator.

It's like reading a story by a novelist whose narrative hints at deeper meanings. Such artists are unknowingly attempting to solve personal conflicts through the various characters' actions and the narrative's dramatic situations, and the novelist does this simultaneously.

A "thoughtprint confession" truly represents a magnificent work of art—a powerful secret story from the same "right-brain" mind, that symbol-dominated subconscious employed by talented writers and artists. A cohesive narrative emerges, one designed to convince police, judges and juries. As her vivid email confession proves, Amanda Knox is a gifted communicator whose super-intel has groomed her as a creative writer.

The Missing Motive

In the end there is one central question and one question alone. Does Amanda's secret story, told in code like a letter from a spy, reveal a stunning confession? Does the email contain the very thing the police need to understand—what Italian prosecutors eventually characterized as a "gone-crazy," drug-fueled "unexplainable crime."

A central problem with the case has been the missing motive. Prosecutors have surmised that Amanda and Meredith had an acrimonious relationship. That Amanda felt put down by Meredith regarding the American's lack of cleanliness, sexual promiscuity, and her tendency to steal. Add drugs to the mix and police have some motives, but they can't explain Amanda's and Raffaele's apparent overreaction. Defense attorneys have contended these are not strong enough motives for such a brutal killing. Ten thousand pages of court testimony later and the question of the motivation for this slaughter is still unresolved.

Clearly Amanda's super-intel, using a classic denial, will inform the police, "I'm the one who knows the most out of everyone" involved in the case. If you hear her messages, the case will open up like a clam exposed to heat.

Beyond the horrific tragedy—for Meredith the victim; for her family who experienced having their daughter, their sister, their baby girl murdered; for Amanda's own family about whom her super-intel has much to say—Amanda's hidden messages make one thing abundantly clear: the truth shall set you free. And she herself longs to be set free from the prison of her own guilt.

Long before Amanda ever met Meredith, her deeper mind knew this fact about the law. Once you cross the line into taking another human being's life, forevermore in this world you live life on the edge, eyes alert in the back of your mind for anyone who might see your shame. Who might shine the light on your darkness? Amanda's own super-intel spotlights the deepest recesses of her mind, revealing secrets her surface mind can't bear to admit.

No doubt about it—Amanda Knox is still waiting to be heard.

Chapter 6: The Email Begins:
Amanda's Undercover News

Email

"To: My close friends
  "From: Amanda Knox, Perugia

*"This is an email for everyone, because **id like to get it all out** and not have to **repeat** myself a **hundred time**s like ive been **having to do at the police** station. **some** of you already **know** some things, **some** of you know nothing. what im **about to say** i cant **say** to **journalists** or **newspapers**, and **i require** that of anone receiving **this information** as well."*

Pay close attention to exactly how Amanda begins the email. Beginnings inevitably set the stage and provide invaluable clues. Opening with *"This is an email for everyone,"* her super-intel first makes it clear that she's unconsciously addressing the entire world—not only friends, family, the public, journalists, but especially police officers and prosecutors. She's particularly referring to one special investigator who can hear her story, who speaks her symbolic language. Someone who recognizes the brilliance of the super intelligence, which understands from beginning to end that this is one cohesive secret story. In this email she strongly and repeatedly advises prosecutors to find this person or persons.

She puts this information in writing so police investigators can go back over it. She doubly underscores *"this email"*—and such repetition is a major message marker. It's a tell. She's dropping hints to the police, using a major announcement/signal—"email"—to alert them to the fact that they have a valuable forensic document in their hands. How valuable? It's potentially court-admissible evidence. She's pointing them to the most valuable document they have—her five-page email. This is the foundational document—and the first—that sets the stage for all her other super intelligent communications. Barely beginning she has promised a huge secret story referencing *"journalists…newspapers."* Already she's showing how her super intelligence guides authorities to listen every step of the way.

Before long, she'll admit exactly what happened that awful night in her house.

After reading this opening, an astute document examiner trained in decoding the super intelligence's metaphoric language would certainly suspect a hidden confession. "Some of you may know some things. Some of you know nothing," but rest assured, Amanda's truest self is clearly ready to talk.

Email Crucial Forensic Document

Email near end—

*"Spoke with my remaining roommates that night (last night) and it was a hurricane of emotions and stress but we needed it anyway. What we have been discussing is bascially **what to do next**. We are trying to keep our heads on straight.*

***First things first** though, my roommates both **work for lawyers**, and they are **going to try to send a request through** on monday to **retrieve important documents** of ours that are **still in the house**. Secondly, we are going to talk…*

*"to the agency that we used to find our house…Ive **been talking** an awful lot lately and im pretty tired…I still need to **figure out who i need to talk to…**"*

Fast-forward momentarily to near the end of "this email" where Amanda's super-intel instructs authorities *"what to do next."* They must get *"first things first."* She consciously requests that they *"retrieve important documents of [mine] that are still in the house"* adding *"going to talk."* That promise is preceded by two other tells: "spoke" and "discussing."

Her deeper self is implying to investigators that she's talking, she's confessing. She emphasizes to them that police have "in-house" an important *forensic document*—her very email. She implies that the email summarizes the story of the crime. Why else would she underscore "documents"?

By stating that she was *"going to try to send a request through"* to them, her super-intel urgently intimates that investigators don't understand that she's talking to them in a disguised symbolic language. Notice how often she repeats the key message marker "talking" — *"going to talk"* ... *"I've been talking an awful lot lately"*... *"i need to talk..."*

In her email, Amanda often uses the word *"document"*—an official term which she uses to introduce legality matters. She makes plain *"I work for lawyers"*—specifically the prosecutors who could use the email in court if they could only hear her encoded messages.

Investigators need a new type of forensic document examiner who fully grasps the way the super-intel code really works. Then they can "retrieve" more significant secret information. She continues to stress the same idea, *"figure out who [you] need to talk to."* Prosecutors, she's saying, you need help. The people who investigated this case were never trained to translate the special language of the super intelligence. This approach represents the cutting-edge of psycholinguistics, the discipline of reading language for deeper psychological clues.[75] The heart of psycholinguistics is thoughtprints—deeper symbolic messages. This is still such a new psycholinguistic method, that most people—including police, psychologists and the mass media—do not even realize the super intelligence exists. As a result, they're missing the boat on a on a great new exploration of the human mind. They're also neglecting to nurture a valuable new way of gathering information.

In her email, Amanda often uses the word *"document"*—an official term which she uses to introduce legality matters. She makes plain *"I work for lawyers"*—specifically the prosecutors who could use the email in court if they could only hear her encoded messages. Far beyond other forensic and legal authorities, Amanda's deeper self knows it is providing them scientific, court-admissible evidence.

Not only that, she went into overdrive presenting authorities with a multitude of unused or unappreciated forensic documents. Besides this email, she wrote two jail statements, a diary, two letters to her attorneys on November 9, and later the memoir, *Waiting to be Heard*. Amanda's parents and attorneys begged her to quit writing, but she couldn't. The super intelligence is obsessive, insistent and determined to reveal the truth however figuratively, and so it is with Amanda Knox.

---

[75]Steven Egger, Ph.D., Professor of Criminology at the University of Houston, called my forensic profiling approach (thoughtprint decoding) "the cutting-edge of forensic science."

Must 'Get It All Out'

*"This is an email for everyone, because **id like to get it all out**…"*

Glancing back to her opening, when she declares to *"everyone"* that she's eager *"to get it all out."* She's predicting she will tell "all"—the whole story of the murder. By writing to *"everyone,"* she suggests that she's constantly living with gut-wrenching guilt which she's driven to confess to the world—to anyone who'll listen.

Must 'Get This Off My Chest'

End of email—

*"in the morning raffael drove me **bck to the police** station but had to leave me when they said they wantrd to take me back to the house **for quesioning**. before i go on, id like to ssay that i was strictly told not to speak about this, but **im speaking** with you people who are not involved and who cant **do anything bad** except talk to journalists, which i hope you wont do. **i have to get this off my chest** because its **pressing down on me** and it helps to know that someone besides me knows something, and that im not the one who knows the most out of everyone. at the house they asked me very personal questions about meredith's life and also about the personalities of our neighbors.*

"[at the house they asked me very personal questions about meredith's life and also about the personalities of our neighbors.]"

Again at the very end of her email she repeats the identical message. Amanda stresses how heavily this crime weighs on her: *"i have to get this off my chest because it's pressing down on me."* Her bookend statements *("get it all out"* from the beginning of the email—*"get this off my chest"* from the end) reveal how desperately she must communicate.

It's as though she's virtually shouting at investigators, pleading with them to review this document and figure out the story, uncover a likely confession. She's simply got to get something off her chest. She's making big promises about what's in this email. Note she promises in her message marker *"police…wanted to take me back…for questioning"* that she indeed answers every question. And there's much more to this section of the email as we will explore.

As the decoding continues, we suspect even more strongly that the email represents a major breakthrough. Attuned to the image of heavy pressure on the chest, we flash back to the crime scene and recall how the perpetrators pulled Meredith's shirt up, exposing her chest—as if to show us, "now we're exposed *too*—the heavy burden of this murder is on our chest, and it's so great we can barely breathe just as Meredith would no longer breathe, ever again."

We might wonder if Amanda's super-intel had simply focused on one of the vivid scenes from her roommate's murder frozen forever in her mind. We should expect to find secret references to the *crime scene details* all through her email because a perpetrator's deeper mind goes over and over the crime endlessly, never able to escape what she's done. Her genius super-intel even suggests how "email" rhymes with "detail"—and a moniker ("email detail") for police to constantly keep in mind the whole story is here.

Remember Amanda's super-intel counsel from her memoir that the smallest detail is important. Her compact non-stop five-page email filled with details confirms yet again this email contains the long-sought specifics of the crime.

Promise to Repeat Story 'A Hundred Times'

> *"id like to get it all out and not **have to repeat myself a hundred times** like ive **been having to do** at the police station."*

Now back to the beginning of her email. Pay close attention to her key denial, "I'd like to…[not]…repeat myself a hundred times."

First read straight through the denial, bypass it and hear the message: in fact, she very much intends to "repeat myself a hundred times." She's compelled to do precisely that. Such a hidden promise to repeat her story fits with the suffocating pressure she's under to "get it all out."

How to Utilize Denials

One of the great ploys of the super intelligence is to get the truth across by slipping it past the conscious mind through a denial. That way the deeper self can say precisely what it really desires to communicate about the crime—introducing the key idea through negation. Psychiatrists realized long ago that denial often surfaces as the most basic "tell." A poker player who comes on strong really has a weak hand. One who slow-plays his cards often holds the stronger hand.

In this case, Amanda repeatedly says, "I wasn't at home the night of the murder"—very possibly introducing the idea, "I *was* at home the night of the murder."

Through her blatant denials, she secretly tells investigators the real truth. *Investigators should quickly read through her denials to establish a working hypothesis—see how well they fit with the known details of the crime.*

Amanda offers another major "tell" specifically about her denials. She promises to *"repeat myself a hundred times."* This fits strikingly well with perhaps the best known read on denial "Me thinks thou dost protest too much."[76]

---

[76]William Shakespeare, *Hamlet.*

In effect Amanda promises to "protest too much" the first of which is "I will not repeat myself." We pay special attention to her numerous protests which are numerous.

I am 'the Police'

*"[...have to repeat myself a hundred times] like ive been **having to do at the police** station."*

Notice her quick promise to repeat my story *"like ive been having to do at the police."* That's another huge "tell" as her super-intel admits that it's talking to the police a lot. Yet another way of predicting a major confession, and she does so with an especially rich image, "at the police." It's another signal that she's constantly talking to the police in code.

"The police" also represents a projection, a part of her. Deep down, she is the police. Her own "inner policewoman"—stationed in her unconscious—has insisted from the beginning that she confess the truth, talk to the official police, and continue to do so.

Her "inner cop" secretly guides this email. Introducing "police" so early in the email strongly implies her wrongdoing, suggesting that her conscience is eating her up deep inside. Those who pay attention to her images will learn exactly how to solve this crime.

She hints strongly early on what the "prison of the mind"—as law enforcement calls it—does to a murderer. She suggests that the email contains her detailed confession delivered under enormous internal duress. The authorities have no idea how deep is that prison inside her mind. As she inhabits that solitary cell, she has her own internal police at her side wherever she goes—seemingly accusing her. Still, she has not yet declared her guilt, only pointed in that direction.

She concludes the email with that same message—multiple references to the police—pleading with them to hear the hidden instructions from the secret policewoman of her soul.

'I Am the Secret Reporter, the News'

End of email—

*"...some of you **already know** some things, **some of you know nothing**.
what im about to say i cant say to **journalists or newspapers**, and i require that of anone receiving this information as well."*

She continues to inform police that she has a lot to say. Her super-intel proclaims that she *"already know some things"* and then reminds them *"some of you know nothing"*—addressing again their lack of expertise about deeper "second-level" communication, in recognizing that the super-intel constantly speaks to them in code. It won't be the last time in this email she tells them this.

Paradoxically if they recognize this, they then become the smartest detectives on the block. Now pay particular attention to what comes next—a crucial message about just how extensive her story is in this email.

*"what im about to say i cant say to **journalists or newspapers**, "*

The marker "what I'm about to say" underscores her announcement disguised in denial, "I can [not] say to journalists or newspapers."

Remember, denials can reveal stunning details. Here she announces her crucial secret role as you read through her second denial and spot her key images, "what im about to say i can say to journalists or newspapers."

Look at it again, "What I'm about to say I can say... journalist... newspaper."

Her main message: "I'm the secret investigative journalist in this story and I can say it—report on it. I am the "talking journalist." This email is 'The Amanda News'—my own hand-written newspaper. I promise a masterpiece of investigative journalism between the lines of this email."

Using rich images, she paints a vivid picture of what she is about in this email. She puts key communication images suggesting a confession right up front early in a forensic document. "Journalist" and "newspapers" are also two sterling message marker images conveying that her super-mind is covering the story full-time as an undercover reporter.

In her email she will reveal her extraordinary unconscious abilities as a secret reporter. We will appreciate how fast and furious she unfolds the details of her hidden story in the rest of the email. Given the sheer brutality of the crime in question, we can expect her "masterpiece," her chronicle of the crime in all its gory details to be revealed in powerful, descriptive terms. We expect the secret narrative of the case.

'I Am A Journalist'

End of email—

"**talk** to **journalists**, which i **hope you** wont **do**. i have to get this off my chest because its pressing down on me and it helps to know that someone besides me knows something, and that im not the one who knows the most out of everyone."

For emphasis she repeats the image of her journalistic role at the end of the email. Again she declares, *"talk to journalists,"* followed by another denial announcement *"hope you won't."*

Secretly she means, "Police, you must talk to me, listen to me, the undercover journalist. Realize I'm talking to you continuously, reporting the entire story."

Now she has doubly promised an exposé of the crime—confirming her earlier message with a bookend match at the email's conclusion. The fact that her email runs five pages long itself suggests a detailed story.

As her message maker, "talk to journalist," indicates, she's challenging journalists the same way she's challenging police investigators. She's speaking to them in code, secretly hoping they hear, hoping that whoever understands this deeper message will report it. In an encouraging turn of events, one journalist actually did hear a few super intelligence messages as we will explore later.

The News: Super–Intel Knows More Than Anyone

*"...it helps to know that someone besides me knows something, and that **im not the one who knows the most out of everyone.** "*

Having announced her secret reporter role immediately she presents the most important news of all, the single biggest scoop in the case, knowledge which *"it helps to know."* Without it, the police are lost. "Know" is the most major of message markers.

She clues them in to the secret, *"Someone besides me knows,"* meaning someone in addition to her conscious mind "knows." Two different minds know. Especially that mind just "beside" her conscious mind—her unconscious super intelligence—knows and can help. The mind that's doing the talking now.

She follows with a denial announcement, "I'm [not] the one who knows the most out of anyone." Reading through her denial, investigators should see a crisp and clear picture of her super intelligence, there in living color with its earth-shaking abilities in full view.

She cannot say it any plainer—given that she has to speak through denial—she knows the most of anyone involved in this case. And she's talking to the police looking through the fantastic lens of her super-intel mind.

By this point she has summarized her major roles in this email: *police investigator and reporter.* And she shows us how she repeats messages to get them across.

Now recall how she described the police from the get-go, and read her message to them in a new way, "***id like to get it all out** and not **have to repeat myself a hundred times** like ive been having to do **at the police** station."*

Listening to their same questions over and over, she tells them that they're repeating themselves needlessly. She's willing to tell them far more than they can know on their own---because it wasn't their super intelligence that was with her every step of the way reading exactly what she did and why. It was her unconscious mind.

Obviously her interrogation by investigators demonstrated a cop's classical battering-ram method. They thought they could break her that way. No question it pressured her into writing the email.

But then they missed how she'd really broken quickly in her email, providing all kinds of details. They would have seen way back then—what they still don't know—if they had only opened their minds and listened. All along she was the main investigator who secretly "asked" and answered all the questions the police have.

Someone Else Knows

Also in her message she writes, *"someone else besides me knows something."* She is hinting that a totally separate person was involved in the crime, pointing strongly to Raffaele Sollecito. Shortly she will connect him directly to the killing.

Chapter 7: A Bloodcurdling Confession

Toward the End of Nov. 4 Email: Discovery of Body

*"...home immediately. while we were waiting, two **ununiformed** police **investigaters** came to our house. i showed them what i could and **told them what i knew.** gave them **ohone numbers** and **explained** a bit in broken italian, and then filomena arrived with her **boyfriend marco-f** and two other friends of hers. **all together** we **checked the houe out,** talked to the **polie**,a nd in a big they **all opened merediths door.** i was in the kitchen **stadning** aside, having really done my part for the situation. but when they opened merediths door and i heard filomena scream "a foot! a foot!" in italian **i immedaitely tried to get to merediths** room but raffael grabbed me and took me out of the house.*

*" the police told everyone to get out and not long afterward the carabinieri arrived and then soon afterward, more police investigators. they took **all of our informaton** and asked us the same questions over and over. at the time i had only what i was wearing and **my badg**, which thankfully had my **passport** in it and my wallet. no jacket though, and i was freezing. after sticking around at the housr for a bit, the police told us to go to the station to **give testimony,** which i did. i was in a room for six hours straight after that without seeing anyone else, **answering questions in italian** for the first hour and then they **brought in an interpreter** and he helped my out with the details that i didnt know the words for.*

*"they asked me of course about the the morning, **the last time i saw her,** and because **i was the closest to her,** questions about her habits and her relationships. afterward, when they were taking **my fingerprints**, i met two of merediths english friends, two girls she goes out with, including **the lat one who saw her alive** that night she was **murdered**. they also had **their prints taken.**"*

111

We look ahead in the email to the crucial moment which deals with the discovery of Meredith's body. Starting in the next chapter we will explore her entire story—in the order she unfolds it.

Key Confession: 'Oh I the one'

*"two **ununiformed** police **investigaters** came to our house. i **showed** them what i could and **told** them **what i knew**. gave them **ohone numbers** and explained a bit in broken italian, and then filomena arrived with her boyfriend marco-f and two other friends of hers."*

When she describes the discovery of Meredith's body, Amanda certainly felt the pressure to confess. If she's guilty, here's where we'd expect her to tell us in a fresh, new way—but speaking in code, of course. We pay extraordinary attention to every single detail in this scene as police burst into her house while the body lays there as-yet undiscovered. Amanda's super-intel has placed this particular section front and center in the lengthy email. If we stay with her details, her images, her confession will leap off the page.

She hints again that she's the real *"ununiformed police investigater"* on the case. Now acting as an undercover cop, Amanda's super-intel investigates "our house." She's investigating her house and her part in the crime.

Amanda's slip *"investigater"* or *"gater"* suggests both "gator/alligator" and "ate her." The slip *"gater"* also suggests "gate." First she hints that she will confess to the specifics of the brutal crime—three gators with razor-sharp teeth who consumed Meredith. Amanda continually refers to dangerous predator animals, primitive images.

She also plans on taking us through the "gate" which surrounded their house at 7 Via della Pergola and opening up the secret story of her roommate's murder. Her super-mind—the gate to the crime—intends to take us through the entryway on a secret tour of the crime scene. Here is what she *really* saw on the night of the murder.

Next she writes, *"I showed them… and told them what I knew. gave them."* For maximum emphasis she uses quadruple message markers: "showed—told—what I knew—gave them [police]." She especially underscores "knew"—the richest of signals. Absolutely stunning new knowledge about the case immediately follows. Indeed she delivers in another one of her magnificent slips, *"gave them **ohone** numbers and explained a bit in broken Italian."* *"Ohone"* suggests "oh one"—"oh, I'm the one." Her super intelligence confesses her guilt as bluntly as it can be articulated. "Phone"—which she meant to write—represents another message marker. At this crucial moment her super-intel phones in the secret answer to police just as an anonymous source would do.

"Ohone" also implies, "Oh hone"—that her super-intel hones in on her guilt. She has in fact shown us who she is ("o hone") for killing her roommate—

112

an *"o"*—a big zero. Amanda suggests that we zoom in to see the secret zero she knows she is.

Even deeper, her slip *"ohone"* also implies "oh home." Not only the message, "oh, I was the one in the home" that night—the killer—but simultaneously, she suggests her underlying pain that actually caused her rage, "oh home"—*that's* where her story *really* started. Something she associates with "home" long ago made her feel as though she was a "zero," a nothing.

Police Have Her Number

*"told them what i knew. **gave** them **ohone numbers** and **explained** a bit **in broken italian**,"*

Amanda follows up with another detail, *"I gave ohone numbers"* translated "I gave my 'oh I the one' number to police." She implies that she has indeed given the police her number, confessed to the crime. They'll realize that if they tune in to her messages.

But *"ohone numbers"* suggest plural and subtly that she's telling them there was more than one killer. As in 'oh, he's one' and 'oh, he's one.'

Immediately before the discovery of the body she writes, *"I told...what I knew...explained a bit in broken Italian"* to two "ununiformed" police at the house.

Again she references speaking a foreign language. *"Broken Italian"* suggests "break down my deeper messages, break the code." *"Ununiformed"* police suggests to them step out of your usual, uniform way of doing things. She implies, "hone in on my hidden messages—don't leave your uniform, your investigative role." Amanda unknowingly presents one vivid image after another.

She has just given police a huge heads-up in code—shouting with all her "tells"—to expect even more major revelations besides "she's the one." It's no accident that she now goes to the discovery of Meredith's body. Now police can potentially hear her explaining everything she knows about what happened to her roommate. Her super-intel wants to be understood.

Marco Polo Game—'marco-f'

*"and then filomena **arrived with her boyfriend marco-f** and **two** other friends of hers."*

Amanda, Meredith's roommate, arrived with her boyfriend in a group. Amanda mentions four people, two by name—*"filomena"* and *"marco-f."* No detail is by accident. The prominent name "Marco" immediately suggests the well-known swimming-pool game "Marco Polo." As Wikipedia describes,[77]

One player is chosen as "It." This player closes his/her eyes and tries to find and tag the other players without the use of vision. The player who is "It" shouts "Marco" and the other players must respond by shouting "Polo," which "It" uses to try to acoustically locate them. If a player is tagged, then that player becomes "It."

The game can also be played on land, with slightly modified rules. It is similar to Blind man's bluff where one person is blindfolded while others choose hiding places around the room.

Amanda suggests they came to play a game with Meredith that night. A unique version of "Marco Polo," specifically they played *"marco-f"* with her. The *"f-letter"* game.

"Marco-f" is such an unusual description. Amanda could have easily omitted his name, but it was a key part of the code. Details.

The *"f-letter"* in this context suggests the *"f-word"* that the game of the night was *"marco-f"* along with two friends. And all three perpetrators tagged Meredith "It." In their blindness they all reached out to touch her while shouting "Marco"/ "M" for "Meredith." It was a tag-team approach where they played polo riding her like a horse, abusing her. In a letter, in a word, they all "f....'d" her. And Meredith screamed for the first time but not the last.

In Amanda's encoded narrative two friends came along with *"marco-f."* The boyfriend, Raffaele, would play the merciless game with Meredith along with two other people. One of those was Rudy and one was Amanda who would play her own version of the new sex game "Marco Polo-f." Crude, yes, but the super intelligence insists on raw truth—the worst word for the worst crime. Again Amanda suggests an order to the three sexual attacks starting with her boyfriend, Raffaele, then either Rudy or herself second and third. Three assailants.

And she further implies at one point in the sadistic game they even made their victim speak—cry out "Polo"—come abuse me. Or even made her reach out and touch Rudy's "private polo horse," as he later implied.

Note again the assault team of three all arrived together at her house by plan. Rudy was clearly invited to the group gathering and has already been convicted of the crime. For the record Amanda also clearly identifies Raffaele as accompanying her at that violent party.

Remember Amanda's counsel, *the smallest detail*—such as the letter "f"— can provide invaluable clues. She uses it four times in succession, including *"marco-f"* and two *friends* along with *"filomena."* Later in the email she will define the *"f-letter"* very clearly as the *f-word."*[78]

---

[77] http://en.wikipedia.org/wiki/Marco_Polo_(game).

[78] To be clear, I am in no way suggesting Filomena or her boyfriend, Marco, was involved in this crime. In this context their names are simply symbolic.

The name *"filomena"* in this context specifically connected to a man in a sexual way also symbolically suggests "fill of men"—that Meredith had her fill of men that night. Amanda could have described her roommate differently, but remember—she promised details. Even Amanda behaved like a phallic woman in charge of the whole game. Even the simple entry, boyfriend/girlfriend coming to the door, suggests a sexual event to come. The bottom line remains: Amanda has unconsciously confessed to the sex game prior to the murder, a scenario matching the forensic evidence. Sex was a weapon in this brutal game but revenge was its intent, as Amanda will tell us.

Of course, Marco Polo is a searching game. Amanda secretly tries to help the police search for the truth. The investigators are truly like the person with their eyes closed crying "Marco," and Amanda's unconscious cries out "Polo— over here and you'll find the killer." For good measure, Marco Polo himself was a famous explorer who brought back to his home in Europe new information that had been unknown before his time. Unconsciously in code Amanda suggests to police they can get brand new information on the case from her super-intel confession.

Not only has she taught police, "Remember details, details—every word has an encoded meaning by design, sometimes even a letter." *She soon prepares them for another major change in one letter of enormous import. Another major slip.*

For good measure Amanda implies that—to one degree or another— "friends" killed Meredith. It was truly an inside job carried out by people she thought were her friends. All three of them, Judases.

More Confession of Sexual Assault

*"**all together we checked the houe out,** talked to the polie,a nd in a big* [word omitted] ***they all opened merediths door***.

"i was in the kitchen standing aside, having really done my part for the situation. but when they opened merediths door and i heard filomena scream "a foot! a foot!" in italian i immedaitely tried to get to merediths room but raffael grabbed me and took me out of the house."

Just before the discovery of the body, Amanda informs us, *"all together we checked the houe out, talked to the polie."* In another revealing slip she suggests the suspected three perpetrators, *"all together...checked the houe out"*—that is, "checked the 'ho'/whore out." Vividly she suggests a three-way sexual assault prior to the murder. She says it in yet another way, *"they [all] opened merediths door and i heard filomena scream."* In other words, they broke her door down— the door to her most private room inside her body, her vagina. Writing in a symbolic "double entendre" code, Amanda implies they all penetrated her sexually. They opened the vagina door, and they entered.

Even further she suggests they initially entered Meredith's bedroom *"together,"* like storm troopers, to carry out maximum humiliation. This never started out as a one-on-one catfight. Amanda's super-intel makes clear it was a sudden group sexual assault. The remainder of the email will give Amanda ample opportunity to confirm it.

Amanda Blanks Out—The Thrusting Stab and the *'Polie'*

As she describes the body being discovered, Amanda unconsciously depicts the exact moment of the murder. She describes fascinating details of the scene of the body being found.

On top of this she refers again to speaking a foreign language—twice. First she had just *"explained a bit in broken Italian"* herself and now her other roommate, Filomena, screams *"a foot, a foot in Italian"* upon discovering the body. As such, Amanda's still shouting at investigators, "Break the secret 'foreign' code in which I'm speaking to you." She's giving them a "foot into the case"—pointing them to her confession.

Then Amanda takes us to the moment of finding the body, *"a nd in a big* **[word omitted]** *they all opened merediths door."* In that way, she confesses that her crime was all too much for her to face. It was so overwhelming that she temporarily dissociated, checked out mentally. She blanked out and could not say the aggressive word—"push" or "shove" but really something much stronger when it came to *"in a big* **[blank-out]** *opened merediths."*

It was too close to that awful moment when she opened Meredith's throat and neck with a sharp knife. She suggests the missing words are **"in a big thrusting stab**—I opened Meredith up." It perfectly matches the crime scene and the horrific open wound on the left side of the victim's neck, a wound that the prosecutor, Mignini, called the worst wound he'd ever seen.

Amanda suggests again that all three perpetrators stabbed Meredith but she was the one who cut her open in a vicious stabbing. Amanda was the angriest, a fact which she will later reveal.

No wonder this is the single most chaotic moment in the email. Like nowhere else here she makes five crucial slips precisely explaining the chaos. Amanda knew exactly what they would find—Meredith's dead body with a gaping stab wound to her throat. Amanda well remembered that wound. She'd seen it over and over that night while she and Raffaele cleaned up the crime scene. She'd looked at it until she could no longer stand it, and Amanda pulled the comforter off Meredith's bed to cover her.

Just for good measure look at two other details—two key slips—just before she blocks out her deed, *"talked to the polie, a nd in a big* [word omitted] *they all opened merediths door."* Her first slip, *"talked...**polie**,"* suggests her confession that she's lying to the police ("po-**lie**").

Meaning to say "police," instead her super-intel insists upon *"polie"*—the slip which sums up her entire email. And she makes the slip at the most crucial place in the email—at the discovery of the body. Unconsciously Amanda stands up and shouts at the police, "Polie. Polie. I'm lying to you, police. I'm lying to you on the surface!"

Her second slip, *"a nd in a big,"* spaces the word "and" into *"a nd."* In context she suggests the message "nd" or "end"—that is, "end in a big stab wound that opened Meredith" and killed her.

When Amanda recreates this moment in her email, the pressure on her psyche was so great she blocked out the wound she inflicted but, with two slips, admitted she had done it.

Her chaotic blank-out also confesses volumes. It was identical to the tumultuous moment the prosecutor Mignini took her back to the crime scene two days after the murder and walked her casually to the kitchen. When he opened the drawers where the knives were stored, Amanda broke down into tears and couldn't speak—as he had anticipated.

If this seems too early to come to such a conclusion, stay tuned. She will quickly repeat the confession *in the next sentence* in sequence with more details.

Continued Confession—'I Stabbed Her'

"all together we checked the houe out, talked to the polie, a nd in a big [word omitted] they all opened merediths door.

"i was in the kitchen stadning aside, having really done my part for the situation. but when they opened merediths door and i heard filomena scream "a foot! a foot!" in italian i immediately tried to get to merediths room but raffael grabbed me and took me out of the house."

Amanda picks up after she briefly blanked out realizing they will find the gory stab wound she inflicted on Meredith.

After she recalls "opening Meredith" up, she tells us, *"i was in the kitchen standing aside, having really done my part for the situation."* Her major slip *"stadning"* suggests both "staning"/"staining" and "stad"/"staid." Now read "I was in kitchen staining and staid—aside." She suggests "I stained Meredith with a kitchen knife, caused her to bleed profusely, with stains everywhere. And I was 'staid' about it, cold-blooded at that moment. " Amanda implies it was a deep cut that stained everything as the crime scene confirms.

Amanda further suggests she was *"aside"* her—beside her—when she slashed Meredith. And Amanda implies she herself was stained by Meredith's blood.

After it was over Amanda stood up but left Meredith bleeding lying on the floor. We will see later how Amanda confessed again in her email that she stabbed Meredith with a kitchen knife. She confirmed not only the stabbing but the weapon she used and where she was situated—details perfectly matching the crime-scene evidence. She had to tell us consciously "I was standing in the kitchen"—to suggest "where the knives are."

She again establishes that in her email, often *"kitchen"* is code for "Meredith's bedroom"—where they murdered her, where they consumed her. Again "I was in the kitchen staining"—where I cut her.

Her slip, *"standing,"* also suggests, "I was in the kitchen appearing 'staid' and uninvolved, trying to cover-up emotionally. Various people including her roommate, Filomena, as well as Filomena's mother, Meredith's friends, and her boss, Patrick, spoke of how cold and detached Amanda could be. Just as she calmly conveyed her cover-up story to police.

> Amanda refers to *"house"* again, hinting again at the murder's deeper motive. All three of them—Amanda, Raffaele and Rudy—had been taken out of their own homes and abandoned many years ago.

Amanda follows with the phrase, *"having really done my part for the situation."* She confirms her part in the murder, virtually yelling it out. She also informs the police simultaneously in yet another tell, *"having...done my part,"* that she has told them everything she can to help them, implying "now do your part."

Yet Amanda's super-intel promised major confessions, major gifts for the police in this section of the email. She has one huge surprise left. Look one last time at her slip, *"stadning"* and think how close the letter "d" is to the letter "b" in shape, long tall straight letters— almost like swords with an enclosed handle on them. In that light *"stadning"* suggests "stabning" or "stabbing." The full message translated: "I was in Meredith's bedroom ['kitchen'] positioned beside her, stabbing her with a kitchen knife. I really did it, my part in the murder." With near supernatural speed the gifted super-intel makes brilliant confessions with the smallest detail, the slightest adjustment in words, And it makes suggestions by simply moving one letter around—a mental Charades "sounds-like, looks-like" process. Show and tell.

Amanda could never, would never, get over that moment when after taunting Meredith with superficial cuts to the throat, her knife ripped into Meredith's flesh and blood erupted like a volcano in a shower of red, bright red. Suddenly her fantasy game with Meredith became living, breathing reality. It was a reality for which Amanda was unprepared, a horrible reality that still consumes her to this day. This is the pressure on her chest she simply must get out on the table as her email announced. If her conscious mind won't own her deed, her great super intelligence certainly will.

Amanda's undercover reporter, her super-intel, clarifies the brutal stab wound discovered when they opened Meredith's room—repeating twice "opened Meredith's (door)." Here she closely connects "opening Meredith" with cutting her, making certain we understand a central meaning of "opened" her, just as surgeons refer to the initial incision as "opening" and suturing the incision as "closing."

The super-intel is amazingly sophisticated in its creative communication yet equally plain. Unconsciously Amanda has found several creative ways of describing a severe stab wound with major bleeding: a slip *("stadning"),* another show-and-tell slip (a completely blank space), a metaphor *("opened Meredith"),* linked it to a specific room *"kitchen"* suggesting "kitchen knife" and further linked the kitchen to Meredith's bedroom. Now she's on the verge of linking it to a scream and a key message marker. All this is connected to the moment Meredith's body's discovered. And we have only just begun. Amanda will confirm this in multiple ways in the rest of the email. Some observers believe all of this symbolic communication is pure coincidence. But such a belief is naïve at best and misleading at worst.

The Stab and the Scream—'Merediths'

*"but when they **opened** merediths **door** and i heard filomena **scream 'a foot! a foot!' in italian** i immedaitely tried to get to merediths room but raffael grabbed me and **took** me **out** of the house."*

Amanda's three back-to-back message markers, *"opened door," "scream,"* and the dramatic *"'a foot a foot' in italian"* means she's widely opening the door to her unconscious mind. She's shouting at police, "Here is a big footprint." She wants their attention. She insists they decode her message.

Here Amanda suggests that we read *"me"* as "Mez" or Meredith since she's used her name twice and continues to speak for her. Amanda is yelling, "I opened her up—stabbed her, I took her out, and she screamed." Amanda emphasizes, **"I heard…scream…merediths."** She still hears that resounding scream every moment of her life. Her super-intel confirms for police, "You had it right—Meredith screamed when I stabbed her." Was this the same terrifying scream neighbors claimed to have heard? Amanda implies it was.

In the process, Amanda links the murder to her own personal trauma, *"took me out of house."* She's again hinting at her deepest pain.

Images Confirm Story

[*"when they opened merediths door… scream…"*] *" i **immediately** tried to **get to merediths** room but raffael **grabbed me** and took me **out of** the **house.***"

Amanda concludes the body discovery scene with more confirmation of the ferocious killing. First in *"i immediately tried to get to merediths room,"* her super-intel presents another revealing slip *"immedaitely"* which draws attention to the correction "ate" instead of "aite" in the word "immedi**ately**." Suggesting: "I immediately tried to get to Meredith and ate her—when I first entered her room." Amanda's screaming that the motive for attacking Meredith was completely one-sided from the get-go.

Finally she writes, "*tried to get to merediths….but raffael grabbed me and took me out of the house.*" She suggests they each grabbed Meredith at different points in the assault. Amanda confirms that she grabbed her by the throat and choked her severely—and the crime scene evidence revealed that hands her size had indeed strangled the victim. In the end they both grabbed Meredith and removed her from the house and from life.

Amanda refers to "*house*" again, hinting again at the murder's deeper motive. All three of them—Amanda, Raffaele and Rudy—had been taken out of their own homes and abandoned many years ago.

Note: *We move ahead in the email to where Amanda confesses again to the brutal murder.*

'Whoever…Did This…Slit Her Throat'
Email [brief section further below]—

> "*i also **talked** with the rest. especially to find out what exactly was in merediths room **whent hey opened it.** apparently*
> *her body was laying under a sheet, and with her foot sticking out and there was a **lot of blood. whoever** had **did this** had **slit her throat.**"*

Amanda continues confessing "*I talked.*" Adding "*talked with the rest,*" that is she's speaking for all three killers. Indeed she confirms she has just told police specifically what happened and will confirm the matter with her third reference to "opened Meredith." She will again tell us "*what exactly was in merediths room whent hey opened it.*" Here she makes plain precisely how she opened Meredith up.

Again "*her body was laying under a sheet…her foot sticking out and there was a lot of blood.*" Amanda is symbolically sticking her own foot out—another communication marker highlighting her message especially here. And now for the punch line, "*whoever had did this had slit her throat.*" Amanda knew when police found the body they would find the enormous wound that she had opened when *she* slashed Meredith's throat.

Then she makes another crucial slip. In telling the police, "*find out what exactly was in merediths room whent hey opened it,*" Her slip "*whent hey opened it*" suggests "hey, I went and opened it—I was the one who slit her throat." All that blood that spurted from that stab wound haunts Amanda. She "*had did this,*" she "*had slit her throat.*" It was all in the past and she couldn't undo it. She must confess "I did it" over and over again.

During the interrogation of Meredith's friends immediately after the body was found, they were all struck by Amanda's aloofness and the way she joked around with Raffaele. Mournfully, the roommates expressed the hope that Meredith's death was quick. That's when Amanda suddenly erupted, interposing into their conversation, "What the fuck do you think? They cut her throat. She fucking bled to death!"[79] The roommates were horrified. But Amanda, the killer, could not stop bluntly describing what she had done to Meredith with a knife. She had opened her up allowing her life's blood to pour out of her.

Confession Heightens after Discovery of Body

*"the **police** told everyone to get out and not long afterward the **carabinieri arrived** and then soon afterward, **more police investigators**. they **took all of our informaton** and asked us the **same questions** over and over."*

Now we return to where the decoding left off before Amanda described, *"what exactly was in Meredith's room"* and *"whoever...slit her throat.*

She writes about police and more police. With an identifiable signal, *"police told,"* Amanda insists that, *"everyone get out"* of her way. Referencing the best detectives—police investigators—her super-intel again announces its presence as the "super-police." Her super-intel—the real investigator—has arrived on the scene, right after her description of the discovery of Meredith's body.

Very subtly she *also* drops a brief hint about a deeper motive from her past. The authorities *"told everyone to get out"* of the house. Does that voice take her back to a significant time in her life—when *she* was told to get out? Keep listening. "House" and "home" are recurrent images linked to key parts of Amanda's childhood trauma.

She repeats the hidden message, *"they took all our informaton."* Her slip, *"informaton,"* suggests "inform-a-ton"—confirming that unconsciously she is revealing, a "ton" of information on the crime, everything she knows. More subtly, her slip *"informaton"* also suggests info- **rmat**-on" or "info on roommate." Impressively this compact slip comes on the heels of a description of Meredith's death.

They have taken all *"our information."* Note she uses the plural *"our* information" suggesting more than one killer.

They *"asked the same questions over and over,"* meaning Amanda has already asked and answered all the major questions including her deepest motives as we will later clarify. Already deep into her email, she reminds police to go back over it, "you already have my confession."

She implies that the one overriding question that now exists is, "Who killed Meredith?"—just after the discovery of the body. Then, to answer that most pressing question, she points directly at herself.

---

[79] Follain, p. 212.

'I Am Bad, I Am the Killer'

*"at the time i had only what i was wearing and my **badg**, which thankfully had my **passport** in it and **my wallet**. no jacket though, and i was freezing."*

Immediately she links herself to the crime. Amanda reminds them in vivid imagery that she has exposed the cold hard truth about herself—she is freezing without a jacket.

In a key slip she announces, *"I was wearing...my **badg**"* suggesting that, like police officers, she has a "badge," and she's now investigating the crime. Importantly a badge also identifies a person by name, and her *"badg"* suggests her name is "bad." As in, "I am bad, I am a killer." That's the name she's wearing.

But her "bag"—she meant to say—*"thankfully had my passport in it and my wallet."* Quickly she has shown them a second personal identification—her passport—with her name, "bad," on it. She is naming the killer for police again, if only they could see it.

She has just given the police her passport on the journey to the crime's solution, the passport to enter her "foreign" deeper mind and identify her and her accomplices as killers. Again she provides a vivid image of a foreign country where people speak another language—the land of the super intelligence.

She instructs them, "Decode the messages I've just given you, and the case is in the bag."

Another Hint at a Trigger Motive

We find one last seemingly insignificant image, *"wallet."* But pay attention. The super-intel's secret motto is "details, details." We must hang on every word, every single communication, every slip.

She suggests, "I was wearing my 'badg(e)'—my name 'bad' on it—and I had in my bad bag my bad passport also with my name on it and my bad wallet. Something in my wallet was bad identifying me as the killer."

In the context of lacking adequate clothes, *"at the time i had only what i was wearing...no jacket though...I was freezing,"* she suggests being poor and unclothed. Put the story together. She strongly implies that she lacked in money, was worried about going broke and has further confessed that she possessed bad money in her wallet.[80] It was money she'd stolen from Meredith. She identifies another major reason for being judged and rejected by Meredith possibly even involving the police. She presents a compelling reason for a conflict with Meredith that night.

---

[80] At the time Amanda had just 3000 euros in bank to last her seven months. Her rent alone cost 300 euros per month.

Instructs Police: Get an Expert Decoder

Again she uses the familiar metaphor of speaking a foreign language and of needing an interpreter, *"they brought in an interpreter and he helped my out with the **details** that i didnt know the words for."* She stresses to police, **"Get an expert in decoding the super-intel now,"** implying that only then will they understand the details which she's providing.

Key to the case—super-intel exists, reveals details

> *"after sticking around at the housr for a bit, the police told us to go to the station to giv testimony, which i did. i was in a room for six hours straight after that without seeing anyone else, answering questions in italian for the first hour and then they brought in an interpreter and he helped my out with the details that i didnt know the words for."*

Now more message marker signals, one after the other virtually non-stop shouting "guilty, expect crucial messages." These signals reflect the tremendous pressure on Amanda at this moment.

Despite feeling the heat, Amanda's deeper self is "giving testimony"—straight, telling the absolute truth. In fact, she has been testifying non-stop for *"six hours"* meaning that's what she'd been doing throughout this lengthy email (which was written late at night, the email time-stamp showed 2:45 a.m. — Amanda was so driven to confess that she couldn't sleep). But she builds up to the momentous testimony exactly as if she were in court. Deep down, she's "swearing on the Bible" like never before.

> *"i was in a room for six hours straight after that without seeing anyone else, answering questions in Italian for the first hour"*

And how is she answering questions? In *"Italian,"* the foreign super-intel language of symbolism.

> *"and then they **brought in an interpreter** and he helped my out with **the details** that i didnt know the words for."*

Again she tells them [the police] to get an interpreter for her hidden messages. She does so by holding up as plain a model as possible—a foreign language which must be interpreted. Her powerful images and hidden stories must be translated, decoded.

"Details" itself represents a crucial marker and announcement that she's about to provide crucial details, the symbolic details, and if they are properly decoded they will *uniquely point to her.* Remember she's in the midst of a tremendous unconscious confession: giving testimony, providing all her secret information, revealing her personal identifications as the killer including showing us her "bad" badge. What comes next has to be vital information.

Linking "details" to the marker "words" strongly instructs us to pay close attention to her words here, words and key phrases which we can track throughout her email for valuable matches and understanding.

Fingerprints Point to 'Thoughtprints'

*"they asked me of course about the the morning, the last time i saw her, and because i was the closest to her, questions about her habits and her relationships. "afterward, when they were **taking my fingerprints**, i met two of merediths english friends, two girls she goes out with, including the lat one who saw her alive that night she was murdered. they also had **their prints taken.**"*

Amanda's multiple identification images build up to *"fingerprints"*—the most powerful identification marker in the case with tremendous legal implications. Unconsciously Amanda then links her "fingerprints"—a completely personal identification to the crime, to her mental fingerprints: "thoughtprints." It's as though she's saying, "See? I'm telling you I did it, and my thoughts prove it."

In their own way, thoughtprints are equivalent to fingerprints. In the symbolic language of the super intelligence "fingerprints" are "thoughtprints"— unique, personal thoughts which identify a particular person.

Here "fingerprints" are yet another rich symbolic image guiding investigators to comprehend "thoughtprints," a new way of profiling, of listening. She suggests her mental fingerprints—"thoughtprints"—are matching symbolic messages unique to this crime. Clearly she has offered prosecutors her valuable mental fingerprints—the way she confesses in code.[81]

'Last Time I Saw Her'

*"they **asked me** of course about **the the** morning, **the last time i saw her**,and because i was the **closest to her**, **questions** about her habits and **her relationships.** afterward, when they were taking my fingerprints"*

Next she goes right to "The Question" which police ask—really her super-intel asks in the email— *"the last time I saw her* [Meredith]." The central question in the case which immediately makes Amanda anxious, she stutters, *"the the morning, the last time i saw her."* Obviously, she's also nervous about what she's going to confess. How she unfolds the answer to her question will be interesting.

---

[81]Richard Regnier, an outstanding California trial attorney and former district attorney, recognized in a previous forensic report of mine detailing the unique matching patterns of thoughtprints—so specific to an individual in a given context—that they are comparable to DNA. He practices in Ventura County where DNA was first admitted into evidence in a courtroom and has an appreciation for new forensic techniques. He also well recalls how strongly police investigators initially opposed the use of DNA evidence.

Crucial Detail—*'Closest to Her'*

Then she continues, *"they asked me... about the last time i saw her... because i was **the closest to her**."* Immediately she casts suspicion on herself. Her immediate answer to *"the last time I saw her"*—*"I was the closest to her"*—implies another confession. Most basically Amanda suggests a powerful motive, "the closest person to her"—but something had happened to make Meredith far away from her, emotionally. Those familiar with the two of them had witnessed exactly that—and once Meredith had been the closest one to her in Perugia, her roommate. Amanda suggests again a separation between the two of them had triggered her rage.

Astute detectives know that people are frequently murdered by those closest to them, by people who live with them, by people with whom conflicts arise. And Perugia had a very low murder rate heightening the possibility of an internal conflict in the home. Yet the murder was so brutal that its ferocity initially threw investigators off—as it did the American media. But that brutality was a clue that this was a crime of passion—a major conflict which triggered Amanda's rage at her roommate—far beyond the immediate rejection and separation from Meredith.

Right off Amanda suggests that immediate trigger really touched on a deeper "time-bomb" motive related to separation, related to her deep sense of abandonment. Abandonment by someone she had been *"closest to"* herself. She points toward her father who walked out on her but her mother also. But investigators simply aren't trained in spotting the deeper motives in the psyche which was why they were so puzzled. Amanda is trying to teach them—deep down she knows everything she's been through her entire life. Secretly she looks at all her past pain through her sterling super-intel lens—she sees the good and the bad.

"Closest to her" also suggests that Amanda was the murderer closest to the victim, the one who inflicted the severest wound.

Amanda's relationship with Meredith

*[they asked me of course about the the morning, the last time i saw her,] ... i was the **closest to her**, **questions** about her habits and **her relationships**.*

Next she follows with key *"questions about her [Meredith's]...relationships"* implying "question her relationship with me." Brilliantly, her super-intel continues to highlight motives—first the immediate trigger motives. Evidence clearly indicates Amanda had significant conflicts with Meredith, and she outright lied about those disagreements. Meredith's parents, friends and roommates, however, knew about them.

Amanda then suggests specifically *"question...habits"*—question her habits for out-of-control, angry behavior. Amanda was clearly in major conflict with her roommates and especially Meredith over her habits: continually ignoring rules of household cleanliness, neglecting to flush toilets, continually competing with Meredith, bringing strange men home and cheating on her boyfriend. She also has confessed to stealing money from Meredith. This would push Meredith further away from her American roommate. Amanda also hints that her work habits also caused a problem and led to a deeper conflict with Meredith who Patrick planned to hire to replace Amanda.

But again Amanda subtly points to her deeper motives, regarding some basic *"relationships"* that she questioned. Specifically she questioned their *"habits."* We keep in mind that something fundamental about her parents' habits hurt Amanda badly. It's no coincidence that she began her memoir by writing about the pain that had long permeated the family.

Unconsciously Amanda has now provided some motives for the murder linked to her idea of the last contact with Meredith.

'Last Time I Saw Her Alive'

From the beginning of her email Amanda has been preoccupied with the idea, *"last time I saw her* (Meredith)"—a unique personal thoughtprint, a recurring idea. There she describes, *"**The last time i saw Meredith**... was when i came home from spending the night at a friends house."* Shortly she writes, *"Meredith...said bye and left for the day. it was **the last time i saw her alive**."*

Now continuing sequentially in the "body discovered" scene at the end of her email, we find the same idea as we look at her next sentence. The last time she saw Meredith remains frozen in her mind forever. She simply cannot get over it. Now she will tell us why.

*"when they were **taking my fingerprints**, i met two of merediths english friends, two girls she goes out with, including the **lat one who saw her alive** that night she was **murdered**. they also had **their prints taken**"*

Remember here she is in the process of answering the question, when was "the last time" she saw Meredith and now picks up the identical theme. Unconsciously Amanda—guiding us to skip ahead to matching phrases as we track her unique thoughtprints—links *"last time I saw Meredith"* to *"the lat one who saw her alive that night she was murdered."* Links "last time to see" to "last one to see." She reminds us of her thoughtprint confession in the beginning of this sentence, *"they were taking my fingerprints"* suggesting "my mental fingerprints, my thoughtprints are all over what I'm about to say—pay attention."

For the first time Amanda then mentions *"that night she* [Meredith] *was murdered."* Unquestionably, the word *"murdered"* represents the most powerful thoughtprint in her email, used here one of two times. Amanda's super-intel continues to tell the story of the murder. Revealing what exactly happened when Meredith went from *"alive"* to *"murdered."*

She links the most powerful single thoughtprint, *"murdered,"* to *"my fingerprints"*—the strongest physical personal identification. It's as though she's saying, "My fingerprints/thoughtprints are all over this murder. I did it."

The first thing we note is that Amanda *"met two of merediths english friends, two girls she goes out with including...that night."* Subtly Amanda is alluding to the previous night when Meredith and her friends went out partying without her—*"that night."* She's hinting again at the most powerful immediate motive for the murder—utter rejection by her English roommate, Meredith, her British friends on Halloween night. Amanda clearly viewed these "proper" English girls as snobbish and judgmental of her, oblivious to her own provocation.

Then she emphasizes one girl, one friend, in particular, *"... the **lat one who saw her alive** that night she was murdered."* We note her slip *"lat one"* instead of "last one" in passing. The slip also marks the embedded message, *"lat one who saw her alive... murdered."* The blatant phrase itself—a hallmark of a super-intel confession—suggests a friend had murdered her. It's a near-conscious confession. Obviously the murderer was the last one to see her. Amanda's slip identifies her as the last one.

Additionally there is one letter difference between *"murdered"* and "murderer" and Amanda's super-intel frequently uses closely linked words in an embedded "sounds-like" message. Read now, *"the **lat one who saw her alive** that night she was ~~murdered~~ murderer."* (Or reading it another embedded way by skipping a word, *"the **lat one who saw her alive** that night...murdered."*) Amanda confesses that indeed she was that girl who last saw Meredith alive, *she* was the murderer.

Amanda establishes that she last saw Meredith alive *"that night"* not earlier that day as she claimed. She saw Meredith die when she murdered her. No wonder she can't wash that memory from her mind.

For the record Amanda also declares plainly that a girl killed Meredith in *"girls she goes out with... the lat one who saw her alive that night."* It will not be the last time she confirms that a female killer was involved, matching the opinion of Italian investigators.

Three Unique Identities

But she identifies herself in even more unique ways. We return to Amanda's major slip *"lat one"* knowing how invariably she reveals crucial information this way. Her slip *"lat one"* suggests:

- First **"late one."**
- Secondly it suggests **"that one"** which matches ("who saw her alive) "that night."
- Thirdly she meant to say **"last one."**

- **She has three different names for the killer, "late one—that one—last one."**
- And one final name: "lat/late one" suggests "ate one"—one who ate Meredith, consumed her. The vampire killer.

Her stunning super-intel suggests a cohesive story with these names.

First Amanda further identifies the killer with the unique phrase and slip, ***"including** the lat one."* She suggests the killer was previously "the late one" to the party. The one really not included the night before by Meredith and her friends when they went partying. The murderer was the "last one," the left-out one, the one all alone. "That one." Remember, Amanda was running later than Meredith and her friends the night before yet begging to be included.

Again the magic word "including/included" points to not being included—being abandoned—which she was on Halloween night. It was a situation the desperately needy Amanda could not tolerate. That experience the night before stuck painfully in her throat—vengefully, she included herself in the group that came to assault Meredith. That group came to specifically make their victim feel "not included."

A Late Visit to Meredith

> *"when they were **taking my fingerprints**, i **met two** of merediths english friends, two girls she goes out with, including the lat one who saw her alive that night she was **murdered**. they also had their prints taken."*

"Late one" also suggests time, the one who came late. That one, the late one, was also the one who came late with two other girls. With the message marker *"i met"* Amanda suggests, "now meet the other two 'girls,' friends of Meredith, who came late with me the night of the murder." She implies that she controlled the other two killers, Raffaele and Rudy, as though they were little girls waiting to be led. In fact Amanda was the only girl of the three.

We return to the email:

> *"met two of merediths english friends, two girls she goes out with...,*
> *including the lat one who saw her alive that night she was murdered. they*
> *also had **their prints taken**."*

Unconsciously Amanda discloses another important confession. Her super-intel uses a familiar embedded "skip-a-word" message. First she suggests, *"two of merediths ...friends, two girls...**saw her alive** that night...**murdered**. they also had their prints taken."* In other words, her two accomplices, the girl-like guys who saw Meredith alive, also murdered her. She confirms the message by adding, "they took their prints too." Her thoughtprints identify them also as murderers. They were vampires as well.

The crucial identifier "fingerprints" are on both sides of this part of her story and used here for the second time. She separates out "her fingerprints" from "their fingerprints" to identify different killers.

But again her image "my fingerprints"—really her thoughtprints—identify her as the primary killer.

Chapter 8: Secretly Speaking for Her Victim

Like a gifted investigative reporter, Amanda Knox's super intelligence goes into great detail, using incredibly vivid imagery to tell her secret story. She will demonstrate that her thoughtprints—so completely unique to her—reflect a compelling legal testimony. And in the end she will, in fact, spotlight the legality of her confession. She revels in the excitement of the chase—and of discovery— as we hang on her every word, never knowing where she will take us next but certain it will continue her stunning confession. We understand one basic fact. We are listening to a literary genius, her super-intel, when it comes to her images, metaphors, stories-within-a-story, and memorable denials.

> *"[...what im about to say i cant say to journalists or newspapers,] and **i require** that of **anone** receiving this **information** as well.*

Near the beginning of her email, Amanda's first slip, *"and I require that of anone,"* is revealing.

Reading through her denial just before this she points out she "can say" the truth and that she's secretly reporting it as an undercover journalist. Then she adds, *"and i require that of anone receiving this information."* Her slip *"anone"* [versus "anyone"] reads "an one"—one particular person who must speak up. One person to report the truth—only one, she herself who knows the truth. We can hear her inner policewoman, her super-intel, demanding she confess and reveal her secret "information."

To highlight the matter, recall that at the very end of the email she used the same metaphor, *"the police...took all of our informaton."* No question she has "all the information," and she's telling all. By now a good investigator would be expecting a full confession, the whole truth however brutal it may be. Details and more details.

Don't overlook her continual request for a special super-intel investigator *"anone receiving this information"*—a person who can decode the messages. She finds plenty of ways to plead for an investigator who can understand her message. This time she demands that he or she decipher her confession and report the truth "to journalists" and "newspapers."

'My Account of How…Roommate Murdered'

*"this is **m account** of how i found my roommate **murdered** the morning of friday, november 2nd. The last time i saw Meredith…"*

Here's the major second slip, *"this is m account"* when she meant to say "my account." Keep this slip in mind.

First she offers "my account" of the murder—an extremely strong signal, a major message marker. Giving "an account" implies meeting stringent criteria with details, precise details, deeper details than first meet the eye. It also subtly asserts that "I was there." "My" account and "my" roommate suggest especially personal involvement. To give an account also suggests a confession.

Amanda goes straight to the heart of the matter as she's compelled to utter, for the first time, the word *"murdered."* It confirms how heavily her guilt weighs on her, and the use of the word dramatically raises the stakes as her story unfolds.

She uses *"murdered"* only two times in the entire email like matching bookends—at the very beginning and near the end.

Her super-intel signals this

> Amanda goes straight to the heart of the matter as she's compelled to utter, for the first time, the word *"murdered."* It confirms how heavily her guilt weighs on her, and the use of the word dramatically raises the stakes as her story unfolds.

is an extremely crucial section of the email. That she will tell how her roommate was murdered again—as she did at the end of the email. She promises the story: *"my account of how I found…my roommate murdered"* which suggests she knows how Meredith was murdered. Notice she doesn't use the much more appropriate phrase, "how I found my roommate's body." She must use *"murdered,"* the bloody reality, and officially link it to herself with the phrase "my account."

"Found" implies "discovery"—yet another key message marker combined with the key marker *"how"* and then *"how I."*

In fact the police, and not Amanda, found the body the afternoon of November 2nd. She was in the back of the crowd in the house and couldn't even see the body in the room. Her insistence on saying "I found [her] murdered" implies she had indeed *seen* her murdered; she was there when it happened.

In addition "how I found" suggests "how I can be found (out)" by decoding this email confession. The marker *"found"* (or "discover") signals "find the hidden messages in this sentence."

'Last Time I Saw Meredith'

Amanda's crafty unconscious runs circles around the conscious mind cover-up by simply arranging a blatant skip-a-word sentence. Skip the one word, *"found,"* to read it this way: "My account of how I…my roommate murdered." Or more plainly, "my account of how I… murdered my roommate."

Shrewdly Amanda's super-intel also utilizes run-on sentences to confirm the message in *"… my account of how i …my roommate murdered….The last time i saw Meredith…"*

The confession is thus doubly confirmed: she murdered her roommate, and that was the last time she saw her.

Matching Bookend: *'Murdered'*

Recall just the second time she uses "murdered," at the end of the email, we find corresponding thoughtprints. The keyword "murdered" fits hand-in-glove with her matching confession there.

> *"[two girls she goes out with,] including the **lat one who saw her alive that night she was murdered.**"*

Read the embedded confession, *"**lat one who saw her alive… murdered [her].**"* Amanda was that *"lat one"*—that one—the last person to see her alive, her haunting signature phrase/idea.

Now let's examine another critical slip.

Killer Speaks for Victim: 'M' is for Meredith

By writing *"this is **m account** of how i found my roommate murdered the morning of friday, november 2nd. The last time i saw **Meredith**…"* Amanda answers the question, "Who is 'M'?" Amanda provides the answer in the very next sentence. "M" is for Meredith. Families often refer to a family member who has a somewhat lengthy name with an initial, i.e. "M." Meredith Kercher's own family shortened her name to "Mez."

Plainly, Amanda announces with her slip, "this is M's [Meredith's] account" of the murder, not only Amanda's account. Amanda is so burdened with guilt, she's compelled to speak for Meredith. A perpetrator's super-intel always speaks for his or her victim in some way.

In the ransom note left at the scene of the JonBenét Ramsey murder, the perpetrator was speaking for little JonBenét. The distinct hand-printed note began, *"we represent a small foreign faction."* The writer's super-intel was admitting that it represented—spoke for—the little girl with the "foreign" name, JonBenét.

Now Amanda's use of the word *"account"* takes on far more meaning. All along she has been giving "Meredith's account" of her murder as Amanda's conscience speaks up for her suddenly slain roommate.

She speaks for her victim all the way to the very end of her email and her last words *"hope you...well"* unconsciously revealing Meredith's "wishes." Don't you think Meredith doesn't wish she was well, still living? So does Amanda—now, so badly that she has to go on and on in this email, continually pleading with the police to hear her confession.

Notice how early her slip *"m account"* comes in the email. Imagine what investigators could learn after they realize just how strongly a perpetrator is compelled to speak for their victim.

'The last time I saw Meredith...day after Halloween'

> *"(this is m account of how i found my roommate **murdered the morning** of friday, november 2nd.)*
> *"The last time i saw meredith, 22, english, beautiful, funny, was when i came home from spending the night at a friends house. It was the day after halloween, thursday. I got home and she was still asleep,"*

Amanda's secret saga continues. First she says she'd been at a friend's house—a friendly home that welcomed her. But she suggests when she returned home the morning after Halloween and her roommate was still asleep, it aggravated her. Again she hints at the severe rejection by Meredith and her friends the night before—emphasizing *It was the day after halloween thursday."* She was acutely reminded of it when Meredith was still asleep from partying having a fun time with her English friends. And *"meredith was still asleep"* indicates that, on the night before, Meredith had been completely tuned out and totally unaware of Amanda's needs.

Finally, that led to Amanda's raging attack on Meredith whom she put to sleep for good later that day. Furthermore *"murdered that morning"* suggests Amanda's murderous rage continued building when she first returned home from Raffaele's and found Meredith "still asleep" as in "still rejecting me."

Her rage was exacerbated after *"spending the night at a friends house"* when she got home that morning. She went from a warm acceptance by a friend to severe rejection by her roommate. Appreciate her three references to "home" and "house."

Keep in mind that phrase *("when I came home")* because she's telling us, she came home mad that day. Real mad—and it got worse. This was a crime of passion. And what environment stirs up enough passion to prompt such a severe stab wound and multiple cuts and bruises on the victim? There's no place like home to do it—one way or the other. Home was associated in Amanda's mind with the worst rejection imaginable.

Three Traumatic Days—Reminders

She also mentions three specific days: Halloween, the day after— *"thursday,"* and also *"friday, november 2nd."* She does nothing by accident.

Every word is carefully planned.

She suggests that each of those three days symbolized something crucial about the murder. And it helped set Amanda off, her super-intel admits. It ignited a killing spree.

She linked the rejection by Meredith with these three days and linked it to far more powerful "time bomb" triggers for the crime, triggers with roots deep in her past.

> *"this is m account of how i found my roommate **murdered the morning** of friday, november 2nd. The last time i saw Meredith.... It was the day after halloween, thursday. I got home..."*

Don't miss an important message regarding her deeper motive that prompted Amanda's uncontrollable rage. Read the embedded phrase, *"this is m [my] account of how I found... murdered... the day after Halloween... I got home"* as "how I…was murdered the day after Halloween when I got home." She suggests her own pain was driven by a near-death experience so powerful it was as if she had been murdered. For some reason she links those early November days with personally traumatic events.

First she highlights Halloween, the day of the dead, the mythical day on which all monsters—including vampires—are released from the otherworld to roam the globe freely, consuming innocent victims. In raucous Perugia, Halloween was a night of dressing up like ghouls.

It was a time of lose-your-mind intoxication, of invoking great levity to lift herself above the most painful realities of life. The basic underlying Halloween code was that you should become the monster instead of fearing the monster.

Importantly, in Italy All Hallows Eve is especially symbolic of death. The public holiday—All Hallows or All Saint's Day which recognizes Christian saints and martyrs—follows on November 1st. On its heels comes the somber All Soul's Day on November 2nd during which the living pray for the souls of deceased relatives. Often they continue to mark All Souls day with a visit to loved-ones' graves, even leaving flowers or food. Thousands of Italians throughout the country took long weekends during 2007's manic-depressive celebration.

Anticipating the Halloween merriment would have left someone like Amanda—someone with major loss issues—extremely stirred up and vulnerable to acting out. The same went for her Italian boyfriend whose family background was full of similar pain.

Last Mention 'Meredith Unaccounted For'

> *"which meant the only one who had spent the night at our house last night was **meredith**, and she was as of yet **unaccounted for**."*

Toward the end of her email she returns to that haunting word, "account," when she describes Meredith's disappearance just before her body is discovered. In the phrase *"she was of yet unaccounted for"* Amanda announces that she has yet to publicly account for Meredith's death.

But reading through her denial *["unaccounted for"]* Amanda's unconscious message becomes "all through this email I am constantly accounting for Meredith's murder in code to the police—I did it, we did it." In some major way Amanda suggests her crime stemmed from being unaccounted for herself. Certainly Meredith had not accounted for her the night before, on Halloween. But Amanda implies that for a long time she saw herself as set aside in the most basic ways—as though she didn't count, as though she just didn't matter to those around her. That Halloween rejection was enough to rekindle deep feelings of rejection from Amanda's childhood, feelings that would explode in uncontrollable rage.

Chapter 9: The Vampire Killers

The Moment of Death, Used 'Kitchen Knife'

*[I got home and she was still asleep,] bu after i had taken a **shower** and was* **fumbling around the kitchen she emerged** *from* **her room** *with the* **blood** *of her costume (**vampire**) still* **dripping down her chin**.

As her story goes, Amanda had just come home and her roommate was asleep. On the heels of *"murdered...last time I saw her...[day after Halloween...],"* Amanda tells us, *"I got home and she was still asleep. bu after I..."* In other words, "I got home: Meredith was still—asleep—dead."

Right away Amanda blatantly suggests she killed her when she came back to her house. Her follow up slip *"bu"* suggests "be you" transparently confirming her confession. Read it this way: "That would be you, Amanda, who put Meredith to sleep." She follows *"bu"* [be you] with *"after I"* again announcing "after I did it."

Quickly she confesses how she did it.

"I was fumbling around the kitchen"—where the knives are stored. That phrase further suggests, "I was fumbling around with a kitchen knife" and *"after I had taken a shower."*

Amanda implies Meredith had died *after* she stabbed her with a kitchen knife, and Amanda ended up taking a blood shower which spewed from the wound. Unconsciously she confirms one of the key details in the crime—she used a large kitchen knife.

Immediately she validates her confession. She mentions Meredith *"emerged...her room with... blood...still dripping down her chin."* Amanda's super-intel has "emerged" (a key message marker) and introduces two powerful images of "blood dripping"—and where? *"down her chin."*

Unconsciously she describes the precise death blow. What's she's really saying is "Meredith's blood was dripping down her chin when I killed her with the kitchen knife."

The first of many times Amanda uses *"shower"* she links it to herself, a particular knife and to Meredith's blood. And she establishes where she killed her. Immediately she links the kitchen indirectly to Meredith's bedroom where her roommate has *"just"* been and thus to "kitchen knife." She's making plain throughout her confessions that *"kitchen"* is code for "Meredith's bedroom" where the crime took place.

The message marker image *"her costume"* reflects "Amanda's costume," her cover-up story.

Can you imagine Amanda priding herself on her creative writing skills as she glibly glosses over her crime? Writing her cover-up email and in the process connecting herself in a *"shower"* to *"blood dripping down* [Meredith's] *chin"* to Meredith's bedroom and speaking of *"fumbling around the kitchen"* virtually shouting "kitchen knives" at us—and overlooking the sheer power of her images.

She brings her readers so close to the crime scene they could shut their eyes and envision it. The whole story's told in a breathless string of word-pictures. Reflecting the heavy guilt she just described earlier, *"I require...this information,"* she's saying, "I require this confession." The burden of her enormous guilt drips from Amanda's figurative pen just as the blood dripped from Meredith's chin.

Vampires

*"...she emerged from her room with the blood of her costume (**vampire**) still dripping down her chin."*

Amanda's super-intel introduces another image of horrific violence, slipping it in ever so subtly. But she highlights it with a message marker parenthesis which sets it off. The word is *"vampire,"* those monsters who must consume human blood in order to survive. At the first mention of Meredith, she immediately cites vampires.

Oh so naturally. Oh so casually. And oh so guiltily. Convicted by her own words and images. Amanda is a vampire. She could easily have left that one word out, but her super-intel insisted on it.

Amanda's clearly confessing that she herself was a vampire that night, and it was no costume! She consumed Meredith, preying on her neck as a vampire would, reveling in her blood. This single, key word sums up this case—*"vampire."* They're cunning monsters which prowl under the cover of darkness, night demons which consume and enslave. Indeed the crime scene reflected the worst vampire imaginable had just left the room leaving behind a shower of blood from the bite.

Again Amanda's image, *"costume,"* represents the continual phony cover-up role she dons for the public and the media, covering up her secret, deeply violent nature. But keep the image *"costume"* in mind. She will make repeat confessions in show-and-tell costumes.

Halloween Again

Halloween, the day of the vampires, simmered in Amanda's and her accomplices' collective psyches—as did the day of the dead that followed. Something horrific—a deep-seated passionate rage—was stirred up in all the three killers by the spirit of the season. But that was part of only one immediate motive. It pointed back, however, to a time-bomb motive from Amanda's past. She will explain this clearly in her email and other key communications.

Amanda further suggests that she herself was consumed, violated severely by an emotional vampire from her past and continually haunted by the terror. Now she had the blood of a vampire and she focused her blood-lust on Meredith. Before long Amanda will tell us who the vampire was in her life. After all, the vampire image itself first implies Dracula, a powerful, even magical, male figure. But are there other vampires in her past?

Going even deeper Amanda suggests that her buried traumas left her terribly bloody emotionally as if she had been stabbed and was living in a constant shower of blood. And she was in great need to wash the blood from that trauma off herself, to be cleansed and free.

Think of Amanda, the great mystery writer, who unravels her story bit by bit—a clue here, a clue there—challenging us to put it all together.

Amanda's super intelligence dances circles around the police. Already she hints strongly at motives. The story is all about *"vampires."* She repeats key words: *"shower"*—eight times, *"blood"*—eleven times, and *"kitchen"*—six times.

Way 'Out Of The Ordinary' Crime

> *"We **talked** for a while in the kitchen, how the night went, what our plans were for the day. **Nothing out of the ordinary** "then she [Meredith] went to take a shower and **i began** to **start eating** a little while i waited for my friend (Raffaele-at whose house i stayed over) to arrive at **my house**."*

Amanda's unconscious makes plain in another striking message marker, *"talked,"* that she is talking/confessing about Meredith. She predicts a crucial message between the lines: she is talking about "in the kitchen/Meredith's bedroom" and how "the night of the crime went and what our plans for the day" were. She suggests that the crime involved a certain degree of planning by several people *("our plans"),* implying the three murderers.

Her blatant denial, *"nothing out of the ordinary,"* tells us the assault on Meredith involved an extraordinary event: some very strange plans that night and also deeply disturbing emotional matters resulted in a crime far from ordinary.

Quickly she informs us exactly about that's night's unique moment. Amanda unconsciously links two events. This time *"she went to take a shower"* and *"I began to start eating."* Read Meredith suddenly "went," left, and quickly died in a shower of her own blood when Amanda began eating/consuming her. Amanda thus confesses, "I was the one who stabbed her and started the massive bleeding." When Amanda, the vampire, took a savage bite out of Meredith's neck—that was the crime's most extraordinary moment.

She suggests twice—*"I began"* and *"to start eating"*—that she consumed and attacked Meredith. While eating represents a benign image on the surface, she returns to more overt vampire images throughout the email.

In a flash, she links *"eating"* to her gruesome image *"vampire"*— completely oblivious to dropping some obvious clues. On top of that, she links it to *"blood dripping from Meredith's chin."* Of course, that's precisely where vampires crudely attack—just under the chin—and where Meredith suffered her worst wound.

Amanda's super-intel cannot be stopped from testifying—early and often. Her conscious mind becomes blinder by the minute.

The Next Vampire Arrives

"then she [Meredith] went to take a shower and i began to start eating a little while i waited for my friend (Raffaele-at whose house i stayed over) to arrive at my **house.**-*"He came right after i* **started eating** *and* **he made himself some pasta**. *as we were* **eating together meredith** *(came out of the shower...)"*

Amanda repeats twice *"started eating"*—or start eating—associated with Raffaele's arrival.

Raffaele immediately *"made himself some pasta"* which again suggests they had smoked cannabis and used other drugs prior to the attack. Remember, at Amanda's house the word *"pasta"* was code for pot—marijuana.

Quickly Raffaele joined Amanda in *"eating"*/consuming Meredith, confirmed by the striking phrase, *"as we were eating together Meredith."* Translate it this way: **"we were eating Meredith together."** This stands as an especially powerful thoughtprint match, *"vampire"* and "eating together Meredith." (In Chapter 16 we'll see Sollecito confess to the murder unconsciously in matching thoughtprints—using identical vampire images.)

Eating after a death—which the day of the dead would remind them—also suggests a wake, a party. Amanda and Raffaele were always secretly at a wake, always escaping their pain in some form of addiction and false revelry. Was it any accident that this Italian holiday was the day of the murder?

Amanda's super-intel can barely wait to tell us who else stabbed her roommate. She waited all of two paragraphs in her email to introduce her primary co-vampire—to emphasize he too was eating hungrily like a desperate predator.

On the surface she thinks, "I'll just casually have Raffaele drop by in my cover-up story," but her imagery paints the picture of their involvement in the murder. Her unconscious has its foot on Amanda's neck. "Right after" she

Not so subtly she reveals all her vampire ways—sex, drugs and money---as her actions have detailed. Clearly Raffaele's father, in interviews he gave after the murder, clearly saw Amanda as a vampire who had destroyed his son.

started writing, her special internal prosecutor tells her, "say it, say it." Implying make it "right after" all.

Also her phrase "came right after" suggests impulsivity on both their parts. They both pursued Meredith like a vampire would. And now her super-intel must "impulsively" confess—meaning quickly confess because it processes guilt in a millisecond. Now her guilt pursues her.

Subtly, Amanda hints again at a deeper motive and her personal trauma. At one time someone came "right after her," dangerously pursuing her. Her clue—it occurred right after *"I started eating,"* implying when she was very young. She suggests something horrific happened to her at an exceptionally young age.

Sexual Pursuit

In another meaning, she suggests sexual excitation—in *"he came right after"*—and sexual abuse as part of their conjoined vampire-like actions. Bringing in a second party, Amanda leaves room for another person to join her charade—Rudy Guede, who has already been convicted. Never forget that double entendres are a staple of the super intelligence.

And remember, one of Amanda's central defenses is sex, which is another way of consuming. She was very sexually aggressive—she *"came right after"* the men she wanted. And her partners described her as extremely aggressive in bed. And we know that she was aggressively in her roommate's face about her sexual freedom.

Not so subtly she reveals all her vampire ways—sex, drugs and money---as her actions have detailed. Clearly Raffaele's father, in interviews he gave after the murder, clearly saw Amanda as a vampire who had destroyed his son.

There are so many clues in her words that see so deeply into her psyche—and they all fit.

'my house'—The Deeper Motive

"then she [Meredith] went to take a shower and i began to start eating a little while i waited for my friend (Raffaele-at whose house i stayed over) to arrive at my house."

Amanda again references *"house"* twice, the difference in staying at someone else's house and her house.

And she *waits* on a person to arrive from his house. Subtly she's suggesting that sometime in her life she'd been separated from, an important man she needed and waited on "to arrive," someone who even now remained at his house not hers. She alludes to her father. Amanda continues waiting.

On this special day of loss and death she was vividly reminded of her own deep sense of loss, losses so severe they drove her to inflict the ultimate loss on her victim.

This matches precisely what we have learned utilizing the super intelligence in the "new depth psychology." Emotionally traumatized human beings often experience deep separation and loss especially in early childhood or even adolescence. And they experience it as if they're being cannibalized—consumed by their trauma—prompting a need to do the same.

Such primitive emotions simultaneously make her story incredibly powerful yet very difficult to hear. Who wants to delve that deeply into the dark side of human nature?

Her continued use of cannibalistic imagery—repeated references to eating and consuming—suggests primitive motivation and early wounds in both of them which fueled the crime.

Still Amanda's idea of *"fumbling around the kitchen"* implying with a kitchen knife suggests that she didn't consciously mean to fatally stab Meredith. But something terrifying—an inner vampire—took over unconsciously and triggered her rage, a rage no one had ever come close to seeing. In the daytime, vampires remain completely out of sight, lying in wait—much like buried unconscious traumas. Especially near-death traumas. Vampire traumas.

Cat-and-Mouse Game—Disguised Vampires

Amanda continually reveals powerful engulfing imagery in different ways. She brings us back to her *"costume"* image. She dressed up like a cat on Halloween the night before the murder, and in her memoir describes the police playing 'a cat-and-mouse game' with her during interrogations. That suggests the exact game she and the others played with Meredith on that fateful night. Keep in mind the way cats toy with their prey before killing and consuming them.

On her first Halloween out of jail in October 2013, free on appeal, Amanda dressed up in all black like a cat or some said a cat burglar. Her costume suggests another confession—that she had stolen Meredith's life and gotten away with it. Furthermore her super-intel implied, "Prison is where I belong, so I'm dressing up like I did the night before the crime, like a criminal. Please catch me and send me back."

In her memoir we find an even more striking confession.

Amanda the Cat Attacks Prey

Amanda described one of her cellmates in prison who collected food wrappers and inkless pens, *"which she stored in her clothing locker, like a squirrel hiding nuts,"* and *"tried to take care of me, in the same way a pet cat that drops a freshly dead rat at your feet thinks it's giving you a gift."*[82] Amanda announces "I am a cat...I am a sneaky killer...secretly I held Meredith's dead body in my teeth after I destroyed her—I am a vampire... and finally I am a rat." We ask for good measure how do cats kill their prey—by grabbing them around the neck, the throat—cat vampires, really.

She is symbolically dropping "the rat"—her victim Meredith—at the feet of the police as a gift, pointing at the dead body to say, "Look what I did!"

Parenthetically in his review of her memoir, New York Times book critic Sam Tanenhaus defended Amanda as a victim of great injustice perpetrated by the Italian court system.[83] Like Amanda, he could have written whatever he wanted, but his super-intel honed in like a bat heading for a cave going to the most powerful secret confession imaginable in her 459-page book. He focused precisely on Amanda's story about the "pet cat" dropping its dead prey at your feet. Intuitively Tanenhaus called it "genuine writing."

In short his super-intel picked up on the genuine truth. Amanda was hiding the truth locked away in her mind like a squirrel hiding nuts—alluding to her deep pain and inner madness that drove her squirrely murderous behavior. Tanenhaus also recognized unconsciously in his denial how, like many in the American media, he protected his little pet Amanda refusing to examine the facts. He couldn't face the fact she was a brutal murderer.

In a litany of violent predator images Amanda has announced she is a cat who proudly captures her prey, a fox who sneaks up on her prey, a burglar who steals lives from others and, all in all, a vampire. How well this fits with a college acquaintance who described her as a "maneater."

For his part, Rudy admitted that at a Halloween party he had described himself to Meredith as a vampire who wanted to "suck her blood." Almost certainly this never actually happened, but it nevertheless represents Rudy's admission to his part in the crime, confirming his own need to cannibalize Meredith.

Grabbing Meredith—Some Details

> *"(...as we were eating together) meredith* came out of the shower and grabbed some laundry or put some laundry in, one or the other and returned into her room after saying hi to raffael."

---

[82] Knox, p. 168.
[83] Sam Tanenhaus, *New York Times,* May 5, 2013.

Amanda continues sharing details of the murder in the context of "eating/consuming Meredith together." First she suggests specifics of the sexual taunting and assault with a series of sexual images. Keep in mind that the female genitalia are archetypically referred to as a box or a container.

Distinct images of *"came out,"* grabbing, of putting something into a container (washing machine) and taking it out and returning *"into her"* container (room) all suggest sexual penetration. She links this aggressive "grabbing" activity to *"after"* and *"saying hi to Raffael"*—suggesting how they taunted Meredith during the sexual assault: "Now say hi to Raffaele, welcome him to return to your private little room."

Amanda also implies in her confusion *"grabbed some ... put some...in, one or the other"* that she and Raffael both penetrated Meredith—as did Rudy Guede, whose DNA was found inside her. It was a gang assault. "Came out" suggests lesbian activity on Amanda's part. In a later writing, Amanda will recall how people thought she was a lesbian in high school.

But the sexual assault was really about power. It was intended to humiliate the victim. Amanda continues to show us all of her psychological tricks, her coping mechanisms. All of which led to covering up the core of her personhood—hiding her secret terror.

The laundry allusion suggests that Amanda is airing the dirty laundry about the crime and how they dirtied up—desecrated—Meredith sexually before they cut her, cannibalized her and took her life. And laundry (washing) suggests something that needs cleaning, and that Amanda is now coming clean.

Not far into the email Amanda becomes unconsciously preoccupied with cleaning—taking a shower, washing laundry. Quickly the super-intel announces what it stands for—getting cleansed of guilt by confession. The police could never have a better ally. But they have yet to meet this mind, the best mind on the case.

Amanda Confirms the Taunting

"after a little while of playing guitar me and raffael went to his house to watch movies and after to eat dinner and generally spend the evening and night indoors. we didnt go out."

Amanda must recap the way she and Raffaele specifically toyed with Meredith continuing the sexual assault imagery. First she relives the taunting phase of the attack which included stripping their victim of most of her clothes—and then she suggests they played the *"guitar me/Mez (Meredith's nickname).*

(Already Amanda has referred to Meredith as "M"—"me" or "Mez" would be similar.) They played Meredith like a guitar, an instrument exposed on display. She was their party music. Guitar players use the fingers of both hands to play the instrument, suggesting that Amanda digitally penetrated Meredith. Clearly she hints again at Rudy's digital penetration of the victim as well—suggesting how he left his DNA inside Meredith.

They all watched her for a while regaled by "the movie scene"—the evening's entertainment—until finally *"after a while...of playing"* they ate her (*"after to eat dinner"*), finished her off.

Her super-intel must tell all. She cannot stop herself—she must repeat *"eating"* over and over to make the case for "Amanda the Vampire." Amanda's hungry—and wounded. Time and again she will unconsciously bring us back to this central vampire role and how it all started long before she ever met Meredith.

We must pay close attention as to where Amanda, the undercover reporter, has taken us. Again she has introduced "Raffaele's house" and her house, pointing to their respective childhood "homes"—where their pain started.

She strongly links their personal homes and "watching" movies unconsciously to the crime scene. In *"went to his house to watch movies,"* she first suggests watching Raffaele's "family movies." Likewise she implies, "We went back to my old house to watch movies too. We both saw the same horror movies."

"Movie" suggests for each of them the story of their home lives. "Movie" also suggests they were both actors in a reenactment of their pain on Meredith. She was the evening's entertainment. In essence, they were reenacting "family movies" at the crime scene.

In the back of their minds they experienced a constant flashback like a movie, watching themselves as victims. Now they changed roles, and Meredith became their victim.

"Movie" is a major message marker, "See this. Pay attention, key story about us, key story about our victim and what motivated our murderous rage." Remember all three perpetrators were into making videos/posting Internet pictures about themselves, underscoring a strong need to act out payback fantasies.

One Flashback from the Past

She further suggests that a key part of the story unfolded when she left her house and went to *"his house"*—a man's house. Often she refers to his "apartment," but here it's *"his house"* to more strongly make her point. What does *"his house"* symbolize to her?

Her memoir points out how traumatic had been her weekend custody visits to her father's house. Recall when her two half-sisters grew older, Amanda and her sister were moved from a bedroom to the living room for their sleep-overs. She called these sisters the "replacement" children, and shortly she and her sister quit visiting her father. Bedrooms would now carry enormous resentment deep down for Amanda, especially bedrooms in a man's house or other girls'

144

bedroom. It was no accident she killed Meredith in the bedroom.

Crime-Scene Guidance

Unconsciously Amanda provides key markers in her email such as stayed *"indoors"* and *"didnt go out"* to communicate: "Don't leave the murder scene. I'm still talking about it.

She implies that she and Raffaele had not left her house for long after the murder. They waited until the coast was clear and returned. Then Amanda and Raffaele stayed *"indoors"* cleaning up the crime scene in the long night after the murder. *"Indoors"* also suggests this crime was an "inside" job.

Also the images of *"indoors"* and *"didnt go out"* fit both Amanda and Raffaele in another way. She suggests that neither one of them really had a life beforehand in some very basic ways.

Grabbing Their Plaything

> *"...the next morning i woke up around 1030 and after grabbing my few things i left raffael's apartment and walked the five minute walk back to my house to once again take a shower and grab a chane of clothes."*

In *"back to my house"* she is still describing the crime scene at her house— as her next sentence also discloses. She uses a vital message marker—*"woke up"*—alerting the police to wake up and hear the secret story she unfolds. Specifically she tells them, "Wake up. I'm confessing that the murder took place close to 10:35 p.m. The time I got home and Meredith was 'still' asleep—that is, dead" (around the same time estimated by the forensic pathologist, Lalli).

Changing clothes hints that she's trying to change her appearance as the murderer and consciously proclaim her innocence. But changing her clothes also means she first took them off—right in front of the authorities—to show them she is exposing herself at this exact moment in a confession taking you back through the gory details. References to "changes" and "exposure" are major message markers.

Again she suggests that they grabbed Meredith, treating her like a plaything to be used for their own purposes. Notice the familiar keyword *"shower"* in *"take a shower and grab."* She confesses again that they grabbed Meredith during the murder, experiencing *"once again"* a deluge of blood. And she paints the picture of an overall hasty event implying the entire assault occurred over a short period of time. She also hints that she took a quick shower to wash the blood off as quickly as possible before leaving her house—implying she changed her bloody clothes and grabbed them to take with her, discarding them shortly after the crime.

For good measure her slip, *"grab a chane of clothes"* suggests "a chain of clothes"—as in "chain-gang clothes." Amanda's super-intel instructs police:

"Grab me. I need to change clothes and go to jail." Deep down she seeks relief. Deep down she insists that only jail will begin to set her free. But that's only her super-intel wisdom. Consciously she's still chained to her false beliefs that she should keep her "cover-up costume" on. Consequently she remains chained to that violent *"shower"* she cannot get off her mind.

Amanda's image of being nude in a shower takes us back to long ago into her past when she was in her birthday suit. *"Chane"* (and Amanda meant 'change') suggests the major changes in her early life that so greatly affected her and imprisoned her in fear.

Secret 'Home Movie' 20 Years Before

At the moment she's describing the murder of her roommate, Amanda's key message markers—especially *"i woke up"* and exposing herself (her image of nudity in a shower)—highlight a phenomenally crucial confession. Unconsciously she's waking up to what caused her to be such a taker. Explaining what caused her to be the lead actor in the brutal reenactment of their pain to the point she would take the life of another human being.

On the heels of now envisioning a "home or family movie" (*"went to his house to watch movies"*) she continues to present her reasons—her secret family story in detailed imagery. Her striking message marker command, "watch movie" combined with *"woke up"* underscores the importance of the next message.

Again she mentions *"back to my house,"* with the vivid image of someone who is only home long enough to take a quick shower, grab a few things, and leave to meet a lover. She suggests how she experienced her father suddenly leaving when she was one year of age. He was, as she knows, leaving for another woman. Amanda suggests deep down she was just a plaything, not to be taken seriously, her needs be damned.

The five-minute walk between two homes also pictures how her father indeed moved only blocks away, living there with the other woman for most of Amanda's life. Maybe, too, she's looking back and telling us about how long that short *"five minute"* walk felt like when she was growing up, when she left her father's nearby house—her temporary place—to return home every other weekend after visitation. Leaving his replacement children secure in their home, Amanda and her sister felt like afterthoughts.

And she suggests he left behind some bloody clothes and family members in the process, again matching a vampire-style attack. She was indeed consumed in the process. Or, reading it another way, it was as if she'd been grabbed and taken from her home. And she explains why she was fixated on getting her father's love her entire life.[84] She was constantly seeking his attention. She still needs it. Remarkably she has not given up hope.

---

[84]Burleigh, p. 31.

Unconsciously she takes responsibility for her actions and yet points to the powerful forces that shaped her life. Isn't that the way it goes for all us? No excuses but reasons, understanding which leads to some compassion for both the murderer and her parents who certainly couldn't have realized how deeply they were wounding their daughter. But Amanda, the forthright reporter says, "Look at the story I am uncovering. Look we must."

Later she will admit to intellectualizing the pain of her father's abandonment, but her super intelligence knows and tells—so that she might understand what it was like. She shows us the power of an early emotional hurt—just how bad the pain can be. It helps explain how a bloodless crime against her led her to commit a bloody crime.

'Amelie of Seattle' or 'Amanda the Ripper'

As revealed in Amanda's other communications, the particular movie Amanda and Raffaele supposedly watched was *Amelie*—a seemingly light-hearted film about an innocent young British woman. Amelie's winsome personality allowed her to get people to do what she wanted while she tries to help them improve their lives.

But the movie had a dark side which fits Amanda in striking ways. Her super-intel presents another clue: decode the meaning of the movie to hear her deepest secrets.

Amelie's father was cold and distant. Her mother had committed suicide. In the movie the transformative moment in Amelie's life comes later after another death. She was devastated by the unexpected death of the British princess, Diana, an idealized royal figure whom Amelie looked up to as a woman. The movie itself suggests Princess Diana's loss was really a displacement, a cover for the loss of Amelie's mother, the ideal woman who violently abandoned Amelie. Surely the suicide of a mother would be far more personally relevant than the death of a public figure she never knew. Amelie symbolizes how quickly people tend towards denial of powerful losses.

Suicide is experienced as a violent attack by surviving family members, as though they were killed themselves in a way—a strikingly powerful abandonment. Apart from the sadness of it all, suicide is a selfish act. In the movie, Amelie's mother also picked a distant, unavailable man to be her father causing Amelie more pain and another rejection.

Amanda resonated with Amelie's story because she experienced her father's abandonment as a type of death and assault. But in the film, Amelie's mother is more absent—also violent and destroyed herself. Unconsciously Amanda suggests in ways she experienced her mother as even more violent and abandoning than her father. And Amanda's mother, like Amelie's mother, picked a scoundrel for a father which a kid experiences as a destructive choice.

Amanda strongly suggests that there is more to her mother's abandonment. In the same way, she sees her mother as violent. For sure Amanda unconsciously felt abandoned by both parents. Yet, like Amelie, she must deny it.

Even deeper still, Amanda experienced the deep abandonment not only as an assault but as her own death. She was the "Angel Face Princess," the pretty girl from Seattle who died. Just as Princess Di died a violent death when the car in which she was riding crashed, Amanda's super-intel has consistently pointed to another supposed secure space that had been wrecked—a home that had been severely broken. And in the end she died in that assault in a real way—and moment by moment is about to again. Like victims of post-traumatic stress disorder, she experiences being dead and alive simultaneously.

At trial Raffaele's defense attorney, Giulia Bongiorno, attempted to portray Amanda in an innocent light, similar to the title character in the movie. She declared that Amanda was "Amelie from Seattle" not "Amanda the Ripper" alluding to the still-unsolved crimes of Jack the Ripper in London in the 1880s. Choosing to introduce the image due to the sheer brutality of the attack on Meredith, the attorney was unconsciously picking up on Amanda's crime and joining her in an unconscious confession—using denial, of course, exactly as Amanda does time and time again.

But the brutal crime scene—the most severe stab wound the prosecutor had seen—was indeed reminiscent of the Ripper's brutal slashings. Referencing Amelie in the movie, Amanda secretly tells us how she was "Amelie of Seattle" on the surface but "Amanda the Ripper" underneath. How well her repetitive violent vampire image fits the Ripper.

This explains why *Amelie* was her favorite movie, and why she was preoccupied with it. On the surface they both had similar three-syllable names and an unusual persona. But deep down Amanda was trying to resolve her unconscious issue, the powerful abandonment assaults she experienced. Unknowingly every time she saw the movie it was another attempt to understand what happened to her and simultaneously to bury it as did the innocent Amelie herself. But as hard as she tried she couldn't bury the terrifying truth about the pain—and the rage—that controlled her deeply. What you don't own, owns you.

In a real way Amanda has given us a quick glimpse at the family movies she secretly shows us, with more to come.

Shortly Amanda will make known just how "mad" she and Raffaele had gone at the moment of the murder. She will continually present signs of a very disturbed—deeply traumatized—personality, frequently alluding to her madness and to his—and where it originated.

She demonstrates how the super-intel can take you back, in half a heartbeat, to a person's childhood 15 to 20 years earlier. Like it's got a constant swivel on its head looking back to the distant past and looking forward to the immediate present as if it possesses two sets of eyes, one in front and one in back of its head.

Her brilliant super-intel unfolds her story in an absolutely logical fashion, admitted that, "We toyed with Meredith, watched her like family movies, then

148

consumed her—destroyed her as we were destroyed. Now see my story all about my home—cluing you in as to why we did it. Why I did it. Maybe now you can get a hint of why I'm secretly so furious."

Chapter 10: 'I needed to grab'—
The Pain that Simmers

Gruesome Details from the Start

> *"...woke up around 1030 and after grabbing my few things i left raffael's apartment and walked the five minute walk back to my house to once again take a shower and grab a chane of clothes.*
>
> *"...i also needed to grab a mop because after dinner raffael had spilled a lot of water on the floor of his kitchen by accident and didnt have a mop to clean it up. so i arrived home and the first abnormal thing i noticed..."*

Amanda cannot stop talking about the crime scene and the voluminous bleeding. She now clarifies the moment the taunting game exploded in all their faces. Her super-intel thoughtprints are detailed and consistent.

Her description of *"a lot of water"* being spilled in Raffaele's kitchen confirms that massive quantities of Meredith's blood were spilled on the floor of Meredith's bedroom—a.k.a "the kitchen."

From water everywhere Amanda soon mentions blood everywhere—and spilled on the floor. Amanda's preoccupied with liquids. Already she's mentioned blood on Meredith's chin from the night before. And she thinks she can get away with murder by glibly going on and on, from scene to scene. The more she talks, however, the more she gives herself away.

She reflects, *"I also needed to grab"*—that she "also" grabbed Meredith and was in on the crime. "Grab a mop" also suggests that perhaps Amanda at one point grabbed a mop of Meredith's hair to control her—likely when she choked her. She remains fixated on "grabbing" but consciously overlooks the fact that she repeats the word, the idea, at the core of the crime—confessing her desperate rage to grab and choke Meredith. Over time, she will describe several versions of this scene regarding the spilling of liquids/blood.

This first version is the most important and accurate because she describes that Raffaele had an *"accident"*—linked again to *"after dinner,"* after they began assaulting Meredith. All other versions of this scene portray him in a passive, uninvolved way, a victim of a simple plumbing breakdown. Amanda strongly implies that the initial stabbing was *"by accident,"* an accident caused by Raffaele. *"The first abnormal thing"* suggests the accident was indeed abnormal and that Raffaele was the first one who took things too far with his knife. The last thing she wants to do is allude to the murder weapon in any way, yet her super-intel insists on bringing it up first thing

And she has just implied an accident on her part—*"fumbling around the kitchen"* (that is, "with a kitchen knife"). Surely, both she and Raffaele got carried away. We now have two powerful indirect references to cutting—fumbling with a kitchen knife and spilling blood.

'I needed to grab'

But we must not miss her crucial phrase—*"I needed to grab"*—comes out of her theme song, *"I needed."* That omnipresent neediness started when she was a child, when her deepest needs remained unmet.

She needed because she had been spilled—not held. Her basic needs were spilled on the floor as if she were nothing more than meaningless, amorphous water—accidentally discarded. She sees herself as nothing more than an accident. Amanda also knows she was an accident, the consequences of an unintended pregnancy, but there's more to her lack of nurture.

We follow the clue, *"grab."* What's the first thing an infant does seeking nurture? She grabs with her mouth even before using her hands, seeking the mother's milk, the most basic image in the world. When that infant can't get her needs met, she will search in desperate fury attempting to grab on to the mother with her mouth.

Enormously frustrated, akin to a needy, frightened infant throwing a frantic temper tantrum, Amanda now tells us, *"I needed to grab"*—the second verse to her theme song. She implies, "I desperately needed to consume out of the deep hole in the center of me, a basic unmet-need-for-nurture" that occurred at some crucial point. Those unmet needs left her so enraged she had to grab life by the throat to survive. In fact, she had to grab someone by the throat and kill her. Translate it one step further, "I needed to grab—like a vampire." She became a vampire to survive, substituting blood for nurture.

Then Amanda turned her rage loose in her sexuality, another way she could grab and bite. There is the well-known myth of the "dentate vagina" or *Vagina dentate*—a vagina with teeth, a vagina that grabs and bites. Wikipedia defines it as "a folk tale in which a woman's vagina is said to contain teeth, with the associated implication that sexual intercourse might result in injury or castration for the man involved."[85] It's a picture of a dangerous woman.

Amanda used her reckless femininity to seduce, then consume. She became a vagina vampire. She consumed men and had just consumed Raffaele. A silent blood-letting that was going on since the moment she seduced him, and he was totally oblivious to it. Later his father could see it clearly, railing about how Amanda had ruined his son's life. Secondarily she consumed Rudy Guede as well enticing him into the crime.

Her image: *"grab a mop,"* a tool with a long handle and soft spongy head on it even suggests "grab a phallic mop and become the man in charge." The power person. The woman who is secretly enraged.

Stay with her images. They will take you to her soul, to the very center of her being.

Autopsy Review

Before continuing our decoding of her email we review the findings of forensic pathologist Dr. Luca Lalli, who worked the crime scene and performed Meredith's autopsy. There's nothing like the brutal crime scene to provide a reality framework to better hear Amanda's secret messages.

Meticulously Lali counted 23 wounds on Meredith's body and multiple scratches to her face, neck and hands. Lalli found bruises on her right nostril, lips, and left check. Bruises on both sides of her neck revealed she had been strangled. Bruises also were found on Meredith's right forearm and left thigh.

On genital exam, Lalli found small scratches on the victim's inner labia and bruises to her lower belly and inner thighs. These suggested the possibility of "rough, quick-sex" with lack of sufficient arousal and protective vaginal secretions. No semen was found overtly. Lalli estimated the likelihood of rape, "Fifty-fifty until DNA results." Those results revealed no semen but a minimum of digital penetration by Rudy Guede whose DNA was found in the vaginal vault.

Most significantly, there were four knife penetrations, three in the neck and one in the hand. One of the neck wounds was a superficial prick to her chin. There were two prominent stab wounds.

In addition, as Dr. Lalli opened the chest, he found no bleeding as usual because of the severe blood loss during the crime. Blood was found, however, inside the victim's lungs which had prevented air from entering the lungs. Meredith had drowned on her own blood. That was the immediate cause of death. Distended small air sacs (alveoli) in her lungs indicated signs of suffocation by strangulation.

Additional findings: Blood droplets, not pooling of blood, found on the victim's exposed chest suggested the killers had cut her bra and exposed her

---

[85] http://en.wikipedia.org/wiki/Vagina_dentata 6/3/14.

breasts after the severe stabbings just before she expired.[86] This suggests staging to support an unknown intruder theory. Ironically, at the crime scene the victim's wounded left hand was raised and pointing toward the severe left-sided stab wound on her neck as though announcing, "This is how I died."

Email Compared to Statement to Police

Amanda's other writings from jail present a golden opportunity for comparison with her email.

In that light we quickly glance ahead *for a brief review* of her handwritten statement to police on November 6, 2007—the day she was arrested. She provides multiple compelling matches. Here Raffaele clearly had blood on his hands and "water" implying blood "flooded the floor."

November 6, 2007 statement to police:

*"One of the things I am sure that **definitely happened the night** on which **Meredith** was **murdered** was that **Raffaele and I ate** fairly late....After dinner I noticed there was **blood on Raffaele's hand**, but I was under the impression that it was **blood from the fish**. After we ate_Raffaele washed the dishes but the pipes under his sink broke and water **flooded the floor**.*"[87]

But Amanda has changed her story from the one she told two days before in her email of November 4. Now she portrays Raffaele's sink as the problem instead of Raffaele accidentally spilling "water." It's a conscious, intentional cover-up. Still her super-intel must confess the *real* truth.

Unconsciously she insists on repeatedly mentioning *"blood."* It had no relevance to this cover-up story, but she had to use the word several times. And in cover-up mode she would be wise to avoid discussion of vast amounts of liquid spilled on the floor. But, oblivious to her repetitive words and ideas, Amanda plows ahead. Her super-intel demands, "We're going back to that murder scene, Amanda."

'definite' Details of Murder

First notice her strong message markers, *"One of the things I am sure that definitely happened"*—doubly underscored with *"sure"* and *"definitely."* She links this to the horrific keyword *"murdered."* Amanda's super-intel announces again this will be a definitive confession of exactly how Meredith was murdered. Amanda's great unconscious constantly searches for message markers to shout about her crime. She must—must—use that keyword *"murdered."*

Once we see her super-intel speaking, her cover-up conscious thinking becomes patently obvious. What follows are extremely important thoughtprints.

---

[86]Russell and Johnson, pp. 68-78.
[87] http://www.telegraph.co.uk/news/worldnews/1570225/Transcript-of-Amanda-Knoxs-note.html?fb.

First she confesses, "*Raffaele and I ate fairly late*" translated the two of them consumed/murdered Meredith late at night confirming the time of the slaying. And vampires come out to eat at night. Her super-intel never misses a detail.

Then she describes with a more overt reference to stabbing/cutting, "*there was blood on Raffaele's hand...blood from the fish.*" The blood on their hands was actually from another human being, Meredith Kercher. Notice also "*under...blood from the fish*" suggests they stabbed their victim underneath them. She repeats "*under*" twice: "*...I was **under** the impression that it was blood from the fish. After we ate Raffaele washed the dishes but the pipes **under** his sink broke...*"

> Her super-intel has now presented three different references to severe stabbing and sudden, massive bleeding. Based on this, Amanda suggests how police can match the details in these documents with the pathologist's report.

Amanda's thoughtprints continue to present matching pictures of the crime scene. It never dawns on Amanda that she has mentioned the tell-tale phrase "blood on his hands" and a reference to a body position. She couldn't wait to link "*blood*" to Raffaele's hands and hers—after leaving it out of her first story in the email. But she has no conscious awareness that her super-intel continues squeezing her like no other interrogator could.

Amanda's vivid imagery now implies they entrapped Meredith—grabbed her when they entered her room, and shortly cut her throat near her mouth, the way you catch a fish with a vicious jerk of the hook. (And you use a knife to prepare the fish.) Meredith was a dead fish.

While she and Raffaele were then desperately cleaning up the crime-scene evidence throughout the long night, Amanda was constantly staring at the left-side neck wound—the one the pathologist described as a mouth on Meredith's dead body. It was the wound Amanda had inflicted. It's no wonder she thought of Meredith as a fish with a huge open mouth. A fish out of water also suggests a victim unable to breathe, a subtle hint of the strangulation that took place during the attack.

Amanda's vivid fish image confirms that she confesses in one communication after another. Both her November 4 email and her November 6 written statement were considered forensic documents—part of the court record.

Her super-intel has now presented three different references to severe stabbing and sudden, massive bleeding. Based on this, Amanda suggests how police can match the details in these documents with the pathologist's report.

Matching Confession to Autopsy

At the time of the murder Meredith was physically situated beneath the two primary perpetrators. The most severe stab wound on the left side of the neck fits the size of the kitchen knife Amanda likely used, and the less severe wound on the right fits the size of the knife Raffaele routinely carried. Thus Raffaele was positioned on Meredith's right holding his knife sharply against her throat with Amanda positioned on the left holding the kitchen knife against Meredith's chin and neck as they both taunted her.

Raffaele first loses control and "accidentally" cuts Meredith superficially during the taunting. This was probably when he nicked her chin as discovered in the autopsy. She also suggests Raffaele was the first to get blood on his hands. Amanda was already furious with Meredith, and after Raffaele cut their victim—crossing a major line—she then exploded and stabbed Meredith with a vicious backward and upward thrust.

This fits precisely with her earlier reference to vampirism and spotting "blood" on Meredith's chin. No wonder Amanda referred to her actions so chillingly, as a given matter-of-fact, *"whoever did this had slit her throat."*

The thoughtprint evidence supports the conclusions of forensic pathologists who analyzed the autopsy evidence and the forensic DNA evidence. The thoughtprints match the DNA at the crime scene.[88]

'wide open'

> *"so i arrived home and the first abnormal thing i noticed was the door was wide open."*

Now we return to the email in sequence. Amanda unconsciously implies that when they arrived at her house that night they were *"abnormal"* from the get-go. They harbored dark, deviant intentions.

At this crucial point the *"first abnormal thing I noticed"* contains a vital message marker—*"noticed"*—suggesting "notice the abnormal." Now she quickly sums it up, *"the door was wide open.* She's saying, "I'm opening the doors to our minds, summing us all up that night in two words, *'wide open.'"* Amanda, Raffaele and Rudy were now out of control. They committed a brutal gang assault, an act of sheer madness reflected in the deep *"wide open"* stab wound to Meredith's chin. They had now entered the realm of murderous criminality and were completely *"abnormal."*

Such violence underscored their collective madness—driven by extreme payback revenge, especially Amanda's. It was a crime of enormous passion. Only extremely wounded killers inflict extreme wounds. Such killers commit personal crimes directed at someone who reminds them of another person. The victim had really hurt none of the three, and this was not a random serial killing. Nor was it a robbery—although that staged cover-up told us just how severely

---

[88]Several forensic colleagues who embrace the thoughtprint method have compared it to DNA—the image they chose to reflect the scientific nature of the approach. This includes legal expert Richard Regnier and the late Irving Weisberg, Ph.D. (See appendix).

the three killers had been robbed personally in the deepest of ways.

Interestingly the initial review of the evidence by the three-judge panel in Italy resulted in a stunning conclusion. They described Amanda as "being capable of satisfying her every whim, even if they were to turn to violence."[89] Her past behavior in Italy reflected her enormous potential for becoming dangerously uninhibited. She confirms the opinion: *"abnormal...wide open."* Her message, "Judges, you have no idea how secretly violent I am; how close to madness I am."

Ironically, after the murder Meredith's eyes also remained wide open in a "dead-fish" stare, as one author described it[90]—as if, in death, she continually glared at Amanda, silently condemning her. The dead eyes testified that Amanda had stolen Meredith's soul. And reminding Amanda of how wide open—how irrational her revenge-sated mind had been. It was another reason Amanda covered the body while they were cleaning up. She couldn't stand to look at the vicious wound and those wide-open eyes gazing at her own madness.

Abnormal Home

As Amanda reports, *"so I arrived home...the first abnormal thing,"* she unconsciously comes back full circle to the place of her own childhood wounds—*"home"*—where abnormal, unhealthy things had indeed happened to her. There was madness in her home, and she has promised to show us that madness.

She brings us back to a familiar story: *"I arrived home and the first abnormal thing I noticed was the door was wide open*—and my father gone." And there was Amanda with her needy mouth *"wide open."* Her desperate needs, still unmet to this day, were reflected in her numerous oral fixations (marijuana, preoccupation with eating, and later references to *"starving"*). She had suffered a severe enough wound early in her life to leave her a dangerous, open-mouth vampire. And her super-intel mind is now wide open, revealing where it all started for her—so poignant, we can almost hear it speaking out loud. Yet *"**first** abnormal thing"* suggests there was another abnormal, extremely painful event also motivating her.

The abandonment by her father occurred shortly after her birth when she was brought home—and when her sister was about to arrive. In her mind the events would have occurred immediately since she was one year old when he left—she has barely arrived in the world, and he's already gone.

Remember it was a particularly brutal abandonment. Leaving when the mother is pregnant again with her sister conveys an enormous lack of nurture and protectiveness. It communicates he never wanted to be there in the first place, especially since he waited for five months to marry her mother after

---

[89]Russell and Johnson, p. 320.
[90] Burleigh, *p. 23.*

Amanda was conceived. Then he left for another woman whom he eventually married, and he proved repeatedly reluctant to provide child support.

She also hints how she would have blamed her "arrival at home" for her father leaving. She was the "first abnormal thing" in his life—it was *her* fault. She was unwanted in his otherwise "normal life." It's another self-image devastation for Amanda. She continually links her story to *"home"* trying to show us just how badly she was wounded. She can't say it enough.

Broken Door, Broken Family, Broken Amanda

*"so i arrived **home** and the first abnormal thing i noticed was the door was wide open. here's the **thingabout** the door to **our house**: its **broken,** in such a way that you have to use the keys to keep it closed.*
*"if we dont have the door locked, it is really easy for the **wond** to blow the door open, and so, my roommates and i always have the door locked unless we are running really quickley to bring the garbage out or to get something from the neighbors who live below us."*

Think of how strange is her cover-up story. She arrives home at her house in Perugia on the morning of November 2nd, and the door is wide open with her soon-to-be-discovered dead roommate inside. Shortly police discover Amanda outside with the door open, dumping some water, still supposedly oblivious to the dead body inside which is when her saga with them begins. She suggests that flimsy story can easily be seen through, that she is really an open book (both in words and deed) and can't lock that story down.

But first, in her *"door open"* image, the first message: Amanda is a broken person opening the door to that pain-wracked mind. The second message is that the code can be broken. But why is *she* so broken?

Again Amanda mentions *"home"* and *"our house,"* revealing her unconscious obsession with *"home"* and all its meanings. In one of the most poignant sections in the email Amanda distinctly opens wide the door to her mind, elaborating on her pain. It was the opposite of a secure home, extremely wide open, reflecting the large hole created inside her when father left. She adds *"here's the thing...our house is broken."* Specifically, *"the door...its broken."*

The front door symbolizes the main way you enter the family dwelling, and once inside it's what you lock to make the space secure. It's a picture of marriage—a strong, secure commitment people enter into in order to raise a family.

The front door also symbolizes the father, the one who leads his family into the house, locks the door and then acts as the central protector once everyone's inside. He's a central key to the family's security. Trouble comes knocking on the door and the father is the one who answers it. Amanda paints a clear picture of the crucial role of the father in a family.

She should know because the front door in her family life was broken. First her life began *five long months* before her father and mother ever locked the door, secured the commitment and married. Then, before she could turn around, her father—also the front door—was broken. A main key to the house was gone leaving the home's security blowing in the wind. Amanda gives us the primary rule of making families maximally secure and the central role of the father, *"in such a [particular] way you have to **use the keys** to keep it [the door] closed."*

And here's what happened to her when the door to her house was broken by an absent father, *"if we dont have the door locked, it is really easy for the **wond** to blow the door open.* Notice her slip, "it is really easy for the **wond** to…open," suggesting "wound," and how easy it was to suddenly open, like a cold harsh wind blowing open an unlocked door.

How perfectly her super-intel has shifted from *"first abnormal thing"* to insecure *"wide open"* door to *"broken door."* Painting one vivid picture after another of her inner world long ago—in record speed—so that we feel her pain. She's like a verbal Michelangelo.

Living Abroad a Major Stress

In her trip abroad to Perugia, Italy, in the summer of 2007, Amanda had a plateful of stresses including a major separation from both parents which would trigger her deep brokenness.

No wonder her parents intuitively worried about Amanda being injured abroad. That worry was their unconscious confession of how they had both contributed to breaking her, injuring her. They knew deep down they had not prepared her to handle separation.

Amanda remained rejection-sensitive and simultaneously prone to provoke rejection. She was enormously sensitive to money issues—her substitute security—and was quickly running out of cash. In a nutshell, Perugia wasn't a light breeze for Amanda but a veritable *"hurricane of emotions and stress"*—her own images in the email—culminating on "that last night" of Meredith's life.

Ready and willing to cut a *"wide open"* wound—a hole—into her "unreliable" roommate, a hole matching the "wide open" hole in Amanda, she broke Meredith just as she was broken.

The crime itself exposed Amanda to the world, revealing just how precariously fragmented she really was. Her super-intel reveals another fact as it deeply probes the psyche to tell the plain, awful truth.

Her Mother's Failures

Of course mother—fundamental to a good home—has the other key to the house. In a way, the mother *is* the house. Amanda referred to both parents, *"you have to use **the keys** [plural] to keep it—the door—closed."* She suggests neither mother nor father secured the family—that mother didn't use her key either. She got pregnant before the marriage and family were even in place, and she took her sweet time securing the door, finally marrying when she was already five months pregnant. Her mother herself was divided about establishing a strong home. So when the father leaves, he partially reflects the mother, the message he was getting all along—let's don't really lock the door. These are the innate rules of family and of valuing oneself, as Amanda so clearly teaches.[91]

In Amanda's life, rules were meant to be broken, but that was only because she had been broken deep down. As a result, she had to reflect her basic flaw by becoming a habitual rule-breaker. It was the only way she could excuse her parents, the only way she could cover her anger. But in her heart of hearts she cries out for security, boundaries, commitment—rules.

Rules are just another super-intel word for security, being tucked in tight by her makers, locked in a home at night when it's dark, her home. Free of wounds. Safe. She's a poster child for the very real need for dynamic secure boundaries. In her case, that security had been deeply violated. Consciously, she spits on the rules of life and in the end she was wide open, wounded and out of control—so badly that she wounded others.

Time and time again Amanda returns to the image of *"the door"*—to convey whether a particular relationship is safe and secure. To identify who her chief role models were and what they built into her regarding self-control. Was she a safe secure person capable of abiding commitment, or was she a loose cannon?

She's also a case study of the vast imperfections in every human heart and how an adult makes her own choices.

Her Garbage Dumped 'Quickley'

*"and so, my roommates and i always have the door locked unless we are running really **quickley** to bring the **garbage out** or to get something from the neighbors who live below us."*

Amanda's saying, "When we all came unglued and killed Meredith, we were secretly on the run, impulsively trying to eliminate the garbage in our lives, dumping our rotten garbage on Meredith. In fact, we were trying to run her out of town, out of the house and out of life. Dump her like garbage. Moving so fast we didn't really think about it."

And her slip *"quickley"* suggests the embedded word and message marker "key"—and the complete message "quick—the key." Miss the slip and you miss the guidance. She will repeat the slip four times in her email each time stressing a critical secret.

---

[91]Therapists who utilize the super intelligence in therapy universally confirm that it operates on definitive boundaries of maximum commitment for maximum security and health. See my book, *The Deeper Intelligence,* Thomas Nelson Publishers, Nashville, 1994.

'bring out the garbage'

After being dumped like garbage as a child, now Amanda's wounds reminded her that she was *still* garbage. She had experienced herself as unwanted by her family. Unprepared to handle the stress, she surely experienced her parents permitting her go to Europe as another way of dumping her.

Again the super-intel is brutally honest when that honesty can set you free. It reports things only it can see—and only it can say, doing so indirectly in striking images and stories. As tactfully as possible to say what must be said that nobody in the room or the family will say. Here Amanda tells us how hurtfully her parents treated her all those years ago—and how they repeat the pattern without knowing it.

How ironic then Amanda was discovered by the police dumping water outside her home just as she would dump garbage. This was her very first contact with them, and it vividly defined her self-image. It also painted a picture of her crime.

Her self-image of "garbage" helped create a "vampire"—the other word that sums up the case. "Take me out like nothing but garbage and I take others out. I destroy them—vampire them—just as I was destroyed." Garbage and vampires, refuse and vultures go hand-in-hand.

Amanda's also describing the other two killers—Raffaele and Rudy who deep inside thought they, too, were nothing but garbage. For a long time now, they had all been running from themselves and their awful self-image. Still each and every one made their own choices.

In light of the garbage in their lives Amanda reports they were the running *"to get something from the neighbors who live below us."* They were running to get a life and to find power by taking something from their "neighbor," Meredith. They stole not only her money but her life, all to make her feel *"below us."* It mirrored the way their lives had been stolen from them. And now Meredith was truly *"below"* them in her grave.

Amanda's crucial slip *("quickley")* also meant the police had the key to the case in their hands—her email confession—and didn't know it. They could have saved themselves and the court a lot of trouble if only they had heard Amanda. Yes they got it right but overlooked an expert witness informing them that Amanda secretly saw herself as garbage.

Historically cops see such trauma as excuses—and miss the real motives. The secret intel provided the key to this case: understand Amanda's pain, understand her motive.

Secretly Searching for a Role Model

But come back to the slip *"running really quickley* …the garbage...*(or to get something from)* the neighbors who live below us,"* for another central message, another secret key to Amanda's mind.

160

She now sees the neighbor who lives below them as Meredith, the roommate neighbor. The one they buried in the ground below them.

But she sees Meredith as still alive *("neighbors **who live** below")* implying in the next world. In another communication Amanda describes her talks in jail with a visiting prison nun and priest about the afterlife. There she reveals more openly her deep belief that Meredith is very much alive there. Even Amanda's interest in vampires suggests an interest in life after death, but this terrifies Amanda.

But in trying *"to get something from the neighbors who live"*—Amanda says that she's trying to get something from those who live right. All three killers were secretly searching for a better role model, someone who loved and didn't hate. Lacking those positive models, they followed the "reverse golden rule" so typical of wounded people—"do unto others as was done unto you."

But deep down everybody knows to do right by your neighbor. Amanda suggests that the downstairs neighbor reflected the unconscious super-intel which possesses extraordinary wisdom. The super-intel points them all in a better direction, *"to get something,"* none of the three had.[92] To treat neighbors right, and to treat yourself with similar respect.

That's what her entire confession is all about—making things right even though her conscious mind simultaneously fights it. Her super-intel continually urges her to come clean and publicly admit her guilt.

How ironic that the trial of Amanda and Raffaele took place with the backdrop of a huge painting of the Madonna with child—a picture of Jesus, if you will—silently speaking the golden rule.

Amanda unconsciously suggests the same wisdom in her idea to *"bring the garbage out."* They were in denial of who they really were, three broken people impulsively dumping their garbage on their victim.

A popular book portrayed Amanda as a beauty who intimidated people who couldn't handle the way she lived her own life as she embraced her freedom as a feminist.[93] She was portrayed as coming from a long line of repressed women. But Amanda's super-intel declares that couldn't be further from the truth. She wasn't looking for freedom but for boundaries. That desire began with her need for parental control, something she never really got. Her mother and father's collective freedom had caused her trouble and repressed her in other ways. Repressed—shut down and shut out.

We note another confession in her *"garbage"* image. She hints that her cover-up story smells.

---

[92] As clinical studies show, the super intelligence possesses a deep wisdom and attempts to guide people in beneficial directions and toward healthy repairs for their flaws. Dr. Robert Langs, who discovered the super intelligence, called it "the deep wisdom center." See Robert Langs, *Fundamentals of Adaptive Psychotherapy and Counseling,* Palgrave McMillan, New York, 2004, p. 212.

[93] Burleigh, *p. 305.*

Opening up her *'strange'* mind

> *"(another important piece of imformation: for those who dont know, i inhabit a house of two stories, of which my three roommates and i share the second story appartment. there are four italian guys of our agebetween 22 and 26 who live below us. we are all wuite good friends and we talk often. giacomo is especially welcome because he plays guitar with me and laura, one of my roommates, and is, or was dating meredith. the other three are marco, stefano, and ricardo.) anyway, so the door was wide open. strange, yes, but not so strange that i really thought anything about it."*

With two striking message makers—*"important imformation"* and *"for those who don't know"*—Amanda announces that she inhabits a house, a structure with a basement and an upstairs, a mind with two stories. Consciously she lives on the upper floor, but her super intelligence lives deep below in her subconscious. Amanda's mind works on two levels. She lives her life on two levels. She sets this message off with another major "oh by the way" marker—parentheses.

She continues shouting at the police, talking to them in code—those special people *"who don't know."* Amanda reveals that the unconscious contains the secret pain people cannot face, the pain which secretly drives anger that can result in criminal behavior.

Now she goes to another immediate trigger motive—an important message—and another key reason she dumped Meredith. She referenced the four Italian guys in the apartment below them but made plain *"giacomo is especially welcome."* First note he *"is"* (present tense) welcome—*"because he plays guitar with me [and laura, one of my roommates]."* But Laura was no threat and Amanda liked making music with Giacomo.

Now Amanda makes a key slip, Giacomo *"is, or was dating Meredith."* Her slip means she has changed the reality "is dating Meredith" to *"was dating Meredith"* by eliminating Meredith. Dumping Meredith to make certain she no longer was dating Giacomo. The message marker *"especially"* reveals that now Amanda has Giacomo back for herself. In so doing, she demonstrates the dark, vengeful, murderous motives—the shadow side of the unconscious.

Amanda did not kill Meredith simply over Giacomo, but it was a factor. She did not take kindly to losing anything to anyone—and due to her deep "father hunger," losing a man was especially hurtful. She is intensely competitive. Competition was how she dumped on others, thus confirming in her mind that she wasn't the garbage they were. And Giacomo was hers in the first place—she was playing music with him. No wonder Amanda was so insulting to Meredith about "letting her have Giacomo."[94]

Amanda wants us to believe that she thought nothing about her strangeness.

---

[94] Russell and Johnson, p. 155.

Again we read straight through her denial to reveal her deeper, truer thoughts, *"strange, yes but [not] so strange that I really thought [anything] about it."* She repeats *"strange"* twice to encourage investigators to see through her denial—really think about it. She admits how strange is her mind and how ridiculous her cover-up story. Not only that, she specifically informs us her super-intel has thought more about this crime than we can ever imagine.

Repeats Slip 'Talking Quickley'

> *"i assumed someone in the house was doing exactly what i just said, **taking out the trash** or **talking really uickley** [meaning "quickley"] to the neighbors downstairs. (so i closed the door behind me but i didnt lock it, assuming that the person who **left the door open** would like to come back in.)*

Amanda continues secretly reviewing the details of the murder. Again her unconscious, her downstairs neighbor in her mind, is *"talking really uickley"* and easy to miss.

This time her slip *"uickley"* actually contains two slips. First she meant "qui**ckley**," her familiar embedded message marker ("key") that underscores a vital secret. She then emphasizes language—how to hear her unconscious messages. She's saying, "go deeper."

She reminds authorities that her all-seeing super-intel quick-reads matters in a millisecond. Then it **"quick speaks"**—patterns secret symbolic messages—about what it sees. It works so fast, at lightning speed—"talking quickly"—that at first all we see are her surface messages. For all the world, it looks as though her conscious mind is doing all the talking. But follow the symbology.

The two slips in one *("uickley")* tell us she's talking especially quickly here as she simultaneously delivers two separate messages. She's providing a key for two different locks which keep her secrets hidden.

When she was growing up somebody in her own home was *"taking out the trash"*—trashy Amanda. Someone was dumping her, getting rid of her, degrading and devaluing her.

In turn this led her to control Raffaele and Rudy into *"doing exactly what I said."* She led them to dump all their enormous pain on their victim Meredith. Treat her like trash and remove her from her home, take her out—destroy her. Treat her as though she was below them (*"the neighbors downstairs"*). Amanda confesses she was the mastermind behind it all. We wonder: Would Raffaele and Rudy have killed without Amanda's authoritative control?

Her imagery hints at another detail. She confesses that she and Raffaele tried to take as much evidence as possible away from the crime scene in a trash bag and dump it as police suspected.

*"taking out the trash ...**talking really uickley** to the neighbors downstairs..."*

Now come back to her second slip in *"uickley"* in her message which suggests "wickley" or "wickedly." Read her confession: "wickedly we took her out like trash, killed her." She is *"talking ...to the neighbor(s) downstairs"* to the dead Meredith in her grave. Not only speaking for her but this time talking *to* her, as if Meredith was actually alive somewhere. Imagine what Amanda would say to her now. She has just told us—"I was wicked—very wicked."

Remember Amanda has publicly requested to talk with Meredith's parents and visit her grave. Deep down she desperately needs to say out loud just how evil she was, how beastly. A real-life vampire.

'come back in'

*"...so i closed the door behind me but i didnt lock it, assuming that **the person who left** the door open **would like to come back in**."*

Amanda's story takes a turn. Her next image of a *"person who left... would like to come back in"* again represents another confession that, after leaving, she and Raffaele quickly returned to the murder scene.

And again she is leaving *"the door open"* to her mind—unconsciously confessing. She poignantly affirms that she continues to speak for her victim, *"the person who left... would like to come back in."* Amanda confesses so strongly that Meredith has now momentarily returned to tell us what happened.

Simultaneously, she mournfully points to her absent father, *"the person who left...would like to come back in."* She reveals her longstanding wish that one day her father would return home. In her mind he's still gone.

And Amanda's deepest wish is that somehow she'd be allowed to come home herself. When her father left, in a real way taking the home with him, she left home too. Still she suggests something else caused her to feel set aside, set outside and she would like to come back in. She longs to be somebody besides discarded trash or garbage. She wants to come back to life. Come back from the dead, the land of the vampires.

Blood Shower 'Right Next' to Her

*"when i entered i called out if **anyone** was **there**, but **no one responded** and i assumed that if anyone was there, they were still **asleep**. lauras door was open which meant she wasn't home, and filomenas door was also closed. my door was open like always and meredith door was closed, which to me **weant** she was **sleeping**. I undressed in my room and took a quick shower in one of the two bathrooms in my house, the one that is **right next** to meredith and my bedrooms (situated **right next** to one another)."*

As she now enters the house, numerous death images stand out: nobody was there, *"if anyone there they still asleep,"* and finally *"meredith door was closed"—"which to me weant she was sleeping."*

Note Amanda's major slip and super-intel confession *"weant"*—suggesting "went" and that Amanda knew Meredith had "went"—gone—died, was sleeping. The door to Meredith's life was now closed and Amanda had closed it.

Again Amanda announces *"I undressed"* announcing that she is exposing herself at this exact moment, and she knows it. Looking back she has just informed us that she had experienced deep down a powerful near-death trauma herself. Just as she strongly described Meredith's death—she also alludes to her own experience. She hints at something even more powerful than her father leaving and her parents marrying after she was conceived. Those repeated images of being *"trash"* and *"garbage"* suggest something you get rid of permanently.

Amanda then takes yet another *"quick shower...right next to Meredith,"* as Meredith's blood poured over her from the sudden knife-wound. Amanda repeats her location *"situated **right next** to one another."* Referring to each of their rooms Amanda unconsciously is referring to each person.

She cannot stop thinking about the blood shower that gushed from Meredith's wound when Amanda stabbed her roommate after holding a knife *"right next to her,"* on the right-side of her neck as Amanda faced her. She was immediately next to Meredith when she died. Amanda repeats Meredith's name, honoring her promise to speak for her victim.

'Noticed the blood'

*"it was after i stepped out of the shower and onto the mat that i noticed the **blood** in the [bath] room."*

She continues with a vital "tell"—*"after...shower...noticed the blood."* Read "notice the order of things closely." That bright red liquid shower initially shocked Amanda as it suddenly soaked her. Only then, stepping back and wiping the blood away, did she comprehend exactly what she had done—the vicious stab wound. It was an impulsive, insane act.

Blood from Amanda piercing Meredith

*"it was after i stepped out of the shower and onto the mat that i noticed the **blood** in the bathroom. it was on the mat i was using to dry my feet and there were drops of **blood** in the sink. at first i thought the **blood** might have come from my ears **which i had pierced extensively not too long ago**, but then immediately i know **it wasnt mine** becaus the stains on the mat were too big for just droplets form my ear, and when i touched the **blood** in the sink it was caked on already. there was also **blood** smeered on the faucet.*

*"again, however, i thought it was strange, because my roommates and i are very clean and we wouldnt leave blood int he bathroom, but i assumed that perhaps **meredith** was having **menstral issues** and hadnt cleaned up yet. ew, but nothing to worry about."*

Next we have one of the most important confessions in the entire email. Amanda describes a blood-soaked room, with blood everywhere: on the mat, caked in the sink, smeared on the faucet. And the reason for all the blood, her first thought: *"blood might have come from...i had pierced extrensively."* She caused it by piercing her ears extensively *"not too long ago."* Her slip *"extrensively"* suggests "extrinsically" – that she had pierced someone extrinsic or external to herself, namely Meredith, and recently. Above all she links all the blood in the bathroom to her actions.

Her super-intel insists on the truth. The disguised truth, the only way the unconscious mind can tell it. And it insists on violent images to give us the raw truth. The last thing a murder suspect who killed with a knife wants to do is mention piercing flesh with a sharp weapon and subsequent bleeding. Her conscious mind again goes blind and misses blatant tells. Trained investigators can learn this.

Additionally, Amanda confesses that *"but then immediately i know it wasnt mine becaus the stains ...were too big for just droplets form my ear."* She knew it was Meredith's blood because she tells us, *"i assumed that perhaps meredith was having menstral issues."* The big stains of blood from Meredith's body were far too large to be mistaken for *"droplets"* but here Amanda links her piercing of a body to Meredith's blood, thus suggesting she stabbed Meredith, dropping her in an enormous pool of blood. Amanda had opened a faucet of blood.

For good measure Amanda adds *"...i touched the blood."*

*"there was also **blood** smeered on the faucet. again, however, i thought it was strange, because my roommates and i are very clean and we wouldnt leave **blood** int he bathroom..."*

We read through her major denial, *"my roommates and i are very clean and we wouldnt leave **blood** in the bathroom."* That's another denial confession that the three perpetrators *did* in fact leave blood in the bathroom. Repeating the key word *"blood" six times*, the shower of blood, the way it drips and rubs off on everything, the guilt that it represents replays itself over and over in her mind. Indeed Meredith's blood was everywhere. They had to clean up the blood stains, blood that was caked on things and smeared various places—as Amanda confesses, *"I touched it."*

Meredith's *'menstral'* Blood

By mentioning Meredith's *"menstral"* bleeding on the bathroom floor, Amanda further suggests that she felt threatened by Meredith's winsome

166

femininity—just as she had over Giacomo. After all, Amanda had just lost her job—at least her main money-making hours at Patrick's *Le Chic* bar—and it was rumored that Meredith would replace her.

In his book *Meredith*, John Kercher reflected on Patrick's comments about the bad blood between the two girls: "Lumumba was later quoted as saying: 'I think that Amanda wanted to derail the investigation...Amanda hated Meredith because people loved her more than Amanda. She was insanely jealous that Meredith was taking over her position as Queen Bee.'"[95]

Denial 'blood wasn't mine'

*"...at first i thought the **blood** might have come **from my ears** which i **had pierced extrensively** not too long ago, but then immediately i know **it wasnt mine** becaus the **stains** on the mat were too big for just droplets form my ear, and when i touched the **blood** in the sink it was caked on already. there was also **blood smeered** on the faucet.*

*"again, however, i thought it was strange, because my roommates and i are very clean and we wouldnt leave blood int he bathroom, but i assumed that perhaps **meredith** was having **menstral issues** and hadnt cleaned up yet. ew, but nothing to worry about."*

Amanda presents a striking denial regarding the blood in the bathroom, *"i know it wasnt mine."* She suggests another aspect to her story unconsciously—that indeed her blood had been shed all over the bloody bathroom. For some reason she viewed herself as having experienced a bloody attack. Amanda further implies that she had been *"pierced extensively not too long ago."* Read through her second denial, *"long ago"* is when it occurred. Again she points to her deep father wound years ago.

Her super-intel uses multiple message markers—"noticed (the blood)," and two references to *"my ears"* implying "hear me"—challenging authorities to figure out how she was so wounded.

Even her message, *"blood....droplets form my ear... i touched,"* imply she's starting to get in touch consciously with what happened to her and again encourages investigators to do the same.

Then her crucial image, "menstrual" blood, clearly implies she was wounded in ways beyond her father, specifically by her mother. She implies her mother particularly had *"menstral issues"* about Amanda. Menstrual blood means menstruation as opposed to pregnancy. Clearly her mother had a major "menstrual issue" when she got pregnant unexpectedly with Amanda all those years ago. Her misspelling *"menstral"* instead of "menstrual" even suggests her mother had made a mistake. Amanda suggests powerfully that her mother had

---

[95] http://www.dailymail.co.uk/femail/article-2129717/Meredith-Kerchers-father-Its-Amanda-Knox-justice-daughter.html

been scarred by that "bloody" identity of being an unmarried mother for so long (five months)—stained ("*the **stains**...were big*"), a label "caked on" her, and her reputation "*smeered.*" The slip further suggests "sneered at."

In turn this left Amanda with a shaky identity. Her mother's blood was "caked on" her, had stained her, and "*smeered*" her, causing her to be "sneered at" at least by herself. Her super-intel strongly implies deep down she felt trashy as though she had been treated like excrement—totally unimportant. She experienced in another way a deep abandonment by her mother for not giving her a more secure home from the start. In part she saw her home as unlocked and not safe.

Think back to her statement, "*so i arrived home and the first abnormal thing i noticed...*" She's right back at her birth, her arrival in this world. She saw herself secretly as the "*first abnormal*" one. This was only heightened when her sister comes along a year or so later after her parents had married. Looking back, five months especially stands out as a long time to wait to get married— her long wait for validation as a person.

Consciously in this day and age our culture tells us that it's no big deal if a woman is pregnant and not married. But it's not so easy to wish the great unconscious "other 90 percent" of ourselves away. Amanda explains why she viewed both her father and her mother as quietly assaulting her—leaving her all bloodied up. Of course, consciously she'd deny it to this day, but we're into a whole other world, a deeper world we inhabit whether we know it or not. We still wonder, is there still something deeper. Is there something even bloodier in her life? We've met with one surprise after another.

Lastly, for the record, a woman can menstruate or have uterine bleeding when pregnant. Often it means an insecure pregnancy. She could lose her child at any moment. Even in that way Amanda's image of "*menstral issues*" presents another picture of her insecure home. Amanda may have even heard later that her mother had experienced some unexpected bleeding during the pregnancy. This would contribute further to an underlying shaky identity. It is no accident that in her memoir Amanda focuses on a character named "Shakey." Symbolically, the word itself reverberated deeply in her psyche.

Drying Her Hair

"*after i got dressed i went to the other bathroom in my house, the one that filomena dn laura use, and used their **hairdryer** to obviously **dry my hair** and it was after i was putting back the **dryer** that i noticed the shit that was left in the toilet, something that definately no one in **out house** would do.*"

Her preoccupation with "drying" suggests she remains obsessed with the massive bleeding which soaked the scene when Meredith was murdered. Indeed, it was a bloodbath which included Meredith's hair being drenched in red.

Secretly Amanda wishes to dry up the ever-present blood—and clean Meredith's hair. And she reminds us of the sheer abundance of blood she and Raffaele encountered during their lengthy efforts to clean the crime scene.

That memory haunts her just as it haunts the convicted Rudy Guede.

From his German cell in Schifferstadt immediately after his arrest in November 2007, he wrote, "I can't sleep...I can't close my eyes. I see everything red. I have never been able to overcome all that blood....I was covered in blood...It is not right that I have lived and...sweet...Meredith be cut off. I am breathing this air but she should be breathing it. I hope that up there she will forgive me because up there I will never go because of my cowardice."[96] Both Amanda and Rudy suffer from post-traumatic stress syndrome with intrusive images of that horrific night.

'Shit in toilet'

In her next image, *"i noticed the shit that was left in the toilet...,"* Amanda suggests that she is a 'shit' for what they did to Meredith. While denying that the unflushed feces in the toilet related to her or those with her, the simultaneous slip *"something that definately no one in **out house** would do"* betrays her. Unconsciously she insists, "one person from our house who was from an 'outhouse' definitely did this" pointing the finger again particularly at herself, the leader of the crime. She admits that all the perpetrators were from an *"out house"* and left a vivid sample just to prove it. In so doing she quickly takes us back again to her house of origin, calling it the most primitive thing imaginable.

With the imperative message marker "notice," she emphasizes, "I'm from the biggest shithouse imaginable." Someone in that household crapped upon the whole family, leaving the rejected Amanda to see herself as unflushed feces, the lowest of the low. These are her words, and they point specifically toward her experience of being abandoned by her father and unrespected by her mother. And possibly something worse.

While leaving the feces unflushed implicated Rudy, the greater message was, "See who I am deep down. I'm telling you what led me to commit this murder." Ironically or not, recall that on his MySpace page her step-father, Chris Mellas, described his two step-daughters as "shitheads," but "I love them anyways."[97]

After his daughter's death, John Kercher wrote, "We knew Meredith had not got on with Knox. Meredith had expressed irritation to us and to her friends in Perugia at Knox's personal habits, because she frequently failed to flush the lavatory and Meredith had concerns over how Knox would 'bring strange men back to the house,' but the idea that this irritation could lead to murder seemed

---

[96] Russell and Johnson, pp. 280-281.
[97] Nadeau, *p. 26.*

preposterous."[98] Unconsciously he's picking up that something far deeper than her conflicts with Meredith drove Amanda to murder.

Summing up, we see that in short order, Amanda offers three powerful self-images: *"garbage," "trash,"* and *"shit."* All of which you get rid of—remove from the home—quickly.

Another quick glimpse?

Her images suggesting the golden rule, a neighbor who has something she needs, her confessions of guilt treating Meredith's precious life like nothing more than trash you casually throw away, going downstairs to visit a neighbor and someone wanting to come back in the house evoke spiritual images of another world. Spiritual images Amanda will address plainly in a follow up letter to police.

On top of this she suggests *"quickley"*—a brief glimpse into another unusual "strange" but not so strange world, the unseen spiritual world she is certain awaits her. The next world just around the corner. Is her super-intel quick-reading that reality as well?

Briefly then we consider that quick glimpse—that she's reporting on her "next-world" take as well. Her images fit. Her colossal guilt over killing, destroying her roommate in a bloody hands-on—up-close and personal—murder looking her in the eye weighs on Amanda like an elephant sitting on her chest. Overcome with her guilt she has to get it off with one long repeated confession. She's in a hell of a jam and soon will use that image itself so we entertain the possibility now especially since her imagery alludes to it here.

Amanda suggests that the next world is vividly real to her and that not only has she buried her roommate in the ground—*"downstairs"*—forever in this present world, but that for her crime, heinous as it is, she herself belongs "downstairs" in a special hell all her own. Do unto you as you did unto others. She cannot escape that deeply embedded code seared on her conscience belying her insistence she wasn't concerned about social consequences as others were. Not only concerned she's obsessed with the "social" consequences of her relationship with M.

Already she can hear the great question when the day of cover-up has ended, "Say, Amanda tell us how you really treated Meredith socially?"

Amanda is totally without hope, has nary one thing she can bargain with while nothing but Meredith's shed blood weighs down the other side of justice's blind impartial scale. Yet Amanda cannot give up, just cannot. She of all people wants to come back in the house. She wants to be invited back into life, into community, into protection yet knowing she is broke as a pauper. Later she envisions herself as cold and with nothing on but rags. But she remains fixated

---

[98] http://www.dailymail.co.uk/femail/article-2129717/Meredith-Kerchers-father-Its-Amanda-Knox-justice-daughter.html.

that there's some kind of key that will get her back in the house.

At the same time she's fixated on *"blood."* She even mentions her own blood suggesting it will be required for how careless she was with Meredith's. Specifically Amanda notes piercing herself and spilling her own blood.

In this sense Amanda reminds me of attorney Christopher Darden who prosecuted and lost the O.J. Simpson murder case. Darden felt the pain of the viciously murdered victim, Nicole Brown Simpson, for whom he fought so hard to achieve justice. He later wrote these words repeated in large print on the back cover of his book about the trial, "I take great comfort in knowing that O.J. Simpson will one day stand before a higher court."

Still there's more of Amanda's story to come

Chapter 11: Amanda's Deepest Pain

A Surprising Primal Trauma—Her Near-Abortion

Reflecting further on her primitive bathroom scene with menstrual blood all around, Amanda strongly suggests another major emotional trauma. Her images of *"shit that was left in the toilet"*—nearly flushed but not quite—suggests a near-abortion. Flushing an aborted fetus down the toilet is a common way women frequently experience early miscarriages or abortions. At times in the past women visited an abortionist and were sent home to discharge the embryo in the commode. Additionally flushing the toilet itself vividly symbolizes an abortion, a flood of amniotic fluid released as a fetus comes rushing out. A near-abortion would indeed lead to the idea that she was nearly "out of the house" creating the distinct impression that her home was an *"out house"* and she was simply feces.

When someone realizes he or she had nearly been deprived of life, they suffer a near-death experience—as Amanda will confirm. Ask any kid if he or she wants to live, and of course they'd say yes. That's what we're talking about.

We must understand one thing. Amanda's mother decided to have her unexpected child. She eventually made a definitive "choice." Amanda remains extremely grateful. Again the operative word for the moment is "choice." Never overlook that reality—because the powerful issue of abortion is destined to stir up deep-seated passions immediately.

It is time for all of us to be the adult in the room. It is time for Amanda to be the adult in the room. And it is time for her parents to do the same. Truth insists upon it. From beginning to end of this email and the rest of her story her super-intel insists upon it.

It's an established fact that Amanda's parents didn't marry until her mother was five months pregnant. Can we believe that abortion was never discussed—seriously discussed? In 1987 abortion was widespread. That year, 1,353,671 legal abortions in the United States were reported to the Centers for Disease Control and Prevention. Almost certainly the topic was never openly discussed with Amanda (and at best only superficially) but she certainly concluded that it had been a very real option. Unconsciously children invariably learn about such family secrets even as they consciously cooperate with the family code of denial.

In this light, Amanda's habit of neglecting to flush the toilet in the bathroom she shared with Meredith represents a powerful message and model of correction. She implies, "Mother and father, you should have kept me from the beginning, not treated me like crap and flushed my life away."

Amanda particularly blames one person for the near-abortion, again her denial message, *"something that definately ~~no~~ one in out house would do. "* Read "something that only one person in my house would do." That would be her mother, the person who definitely had the final say.

There are two key slips here also confirming the near-abortion. Her first slip, *"definately...one in out house would do [it]"*—strongly combines with her second slip *"out house."* Unconsciously she clearly conceals "ate" in her misspelling of "definitely" implying "definitely my mother 'ate' me—consumed me—in the outhouse in which I grew up." Amanda will secretly embed the word "ate" in numerous slips.

Thoughtprint Profiling Surprises

We are now viewing the email through a new lens and a new trigger—a near-abortion event—a particular trauma in Amanda's life. Previously we looked at many of the same thoughtprint images through the lens and trigger of her father's abandonment. Now we see that many of those same images also apply to her mother and father regarding a near-abortion—a deeper abandonment.

In the same way, when we considered the trigger of Amanda murdering Meredith we found that the thoughtprint images matched that event as well. Now we read the images Amanda used to describe how she murdered Meredith on a deeper level—as reflecting the violence she experienced with the near-abortion.

Again the same words have different meanings depending on what trigger/reality event the super-intel is describing. Each particular reality event is one key to the story.

The sudden discovery of surprising new information underscores the super-intel thoughtprint profiling method.[99] Suddenly a new idea, a new revelation and a major key to the crime surfaces in a much clearer way.

Right off, a near-abortion trauma reflects a far more powerful truly life-or-death trigger than father abandonment as painful as it was—and it points toward an even deeper "time-bomb" motive.

---

[99]We first learned this in therapy with patients utilizing their super intelligence, light years ahead of the conscious mind. Invariably, patients would surprise the therapist with startling insights about their hidden motivations. It changed therapy from a stodgy, stale, repetitive process to an unbelievably dynamic one whereby a therapist listened to his patients' brilliant super-intel unfold the truth moment by moment, the painful truth they needed to face but couldn't consciously access. See Robert Langs, *Fundamentals of Adaptive Psychotherapy and Counseling,* Palgrave McMillan, New York, 2004.

Immediately we look back and realize Amanda all along has been repeatedly presenting a powerful hidden story about her near-abortion. In the same bathroom scene, just prior to describing the toilet in the email, Amanda paints a memorable word picture of that event.

Abortion Frozen in Her Mind

> *"it was after i stepped out of the shower... that i noticed the **blood** in the bathroom. it was on the mat i was using to **dry** my feet ... drops of **blood** in the sink....i thought the **blood** might have come from my ears **which i had pierced extrensively not too long ago**... immediately i know **it wasnt mine**... the stains... were too big for just droplets form my ear... i touched the **blood** in the sink it was caked on already. there was also **blood** smeered on the faucet.*
>
> *"again, however, i thought it was strange.. but i assumed that perhaps **meredith** was having **menstral issues** and hadnt cleaned up yet. ew, but nothing to worry about."*

Amanda persists in looking back at her life through her magnificent super-intel lens. She's trying to understand the brutal murder she directed. As William Blake said, we live our life going forward but understand it looking back. Her story continues.

First she takes a shower in a bathroom. She's nude, surrounded by water, and unprotected. She suggests a picture of the womb. Suddenly she sees blood all around her suggesting a blood shower. She links this first to her flesh being pierced by a sharp metal object (ear piercings)—extensively—and *"not too long ago"*—and then to her roommate's *"menstral"* bleeding. She refers to bigger droplets of blood than those causes could create. She suggests her mother aborting her—dropping her from the womb as a large fetus. She sees herself as spread out and smeared into a million pieces, nothing but a bloody mess all over the floor. Undefined.

All in all, she continues to describe an abortion in process, how she views it deep in her mind reflecting on the past. Her unconscious belief is that she was almost the victim of a menstrual storm—an abortion performed by an abortionist with a vicious instrument. In her mind she's nothing but a pile of feces about to be flushed away. On the edge, "ew, nothing to worry about" indeed. Almost dead and barely alive. This is Amanda's secret world deep inside, always haunting her. As she tells us about her piercings—"not that long ago," her trauma is ongoing.

Amanda's PTSD

Amanda's super-intel sees the reality of her near-abortion so plainly and in depth that it makes the experience powerful beyond words; traumatic experiences become etched indelibly in the mind. The horrors of battle, for instance, are brought home by soldiers suffering *post-traumatic stress disorders* (PTSD). In their mind, they're still on the verge of being shot—and nightmares plague them every night when the unconscious reveals itself so plainly.

> Amanda's super-intel sees the reality of her near-abortion so plainly and in depth that it makes the experience powerful beyond words; traumatic experiences become etched indelibly in the mind.

Titanic survivor Michael Navratil demonstrated well the lasting effects of a PTSD experience. As a four-year-old in 1912 he survived the famous sinking of the "unsinkable" ocean liner along with his two-year-old brother. Michael vividly recalls being placed in a lifeboat by his father who remained on the ill-fated ship. Michael watched RMS Titanic go down and could hear the screams for the rest of his life. Sixty years later, when asked what it was like to be a Titanic survivor, he replied, "I died at four." When he lost his father and nearly lost his own life, it was as if he himself had died on that day.[100]

Amanda reflects a similar PTSD near-abortion syndrome. In one part of her unconscious she constantly sees herself about to be aborted. People say she should be glad to be alive and that's the end of the story. They fail to grasp how the vast unconscious processes powerful experiences and how near-death experiences become frozen in time.

Of course she realizes she lived. But psychologically she sees herself as both dead and alive. People who wonder why she is so troubled, since she lived, don't understand what trauma does to the mind.

She has a "Near-Abortion Trauma Syndrome." And she will continue to confirm how in her mind she died—or was so close to it that it left her constantly on the ledge of "it's about to happen again."

Womb-Mates—The Mother Next Door

Email [reviewing]—*"my door was open like always and meredith door was closed, which to me weant she was sleeping.*
*"I undressed in my room and took a quick shower in one of the two bathrooms in my house, the one that is **right next to meredith and my bedrooms (situated right next to one another).** it was after i stepped out of the shower and onto the mat that i noticed the blood in the bathroom."*

Now observe the scene *immediately preceding* the blood in bathroom story.

First she described undressing—being exposed—but safe in the room where she sleeps. Her roommate in her bedroom is "situated right next" to her, she tells us twice. She pictures two individuals in two rooms who sleep in peace.

---

[100] Andrew Wilson, "Shadow of the Titanic," *Smithsonian*, March 2012, p. 84.

Amanda suggests the womb located right next to "m" or "mother." She pictures her roommate-mother alive and well. Again they are "next to one another."

These roommates—or womb-mates—share a bathroom. She suggests both she and her mother jointly occupy the womb-room and had equal privileges. But this shared room/womb suddenly became the bloody room, the abortion room. Suddenly her mother, living just beside her, becomes the dangerous womb-mate. Amanda's informing us again how her mother nearly ended her life.

Note her references to doors just before this, *"my door was open like always and meredith door was closed, which to me weant she was sleeping."* Deep down she sees her womb door was constantly open, again implying that her mother was about to drop her. She then speaks of her roommate—but in the context of a near-abortion she's talking about herself—who has "weant" (went, or left), was sleeping, and her door closed. All death images. Again looking back Amanda saw herself as dead or on the verge. We will return to doors in a moment.

Here Amanda also explains how she became the dangerous roommate who did to Meredith what she envisioned (almost being) done to her by her mother—being aborted, being destroyed. And she did it up close and personal, *"right next to Meredith...(in her own) bedroom."*

Yet the tension between them often centered around the bathroom. And we can see how ripe the bathroom was for expressing her conflicts with Meredith. Why Amanda mistreated Meredith in their shared bathroom just as she had been mistreated in the womb. The bathroom symbolized the dangerous womb for Amanda (where she bathed)—a highly toxic, dangerous environment.

How true her super-intel descriptions, her word pictures, of the womb are to the biology of a fetus existing in a pregnant female.

Next she mentions going to another bathroom.

Needs a 'Dry, Not Bloody' Womb-Room

*"...after i got dressed i went to the other bathroom in my house, the one that filomena dn laura use, and used their **hairdryer** to obviously **dry** my hair and ... i was putting back the **dryer** ..."*

Back in sequence after the vivid abortion scene, Amanda then visits another bathroom. Notice her images. In the process she is preoccupied with drying herself—her feet on the mat, her hair in the other bathroom. She makes three references to drying.

She sees herself as bloody, wet, just aborted, just delivered in a blood shower, and now she needs drying. Instead of drowning in blood, her life being splattered all around, she needs a strong secure womb. Telling us she put the dryer back in place, she needs to be put back in place. She reflects on her urgent need for the "dry womb-room" free of blood where she's safe. It would truly be a relaxing bathroom where she'd be constantly bathed, surrounded by nourishing amniotic fluid in the "womb room" bathroom.

Her image of an unflushed toilet suggests the womb where she survived—in the end her life was not flushed away. But always she remains nothing but feces about to be cast away into oblivion. The same story of "I'm dead, no—'ew'—I'm alive. Barely."

Searching for Matching Thoughtprints

> *"The last time i saw... when i...home... the day... was still asleep, bu after i had taken a shower...* **fumbling around the kitchen...***emerged from...room with the blood of ...vampire still*
> *dripping down...chin. .... Talked...kitchen... what our plans were for the day."*
>
> *"Nothing out of the ordinary. then (Meredith) went to take a shower and i began to start eating a little while i waited for my friend..."*

Now we return to the *very beginning of her email* looking for more near-abortion thoughtprints. The discovery of this new deeper motive dictates such a review.

Her images come into focus right before our eyes. Every image now represents Amanda the near-abortion victim—as her super-intel looks deeper at Amanda.

Mother the Vampire—and Father

First she describes, *"after I had taken a shower"*—immediately suggesting a blood shower. Then she adds, *"I...fumbling around the kitchen... emerged from... room with the blood of...vampire still dripping down...chin."*

The keywords, *"her room,"* suggest her deeply painful view into her womb room: suddenly her mother turned into a vampire in disguise. "Kitchen" also symbolizes the womb and the home mother creates as a home-maker. Pregnancies are often referred to as "something cooking in mother's oven."

Again Amanda reveals she experienced the near-abortionist's instrument sanctioned by mother as a kitchen knife about to attack her. The very weapon she chose to kill her roommate points uniquely to Amanda and her deepest most pain-filled trauma. The kitchen knife suggests a woman's knife.

In this opening scene the sheer brutality of her trauma remains paramount in her deeper mind. Amanda viewed herself as good as dead, always on the threshold of being destroyed.

The Moment of Conception—The Next Vampire Arrives

> *"Nothing **out of the ordinary**. then she **went to take a shower** and i **began to start eating** a **little** while i waited for my **friend** (Raffaele-at whose house i stayed over) to **arrive** at my house. He came right **after i started eating** and*

*he made himself some pasta. as we **were eating together** meredith came out of the shower and grabbed...meredith came out."*

She continues with shower stories—her womb story—and takes us to the extraordinary moment in her life with a denial announcement, "nothing out of the ordinary." A signal to pay very close attention. Amanda's super-intel continues to focus on the ferocious trauma she experienced.

Now for the key moment, *"went to take a shower...I began"*—Amanda describes her conception. She has just entered the womb-room, the shower surrounded by warm, nurturing water confirmed by *"at whose house I stayed...arrive at my house."*

As soon as she arrives, her roommate/wombmate *"began to start eating a little."* Here in the translation, Amanda continues to be the victim, her mother is the aggressive consumer. As soon as Amanda is conceived, she sees her mother then planned to eliminate her as a vampire would. Her mother began to *"start eating a little"*—little Amanda, very little Amanda. But that's not all.

Her mother waits for her boyfriend *"my friend (... at whose house i stayed over) to arrive."* She suggests with a special parenthesis marker her father at whose house she would later stay over on weekends. Indeed he was only mother's casual boyfriend when Amanda was conceived.

When Amanda started eating, thriving in the womb, that's when she saw her father joining mother in the Amanda meal. As she tells as, *"he made himself some pasta. As...[they] were eating together me...."*

She confirms the picture, *"came out of the shower...grabbed"*—jerked out of her warm, nurturing amniotic bath.

Unconsciously Amanda pictures being attacked in the womb by *two* people, suggesting her mother and father both were full force behind her near-abortion. Amanda's 'womb-room' was a war room.

But still she can see that eventually they both allowed her to "stay over...at my house"—she lived, again barely. Yet powerful traumas make for powerful memories.

She has revealed the unbelievable drama surrounding the most unique moment of her life—her conception. She has unfolded how Amanda became Amanda the near-abortion survivor turned vampire and convicted murderer.

A powerful story—and it is extremely difficult to consider such meaning. But consider we must if we want to understand the ruthless committed against Meredith Kercher—and how a pretty American college-girl from Seattle could possibly have done it.

A Lot of Water Spilled in Kitchen

"after a little while of playing guitar me and raffael went to his house... to eat dinner....we didnt go out. the next morning i woke up... after grabbing my few things i left raffael's...walked... back to my house to

once again take a shower… after dinner raffael had spilled a lot of water on the floor of his kitchen by accident…."

In the next paragraph of her email abortion images continue to emerge. She implies in *"after a little while of playing guitar me"* that her parents toyed with her little self, little Amanda, and then *"eat dinner"*—once more consume her like a vampire.

She then mentions *"grabbing my few things"* suggesting "somebody snatching her little life, all she had" out of the womb. She returns home to take a shower—another womb image. But she quickly shifts to abortion. Someone accidentally spills a lot of water on the kitchen floor pointing to her blood being spilled out of the kitchen of her mother's womb onto the floor.

Amanda now views herself deep down as *meaningless spilled water*–that you just mop up and pour out down the drain. Or that simply evaporates as though "it" never existed in first place.

Arriving at Abnormal Home

*"…so **i arrived home** and the **first abnormal thing** i noticed was the door was wide open. here's the **thingabout** the door to **our house**: its **broken**, in such a way that you have to use the keys to keep it closed. if we dont have the door locked, it is really easy for the **wond** to blow the door open, and so, my roommates and i always have the door locked unless we are running really quickley to bring the garbage out or to get something from the neighbors who live below us.*

Next In her surface story Amanda has just entered her home the morning after the murder, *"so **i arrived home** and the first abnormal thing i noticed."* Read "I arrived home and right off I noticed it was abnormal." Again Amanda's describing her conception in the womb. She then *"noticed the door was wide open"* implying her mother's completely unsafe womb.

Amanda suggests a distinct picture of an early abortion. She's saying, "Barely here and my mother's womb starts to open. She's not holding me. I am not in good hands." In retrospect, her mother was the first abnormal thing in her life, the most basic abnormal thing.

Amanda is particularly concerned with the *"door"*—the entrance to the home, *"the door to our house: it's broken…have to use the keys to keep it closed."* She sees her mother as a broken door who didn't use her key—her will and her commitment—to lock Amanda in, leaving her a broken person without protection and security.

Look closer at her slip, *"here's the **thingabout** the door to our house: its broken."*

Everyone wants to know what the crime was all about. Amanda answers it was all in her "birth announcement"-- *"here's the thing."* She was "a thing," nothing more—aborted out the door of her mother's broken womb.

She adds *"if we dont have the door locked, it is really easy for the wond to blow the door open."* Meaning to say "wind," her slip *"wond"* suggests "wound"— how easy it was to reopen her wound, from when her mother nearly ridded herself of Amanda for good. *"Wond"*/wound also suggests the "womb"—where her near-fatal injury occurred in the very first place she stayed.

"Wound" also points to physical violence matching other violent images: piercings, fumbling around with a kitchen knife and a severe stab wound, murder, and vampires.

She gives us one last vivid image of herself and her near-abortion/abortion, *"and so, my roommates and i always have the door locked unless we are running really quickley to bring the garbage out."* Her mother failed to secure Amanda's womb-room but instead was impulsively getting rid of her, dumping her outside her home like she was garbage.

Her powerful image *"garbage"* implies how she views herself deep down—dispensable, of no value, exactly as she treated her victim. About to be thrown out.

Strange Shocking Experience in New Home

> *"...anyway, so the door was wide open. strange, yes, but not so strange that i really thought anything about it. i assumed someone in the house was doing exactly what i just said, taking out the trash or talking really uickley? to the neighbors downstairs. so i closed the door behind me but i didnt lock it, assuming that the person who left the door open would like to come back in."*

She makes a second reference to her roommate taking trash out of the house. First Amanda's "garbage," now she's nothing but *"trash."*

In the story her roommate again quickly talks to a neighbor suggesting her father bought into the potential abortion. Amanda repeats *"the door was wide open...strange"* cluing us in to her pain. She just arrived, and they want her to leave.

Referencing her downstairs neighbor a second time, Amanda's super-intel again holds up a picture of the way her life should have been. She lives safely downstairs in her mother's two-room house. Mother has her separate dwelling/room above her while Amanda has hers down below in the womb. It works the same way once Amanda's born. The idea of stability and security, ownership and identity stay the same from the beginning of life. Everybody gets their own room or their own bed in a shared room reflecting their own life.

Then she reminds us of another vivid image of a house about, *"the person who left... would like to come back in."* She suggests that she was "a person" and was told to leave the home. She didn't want to leave, didn't like the abortion idea at all. She wanted to stay in the womb all along. Deep down she wishes that abortion had never been considered.

Her idea of a person leaving and coming back into the house also points to her ongoing fear that another intruder who destroys would return at any moment and finish her off. This matches Amanda's later description of incessantly banging on Meredith's door—her own experience of the constant danger she herself experienced in the back of her mind.

Again Amanda suggests her deepest longing: I want to come back in my house, the womb. In a real way she did—she lived. But in another real way she didn't, she died. And she's still caught in that trap. And unless she undergoes deeper super-intel therapy—she will never know what really happened to her.

Entering her House—Revisiting the Womb

> *"when i entered **i called out if anyone was there**, but no one responded and i assumed that if anyone was there, they were still **asleep**. lauras door was open which meant she wasn't home, and filomenas door was also closed. **my door was open like always** and **meredith door was closed**, which to me weant she was **sleeping**."*

> *"I undressed in my room and took a quick shower in one of the two bathrooms in my house..."*

Now Amanda takes us further into her home—what it looks like when she enters. Once more she sees that awful early wound revealing just how severe such wounds can be.

She brings us back to the first moment she arrived in the womb, *"when i entered i called out if anyone was there."* Her major message marker "called out" identifies her deepest pain. She's also giving a "shout-out" to police.

Amanda calls out and no one's there—if so, they are asleep to her needs. No one is there for her. Her roommate/mother is gone, not at home and not welcoming. Her womb door is open—again Amanda's on the verge of total rejection, abortion. She adds, *"my door was open like always,"* confirming the picture. The overriding image is one of total abandonment and insecurity. She sees herself asleep, dead in the womb upon arrival.

Two other roommates have closed doors, including Meredith. Amanda first suggests yet another motive for the murder: Meredith had a secure upbringing by comparison—her door was closed. Her mother's womb was secure—she wasn't nearly aborted (she was the third of four children). Whereas Amanda's door to her room in her mother's womb remained completely loose, blowing in the wind, blowing Amanda out at any moment while Meredith was locked down tightly and securely. How that must have galled Amanda deep down—unconsciously.

She underscores how this led her to direct her rage at Meredith. Amanda follows with numerous death images of her roommate: her door closed, when she *"weant"* or left, and *"she was sleeping."*

So in the end, go figure—whom did Amanda really stab? At whom was she most angry? Secretly she raged against her roommate/wombmate mother, her giver of life and her near-taker of life. The power of human relationships—none more powerful than mother and child—is on full display. No other human relationship is more bathed in love, and none more potentially destructive. There's none more giving, yet none potentially more taking. In the end her mother was the one who possessed in her own body Amanda's home. She would be the one who would finally allow her to be taken from the home.

Is there any way Amanda the human being cannot be secretly furious at the person who tried to take away her most precious possession—life?

Dead and Alive

We see Amanda's mixed imagery—security and complete lack of security. Thrown away like garbage or trash but then allowed back in the house. She's dead and she's alive at one and the same time, and she's about to die again. Any minute she expects another near-death experience so close to death that it will actually happen—an experience always arranged by someone she has trusted. Do you think that would be enough to twist your psyche?

The unconscious mind sees both realities, has both powerful experiences of dying/nearly-dying and living. But the initial blow to her was so great Amanda couldn't get over it. She continues to suffer near-abortion PTSD.

She totally buried that trauma, as did her parents. We can be sure they tried to keep it a secret but the super-intel quickly picks up on such crucial family secrets—as Amanda demonstrates so well.

This is where therapy utilizing the super intelligence could come into play. If Amanda had come to understand her enormously tortured existence, she could have owned it and not become a prisoner to her fears. Then she could have verbalized and experienced her understandable reflexive rage and not acted it out with such deadly lethality.

Amanda has given us a virtual tour of the womb through the eyes of a newly conceived person. Then she reveals what an abortion/near-abortion looks like. Her brilliant super-intel looking back has the most unbelievable lens imaginable. Truly a psychoscope for looking inward—quick-reading in phenomenal depth—in its own way as revealing as the Hubble telescope for looking outward at nature. Researchers who have looked through this lens for years estimate that this super-intel mind is up to three thousand times more capable than the conscious mind,[101] just as Amanda shows us.

For example Amanda certainly knew her parents were married on February

---

[101]Seminar presentation and discussion in 2009 with Dr. Robert Langs, the discoverer of the super-intelligence.

21, 1987, with her mother five months pregnant before Amanda's birth on July 9, 1987. That meant she was conceived around October 9, 1986. *Her utterly brilliant super-intel would have figured out in a heartbeat that it was sometime in November 1986 when they considered the abortion.* That month would have had special significance to her and evoked an enormous unconscious anniversary reaction marking her near-death.

Was it any coincidence that Amanda brutally murdered her roommate on November 1st? Or was the month burned deep in her psyche underscoring the day she had died?

Amanda's Plea to Mother: 'Only You Can Make... Life Make Sense'

Amanda told us the same story again of her death, and her rage at her mother especially the night before the verdict in her first trial in December 2009.

Then she wrote a letter to her mother in case she had been found guilty.[102] In the letter she addresses the possibility of continued separation and how she didn't want her mother to be "dead inside" because they would be apart.

At first it seems a strange thought—but not really. Read through her blatant denial. Amanda's reflecting on how she ended up in jail, and she's thinking about wanting her mother to die. One and one is two. Unconsciously she holds her mother accountable for inflicting such pain on her. She loves her mother dearly, but despite idealizing her Amanda's suffering comes pouring out between the lines.

> *Dearest Mom,*
>
> *I love you. I'm writing this letter in case you come home and I'm not there with you... in case we didn't win...I won't be coming home for a long time.*
>
> *I want you to know that I'm okay.... because I'm not dead inside...and I don't want you to be dead inside. The shit we can't control. The things that make us suffer...give us the opportunity to survive... be stronger, smarter, better. We are the only ones who know just how much we and our lives are worth, and we must choose to make the most of every passing moment, no matter who we are.*
>
> *I've thought of ways to make my life worth it, and I want you to remember exactly what makes my life worth it. Don't be lost, don't lose yourself. Read...write, breathe, because I will. You'll have to tell me, now that's it's over...what you thought.*
>
> *I can't wait to see you. I love you so much.*

---

[102] Knox, *pp. 435-6.*

Remember it's only you who can make your life make sense. Thank you for always reminding me the truth about love.

I love you always, Amanda.

On the biggest night of her life before the jury declares Amanda's worth—innocent or guilty and condemned—she writes the single most important person in her earthly life, *"Dearest Mom."* But was her mother always so dear? Here is Amanda's story once more. Between the lines, she can't say it any plainer.

The short summary version. She paints a picture of her mother arriving back at her house after following through on the abortion, *"you come home and I'm not there with you."* For Amanda that means, *"I won't be coming home."*

Nearly being aborted also meant Amanda was *"dead inside"* because her mother was *"dead inside."* She notes, *"The things that make us suffer... give us the opportunity to survive."* A picture of how she suffered and almost didn't survive, no opportunity at all. She continues, *"We are the only ones who know just how much we and our lives are worth, and we must choose to make the most of every passing moment, no matter who we are."* How wonderful a choice her mother made not to turn Amanda into a *"passing moment"* as the littlest most insignificant being imaginable. But only her mother and Amanda can appreciate now how little worth she had at that moment of her *"passing"* when she didn't *"matter."* When, in her mind, her mother completely set her aside.

Amanda's obsessed with *"ways to make my life worth it."* She wants her mother to remember *"exactly what... life worth"* and how at the near-abortion moment her mother was "lost," and had "lost herself." Lost her motherhood and her own worth.

She emphasizes that *"it's only you who can make...life make sense."* Only her mother can help stop Amanda's inner madness. Amanda holds up the way, *"Thank you for always reminding me the truth about love."* Amanda reminds her mother of her failure to love her. That the near-abortion contained the message, "I hate you. Good riddance."

Until her mother (and father) owns that she can't move on—nor can her mother. Only then can Amanda hear how much her mother loves her, how much she regrets her actions. Otherwise underneath Amanda will remain frozen in her abiding belief that her mother wants her dead. (And her father.) Only the powerful antidote of *the truth now* can began to thaw the *truth of the moment back then*. Understanding can help detoxify the destruction that controls Amanda's mind. Deliver her from the prison of a powerful belief caused by a powerful reality.

Amanda wants to rise above her pain but in the end it engulfed her and her roommate.

Chapter 12: Amanda Announces Great Tell 'be patient'

The Clean-Up Story

*"i started feeling a little uncomfortable and so I grabbed the mop from out closet and lef the house, closing and locking the door that no one had come back through while i was in the **shower**, and i returned to raffael's place. after we had used the mop to cleanup the kitchen **i told** raffael about what i had seen in the house **over breakfast**. the strange **blood** in the bathroom, the door wide open, the shit lef in the toilet."*

Amanda verifies her confession of murder and motive. She repeats matching thoughtprints to validate her story—like fingerprints found different places at a crime scene. While she tried to wipe the crime scene of fingerprints she left her thoughtprints for the world to see.

Her opening words, *"I started feeling a little uncomfortable...I grabbed...out closet...lef the house,"* reflect another string of abortion images. She suggests "I just started in life, I'm little, and I'm not being comforted. I was grabbed from the closet of the womb, removed from my house." Nothing but a mop to clean up her parents' mess.

Again she saw the *"strange blood in the bathroom...door wide open...shit left in the toilet."* Unconsciously she could still vividly see her impending abortion: her mother strangely, crudely aborting her on the toilet as though she was nothing but excrement.

But in a far corner of her mind she survives. She was in fact left to live—like nearly discarded, nearly flushed-away feces. "Ew, barely alive at least but not much of a self-image."

Quickly she again links her assault to two vampires—her parents—who consumed her for breakfast, one more image of "eating." Her key message marker "out of the closet" corroborates her deepest secret—her near-abortion. Clearly her super-intel has picked up on the matter.

185

Back to the Murder

The flip side of the same images fit the crime precisely. Amanda implies they suddenly surprised Meredith as though coming "from out closet" and "grabbed" her, again that crucial keyword "grab."

Her message *"that no one had come...through the shower"* suggests Meredith did not make it through the shower of blood. They had killed her. "Out of closet" once more suggests Amanda's lesbian assault on her roommate.

Undermining her cover-up story, Amanda confesses in "locking the door that no one had come back through" that absolutely—"lock it down"—no intruder besides the three killers were involved.

In *"I told raffael... what i had seen in the house over breakfast. the strange blood"* she confesses again to their primitive vampire attack on Meredith demolishing her for *"breakfast."* The *"strange blood"* from the murder ever present in her *"strange"* mind. Amanda remains in shock.

After the murder, they left Meredith's room and quickly left the house, *"closing and locking the door that no one had come back through"* behind them—an important detail. They had locked Meredith's door with a key to prevent anyone from coming into the room by chance and to provide Amanda with an alibi if needed.

> Undermining her cover-up story, Amanda confesses in "locking the door that no one had come back through" that absolutely—"lock it down"—no intruder besides the three killers were involved.

Her reference to closing and locking the door represents another clue to investigators—they have a closed case. They can lock it down.

Party and Unfinished Business

*"he suggested i call one of my roommates, so I called filomena. filomena **had been at a party the night before** with her boyfriend marco (not the same marco who lives downstairs but we'll call him marco-f as in filomena and the other can be marco-n as in neighbor). she also told me that laura wasnt at home and hadnt been because **she was on business** in rome. which meant the only one who had spent the night at our house last night was meredith, and **she was** as of yet **unaccounted for.**"*

What do you do when you're in such pain as Amanda? When you barely survive an ignominious death leaving you a degrading self-image—"shit." What to do? You have a party.

With two back-to-back announcement markers (*"called"*), Amanda suggests in *"filomena had been at a party the night before with her boyfriend"* that the crime represented a huge party for both Amanda, Raffaele and Rudy, a

186

party celebrated at Meredith's expense—a manic acting-out of their own brutal pain. *A power party* instead of being victims at someone else's party.

In referring to her other roommate, Laura, being away on *"business,"* Amanda suggests the crime was all about the unfinished business from her past, the same being true for her two cohorts in crime.

Next she takes us back to Meredith being *"the only one who had spent the night at our house last night."* Amanda implies the three perps got down to business with initial plans to taunt Meredith all alone and vulnerable, her other roommates out-of-town for a long, three-day weekend.

Condensing her comment, Amanda points quickly to Meredith's death, *"the one who had spent...[her] last night was Meredith."* Or even more succinctly, *"last night...Meredith,"* implying the last night she was alive.

Party Parents with Jobs

Again we shift to the other deeper trigger, the lens of her near-abortion, to see if a cohesive story emerges.

First she mentions a roommate, a woman away from home on a pleasure trip partying with her boyfriend. She suggests a picture of her mother away from home partying with a boyfriend which fits with her idea of how mother got pregnant with her.

She saw her mother—her roommate/womb-mate—abandoning her because she would rather party with the father. She implies they both considered an abortion because she interfered with their good times. They were two hard-partying parents offering no home for Amanda.

Introducing her next message with a major tell, *"she told,"* Amanda mentions another roommate who *"wasnt at home"* and away *"on business."* Again she implies her "womb-mate" mother had other work to do as a career woman, another reason to abort Amanda. All perfectly logical ideas, ideas which her super-intel could easily conclude.

She also sees her father abandoning her mother. He was away on business, out of the home—that is with another woman. He was two different men to her mother and to Amanda. She mentions two men connected to her absent roommate "filomena"—a boyfriend and a neighbor. She again suggests her father who was initially her mother's boyfriend and later her neighbor; he ended up living blocks away from Amanda's house after the divorce.

Unconsciously looking back, it was now obvious to Amanda that her father was never really there for her mother. And his leaving was a symbolic abortion. Repeating *"filomena. filomena"* back to back specifically connected to a boyfriend and a party Amanda now suggests that both she and her mother had their fill of men. Brilliantly, her super-intel introduces "men" into the picture.

Amanda sees herself as dead or about to die—the constant recurrence of that crime in her mind. On one side of her mind she just died in her very own home, in her own bed, in her womb-room. Amanda's super-intel reveals her fixation in this constant predicament, explaining how she was set to go off at any time. And Meredith was a perfect target for Amanda on that particular night. Totally alone and in danger in her own house—Amanda saw herself.

She takes us back to her own pain, *"as of yet unaccounted for."* Deep down, she never really counted. Abortion means you never really existed.

The exact way she treated Meredith. And in a bizarre, perverted way, her act of defiance and destruction was her statement: "I count as a person. See how powerful I am. "

Strangely, Amanda still holds out hope for herself, *"as of yet unaccounted for."* Deep down she suggests *"yet"* another way of finding validation as a person—an as-yet untold part of her story.

Three Phone Calls—Meredith 'Out Of Service'

*"filomena seemed really worried, so i **told her id call meredith** and then call her back. **i called both** of merediths phones the **english one first and last** and the **italian one between**. The first time i called the english phone is rang and then sounded as of there was disturbance, but no one answered. i then calle the Italian phone and it just kept ringing, no answer. i called her enish phone again and this time an **english voice** told me her **phone was out ofservice**. raffael and i gathered our things and went back to my house."*

Amanda's reference to *"told...id call meredith"* suggests she speaking for her victim, fulfilling an unconscious promise to Meredith, "told you I'd call police." Her six references to "call" reflect her urgent confessions to the police.

Next Amanda reports that she was unable to reach Meredith on either her English or her Italian phone. Amanda reminds police again that she's speaking to them in two ways, two languages. Consciously she speaks literally; she lies. Unconsciously she speaks the truth to them in code, her symbolic figurative language. This is the heart of forensic psycholinguistics.

Next she drops an even more specific hint, *"i called both of merediths phones the english one first and last and the italian one between."* Telling the police they should read the code between the lines.

The police would be a third major reality trigger in Amanda's life at this time. Once she'd murdered her roommate, Amanda's super-intel was constantly focused on police officers. She was constantly confessing to them, her super-intel continually talking to them throughout her unconscious murder confession, urging them to catch on.

Her familiar images, *"The first [call] phone...there was disturbance, but no one answered."* Second call, *"it just kept ringing, no answer."* Third call, *"an english voice told me her phone was out of service."* The images *"disturbance no one answered...no answer....out of service* (basically the line is dead)" all convey Meredith has died—caused by a major disturbance with an English voice who put her *"out of service."* That would be Amanda.

She again drops a major hint to her immediate motive, *"i called... merediths... first time i called...there was disturbance...no one answered."* Three short days ago before, on Halloween, Meredith had greatly disturbed Amanda when she didn't respond to repeated texts/calls to be with her.

Amanda's three calls to Meredith point to three callers—the three killers who paid a call on her that night.

The first one, Raffaele, disturbed Meredith with his sexual attack. Rudy, the second caller, continued more of the same—"kept ringing" her. Finally Amanda, the English-speaking caller, became the primary killer.

She also implies she and Raffaele tossed the cell phones which were discovered—tried to put them *"out of service."* Another detail of the crime hidden in her email.

Amanda Calls Both Parents

Remarkably Amanda continues to explain her deepest motives at the same time. Her super-intel rapidly processes everything. Consider the abortion trigger again. She's worried about her roommate—missing from home—suggesting Amanda's missing "womb-mate" mother who Amanda was certain had planned an abortion.

Amanda suggests a scenario of how such an event then played out deep in her mind with three distressed "phone calls." Desperate, she then called her English-speaking father hoping he would come to her aid—her father whose attention she constantly sought lifelong.

Isn't that how kids think? If one is hurting them badly, they reach out to the other parent. But there was a disturbance in the relationship, he was gone and didn't want her either. So she tries her German-born mother, hoping she has reconsidered but no luck, the same silent answer—not home, abortion.

Finally in her mind she calls her English-speaking father one last time. But again he refuses her request and finally announces he agrees with her mother on putting her *"out of service."* Neither parent wanted to serve her. Neither parent heard her calling out to them silently from the womb. At that point Amanda envisions her near-abortion. The line goes dead. She's about to die.

Amanda Announces Special 'Tell'

*"...raffael and i gathered our things and went **back to my house**.
"i unlocked the door and im going to **tell** this **really slowly** to get everything right so just **have patience with me**."*

Right off, Amanda alerts us there's much more to her secret story. In a startling message marker she announces with triple emphasis that she has now *"unlocked the door"* to her mind, and *"I'm going to **tell** this really slowly,"* especially pleading with police to *"have patience."* Clearly she's announcing a "special tell" in the email.

189

She desperately wants to *"get everything right."* This will be a crucial moment in an email filled with crucial confessions—*"everything"* will come out, major revelations.

What else does she want to emphasize? What could she add?

Her brilliant unconscious needs to establish that she is speaking "the God's truth" reflected in her intentions *"to get everything **right**."* One word—*"right"*—sums it all up: make it right, get right and get justice right, for example.

She predicts that she will take us to the moment of the murder with vivid images. We anticipate she would add crucial details of the crime, to further elaborate on her motives and to provide convincing evidence that a jury could *"get everything right"* and find her guilty—but with compassion for her pain that controlled her rage.

Her plea, *"have patience with me,"* suggests more about her near-abortion trigger—the most painful lens she looks through. Above all, a baby growing in the womb needs patience—nine months' worth. And Amanda herself needs patient understanding for her horrific crime, a tincture of empathy.

Amanda's Mind and Motives

"…*went **back to my house**. i unlocked the door and im going to **tell** this **really slowly** to get everything right so just **have patience with me**…*

"*the living room/kitchen was fine. looked perfectly normal. i was checking for signs of our things missing, should there have been a burglar in our house the night before. filomenas room was closed, but when **i opned the door** her room and a mess and her window was open and completely broken, but her computer was still sitting on her desk like it always was and this confused me. convinced that we had been robbed i went to lauras room and looked quickley in, but it was spotless, like it hadnt even been touced. this too, i thought was odd. i then went into the part of the house that meredith and i share and **checked my room** for things missing, which there werent.*"

'Unlocking the door' also suggests she's taking us deep inside her mind. She uses rooms in her story as images—metaphors—to show us different parts of her "confused" mind, the two primary ways she experienced her near-abortion.

'Unlocked door' also definitely represents code for her mother's unlocked womb on the verge of aborting Amanda. She follows this key image with a detailed look at the various rooms in her house.

Unconsciously she reveals two powerful experiences inside the womb. Her super-intel saw one thing and then another in her most private room inside her mother: death and life simultaneously.

In the first room—*"the living room"*—she sees herself alive and everything looks *"perfectly normal."* She indeed has survived, is living and all is well. End of story—but not quite.

The living room is also the *"living room/kitchen."* The kitchen symbolizes where the warmth in the home should be and her womb-room most of all. At first it appeared to her everything was fine in that protective cocoon in her home. (But recall "kitchen" was also where the knives were stored, hinting at an assault.)

Then her super-intel starts checking the rest of her mind and immediately plainly sees her near-abortion/near-destruction. She enters a second room, a roommate's bedroom, after opening the door to find an open window suggesting twice more that she's opening the secret window to her mind.

We can imagine her super-intel mind describing what it sees deep down in the rooms, the compartments in her mind:

> *In my story I next open the door to a roommate's (Filomena's) room—my private room really, in my mother's womb as her womb-mate. The window had been completely broken and destroyed—and me along with it. The room was nothing but chaos—"a mess" strewn about.*
>
> *It was truly as though I had died at the hands of an intruder who had entered the room breaking the window to my womb-room. He or she had come in by tearing open the opaque amniotic sac surrounding me—the only window in the womb.[103] He had entered through my mother's cervix where the opaque window was. It was the abortionist who had completely broken open that window leaving it wide open, leaving me "completely broken" into nothing but "a mess" on the floor, pouring out of my mother into a million pieces. An undefined mess with now nothing to me. No boundaries—no defined parts to me, no body. Truly I was now a nobody—forever.*
>
> *Still looking at that broken window and my topsy-turvy room, I see signs of things missing—namely my life. A burglar had been in my house and robbed me of a home, stolen my life permanently. The sharp broken glass embodies—the abortionist's sharp instrument that destroyed me. The near-abortion was so real in my mind that I died.*
>
> *Do you now understand why I was telling this "real slowly...have patience with me" meaning first listen closely? But I was also telling my parents they should "have patience with me"—and let me keep growing inside that womb.*
>
> *And I'm speaking to all those "pro-choice" people, of which I was*

---

[103]For technical purposes the amniotic sac is inside the placenta attached to the wall of the uterus. But the fetus lives in the amniotic sac filled with fluid. A natural underwater swimming pool in which to grow and play nurtured by the oxygen line of the umbilical cord attached to the placenta.

one. *"Have patience" with my story. Now that I exist and was allowed to grow into a person, can I see nearly losing my life any other way but one horrific frightening mind-shaping event?*

And my parents did have patience—eventually. They kept me around. But not at first in that horrific fight for my life they put me through. That fight left me with a lot of scars. A lot of permanent painful memories.

Amidst the chaos of the "broken" window/room I had another view of that space simultaneously: in my story my computer was still intact. I was still alive in my mother's womb and completely alert, my computer was turned on, my mind was working fine.

But these mixed perceptions of my mother and my private womb room left me utterly confused. Was I alive or dead, intact and nurtured or completely broken? I was both. And I could never stop seeing my death in that room. I was still "convinced that "I had been robbed— destroyed."

Then in my story I visit yet another room in my house—another roommate's (Laura's) room but again really my private womb room— and I see "it was spotless," no blood spots. Everything is fine, I am still alive. My super-intel again from a different view plainly sees I am unharmed, like I had never been touched. But I was.

Next I go into another part of the house "Meredith and I share"— and only briefly allude to another part of my mind, the room where she was murdered and where I experienced being murdered like she did. Shortly I will focus on the details of entering her room and reveal far more.

Amanda's super-intel has given us a moment by moment super lens view of her early womb experience inside her mother—a detailed tour of a near-abortion, unlike anyone has ever seen

Indeed this sterling special intelligence is that capable.

Amanda's great unconscious teaches us about the power of one traumatic event in our lives, and how a person's life organizes around it including the step of reenactment on others.

For example, think back to Amanda staging a phony break-in at the house she shared with five college roommates in Seattle. She left them all a powerful memory of a robbery and then attempted to undo it with "just joking guys." Amanda's "joke" played on her American roommates presaged the far more violent "game" she would play with Meredith in Italy mirroring the terrifying "near-abortion" game played with her, fixated in her mind.

Missing Things

Amanda returns to her other central trigger—the murder—the result of her terror. She describes the crime scene, checking for things "missing" twice, suggesting her missing roommate and her secret confession that Meredith was dead. Her image of a burglar suggests she stole Meredith's life. Describing her entrance to another roommate's closed room she unconsciously confesses exactly what Meredith looked like behind her closed door: "a mess...and completely broken." A massive chaotic disaster with her blood all over the room and Meredith totally destroyed, beyond rescue.

Amanda links her pained mind to what she "shared" with Meredith that night, *"i then went into... meredith and i share... things missing" [in me].* She took Meredith's life from her just as her own life had been taken. She shared a death experience with her roommate.

'Knocked on Meredith'—The Details and the Door Again

*"...then **i knocked on merediths** room. at first i thought **she was alseep** so i knocked gently, but when she didnt respond **i knocked louder and louder** until i was **really banging on her door** and **shouting her name. no response. panicing, i ran** out onto our terrace to see if maybe i could see over **the ledge into her room** from the window, but i couldnt see in. **bad angle.** i then **went into the bathroom** where i had dried my hair and **looked really quickly into the toilet.** in my **panic i thought i hadnt seen anything** there, which to me meant whoever was in my house had been there when i had been there. as it turns out the **police told me** later that the toilet was full and that **the shit had just fallen to the bottom of the toilet,** so i didnt see it."*

Amanda continues to look at the murder.

She writes, *"I [we] knocked on Meredith."* At first they knocked gently, still suggesting she go along with their sexual game. But the more she resisted the louder and louder they knocked on her until they were brutally banging away on her, *shouting her name* in fits of rage, becoming more and more agitated until finally erupting in ferocious stabbings until "no response," until Meredith fell asleep—never to awake again.

We must appreciate Amanda's major message marker, "shouting," that signals to police just how clearly and desperately she shouts to them in code, not just talking to them. Soon she will "scream" at them.

Then Amanda describes *"panicing"* at what they had done when Meredith finally didn't respond/died, *"I ran out onto our terrace to see if maybe I [we] could see over the ledge into her room from the window, but i [we] couldnt see in. bad angle."* She reports her phony cover-up of how she and Raffaele "ran" outside the house and tried to see over the ledge of the window into Meredith's room, but couldn't.

Here Amanda is suggesting they panicked and ran after they killed Meredith. She also implies that she and Raffaele had left the crime scene shortly after the murder but at some point were outside the house trying to look into Meredith's room. Ironically this seems to corroborate the witness who reported seeing them jumping up and down trying to see into Meredith's room from the nearby basketball court. Presumably they were looking to see if anyone had happened onto the crime scene or if police had come. By then, Rudy was long gone.

"Bad angle" suggests that the killers had taken a *"bad angle"* with the knives when they taunted and teased a resistant Meredith. But at some point they lost total control and stabbed her viciously. Amanda implies they pointed the knives at her in error and that further taunting with knives was a bad idea. *"Angle"* itself suggests something sharp. *"Ledge"* suggests edge, that they had Meredith on the ledge of her life with the edge of their blades. *"Bad angle"* implies bad knives, even bad killers.

Amanda Confesses: Low-Down Killers

Not mincing words, Amanda the reporter and the secret policewoman (*"the police told"*) comments on the killers. She describes them in toilet terms, *"shit had just fallen to the bottom of toilet."* She's saying, "we are low-down shits" having sunk to a new level of base violence.

She then writes, *"whoever was in my house had been there when i had been there."* That's a confession, *"i had been there"* when an intruder came into the house with Meredith. She and her two co-conspirators were there all along. They were the intruders.

Amanda Panics: Thought Life Flushed Away

The separate story continues on another level. She then writes, *"whoever was in my house had been there when i had been there."* She suggests that she was there when they tried to abort her. She's back to that primal moment, ever-present in her mind.

First she views her parents as panicking after her mother got pregnant and unable to see who she was in the womb. Unconsciously she envisions what she would have looked like to both parents at that early moment from outside "her room." Speaking for each of them especially her mother she describes, *"I ran out ... to see if maybe I could see over the ledge into her [Amanda's] room from the window, but I couldnt see in. bad angle."*

They needed a window to the womb to see her in there—suggesting a sonogram would have helped. In their turmoil they had a bad angle to what had really happened. In their moment of panic they couldn't see she was alive, that they had created a person.

In the surface story she pictures being unable to see Meredith in her room, Meredith who we know was dead. It's as though she knows her mother and father could not see the destruction of Amanda they were about to enact.

In the end, she survived the near ending of her life. But it left her constantly "on the ledge"—any moment she could die.

And as a result, she would view herself as living in her mother's womb surrounded by contaminated amniotic fluid. We see why earlier she referred to her home as an "outhouse." In Amanda's mind her mother had not valued Amanda or herself.

Amanda now had fallen even lower down in her mind, excrement in the very bottom of the toilet, as low as she could go. So low it was as if no one could see her, as if she were totally unimportant. For the third time she crudely refers to herself as human waste. No wonder she always had to be the center of attention.

But still she existed. And she cries out to be valued, insisting from her vantage point that a womb child is of enormous worth.

Amanda also says to her parents, you were "low-down for dumping me in the near-abortion toilet." They were fooling around with her life after they gave her one.

She reveals the broader targets of her misguided fury directed at Meredith. Her rage at the two people—her mother and now father—who tried to take her life from her.

Amanda promised us the real news on the case, all the pertinent details. Can we hear them? It is indeed a lot of pain to take in, pain she has secretly carried around her entire life.

'Can You Hear Me?'

> *"i ran outside and **down to our neighbors** door. the **lights were out** but i banged ont he door anyway. i wanted to **ask them if they had heard anything** the night before, but **no one was home**. i ran back into the house."*

Amanda continues talking to her parents—unconsciously through her super-intel, her personal downstairs neighbor, her super-special super-intel, the door which she has opened to us.

And her super-intel is speaking to her neighbors, specifically her mother and father. We can almost hear a helpless Amanda banging on her mother's and father's door, but no one was home.

She wants to talk to them about the door to her room—securing it. But they are not there, *"the lights were out."* Amanda notes, *"I wanted to ask them if they heard anything...but no one was home."* She suggests wanting to ask them if they heard anything in the womb—such as a heart-beat.

In fact she knew they had waited five months to get married and considered the abortion for much of that time—surely long enough to hear a heartbeat.[104] Her parents, her neighbors just next to her, and neither one could hear her. Nobody was listening to her needs.

How Super-Intel Therapy Might Have Helped Amanda

Amanda has made plain that the severe assault on Meredith was fueled by the severe assault she herself suffered. If she'd been in psychotherapy she would have mentioned her roommate's "hypersensivity" about her bathroom habits. A therapist who was tuned into her super-intel would have heard her confession.

Amanda Knox would have shortly alluded to more and more overt abortion images such as a friend who had an abortion. Eventually a therapist would point out, "So what are you trying to tell yourself about being flushed feces and an abortion, a woman on a toilet, a woman close to you such as a roommate?"

Following one denial after another, Amanda would eventually discuss her mother's marriage when she was five months pregnant with her. And a therapist then would have showed her the connection, helping Amanda decode her unconscious belief that she had been destroyed, murdered at that time, aborted. That would detoxify her rage enough to help her gain control, help her see how wounded and furious she was. Help her talk about it instead of impulsive acting out.

Until Amanda got to that deep level of her psyche in therapy, she'd still have been prone to act out her rage on others. Until that moment she would never have faced the terror that controlled her. Indeed, what you don't know about yourself can hurt you—and others.

But therapy would ask a lot of Amanda. Could she face such pain caused by the two people in one sense she loved most—the two people who had given her life? No wonder Amanda is always on the run. But she could no longer hide when her rage reached the boiling point. Just as she was certain it would in Italy (see Chapter Three). Her super-intel saw it all and tried to warn her and her parents, but Amanda couldn't see. The price for seeing was pain beyond belief.

Will she see it now? She needs jail—her truth-telling super-intel knows that full well. She talks of wanting to learn different languages in jail. The one language she must learn to find true freedom is her super-intel psycholinguistic language.

---

[104]A fetal heartbeat can be heard as early as seven weeks and clearly by twelve weeks with a fetal ultrasound.

Chapter 13: Cops, Gators, & The 'Bad' Gang of Three

Tried to Break Meredith, Then Cut Her

*"i ran back into the house. in the living room raffael **told me** he wanted to see if he could **break down merediths door**. he **tried**, and **cracked the door**, but we couldnt open it."*

Amanda's undercover reporter describes the scene just before the discovery of the body. She's now running "back into the house," secretly urging us to accompany her back to Meredith's room to see what happened. First we look at the murder.

Right off Amanda's super-intel announces that *"Raffael told"* if police "want to see" what happened. She also mentions "breaking and cracking," more hints that their victim's breaking right in front of them.

Then her image guides us further. Meredith's door represents Meredith herself. At this point Amanda reports: *"Raffael told me he wanted to see if he could break down merediths door."* She suggests that first Raffaele attempted to violate Meredith sexually—break into her private "room"—with Amanda's encouragement. She suggests her command, *"Raffael told....see...break down merediths door."* And he succeeded to a point, *"he tried and cracked the door,"* partially entered her room. She implies a brief, teasing partial penetration.

Yet Meredith resisted the assault. She wouldn't open up, wouldn't cooperate. Then her resistance irritated them, and they shifted from "breaking" her to "cracking" her—when they cut and stabbed her.

Back to Her Deeper Motive

Amanda also takes us back to her deeper trigger for her rage—her own near-death. Unconsciously she tells how they—her parents—tried to break down her door, remove her from the womb

Her parents tried to break her, but they couldn't. Her reactionary rage declared, "You may have cracked my door to the womb, but you didn't get all the way in."

True to her nickname, Foxy Knoxy the soccer player remained constantly on the lookout for openings on offense, seeking a crack in the defense where she could get through with the ball.

Deep down get through life—survive. Always pushing back instead of being the victim.

Amanda, Raffaele Investigators out of Uniform

*"it was then that we decided to **call** the cops. there are two types of cops in italy,carbanieri (local, dealing with traffic and domestic **calls**) and the police investigaters. he first **called** his sister for advice and then **called** the carbanieri. i then **called** filomna who said she would be on her way home immediately. while we were waiting, **two ununiformed police investigaters** came to our house. i showed them what i could and told them what i knew. gave them ohone numbers and **explained** a bit in broken Italian,"*

She repeats her message marker "call" linked to "the police" five times. Having just confessed to cracking/killing Meredith, she insists they should be turned over to police.

Then she describes in her mind two types of police—domestic ("carbanieri") versus police investigators, the detectives who probe more deeply to solve major crimes. Unconsciously she's saying, "Call the real investigators who can look more deeply into the mind." There they would find her super-intel which constantly tells the real story.

She repeats the message in *"two ununiformed police investigators came to our house."* Both she and Raffaele are unconsciously police investigators out of uniform.

On cue her super intelligence adds, *"i showed them what i could and told them what i knew. gave them ohone numbers and explained a bit in broken Italian."*

The message: her super-intel has told them that she knows—everything. If they will just look back at her ongoing story filled with violent images and details of the crime, she has identified the murderers—given the police their number. And she has explained it all in her special symbolic (foreign/*"broken Italian"*) language. Psycholinguistics.

Again her Trauma

Following the second story line—her pain and her motive—the phrase *"broken Italian,"* which Amanda speaks, also pictures "broken person" which she is. Again she has linked the trauma to her past, her familiar "house," speaking of investigators *"who came to our house."*

And she has just described her near-death—cracking into her room, nearly taking her life. At that moment she tells us, *"it was then that we decided to call the cops."* Amanda wants to call the cops on her mother and father—insisting it was a personal crime against her. As the police investigator who knows the most, she "came into the house"—her womb room. She saw the brutal assault on her.

But the other side of Amanda sees that she's alive, *"called **filomna** who said she would be on her way home immediately."* Her slip *"filomna"* suggests "fill ma"—that she was now allowed to *fill* her *mother's* womb, to exist. Her counter-culture mother had finally rediscovered her maternal instincts, and Amanda survived.

Continuing the email in sequence we again review to the crucial scene (see Chapter Seven) in which Meredith's body was discovered.

Gators

As the real *"ununiformed police investigater"* on the case, the secret undercover cop, she makes a telling slip, misspelling 'investigator,' as *"investigater"* or "gater," suggesting both "gator/alligator" and "ate" her.

First she confesses to the heartless crime—being the ringleader of three gators with razor-sharp teeth who consumed Meredith. But now, deeper down, she exposes her own fear of being consumed—aborted, vampired—the mortal fear that controlled her.

Confessing—'I'm the one'

She reminds police of her extensive hidden confession. She writes, *"I showed them… and told them what I knew...gave them."* For maximum emphasis she uses quadruple message markers: *"showed—told—what I knew—gave them."* Then she adds *"gave them ohone numbers and explained a bit in broken Italian."*

Her slip, *"ohone"* instead of phone, tells them "oh one"—"oh, I am the one." It also suggests "Oh home" where her horrendous near-termination traumas took place. Read it, "Oh, I was the one nearly consumed. Oh, I was the one who was broken."

Sexual Attack

> *"...and then filomena arrived with her **boyfriend marco-f** and two other friends of hers. **all together** we **checked the houe out**, talked to the **polie**,a nd in a big [BLANK] they all opened merediths door."*

Next she confesses in code that the three perpetrators sexually assaulted Meredith. Mentioning her Italian roommate coming to the house with two guys, she reveals the assault by the gang of three—Amanda, Raffaele and Rudy.

Then, in another slip, Amanda suggests exactly what they did to their victim, Meredith: *"all together we checked the houe out"*—suggesting "the ho,"

> In another slip, Amanda suggests exactly what they did to their victim, Meredith: *"all together we checked the houe out"*—suggesting "the ho," that they sexually abused her like a whore. A three-way sexual assault.

that they sexually abused her like a whore. A three-way sexual assault.

Her next slip, in the last three letters of *"polie,"* unconsciously declares she's lying to the police.

Next she suggests *"in a big [BLANK] they all opened merediths door"* that all three perpetrators broke Meredith's door down—the door to her most private room inside her body, her vagina.

All three penetrated her in some way, entered her vaginal or anal orifices. It was a "fill in the blanks" clue—confessing that it was all three of them.

Gang of Three Threaten Amanda

As for looking more deeply at her own pain, her messages are clear. Amanda felt ganged up on by a group of attackers about to abort her. They had checked her out, and she was nothing but the product of her mother whoring around. As a result, a gang of three—mother, father, and the abortionist—now were entering Amanda's most private room in her mother's uterus. The uterine room—"for me (mother) and for you, Amanda. This is your room in my house." But they had come to take her out.

But then she suddenly in the end saw it had all been a charade—sort of. She went on living—but it was a gruesome game. Terrifying.

Discovering the Body

*"i was in the kitchen **stadning** aside, having really done my part for the situation. but when they opened merediths door and i heard filomena scream "a foot! a foot!" in italian...."*

Immediately when the body is discovered Amanda again reveals she was the killer, *"i was in the kitchen stadning...really my part."* Read her slip *"stadning"* as "stabbing"— her part in the murder, with a kitchen knife.

In her tell, *"having done my part,"* she has again told police she has done everything she can to help them. She has highlighted her role in the crime implying "now, do your part."

She makes a quick indirect reference to the famous comforter at the crime scene which was pulled over Meredith's body with a foot left sticking out—as she described her roommate shouting in Italian. Going a step further, Amanda implies the decoded message is "I'm shouting that her foot was sticking out because I covered the rest of the body." Many investigators believe the comforter pointed toward one of the killers being a woman with instinctive needs to nurture. Amanda obviously agrees with them.

Amanda Discovers 'Her Own Dead Body'

Amanda must take us deeper into her near-abortion/abortion and clarify just how she experienced the moment of death. No question, a part of her died on that day.

Now she relives the moment that they entered her womb room to take her life. When they open the door she comes unglued, cannot even speak. We envision her story of that moment,

"in a big [BLANK] they all opened my door to destroy me. My part, my role in life was over. I was done. Can you hear me screaming 'a foot, a foot' as they grab my foot?"

Exactly like the true-to-size picture of the clearly formed little feet of a two-month-old fetus in the womb. Amanda has seen that image and uses it here. She hints that she sees herself coming apart piece by piece. Poignantly, Amanda has just described her super-intel's discovery of her own body, her near-destruction—her "virtual death."

Grabbing As They Were Grabbed

"i immedaitely tried to get to merediths room but raffael grabbed me and took me out of the house."

Now we're back to Amanda's keyword "grab/*grabbed*." First follow the idea, somebody—a woman—is grabbed and prevented from getting to the most personal room, the bedroom, signifying ownership, security and peace, rest—and is instead taken out of the house. Again she plainly points to the murder trigger for her thoughts.

She confesses that Meredith was grabbed by the perpetrators and prevented from resting in her room. Eventually they removed Meredith completely from her house, figuratively, when they murdered her.

Deeper Storyline

At the same time Amanda "super-imposed" her own trauma in a second message when she experienced her near-abortion as being grabbed and taken from her home. Her slip *"I immediately"* with yet another embedded "ate" suggests once more she was immediately consumed by her vampire parents right after conception.

Temporarily Raffaele had rescued her from *"the house"* in her past, *"raffael grabbed me and took me out of the house."* Here she suggests that her week of non-stop sexual activity with Raffaele—and her immediate symbiotic relationship with him, going home to his bed mere hours after first meeting him—represented a temporary reprieve from her lingering trauma of cruel abandonment and assault. But "grabbing" onto him was never enough to undo her terror of "being grabbed from the womb."

'My Badg…My Passport…My Wallet'

Email *"the **police** told everyone to get out and not long afterward the **carabinieri arrived** and then soon afterward, **more police investigators**. they took **all of our informaton** and asked us the same questions over and over. at the time i had only what i was wearing and **my badg**, which thankfully had **my passport** in it and **my wallet**. No jacket though, and i was freezing."*

Immediately she links herself to the crime after promising "all her information." In vivid imagery, Amanda reminds them that she has exposed the truth about herself—she is freezing without a jacket—but suggests she has her *"badg"* or badge—like a good investigator—and her passport. She first shows them *"my badg,"* her slip suggests "my badge, my bad." Read "see my badge—I'm bad, bad killer."

But her "bag"—she meant to say—"thankfully *had my passport in it and my wallet."* She has identified herself and the other killers for the police, "Here, see my confession, see who I am, see who we are."

She has shown them her badge and her passport—personal identification. And for that the police can now give her thanks. They now have her passport on the journey to solving the crime, the passport to enter her "foreign" deeper mind and identify her and her accomplices as killers.

Mother's Cold Womb, Bad Amanda

*"at the time i had **only what i was wearing** and **my badg**, which thankfully had my passport in it and my wallet. No jacket though, and i was **freezing**."*

As always she points to her near-abortion. Her slip, *"my badg"* implies "my bad—I'm bad." Her parents had told her so by nearly terminating the pregnancy. She had interfered with their life. In turn her bad parents almost took away her passport out of the womb. At the time *"I had [on] only what I wearing"*—her birthday suit.

No jacket—no outer protection such as the amniotic sac in which she played and thrived. The amniotic sac is commonly known as the "bag of water." Amanda's slip *"badg"* reveals her "bag" was bad. Her womb-mate supervisor—her mother just outside the womb-room where Amanda rested in in her mother's body—was gone. Amanda was freezing, left out in cold. Her no-nurture womb had become like a cold tomb. She was almost buried straight from there. From the womb to a grave.

But in the end, *"thankfully"* her "bag" she meant to say —"thankfully *had my passport in it and my wallet."* In her bag of water she survived intact—barely. She would live after all to make the journey out of the womb to be born alive. And she would have a name.

Find Super-Intel Interpreter

> **Email [reviewing]**—*"after sticking around at the housr for a bit, the police **told** us to go to the station to **give testimony**, which i did. i was in a room for six hours straight after that without seeing anyone else, **answering questions in italian** for the first hour and then they **brought in an interpreter** and he **helped my out** with the **details** that i didnt know the words for.*

Unconsciously Amanda brings us to one of the two most important legal moments in her confession.

She tells of giving a six-hour interview pointing to her unbelievably long email, far beyond a lengthy interrogation. Here she revealed precisely what happened to Meredith. They have *"told her to give testimony,"* and indeed she has. Her unconscious messages represent court-admissible evidence, secret testimony, if only investigators could interpret the super-intel code. Again she advises them to bring *"in an interpreter...help out...details...didn't know words for."*

Read, "bring in a trained decoder of super intelligence language." Her entire hidden confession rests on this fact.

Speaking for Herself in the Womb—Amanda the Interpreter

Amanda now gives a different kind of testimony looking back, saying what she would have wanted to say when her future was bleak and her life on the line amidst her parents' uncertainty and confusion. That moment when she was almost aborted constantly replaying in her unconscious mind.

She speaks between the lines newly conceived in the womb—*"after sticking around at the housr for a bit."* First she wasn't going anywhere. It was her house even if she was just a barely little *"bit"* of a person.

Her super-intel answers her parents' questions about what to do with her—this fact, this unexpected occurrence—whom they can't see. She existed. She was not *"anyone else."*

She's holding out the hope that if they really interrogated themselves they would grasp that one day soon they would see her face-to-face. As if to say to them, "Imagine a new born baby. The magic."

Her great super-intel continues her interpretation with one crucial slip, *"they brought in an interpreter and he helped **my** out with the **details**... **i didnt know the words for.**"* Her slip *"my"* instead of *"me"* speaks volumes. She confronts her parents' confusion. Was she a "my" or a "me?" Could her mother especially or even her father call her "my choice" or was Amanda really a "me," her own individual? Reading through her immediate denial, she leaves no doubt **"i...know."** She was an "I" and a "me" from the beginning. Deep down she knew the meaning of the word "self" even if she hadn't yet learned it. Intuitive instinctive knowledge—super-intel knowledge.

One simple letter defines the matter, "my" or "me." Her mother declaring, "my choice" or Amanda announcing "me, I choose." No wonder Amanda instructed us to read her email slowly with great patience at this very point. In her mind her very life hung on the message.

Remember her motto about her hidden confession, "Don't overlook the smallest detail." Newly conceived, Amanda was the smallest of details but growing larger day by day. People call that living entity in the womb a lot of things: embryo, fetus, accident, unwanted pregnancy, "an intruder into my womb," an "it"—my choice to do with 'it' as I please—and a baby.

Nearly discarded, Amanda saw herself in utero with other names including garbage, trash, unflushed feces, and 'a thing,' but she always referred to herself as "me" or "I." A person. She insisted maybe she was an overlooked inconvenient detail but she was a detail. A reality of life.

And her parents desperately needed an interpreter to recognize that detail—her—and what a pregnancy really means.

Unconsciously she advises parents who together create "a pregnancy"—get an interpreter. She suggests she speaks for the womb child because no one spoke for her for too long a time and that she speaks for parents who might make an impulsive mistake.

No doubt Amanda's trauma shaped her deepest viewpoint. She perceives deep down that the instant a being enters the womb—the conception moment—they are a person. She can see back that far. She knows how close she came to losing her life. In her mind she did lose it. And no one can appreciate having a life so well.

Surely Amanda wonders who spoke up for her in the end. Was it her Catholic mother, her grandmother, or maybe both parents?

Fingerprints and Thoughtprints Identify Killers

Email [reviewing]—*"they **asked** me of course about the the morning, **the last time i saw her,** and because i was the **closest to her**, **questions** about her **habits** and her **relationships.afterward**, when they were taking **my fingerprints**, i **met two** of merediths **english friends**, **two** girls she goes out with, including the **lat one** who **saw her alive that night she was murdered**. they also had **their prints taken.***

Amanda unconsciously links the final image of "fingerprints" to her confession in sequence. From "the last time I saw her" to "question our relationship because of my bad habits" she proclaims, "take my fingerprints." Read "I'm verifying this, think fingerprints—thoughtprints now." She's validating that her secret thoughtprints are again all over this crime. Same repeat message, "I had a major conflict with Meredith and that resulted in me never seeing her again."

She then introduces the other two killers. Amanda suggests meet *"two of merediths... friends, two...she goes out with"*—Raffaele and Rudy. She notes, *"they also had their prints taken."* Her thoughtprints finger them also.

And once more in *"lat one who saw her alive"* Amanda must remind us she was the last one—the last friend and girl—who saw Meredith alive on *"that night she was murdered."* She saw her die, she was the killer.

Amanda verified that fact with more brutal thoughts. She had to use that horrific word, *"murdered"*—saying it for only the second time. Later she will more directly describe, *"whoever...did it...slit her throat."*

Again this is the same dreadful description she blurted out at the police station, staggering all of Meredith's friends. Her shocking language represents a "show and tell" of her actions on the night of the crime.

But we must not stop here. Amanda describes her deepest motive—all the way to the bloody end of her life as she saw it.

Amanda questions

She asks when was the *"last time [they] saw her"* implying before she died. Amanda asks one person in particular, "because *i was the closest to her."* She points toward the one who nearly aborted her, her mother. She questions her mother's bad *"habits and her relationships."* Especially her relationship with Amanda *"afterwards"*—implying after the pregnancy occurred. Unconsciously Amanda declares, "She should have thought of my fingerprints, how that made me a unique individual. No one like me."

Specifically again she suggests her mother—a friend and a girl/woman— was the last one to see *"her alive that night she was murdered."* Strong words but that's how anyone depicts their life taken from them. And mother had help. Amanda notes *"I met...two friends"* who were involved again suggesting mother and father.

As far as she's concerned they should have *"their prints taken."* It was a crime against her. And it was nearly the first and last time her parents *"saw her."*

Chapter 14: Amanda W. 'Whoever' Knox

Motive: in Waiting Room, No Home for Amanda

*"after that, this was around 9 at night by this time, i was taken into **the waiting room** where there was various other people who i all **knew** from varous places who all **knew** meredith. Her friends from england, my roommates, even the owner of the pub she most frequented. after a while my neighbors were taken in too, having just arived home from **a weeklong vacation** in their home town, which eplained why they **werent home** when i banged on their door."*

At the police station Amanda talks about how many people who knew Meredith were there—stressing her popularity, which irritated Amanda and sparked jealous rage especially from Meredith's rejection. She explains her violence, *"I banged on their door,"* unconsciously linking it to her familiar "banging on Meredith's door"—that is banging on Meredith until she killed her.

Amanda returns, inevitably, to the question of her own existence. In *" i was taken into the waiting room"* she suggests the womb, her conception. She didn't invite herself, she was brought in—created, an intentional act. And *"having just arrived home,"* she suggests again her conception. And her neighbors were gone—specifically her mother and father. They weren't home, but she implies they were banging on her door. Again she pictures her parents trying to abort her. Totally unlike her roommate Meredith who had a recent vacation and rest back in her nurturing hometown.

Nobody's home for Amanda. There's no one to hear her pleas—no one to hear her banging on their door. Amanda envisions herself kicking in the womb to announce her presence but no one cared.[105]

She sees herself taken into waiting room/the womb to be thoroughly questioned. Would she be trapped, punished, or freed? Would she be judged worthy of keeping or be judged guilty for destroying her parents' lives?

---

[105]Mothers can feel their baby kicking in the womb starting at sixteen weeks. Ultrasound shows babies moving at seven weeks. Veteran mothers often recognize first-kicks—known as "quickening"—much earlier. Amanda would have every reason to believe that when her parents married after she'd been conceived 20 weeks prior, they could actually feel her in the womb.

Amanda's Secret Masculine Persona

*"later thanthat **another guy showed up** and was taken in for **questioning**, a guy I dont like but who both **meredith** and i **knew** from different occasions, a morracan guy that i only **know** by his **nickname** amongst the girls "shaky"."*

Out of the blue Amanda now mentions that *"another guy showed up,"* a very unusual guy. Her super-intel has chosen this particular symbol to impart key information.

"A guy showed up" suggests her hidden masculine power side. What do you do when you feel as vulnerable and weak as Amanda did? You find a powerful role—choose power over helplessness.

Her inner police have again arrived on the scene with her prominent message marker *"questioning."* She suggests, "Question my guy side, my secret masculine side that showed up in

> Amanda depicts her secret masculine identity as shakily adrift amidst her feminine side. She never really liked that "guy"—that side of her, but deep down that decidedly potent identity was necessary to her survival.

this crime—a guy who declares *'I don't like…Meredith and I knew from different occasions.'"* A guy *"I know"* as "shaky." Amanda links this guy to herself—she knew him but "only by his nickname."

Amanda depicts her secret masculine identity as shakily adrift amidst her feminine side. She never really liked that "guy"—that side of her, but deep down that decidedly potent identity was necessary to her survival.

She prompts us to recall her known nickname, "Foxy Knoxy," and her aggressiveness on the soccer field. She had a secret "power" side that had to outfox others as she attempted to do in this crime—which constantly protected her from being "Girl Shaky," a helpless female victim.

Deep down she also sees the abortionist ever present in her mind. Truly *"a guy I dont like."* His *"nickname amongst the girls 'shaky.' "* He leaves the all the girls he comes after feeling shaky to the extreme. He also leaves mothers who've had abortions feeling shaky as well.

Vending-Machine Vampires

*"then i sat around in this waiting room wthout having the chance to leave or **eat** anything **besides vending maschine food (which gave me a hell of a stomache ache)** until 530 in the morning."*

Amanda's super-intel now returns to a crucial confession suggesting the engulfing imagery of vampires. Immediately before describing the horrific wound to the victim's throat, Amanda unconsciously pictures Meredith trapped

207

in her room, *"...sat around in this waiting room without having a chance to leave."*

Then Amanda confesses I *"eat anything ....vending maschine food which gave me a hell of a stomache ache."* She implies she consumed Meredith like a machine, dispensing her like cheap food. Certainly vampires are depicted as machine-like, enacting their crimes uncontrollably without a whit of conscience.

And we focus on her slip, *"vending maschine food."* *"Maschine"* suggests "masculine." Very few words begin with "masc." Again she confesses that, during the crime, her aggressive, masculine persona flew like a bat out of hell. For that moment, she was Dracula, the Prince of Darkness, the one with all power. This time, she was the consumer, not the consumed.

Momentarily she takes us to one other place—the consequences. Now the prison of her mind, her soul, overcomes her with the enormous guilt that followed the murder. Her soul gives her hell over the egregious crime. We keep *"gave me hell of...ache"* in mind as though her soul, like a judge, is sentencing her to eternal damnation. Indeed, in a later confession, she will return to spiritual issues—specifically her questions about life after death.

'Without Having a Chance'

Amanda's imagery brings a dark picture to light. Again she looks back at herself, *"I sat around...waiting room without having a chance to leave or eat anything."* She sees herself in the waiting room of the womb—waiting on her parents' decision. Would they keep her or not? Her deep belief: she would never have a chance to be born, no chance to leave the womb alive. Her life in constant limbo, her mind fixated on *"without having a chance."*

Can we feel her pain yet? Have her own words convinced us yet?

She saw herself as giving her mother a hell of a stomach ache—an unwanted pain in her life. Amanda even wonders if mother didn't have morning sickness—Amanda sickness.[106]

Her images take us deeper still. Vending machine suggests sexual imagery, conception and delivery. You insert something of value into the machine (the "female" container), you wait and out comes the product. But it's not an expensive product. She sees her parents' behavior as cheapening her.

Her slip *"maschine"* suggests "mash" or "mashes," a machine that chews up its victims, like a mechanical vampire. Considering the crime's violence, Amanda's slip *"maschine"* further suggests "machete." Amanda conveys the deep violence to her person with which she lived. Undeniably Amanda presents a childbirth image followed by a vampire/abortion image.

Keep in mind Amanda herself introduces the concept of hell. Her heartache suggests her parents deserve hell for putting her through such extreme mental torture just as Amanda knows that's what she deserves for killing Meredith.

---

[106]Morning sickness can occur as early as four weeks. It affects three-quarters of women in the first trimester.

The Most Brutal Moment

*"during this time i **received calls** from a lot of different people, family mostly of course, and **i also talked** with the rest. **especially to find out what exactly was in merediths room whent hey opened it**. apparently her body was laying under a sheet, and with her foot sticking out and **there was a lot of blood. whoever had did this had slit her throat**. they told me to be back in at 11am. i went home to raffael's place and **ate** something substantial, and **passed out.**"*

Amanda continues describing the vampire attack on Meredith.

In numerous "tells" she reminds police you have *"received calls"* from me, again *"I... talked."* She instructs them you must *"especially...find out"* that I am going to tell you *"what exactly was in Meredith's room when they opened it."*

Unconsciously she announces—as if using a loudspeaker—she knew exactly what they would find. Immediately after picturing the utter viciousness of her near-abortion she presents the most primitive image of murder in the email—what happened and who caused it.

Now at the email's single-most wicked moment, Amanda tells us, I *"slit her throat."* And the next day she added to it in the police waiting room, when Meredith's friends thought she seemed aloof, uncaring—the only one not crying. Suddenly Amanda erupted, *"What the f.... do you think? They cut her throat. She f...ing bled to death!"*

She validates her confession in run-on sentence fashion, *"there was a lot of blood. whoever had did this had slit her throat...told me."* In other words the person who did this, "they told (me)"— "told you it was me."

In one quantum leap, Amanda's back holding the bloody kitchen knife in her hand and staring at her victim's gaping throat wound. Blood gushed from it everywhere—that ever-present blood.

Amanda points to herself as the one who inflicted the fatal stab wound—an admission that matches the forensic evidence.

She implies a single killer and a single wound—*"whoever had did this."* She repeats *"slit her throat"* after her images *"eat anything—[consuming] vending machine food."*

And she repeats exactly how they would find the body covered, *"apparently her body was laying under a sheet, and with her foot sticking out"*—while attempting to appear ignorant by calling the comforter a sheet. Another confession that *she* was the one who covered the body.

After the primitive description of the wound, she notes the police then *"told me to be back at 11 am,"* once again pointing to the time of the murder around 11 p.m.

What Was in Amanda's Womb-Room?

Email (repeating)—*"especially to find out what **exactly** was in.... room whent hey opened it. apparently her body was **laying under a sheet**, and with her foot sticking out and **there was a lot of blood. whoever had did this had slit her throat.** they told me to be back in at 11am. **i went home** to raffael's place..."*

Now switching lenses, Amanda takes us back to her womb-room, to *"exactly"* what she discovered when her super-intel *"opened it"* looking *"back in [time]...I went home."* Again set off by the message marker "told me," her all-seeing super-intel reveals to her what her deeper eyes viewed.

She saw the same identical picture only this time it was her, *"whoever had did this had slit her throat."* She had been attacked by a vampire—in her womb-room, aborted with a sharp, knife-like weapon. She envisions her little *"body...laying under a sheet"* of uterine sac tissue *"with her foot sticking out"* and *"a lot of blood."* And her total helplessness, her inability to prevent it left her eternally enraged.

She explains why she announced her assault on Meredith as *"whoever had did this."* She was Amanda W. Knox—Amanda "Whoever" Knox. Amanda "Whoever I am," Amanda "Wherever I belong." She was Amanda the lost one, the consumed one—again in her own home—who in turn consumed her victim in her own bed. Not to be forgotten, Amanda implies she was named by "My Whoever Parents, whoever and whenever they wanted to show up." And finally they did show up but not without putting her through hell itself.

In her mind they were the *"whoever (s) had did this... had slit her throat...I went [had gone] home."*

Can we bare to look at her pain anymore? Amanda Whoever insists we must.

But she implies an even deeper story: at her death/near-death *"I went home"*— to another home, a longer lasting next-world home. She expresses the same thoughts about Meredith whom Amanda herself had sent on to the next world.

Third Vampire Image

*" **i went home** to raffael's place and **ate something substantial**, and **passed out**."*

For a third time in rapid succession, Amanda returns to eating, confessing unconsciously that in murdering Meredith she *"ate something substantial,"* consumed an entire person. She implies at that moment Meredith *"passed out"*—passed away.

Distinctly she links Raffaele to the crime, and then she/he *"passed out"* suggesting they were in a mind-altered state of rage. They were all out of their minds and are now trying desperately to block out the harsh reality of their crime, including the indelible memory of slitting a woman's throat.

But going deeper Amanda reminds us that she herself was a substantial meal for the vampire attack on her when she *"passed out"*—died—in the womb. That's the "vampire" attack that always resounds through her psyche.

Third Visit to House: Heavy Guilt Drives Confession

*"in the morning raffael drove me bck to the police station but had to leave me when they said they wantrd to take me **back to the house** for quesioning. before i go on, id like to ssay that i was **strictly told** not to **speak** about this, but im **speaking** with **you people** who are not involved and who cant do anything bad except **talk to journalists**, which i hope you wont do. i have to **get this off my chest** because its **pressing down on me** and **it helps to know** that someone besides **me knows something**, and that **im** not **the one who knows the most** out of everyone at the house."*

In Chapter Six we examined this section of the email which revealed her internal pressure to confess signaled by numerous message markers. Now we can better appreciate why at this crucial junction Amanda shouts out, bombarding us with key message markers.

She has just highlighted the most vicious moment of her crime driven by the horrific realization of the earlier "abortion" attack on her. Nowhere else does she lay out "the so-called missing motive" so vividly reaching the peak of her confession.

Now she must take us back for the third time to revisit her house, her first home in the womb. Here she confirms "The Great Family Secret" and reveals more personal information.

In her story Amanda's back at the police station. Investigators want to take her back to her house, meaning Amanda's inner policewoman is driving her confession. She must tell us more.

She announces with multiple message markers and denials that she's speaking as a secret journalist, to everyone, *"you people."*

She is desperate to confess as her words reveal: *"like to say, strictly told, speak about this, speaking with you, can't do anything but talk—talk to journalists, get this off my chest pressing down on me, helps to know,"* and finally *"I am the one who knows most of anyone in case."*

The guilt pressing on her chest is overwhelming. We anticipate that her murder confession will pick up in her following comments.

The Unspeakable Family Secret

But first, with the lens of her near-abortion trauma now in place, she again elaborates on how she nearly lost her life before it ever started.

She reveals the forbidden family secret that she was *"strictly told not to speak about"*—the near-abortion. Indeed it *"helps to know that someone besides me knows something."* Her mother and father know the truth and Amanda's super-intel does as well.

Sex Crime—'wtf'

> *"at the house they asked me **very personal questions about meredith**'s life and also about the personalities of our neighbors. how well did I know them? pretty well, we are friends. was **meredith sexually active**? yeah, she borrowed a few of my **condoms**. does she like anal? **wtf**? I dont know. does she use vaseline? for her lips?"*

Now Amanda's super-intel announces to police she will answer some *"very personal questions about...[her] life and... the personalities of...[her] neighbors,"* suggesting her co-conspirators in the murder. On a deeper level, she'll answer personal questions about Meredith's murder and about her own "murder" that occurred before that.

Her inner policewoman first asks *"was Meredith sexually active?"*—during the crime—meaning: did you assault her sexually? Amanda answers, *"yeah...borrowed a few of my condoms."* She confirms that the crime indeed entailed a sexual assault and suggests she provided a few people in the assault with a condom, likely Raffaele and Rudy.

Then Amanda secretly asks, *"does she like anal?"* Specifically, was Meredith assaulted anally during the crime? Her answer is *"wtf"*— "what the f...." in popular lingo. This "what do I care" message implies a reckless and careless action, specifically admitting, "of course we f__'d her anally." And crime scene evidence reveals the possibility of both vaginal and anal assaults.

"Wtf" represents Amanda's increasingly reckless life as well as her exceedingly reckless crime. In essence Amanda says, dismissively, "I'll treat you any way I want." And she speaks for all three murderers, each one with the same *"wtf"* attitude about how they treated Meredith.

Finally she asks, *"does she use vaseline? for her lips?"* Unconsciously Amanda is confessing to having loose lips—and providing the police a heads-up. She points them to the question they should be asking themselves about this entire email, "Does Amanda secretly confess in this document?"

She also discloses her deeper wisdom for what her parents should have done in the beginning, *"borrowed a few... condoms."* No wonder she was preoccupied with condoms blatantly displaying them all around—constantly announcing in between the lines, "See what happened to me, see how in the end I was the product of unprotected sex. Prevent pregnancy! Prevent pregnancy!" Yet ironically she also proclaims by her actions, "See how I sexualized my pain and try to turn it into pleasure with unbridled sex myself."

But think back to her early life, and how she was treated as unimportant. Realizing as a child that she was a worthless person, unwanted, nearly aborted after being conceived in a careless liaison, *"wtf"* truly sums up her deepest trauma.

The Phallic Woman

Amanda continues with more unconscious personal revelations about herself. Again she underscores an aggressive, pseudo-masculine, in-charge persona, often referred to as the "phallic female." Shortly after meeting Meredith, Amanda was shockingly exhibitionistic about showing off to her new roommate the condoms and vibrator she kept.

She also provided condoms when Meredith had sex, so something personal of Amanda's was connected to the act. Something she had owned was literally inside Meredith during intercourse. Amanda suggests again that she sexually violated her roommate.

During the sexual assault Amanda saw herself as the in-control phallic female who taunted and raped Meredith. Remember that momentarily she was the "Guy Shaky."

"what kind of person is stefano? nice guy, has a really pretty girlfriend. hmmm…very interesting…

*"we'd like to how you something, and **tell** us if this is **out of normal**."*

Again she suggests she viewed herself unconsciously as a guy with a pretty girlfriend—Meredith.

Her slip *"like to how you something… this is **out of normal**"* suggests "like to show you how" she violated Meredith sexually in an *"out of normal"* way. This fits with Amanda's last written statement to the police from jail in which she mentioned that high-school classmates thought she was a lesbian—another thoughtprint of her sexual attack on Meredith.

Cleaned House Spotless

*"tehy took me into the nieghbors house. the had **breaken the door open** to get in, but they told me to **ingonore that**. the rooms were all open. giacomo and marco-n's room was **spotless** which made since becaus the **guys had thoroughly cleaned the whole house** before they left on vacation.*

Amanda unconsciously confirms details of the crime in familiar thoughtprints. The three assailants all broke their neighbor, Meredith's, door open implying the assault and the fatal stabbing.

Still Amanda adds an important crime scene confession about the staged break-in with the broken window and apparent intruder telling us in another message marker to *"**ingonore that.**"* And most clearly of all places in her email she confesses that *"the guys had thoroughly cleaned the whole house before they left"*—pointing to exactly how she and Raffaele had cleaned up the crime scene all night. Her thoughtprint evidence perfectly matches the crime scene evidence.

Her super-intel again takes us on another tour of Amanda's womb experience. Her parents had broken her womb door totally open, and she was exposed. They wanted to ignore that trauma—leaving for more fun *"on vacation."*

The 'Comfoter'—Bed Stripped

*"stefano's room however, well, his **bed** was **strpped** of linens, which was **odd**, and the **comfoter** he used was shoved up at the top of his bed, with blood on it.*

*"i obviously told then that the blood was **definatley out of normal** and also that he **usually** has **his bed made** they **took note of it** and **ussred me out**. when **i left the house to go back**to the police station…so the reporters wouldnt try to talk to me."*

Amanda continues unconsciously acting as a policewoman back at the crime scene reviewing the murder. She specifically mentions in the next room how a young man's *"comfoter he used was shoved on top of his bed, with blood on it."* Her super-intel points to the bloody comforter she placed on top of Meredith's dead body.

Her slip, *"comfoter,"* suggests "com-footer." She highlights that she had left one of Meredith's feet uncovered. She makes another reference to her madness the night of the crime, the stripped bed was *"odd"* and *"i obviously told… that the blood was definatley out of normal."* Insanely, she had spilled Meredith's blood—her slip *"definatley"* revealing one more embedded "ate," one more vampire confession.

But she must say more about the blood using vital message markers, *"they took note of it and ussred me out."* Her striking slip, *"ussred"* (instead of "ushered") suggests "us red"/ "us bloody" from the murder as we ushered Meredith out of life, just as Amanda's parents almost ushered her out of life in the near-abortion.

She further implies *"us red [bloody] and me [Meredith/Mez] was out when we left the house."*[107] The murderers were dripping with blood and Meredith was *"out"*—dead—when they left. Yes, they. Again she highlights "us" in "us red."

Not only had she lost her mind then, Amanda tells us that her madness began in her *"odd"* bed, in her own womb-room. The same imagery paints the picture. *"Usually …bed made"* but not in her case, the comfort was not there, the nurture was missing. *"Bed… stripped"* tells us that emotionally, in a deep deep way, she had been *"stripped"* naked—in her mind, stripped from the womb.

---

[107]Meredith's family and friend called her "Mez"—very close to "Me."

Most of all she elaborates on the bloody comforter at the crime scene, *"i obviously told then that the blood was definatley out of normal."* Yes, spilling her blood was abnormal for a mother to do to her womb-mate—once more like a vampire to *"definatley"* consume Amanda.

As her super-intel, her own secret attorney, speaks on her behalf, her final verdict *"when i left the house to go back"*— to leave the womb— she suggests her parents should go *"to the police station..."* and turn themselves in, for having almost murdered her in the womb. The super-intel, an impartial judge of pure justice, points to motives and assesses consequences.

Back to Police Station

*"when i **left the house** to **go back to the police station** they **told me to put my jacket over my head** and **duck down** below the window so the **reporters wouldnt** try to **talk** to me."*

Amanda's clearly talking to the police here. She insists *"go back to police station"*—in which she's really saying, "I need to go to jail." Unconsciously she introduces instructions to *"put jacket over my head"* and then *"duck down below the window."* We decode the images.

In this true-crime translation "game of Charades" as regards the murder "jacket over head" itself suggests covering up, hiding the truth, and immense shame. It also points to images of people being arrested. In this case the phrase also suggests "blood jacket," that covered Meredith in blood. Specifically Meredith's fatal injuries were to her head and neck which Amanda has just vividly stressed. And when a corpse is on the way to the morgue—a "jacket," a body bag, is placed over its head. Amanda's super-intel always has the crime scene in view.

In that context, "duck down" suggests dead duck—yet another murderous illustration. Dead duck further suggests being caught dead to rights. Head down, more shame upon shame.

"Duck down below the window" implies her confession that Amanda's ducking out on her guilt, trying to hide the truth from police. But also that Amanda's a dead duck if police see her hidden confession below the surface by looking into the window to her deeper mind.

She continues especially in closing her email to make a final appeal to police to catch on. Yet they have their heads down and can't see through the window she's offered into the case. Their eyes are covered, their jackets all over their head, they are blind.

"Down below" suggests jail itself and the ultimate jail, "hell." *"Duck down below"* suggests Amanda deserves hell and judgment—more guilt thoughtprints.

Simultaneously, *"duck down"* points to her own death/near-death. *"Duck down below the window"* suggests that her parents for the longest time couldn't see "the little duck Amanda swimming in the water of the womb." But she eventually realized she had barely ducked her demise, her ending at their hands. She may have been a wounded duck, but she had survived.

As a new correspondent reporting from inside the womb-room, she describes what she saw, and she saw it all.

Returning to her image of secret reporter nearing the end of her email, Amanda gives us a heads-up that more news is on the way—*"Reporters...try to talk to me."* And one more message to the police, *"try to talk to me"* about my confession.

Chapter 15: Starving Vampire, Closing Confession

Emotionally Starved—and Entitled

*"[so the reporters wouldnt try to talk to me.] at the station **i just had to repeat the answers** that i had givne at the house do they could **type them up** and after a good 5 and a half hour day with the police again raffael picked me up and **took me out** for some **well-deserved** pizza. **i was starving**."*

Amanda makes a powerful closing statement to police—her super-intel presenting evidence like a master attorney. First in a denial announcement, *"the reporters wouldnt try to talk to me. at the [police] station,"* she unconsciously reports to police. Then she adds, *"I just had to repeat the answers."* She promises to repeatedly confirm details of her confession.

Her *"good 5 hour...day with police"* reminds them her lengthy five-page email contains a typed thoughtprint confession with plenty of answers.

She suggests "type them up" and use them as evidence. Her super-intel take on her communication: police have a legal psycholinguistic forensic confession on their hands. Recall she informed them her thoughtprints were compelling like "fingerprints" unique to an individual.

She has something else vitally important to disclose—repeating key information/thoughtprints at the heart of her crime yet using a new image. Here she describes, *"again Raffael picked me up and took me out for some well-deserved pizza. I was starving."* Amanda thus repeats an oral image for a fourth time, this time "starvation." She shows yet again how the desperate vampires were driven to carry out such a deed. In a quick "pick-me-up" they demolished Meredith. She confesses we *"took [her] out"*—killed her.

This fourth food image culminates her recent matching thoughtprint images of vampires:

- eating *"vending macschine food;"* She had consumed Meredith, in a powerful machine-like fashion, mashing the life out of her.
- *"whoever had did this had slit her throat"*—reflects Amanda's confession as the primary perpetrator.
- "at Raffaele's place *ate something substantial"*—they consumed another human being, Meredith.

Finally she tells us that she was entitled to *"some well-deserved pizza"* because she was *"starving."* She and Raffaele and Rudy were all steeped in abuse and starved for love. So they prepared themselves a "well-deserved" meal at Meredith's expense. Their personal pain was so deep they were convinced it entitled them to take their pound of flesh in revenge from whomever they desired. Amanda clearly describes the deep entitlement that often drives victims of abuse.

For her, the crime was all about going home. In a real way *"I went home"*—Amanda went back into her past and reveals the pain she had inflicted upon her victim. And why? She reports, *"I just had to repeat the answers that i had givne at the house."*

Again she explains, *"do [sic] they could type them up."* From the get-go she has been continually weaving her story between the lines of emotional starvation regarding the house in which she grew up. She wants her painful tale typed up, wants a writer who understands her to tell the whole story. Note her slip: *"do [sic]...type them up."*

Here is the answer she wants revealed. Amanda unconsciously verifies her deepest motive with startling clarify in a brief memorable, *"i was starving."*

Indeed this is the frantic theme song of a vampire. She has summed up her overwhelming pain in the most primitive phrase matching the animalistic murder. In one simple phrase she has revealed the passion behind the rage killing, *"i was starving."* She had been starved in multiple ways, never forget it.

In her world of near-abortion horror, Amanda was casually consumed—no more significant than a take-out pizza. Indeed they took her out of her house. They didn't intend to continue feeding her.

In her mind her parents literally starved her, cut her throat. That permanent memory left her perpetually starving. The powerful image *"starving"* describes our most basic need—both physically and emotionally. It takes us to our very core. There is no greater primordial passion. The need for food is truly a life-or-death matter physically just as is emotional food—love. In addition to *"starving,"* her repeated references to "eating" paint a poignant picture of just how desperately needy she was.

Her desperate needs were displayed after the crime by notably oral behavior as she and Raffaele were constantly hugging and kissing, off in another world. Oblivious to the grief around them they constantly sought gratification to ward off any pain. But their kissing faces ironically testified to their coldness, their symbiosis and how—together—they could have carried out such a crime. Their desperate separation anxiety/death anxiety fueled their rage. When we decode it, the couple's post-murder affection was a huge show-and-tell.

Can't 'enter my house'

*"i then bought some **underwear** because as it turns out **i wont be able to** leave italy for a while as well as **enter my house**."*

Now nearing the end of her email, Amanda must confirm her near-death story in vivid imagery. She implies she was turned out of her home, trapped in a foreign world outside her usual home, unable to enter her house. She can't remain in her uterine home. Again Amanda suggests the moment of conception, as soon as she entered her womb-room she was ushered out.

In one final grand sweep, her perceptive super intelligence sums it all up about her starvation, *"I won't be able to...enter my house."* There was no place for her at home. She was locked out, quickly discarded. She never had the home she needed.

Because of this fact, Amanda discloses, *"i then bought some underwear."* Being without underwear suggests nudity and exposure. She needed covering and protection. She needed parents who would buy that fact, but hers didn't. Missing underwear also suggests her biological condition. The amniotic sac that supported and covered her like a big translucent protective diaper was missing—pointing to abortion.

Underwear also suggests "what I'm secretly wearing you can't see" or in her case not wearing. Going a step further Amanda suggests, "see who I secretly am. See how wounded I am." Most particularly, underwear covered her mother's private vaginal/uterine home which Amanda saw herself as having left. In her mind aborting her was like her mother changing underwear. Amanda was simply old underwear.

That's how insignificant Amanda was. She gives us another self-image like cheap vending-machine food or take-out pizza. Enough insults to make one furious, really furious.

Guilt still ruled Amanda for murdering her roommate. Notice her comment, *"it turns out i wont be able to leave italy for a while."* Her conscience turned on her and demanded that she stay in Italy, as she will later tell us, "to help the police." Her inner policewoman has continued to make her presence felt, and Amanda's declaration that she would be in Italy *"for a while"* proved prophetic, as if she were sentencing herself.

At that point Amanda could have caught a flight home. Her mother says that her great regret was that she failed to urge Amanda to leave Italy immediately. But Amanda had to stick around to secretly punish herself.

Amanda the 'Bagan'

*"i only had the clothes i was wearing **the day it bagan,** so i bought some underwear and borrwed a pair of pants from raffael."*

Amanda continues wallowing in her own personal pain. She elaborates, "*i only had the clothes i was wearing **the day it bagan**.*"

Now she takes us back in time to "The Day" it began, to the beginning of her life, to when she was conceived. In her mind the only clothes she had was her birthday suit—naked and stripped, totally vulnerable, completely unprotected.

We read again, "*the day it bagan*" noting her slip "*bagan*" or "bag an." "Bagan" implies "bag" and "bag it," pointing unmistakably toward her being aborted. The day she began, her parents said, "Bag it." She was an "it." Get rid of "it." Put her and her bag out the door of the womb. Bag of water, of nourishment—forget it. Any wonder why Amanda is still starving. You don't get over such a day so easily. The day you began and immediately you're a "*bagan.*"

In light of being a discarded "*bagan*" Amanda needs some cover. She repeats, "*i bought some underwear*" linking it to "*and borrwed a pair of pants from raffael.*" She borrowed Raffaele's masculinity, his secret power, to protect her. Now she was suddenly the one in power implying Raffaele had given up his pants and was now under her control.

She used him like underwear to cover her weakness and in so doing soiled his life.

Unconsciously Amanda reminds us of her missing father and her early pain that led to her distinctly masculine strivings. She had to become the man of the house since no man was around to stand up for her—especially to take responsibility for her as his child instead of considering an abortion. No wonder she took out her anger on Raffaele, misusing him.

End of email—"*Spoke with my remaining roommates that night (last night) and it was a **hurricane of emotions and stress** but we **needed it anyway**. What we have been discussing is bascially what to do next. We are trying to keep our heads on straight.*"

"*First things first though, my roommates both **work for lawyers**, and they are going to try to send a request through on monday **to retrieve important documents** of ours that are still in the house.*"

"*Secondly, we **are going to talk** to the agency that we used to find our house and obviously request to move out. **It kind of sucks that we have to pay** the next months rent, but the **owner has protection** within the contract.*"

"*After that, I guess I'll go back to class on monday, although im not sure what im going to do about people asking me questions, because i really dont want to **talk** again about what happened. Ive been **talking** an awful lot lately and im pretty tired of it. After that, Its like im **trying to remember** what i was doing before all this happened.*"

*"I still need to figure out who i need to **talk** to and what i **need to** do to **continue studying** in perugia, because its what i want to do.*

*"Anyway, **thats the update**, feeling okay, hope you all are well, Amanda."*

Nearing the end of her email epistle, Amanda unconsciously confesses one final time that *"(I) spoke with my… roommate(s) that night (last night) and it was a hurricane of emotions and stress."* She simply must communicate again, in her special symbolic language, that she talked to Meredith on her *"last night"* alive. And Amanda sums up the crime as *"a hurricane of emotions and stress"*—a perfect description of all three killers joining forces in a gang attack fueled by their collective madness. Indeed, recall Rudy Guede had similarly described the murder as the result of "an explosive mix."

They had hit Meredith unexpectedly like a Category 5 hurricane descending on a defenseless populace. Amanda's super-intel adds violent image upon violent image saving the most potent for the end.

She links *"hurricane"* to *"her roommate"* and to *"trying to keep…heads on straight."* Amanda suggests that when she cut Meredith's throat, she nearly decapitated her thus vividly confirming the thoughtprint details of the crime.

"Trying to keep our heads on straight," suggests another phallic image and trying to keep up her typical macho-like bravado, maintain power to make up for her vulnerability.

Her comment, *"It kind of sucks that we have to pay the next months rent, but the owner has protection within the contract"* again implies an immediate motive for the murder. Namely that it sucked that she was running low on money causing her to steal next month's rent from Meredith. She suggests Meredith acted self-protectively feeling that Amanda's behavior "sucked" precipitating an overt conflict that night. Amanda also points to her confession driven by her innate need deep down to protect her roommate who owned her own life (*"the owner has protection"*). She implies an unwritten super-intel contract of the golden rule with her roommate Meredith deep in her unconscious.

She describes how hard the process was *"we're trying to keep our heads on straight,"* and that all three perpetrators are fighting for their sanity in the midst of the hurricane-like assault, especially Amanda. You just don't murder easily and simply walk away from it.

At the same time her image, *"trying to keep… heads on straight,"* suggests the battle to keep herself intact in the womb instead of a late-term (partial-birth) abortion in which the abortionist sucks the baby's brains out. Amanda knows that reality, and she was late term in a way because her parents married when she was five months in the womb.

In another sense, she sees her parents' decision to keep her as them declaring, *"It kind of sucks that we have to pay the next months rent, but the owner has protection within the contract."*

It sucked that they had to "pay the rent"—support the pregnancy economically—but intuitively they knew they had created a person with whom they now had a contract. She had "owner protection." It was her life. As "parental owners" of a child it was up to them to protect/support her until she was on her own. She was only a temporary renter in their home. In the end they reluctantly did the right thing. Amanda knows a baby can be expensive and thinks that money was a central reason behind the near-abortion—and stealing her life from her.

She then thinks of what responsible parents do under extreme economic distress, "going to talk to the agency that we used to find our house and obviously request to move out." They go to a lawyer and an adoption agency and "find (a) house" requesting "to move [the child] out" to that new home. Then they finalize adoption "contract." Again Amanda's super-intel can consider a thousand real-life situations and solutions in the blink of an eye.

One more time she removes all doubts about what her wishes were at the time. She takes us back to her voice then, "I still need to figure out who i need to talk to and what i need to do to continue studying in perugia, because its what i want to do." Amanda declares, "what i need to do…continue"—living. So that one day she can "continue studying…because its what i want to do." She has a will. Again it's her life and nobody else's—owner protection.

Does she speak for all womb children? No doubt in her mind she does.

She had advice for would-be parents who find themselves in her parents' shoes with a surprise pregnancy on their hands, one they know they cannot afford. She would tell them, "I know 'it's *a hurricane of emotions and stress but…(it's) needed.'* You need to understand you just created a person who needs you to protect him or her. One day you will see you both needed them 'anyway.' Discuss what to do next and try to keep your heads straight. Follow a clear direction. Do the right thing."

Amanda returns to the reality of precisely what she inflicted upon her roommate. But she's also unconsciously attempting to go straight and confess. Her super intelligence makes the strongest of appeals to law enforcement. Reading between the lines, we see Amanda first instructing the police: decide *"what to do next"* about my confession. Get *"your heads on straight"* about her deeper communication, she advises.

In particular she specifically addresses prosecutors in *"work for lawyers"* suggesting she has provided them a legal court case. She *"requests"* that authorities *"retrieve important documents of [mine] that are still in the house."* She strongly hints that in this very email investigators have a valuable forensic document still to be decoded. If they retrieve that information, they have her confession, they solve the case.

Then she floods them with a plethora of message markers shouting that she's frantically confessing—repeating the word "talking" over and over:

"spoke...discussing...talking," "going to talk ... "I've been talking an awful lot lately"... "i need to talk...talk again." She adds, *"what I need to do...what i want to do."*

Reading through her denial, she really wants *"to talk again about what happened."* Amanda reminds investigators about this email affirming her confession, *"I've been talking an awful lot lately."* She adds especially *"[I] ...remember what i was doing before all this happened"*— confessing that her portrayals of herself as suffering severe memory lapses are totally false. Clearly she remembers what happened in this crime; she could never forget such a thing.

> She begins to end with "that's the update"—exactly what police desperately need... All along Amanda, the undercover reporter, has been updating the police. And in her varied writings she has been updating herself unconsciously about a new way to truth. The way of narrative. The scientific narrative that reveals universal truths.

Deep down she knows her email can be studied by the appropriate document examiner versed in unconscious communication. The super-intel provides forensic science with both a new type of forensic profiler.

Utilizing official terminology such as "lawyers, documents, agency and contracts" she verifies that her communications should be used against her as court-admissible evidence.

Shortly she shifts into overdrive writing numerous forensic documents—to police—including jail statements, a diary, and letters to her attorneys. Unconsciously her deeper moral compass dictates that she pay the price for her crime, that her roommate in the house they shared was protected by the law.

She begins to end with *"that's the update"*—exactly what police desperately need. They need some key person to update them on the crime, to bring them up to speed and provide missing crucial information. We can read it, "Dateline: Amanda News Bulletin, Up-to-the-Minute Update." All along Amanda, the undercover reporter, has been updating the police.

And she has been updating herself as well unconsciously about a new way to truth. The way of narrative. The scientific narrative that reveals universal truths.

Later she would mention authors whose writings had a profound effect on her in jail, *"Vladimir Nabokov...Dostoyevsky...David Foster Wallace who experiment with narrative and delve into very specific conditions within their characters in order to expose universal truths about humanity."* Precisely what Amanda has been doing in this secret narrative email, delving deep into her mind, revealing the absolute fact that she must confess to the specifics of the murder.

Her all-seeing unconscious continually reveals those dreaded words *"universal truths* about ourselves" from which we run.

In her hidden conversation with police she encourages them to listen with a deeper ear, experiment and develop a new law enforcement method of hearing. Ironicallly, she thinks she catches on, "After reading... I've experienced, learned, identified, been challenged and been provided with insight."[108] But she never owned up to the crux of the matter: her secret narrative was all about her. She never decoded her own insights.

In her email she has one final piece of advice for investigators who must probe deep into their own character and natural blindspots, *"need to do…continue studying in perugia."* They need to *"continue studying"* the email to "figure out" that she desperately "needs to talk to" them—and in fact is doing exactly that. She's confessing from start to finish. Remember the Italian Supreme Court in its rejection of the appeal court's findings recommended that investigators review her memoir for overlooked information. The Supreme Court judges didn't say it, but they were clearly pointing to messages, including confessions, planted between the lines by Amanda' super-intel.

Final 'Good-Bye' to Meredith

With Meredith heavy on her mind, Amanda's final thought, *"feeling okay, hope you are all well, Amanda"* suggests several messages. She thinks of people who are healthy and well but raises the possibility someone she knows might be ill, not well at all. She cannot get her mind off what she did to Meredith Kercher. We can hear the agonizing loss, the lingering guilt Amanda will endure her entire life: "I wish you were well. I wish you were still living. I wish I hadn't killed you."

But we can hear her own desperate plea, as she hopes for herself: "I hope you are all well too, Amanda." She echoes her lifelong cry after teetering always on the ledge of life, about to plummet into oblivion. In her mind, what happened November 1st was a "double murder"—hers first and then Meredith's.

Amanda never actually mentions "abortion," but she paints numerous mental pictures of it. That's exactly the way therapy patients avoid their trauma until their great unconscious finally overwhelms them.

---

[108] http://www.nytimes.com/2013/05/12/books/review/amanda-knox-by-the-book.html?_r=0.

Chapter 16: Matching Thoughtprints—
Amanda's Jail Writings

Amanda began her cover-up in typical bravado fashion using a bold approach that worked like a charm—at least for a few days. She appeared cooperative, seemed to have her story together, and talked of her special memories of Meredith.

She was so confident, Amanda never seriously considered rushing out of the country to her family "in an emotional crisis" as some of Meredith's friends did. She was a rough, tough American who could handle anything. Consciously she said she stayed in Italy to help the police.

Thinking she could live outside social conventions whenever and wherever she wanted, Amanda's own secret moral compass betrayed her. Less than 48 hours after the murder, she was unconsciously compelled to write that November 4th email with the secret confession.

Then a day later at the police station, tired and surrounded by detectives, she was shocked when interrogators informed her that her boyfriend had reneged on the alibi. He now claimed, police said, that Amanda had not been with him the entire night of the murder. Instead of holding firm—his word against hers—Amanda folded. She lapsed into an "I can't remember" routine. (Again not long afterwards Raffaele stuck to his original story providing Amanda the all-night alibi.)

Under pressure, Amanda made the juvenile move of blaming someone else even while placing herself at the crime scene. She fingered her foreign black boss, Patrick Lumumba, for the killing, but she also admitted she had been at the stabbing scene that night. And in the early morning of November 6, 2007, she signed two confessions typed in Italian (1:45 a.m. and 5:45 a.m.) to substantiate she indeed was at her house at the time of Meredith's murder.[109]

Before long she tried to cover up the mistake/confession by lapsing by again reciting the mantra, "I can't remember." Deep down, however, the unconscious mind never changes its secret plan to tell the truth.

---

[109] To briefly decode her 1:45 a.m. statement, she reported using a lot of pot and hinted at also using narcotics. She mentions her black boss was the murderer and sexual assailant but indirectly points to Rudy whom they met at the basketball court. In her 5:45 a.m. statement she again identifies a black guy, Patrick, but really she means Rudy was in on the murder with her and Raffaele present in this version. No question about it, all three killers were there.

You can't take back a signature although Amanda tried in another hand-written statement to police (known as the "first memoriale") later on November 6th. Confident that she could undo any damage to her case, she went ahead and made it worse. Her super-intel provided a major clue when Amanda told policewoman Rita Ficarra, "This is a present for you"[110] as she handed her the letter. It was another secret confession.

In that November 6th statement (which we reviewed in Chapter Ten) we read through the repeated denial "I know I didn't kill Meredith." In that statement she confessed that indeed she had killed Meredith. In another denial, "I don't remember FOR SURE if I was at my house that night" she shouted out in all-caps that she was certain she *was* there. Her thoughtprints declared that she remembered everything. Her memory lapse was nothing but a lie.

Using the same all-caps shout, Amanda's super-intel also informed us, "I KNOW," implying that she knew who killed Meredith. "NEVER asked him [Raffaele] to lie for me" implied the joint cover-up all along; and finally in "Who is the REAL murder [sic]?" she confessed that it was her.

Non-Memory-Loss Amnesia

All in all she presents a case of *"the non-memory-loss memory loss."* A cover-up. Her *sudden* memory loss has no other explanation especially since it was triggered instantaneously by her boyfriend who had apparently undermined her alibi.

All the other thin explanations of such abrupt amnesia fall by the wayside. Not stress or tiredness, and she had functioned far too well for any severe drug blackouts (which she never claimed anyway). Her contention that marijuana affected her memory was bogus, especially given that her email and earlier testimony reflected an impeccable memory. She had been smoking pot like a haystack. There wasn't enough hash in Perugia to impair her memory. (And she will shortly "regain it.")

Her roommate's death bore a striking resemblance to the horrific murder of another young victim in the JonBenét Ramsey case in which another major contradiction existed from the get-go: a *"non-kidnap kidnapping."* The killer allegedly left a ransom note demanding money for the "kidnapped" victim only shortly JonBenét's body was found in the cellar of the house. No kidnapping ever took place. Of course such a scenario offered an outlet for the primary suspects in the case—her parents. And recently their primary defense of an intruder has been blown to smithereens.[111]

---

[110] Knox, p. 135.
[111] James Kolar, *Foreign Faction,* Venus Publishing, Inc, 2012, p. 102. In 2011 Boulder detective Kolar released previously unseen crime-scene video showing spider webs in the broken window downstairs completely ruling out any intruder theory. He also noted extraneous DNA on JonBenét's clothing was insignificant and likely from factory sources. He concluded the Ramseys were involved in the murder speculating the parents were covering up for their son, Burke.

Later Amanda would lie about police abuse and claim a forced confession, but she herself—the part of her mind she never accounted for—is what really forced the confession unknowingly.

Before you knew it there she was in a jail cell with the doors closing behind her. Amanda heard that distinct, unforgettable click. The old isolation technique continued her free fall. All alone in her jail cell, before anybody, especially her mother, could get into the country, her boyfriend off in a cell all his own in another jail, no books, no TV, no distraction. She found herself totally alone with herself—and her crime.

Then she was visited by a priest. As a jail cleric, he had seen it all before, all the cover-up cons, all the denials and claims of innocence. He never challenged Amanda. He simply invited her to Mass and asked her to play her guitar in "God's house." He told her to do "what I felt was right in my heart, because this was what God was," as she reported.

Not long after a nun magically appeared at Amanda's cell door. She was making her prison rounds to comfort those forgotten prisoners in jail and saw Amanda in the worst situation she had ever experienced. The nun put her hands—the 'hands of God'—through the bars separating them. Who would ever reach out to Amanda if they knew the truth? The truth was that she didn't deserve a human touch since she was the last human being to touch her roommate as she took her life. Meredith would never again be touched as a living human being—and now Amanda deserved that same fate.

When Amanda continued her lies and the drama queen performance of her life, proclaiming her innocence, "unable to remember," the nun never flinched. Instead she told Amanda, "God knows everything. He will help you."

Now the idea of God had entered the equation. Was he pressuring her to come clean? Pressure had now come from the most unexpected source, and Amanda couldn't stand up to it a whit. It had taken intense interrogation from investigators to break her, but now a priest and a nun simply spoke kind but firm words, and she suddenly collapsed. Alone in her cell *immediately after the nun's visit* Amanda's memory came back to her in a flash, crystal clear.

Second Letter/Memoriale

Once again she immediately wrote the police another letter (known as the "second memoriale") on November 7, 2007. Of course she continued to lie and had no idea that her super-intel guided her thoughts—secret thoughtprints between the lines which perfectly matched her elaborate email confession. Witness.

Her very first words in the letter are "Oh my God!" She can now remember for certain she was at Raffaele's the entire night of the murder and not at her house.

She remained preoccupied with the disguised cannibalistic theme of eating dinner with Raffaele—consuming their victim Meredith. "After dinner Raffaele began washing dishes," she wrote followed by her all-caps shout-out, "I remember now it was AFTER dinner." Amanda again had to shout it out that they were 'VAMPIRES' who engulfed Meredith. She even linked it to the specific moment of the murder, "must have happened at the time of Meredith's murder."

In this written letter to police "regaining her memory" she reveals new details of the murder. They were all high on drugs as she recalls Raffaele attending a concert with friends all using drugs. She continues with references to "cutting" and "piercing." (Raffaele cut designs in his hair on his head and wore earrings—pierced flesh in the head/neck region.)

Importantly she linked her deepest motives to the murder as she referenced Raffaele's traumatic past and his reaction to his mother's recent death. Remember, Amanda's own rage was driven by the early emotional loss of her own mother. She writes, "We talked about…how she [Raffaele's mother] died and how he felt guilty"—another super-intel confession of her guilt over Meredith's murder.

Jail Diary

Amanda can't stop writing and putting her thoughtprint evidence on paper. Next she writes a lengthy diary over several weeks in prison. Again she confirms the identical confession in her email and previously written jail statements.

Her first entry on November 7, 2007, right after being jailed, is enormously revealing. She describes the sudden recollection of her memory with a powerful unconscious confession filled with egregious images of violence to the head. "I sat down to write and [to] try to remember and then it *hit me.* Everything came back to me like a flood, one detail after another *until the moment my head hit* the pillow and I was asleep the [time] Meredith was *murdered."* Note two strong images of hitting someone in the head, a flood, details, and all linked to "Meredith was murdered." \

Amanda makes yet another reference to pierced ears/flesh, "They took all but two of my earrings and I'm afraid the holes will close, but that's not important at the moment." Her denial tells police in code what she's saying is totally important. Again she suggests that she and Raffaele had pierced—stabbed—Meredith. She describes two holes. She's also revealing the holes in her story.

Trial Testimony—Denial City

At her trial testimony Amanda's thoughtprint confession continued without missing a beat.

Addressing the court she admitted how truly frightened she was, "I'm scared to lose myself. I'm scared to be defined as what I am not and by acts that don't belong to me. I'm afraid to have the mask of a murderer forced on my skin."

Her denials confessed the murderous act belonged to her. She wore the mask of a murderer who forcefully pierced Meredith's skin. No wonder she was terrified. (And yes we can hear her near-abortion trauma images: "lose myself," "defined as what I am not" as in not existing, "acts that don't belong

> Amanda continued in violent image confession mode. *"It was my first day here and reality had punctured my expectations,"* she wrote. In fact the reality was Meredith had rejected her, and in turn Amanda "punctured" her and all her expectations for the rest of her life.

to me," and "murderer forced on my skin." But the current question is "Did you commit murder?")

In her final testimony at the appeal trial, she made more denials. "I had never suffered," she said. "I didn't know tragedy…it was something I watched on television." Reversing the denial reminded the court she knew tragedy all right. She had severe deep-seated pain and rage—a powerful motive from her past.

Defending herself with more denials, "I didn't kill. I didn't rape. I didn't steal. I was not there," she again confessed to all the details of the murder.

Memoir—Amanda Profiles the Murderer

Even after she was released from jail, Amanda couldn't stop confessing. In her cover-up memoir in 2013 she vividly portrayed how she attacked Meredith like a cat attacks a rat (see Chapter Eight).

Amanda again profiled herself for police using that very word—"profile"— in the story about the first meal she shared with her roommate and her friends in Perugia. "At dinner, I discovered that Meredith's friends fit the reserved British *profile*," she wrote. Subtly she hinted at her painful rejection by all the Brits in Perugia and having "Meredith for dinner."

Explaining her roommate's background, "Meredith had been *crushed* when her [British university] *turned her down* for a program abroad," she described how she crushed her, put her down for good. For Meredith there'd be no more school abroad—or anywhere else.

Amanda continued in violent image confession mode. *It was my first day here and reality had punctured my expectations,* she wrote. In fact the reality was Meredith had rejected her, and in turn Amanda "punctured" her and all her expectations for the rest of her life. She elaborated on her rage attack, "I'm sure *I struck* them as a stereotypically *loud* American. I was *energetic* and *outspoken*, even by *nonconformist* Seattle's standards, and I was probably *louder than I meant to be.*" Amanda's super-intel pictured how she unquestionably lost control—angrier, more forceful than she meant to be—and struck/stabbed Meredith in her 'nonconformist" fury.

We have just scratched the surface of Amanda Knox's continued written or spoken "thoughtprint confessions" from one document to another. The inescapable conclusion: she must confess. Her deeper moral compass will prevail.

Raffaele's Matching 'Vampire' Confession

On November 6, 2007, Raffaele first broke from Amanda in a statement informing Inspectors Moscatelli and Napoleoni that Amanda had in fact left his house alone the night of the murder.

His statement included the following as he reviewed the day of the murder.[112] We decode his comments in the context of the murder, a lens his super intelligence insists on looking through.

"In there was Meredith who left in a hurry about 16.00 without saying where she was going." In other words, Meredith died quickly that day during the impulsive murder which rapidly got out of hand. She had no idea she was going away and would never speak again. He implies they did not go there consciously to kill.

"Amanda and I went to the [town] centre about 18.00 but I don't remember what we did. We remained in the centre till 20.30 or 21.00." He suggests they were together at the center of the crime, and were at the crime scene for several hours that night. His denial implies he remembers exactly what they did but doesn't like to think about it.

"I went to my house alone at 21.00, while Amanda said that she was going to the pub Le Chic because she wanted to meet with her friends." This contains a blatant lie—Amanda did not go to Le Chic that night. Sollecito suggests that not long after 9 p.m. Amanda left with him to go meet Rudy in a group gathering—"her friends"—who would pay a visit to Meredith all alone in her house. He suggests they were all on drugs—had visited a pub, symbolic of drugs flowing freely. He suggests the embedded message, "meat for her friends"—that Meredith was "vampire meat" which he confirms next.

"At this **point** we said goodbye. I went home, I made a joint. Had dinner, but I don't remember what I ate. About 23.00…" His super-intel is saying that at the point of knives he and Amanda said goodbye to Meredith—the moment they stabbed her. Again they were on drugs and Raffaele suggests that he had made [laid] Meredith—had sex with her beforehand. They had consumed her like vampires—"ate" her for dinner—as he repeats Amanda's identical oral-engulfing imagery. He reveals how primitive and similar their psychopathology was, even linking it unconsciously to his background, "I went home." Like

---

[112]http://truejustice.org/ee/index.php?/tjmk/comments/knox_camp_illusions_multiple_examples_of_how_rs_and_ak/.

Amanda, he confirms his threatening home of origin—one dangerous place deep in his mind. Once more his denial announces he remembers precisely what happened that horrific night—even down to the exact time "about 23.00 (11 p.m.)" which Amanda mentioned in her first handwritten statement on November 6th. She reported, "…the night on which Meredith was murdered…Raffaele and I ate fairly late…around 11 in the evening."

Raffaele's statement continued: "About 23.00 my father called me on my house phone line." Again he unconsciously links his relationship with his father specifically to the murder—connecting it to his home of origin underscored by the message marker "phone." Also, Raffaele never talked to his father at that time.

"I recall Amanda was not back yet." His phrase "I recall" suggests "doubt me" and his denial ("not back yet") implies that he and Amanda were still together but they had not come home for some time. Coming back suggests they returned to the crime scene later, likely to clean up.

"I web surfed on the computer for two more hours after my father's phone call and I only stopped when Amanda came back in, presumably about 01.00…" Raffaele implies a specific detail of the crime scene, *that he "surfed" barefooted on the towels in the house to dry up the blood on the floor.* He implies he would stop and start when Amanda came into the room doing the same thing, sliding on towel. This explains why a bloody footprint the size of Raffaele's foot was found on the bathmat in the bathroom nearby. Sollecito further implies that the particular clean-up activity lasted a good two hours in the bedroom. His claim to be on the computer for two hours at that time was a blatant lie.

"In my previous statement I told a load of rubbish because Amanda had convinced me of her version of the facts and I didn't think about the inconsistencies." He announces with a hidden tell—"I told"—this new statement was a load of rubbish and filled with inconsistencies exactly like his former statements. Once more he declares he was Amanda's puppet in the entire charade—a role which enabled him to deny any responsibility.

Whether or not Raffaele and Amanda were separated for a brief period of time early that night on November 1st as some evidence suggests is really unimportant. Perhaps she went off to get some drugs. He makes it plain, as does Amanda, that they were both knee-deep in on the murder. By late 2014 they had both changed their stories several times, eventually blaming each other individually for the murder to free themselves—like rats scurrying for cover.

Yet Raffaele's own words in July 2014 once again betray him. Sollecito insisted he wasn't (again) changing his story. "Only a madman or a criminal would change versions, and I'm neither mad nor criminal," he said. "There's proof that I was at my place and I was watching Japanese cartoons."[113] Read

---

[113] http://www.independent.co.uk/news/world/europe/amanda-knox-phone-sex-and-cash-links-to-italian-cocaine-dealer-to-be-used-against-her-in-extradition-bid-9582407.html.

through his back-to-back denials announcing he is indeed "a madman and a criminal. There's proof..." Unconsciously he confirms the message as we read the next sentence run-on with the striking message marker "proof."

At trial: repeated non-verbal confessions
Tight T-shirts

Then we have her behavioral confessions. During the trial Amanda often surprised people with her dress. She wore tight T-shirts and blouses confessing her freed-up sexuality, making her appear the very vixen the prosecutors portrayed. It's as if she were saying, "See my seductive power that controlled the whole sex-game charade on the night of the murder."

Valentine's Day

Behind her quirky dress there were other meaningful messages. Is it any wonder that she would show up on a Valentine's Day hearing in 2009 at her first trial wearing a long T-shirt emblazoned with the title of a Beatles' song, "All You Need Is Love?"

Once again we have a subtle denial confession of how she had failed to show love to her murdered roommate. And now all the guilty Amanda needs is love.

Amanda was displaying, for all the world to see, her deepest motive behind the murder. She was announcing to prosecutors, "See my pain—see my motive," begging them to decode her show-and-tell message. Her all-knowing super-intel summed it up in a phrase which she wore across her chest. From the get-go, in her deepest subconscious she never felt that she was loved. That's what abandonment of the worst kind did to her—it left her shouting "All You Need Is Love," particularly on the day that symbolizes love.

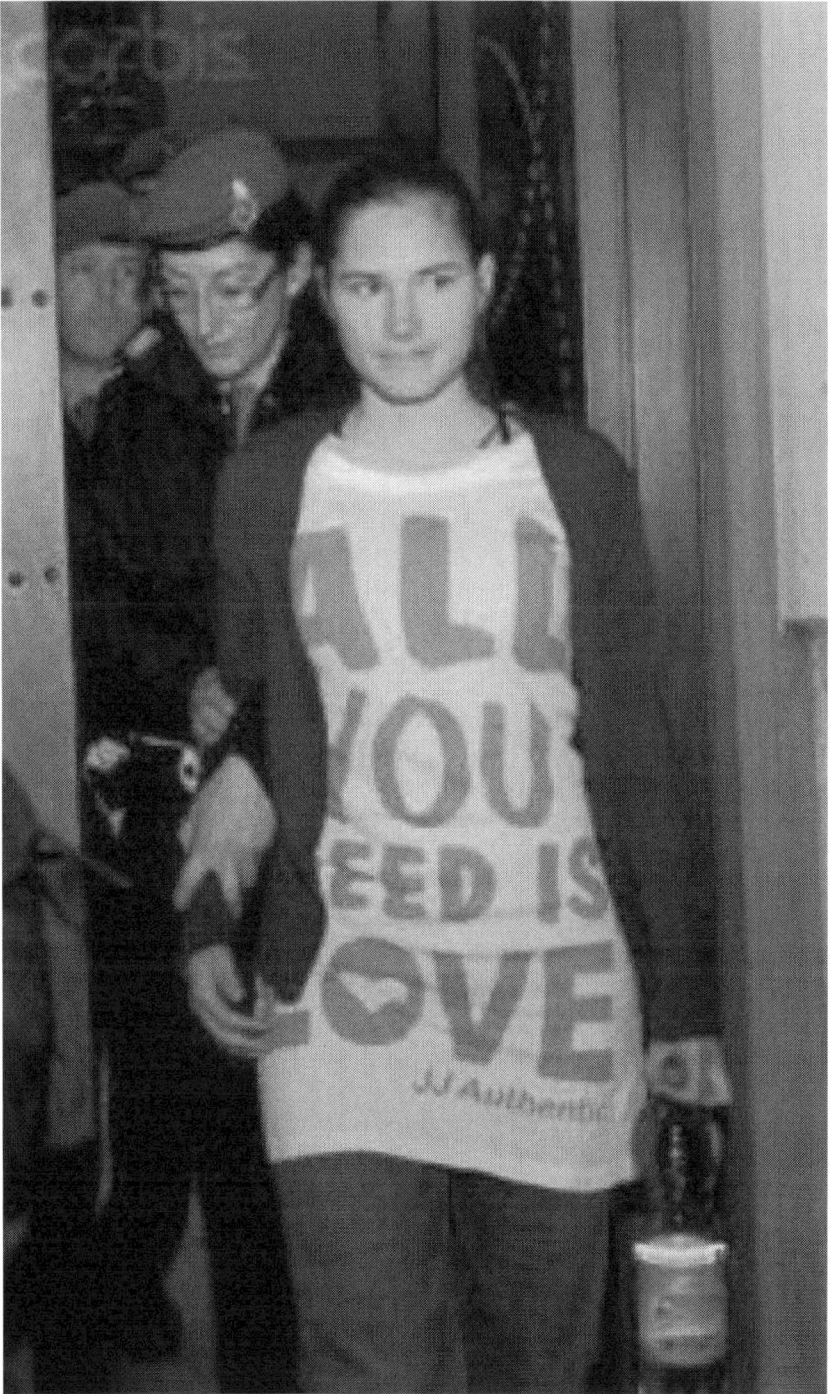

Amanda Knox IN BEATLES T-SHIRT—"All You Need Is Love"

Tattoo

In jail she decided she wanted a tattoo, "Let It Be," another title of a well-known Beatles' song. Consciously she couldn't explain it, but her diary did. Right after her arrest and in prison she though she would soon be out: *"I'm glad something is finally being figured out. It means the creep who did this will go to jail…I want to get another tattoo—the words 'Let it be.' They mean so much to me now. I don't know where I just want them."*

She realized that investigators had determined her guilt. Her powerful images, "creep who did this will go to jail" implies the creep who did this is already in jail and she insists, "let it be." That is, "Let my jail sentence continue." Amanda wants numerous tattoos, but she's just not sure "where I want them." Amanda suggests her neck, returning again to repetitive body piercings. She deserves to be tattooed as she tattooed Meredith.

Halloween 2013

For the record Amanda's behavioral confessions continue out of jail. Recall her "black cat/robber" costume on Halloween 2013. Behind the All-American girl demeanor, she's still a vicious black cat, a vampire killer.

All in all Amanda continued to pretend she was telling the truth, continued her charade through two trials, even learning to speak in Italian to the court for the appeal trial, skillfully lying in two languages. She had corresponded with and been interviewed by journalists, and had her family hire a public-relations team back in the states to magnify her innocence. She appealed to all sexually permissive people, depicting herself as one of them. That was all she had done—engaged in free love. A little promiscuity here, a little promiscuity there. She was simply a modern young woman who liked sex. After all, wasn't that what life was all about? Except for the life she took. And now it was about so much more.

Chapter 17: FBI Profilers Overstep Their Abilities

During her three plus years in jail—2007 to late 2011—Amanda attracted significant media attention in America. Who could believe that this innocent, beautiful, American college girl from Seattle could brutally stab her roommate in such vicious manner it shocked experienced investigators, and had the crime-scene pathologist so stirred up he broke his restrained demeanor? Certain ex-FBI agents proved more than willing to buy her performance.

Noted FBI profiler John E. Douglas weighed in on the case in his book, *The Forgotten Killer: Rudy Guede and the Murder of Meredith Kercher* (January 2014). Basing his theory on supposedly cutting-edge forensic profiling "evidence," Douglas claims Rudy Guede alone killed Meredith. Douglas limits the evidence to crime-scene interpretation with no true validating method. He presents this in a matrix of profilers' jargon and murder classifications. He makes superficial attempts to utilize unconscious clues from the killer(s).

But he ignores the far greater forensic evidence—*verbal communications in the forensic documents* produced by all three convicted killers—which he is not trained to decode. These documents include emails, written statements to police, verbal interrogations, etc. Douglas simply doesn't grasp unconscious super-intel communication which provides substantially more information and secret confessions.

Douglas also established his reputation in profiling mostly serial killers at the FBI Behavioral Science Unit. His methodology in recent years has been greatly challenged. Investigative reporter and author Malcolm Gladwell wrote a revealing article about FBI profilers which revealed a fundamental flaw in their method.[114] They claimed to identify patterns between a killer's life and personality with the nature of his crimes, focusing heavily on the crime scene. From this they attempted to make predictions about identifying murderers, but the method proved to be inconsistent. Their profiles were all-too-often so vague that their predictions fit any possibility.

---

[114] Malcolm Gladwell, "Profiling Made Easy," *The New Yorker*, November 12, 2007.

Gladwell interviewed psychologist Laurence Alison from the University of Liverpool and author of *The Forensic Psychologist's Casebook*. Alison observed that forensic profiling "is a lot more complicated than the FBI imagines." He attributed the FBI profilers' sterling reputation to a simplistic psychology and the way they compiled reports. Alison broke down their profile in one prominent case sentence-by-sentence concluding, as Gladwell wrote, "that that it was so full of unverifiable and contradictory and ambiguous language that it could support virtually any interpretation."

This reminds me of former Wichita Police Chief Richard LaMunyon's comment that "30 FBI profilers means 60 opinions." LaMunyon ran the BTK investigation for 15-plus years and remained active behind the scenes until BTK was captured in 2005. He had unofficially consulted me late in the case not long before BTK's arrest.

FBI's Flawed Approach

Gladwell demonstrated much of the myth behind the work of Greenwich Village psychiatrist James Brussel, a man credited by Douglas as the inspiration for the FBI profiling team he led. Brussel claimed to have identified the mad bomber that terrorized Con-Edison in New York City for more than 15 years in the 1940s and '50s. To profile the bomber, Brussel attempted to utilize his abilities as a Freudian analyst. He reported multiple specific accurate predictions about the bomber and his personal life documented by Brussel in his later memoir, *Casebook of a Crime Psychiatrist*.

But the truth is that most of Brussel's numerous predictions fell far off the mark, and *he had cleaned them up for his book.* In fact the person who actually solved the case was a clerk assigned to comb through Con-Ed employment files to identify disgruntled employees. Going back through the files, she discovered one suspect from prior years who turned out to be the bomber.

Along the way, however, Brussel made two sterling predictions which he based on his observations of the bomber's extremely neatly drawn block letters in his hand-written notes to police. Brussel paired those observations with details of the bomber's crime-scene behavior such as slitting seats in movie theaters to leave bombs. Using his instincts, Brussel declared the bomber would be single and living with a mother figure (he lived with his two sisters) and that he would typically wear a double-breasted suit which would be buttoned. When police found the suspect—later convicted—he fit those two criteria and FBI profilers took off from there. They ignored Brussel's numerous failed predictions and supported the "legendary" accurate predictions. Douglas and his team would adopt that grandiose technique overly dependent on hunches and resort to "telling details" in their profiles—often inaccurate as well.

To both Brussel's and Douglas's credit, they attempted to tap into the criminal's unconscious mind. Later efforts by FBI profilers Douglas and Robert Ressler to look for connections between the killer's life and the nature of the crime also had promise, but they failed to put it all together even though it was right in front of them when the killer's unconscious was speaking to them. In short, the killer's super-intel had to inform them verbally, either in various writings or interviews. The FBI profilers simply didn't know how to read the super-intel's symbolic language or to trace thoughtprint patterns to grasp the deeper trauma that drove a killer.

Douglas and Ressler took their study of serial killers on the road, talking with homicide detectives and murder suspects in local jurisdictions and interviewing notorious murderers in prison. They hoped that information they were gathering about past crimes could shed light on live cases, murders committed by unknown suspects on whom they were offering profiles.

But unable to tap into a killer's super-intel, unable to hear it, Douglas and Ressler often missed powerful motives behind a murder. They couldn't fully plumb the depths of the murderer's psyche—even at the unconscious invitation of the murderer. As a result they didn't appreciate the full extent a killer's personal pain played in a crime, a pain that was at times specifically reenacted at a crime scene.

> Unable to tap into a killer's super-intel, unable to hear it, Douglas and Ressler often missed powerful motives behind a murder. They couldn't fully plumb the depths of the murderer's psyche— even at the unconscious invitation of the murderer.

They also disregarded important clues such as major boundary violations in relationships—a form of violence—in the past history of perpetrators. That's why Douglas reached the wrong conclusion in the Amanda Knox case and earlier in the JonBenét Ramsey case.

Looking back Amanda had warned everyone with her increasingly out of control behaviors—she was secretly doing violence to herself and others. She communicated how vulnerable she was to physically losing control. In thoughtprint patterns Amanda Knox unconsciously communicated to police just how deep her personal traumas went and how they secretly controlled her life. Then in multiple post-crime communications she revealed the entire story over and over again between the lines, but Douglas missed it entirely.

In turn he overlooked her description of both the deeper time-bomb motives and the immediate, less powerful motives in the case. He then failed to see the crime-scene as a reenactment that directly connected the killer's life to the brutal crime. Douglas never grasped how a powerful emotional trauma remains frozen in the psyche as though it had just recently happened, how near-death experiences are so close to dying, it's as though a person actually died.

But why would Douglas know this? He had never been trained in "super-intel" psychotherapy focused on decoding brilliant "all-seeing" messages from the super intelligence. He had never taken the painful journey deep into the human psyche, and neither had Brussel, the "old Freudian" analyst.

Co-author and former FBI agent Steve Moore agrees with Douglas that Amanda Knox is not guilty. Moore also lacks training in how to read a suspect's unconscious confession and settles for his conscious read on Amanda's innocence. He befriended her while in jail and so, he says, he can tell she's innocent.

Both Moore and Douglas linked themselves with "co-authors" heavily biased toward Amanda's innocence and antagonistic toward the Italian justice system. These include: Douglas Preston, who makes excessive claims to understand motives and forensic evidence; Tom Wright, who was a personal friend of Amanda Knox and the originator of the friendsofamanda.org website; and Judge Michael Heavey, who specializes in the study of "wrongful convictions."[115]

Forensic psychiatrist James Raney compared Douglas' work to my thoughtprint decoding method in the JonBenét Ramsey case in a professional journal review of my two books on the Ramsey case. Raney supported my conclusion of Ramsey guilt. He also noted, "Douglas may have met his match in the Ramseys' obfuscation of the case...Perhaps Mr. Douglas [hired by the Ramseys], despite his declaration of objectivity, reveals himself through his "absolutely no evidence" hyperbole as the Ramseys' proxy voice."[116]

Douglas's colleague, Robert Ressler, was interviewed by a reporter about my first forensic profiling book, *A Mother Gone Bad,* on the Ramsey case in 1999. Here I introduced the thoughtprint decoding method focusing extensively on the crucial ransom note, the smoking gun which so puzzles prosecutors that they've still failed to utilize it. Ressler expressed doubt about my method and wondered how in the world a person could write a 200-page book about the ransom note.[117] He failed to grasp the ability of the super intelligence to communicate extensively in detail about a crime providing overlooked motives only known by the brilliant unconscious mind of a perpetrator. As a result he missed confessions from JonBenét's killers and failed along with Douglas to bring about justice for little JonBenét.

In a follow-up book on the case published in 2000, *Who Will Speak for JonBenét?*, I further detailed the killers' confessions. Two forensic colleagues and I sent Boulder prosecutors an eighty-page report and forensic analysis decoding the ransom note with fourteen conclusions identifying the killers. The report was supported by a legal scholar's brief. At the time there was an unusual split between the police and the DA's office which ignored the report. Only

---

[115] John Douglas, Judge Michael Heavey, Jim Lovering, Steve Moore, Mark Olshaker, Douglas Preston, Thomas Lee Wright. *The Forgotten Killer: Rudy Guede and the Murder of Meredith Kercher* (Kindle Single; Amazon Digital Services, Inc.), 2014.

[116] James O. Raney, M.D., International Journal of Communicative Psychoanalysis & Psychotherapy 15:4 (2000). [Who Will Speak for JonBenét? book review].

[117] Thomas Spenser, "Who Killed JonBenét Ramsey?" The Birmingham News, 1999.

years later, in 2012, was it revealed that the grand jury had secretly voted to indict the Ramseys, but DA Alex Hunter refused to go forward.

Brussel and Douglas et al never knew a super intelligence existed. They didn't realize that it communicates extensively in a symbolic language. Sigmund Freud himself had never grasped the true abilities of the unconscious and could only decode its messages in limited fashion.[118]

In short, the FBI profilers lacked the skills needed to accurately decode super-intel messages. Instead, they would add details to their profiles based on hunches and instincts producing extremely mixed and unreliable results. At times, Douglas's instincts were excellent. At other times, he strayed way off base.

Personally, however, I owe John Douglas a great debt of gratitude. In the late-1990s, I happened to meet an FBI agent who had become interested in my clinical work after we'd learned that the super intelligence insists on telling the truth. The agent suggested I consider applying my clinical work to forensic profiling and recommended Douglas' first book, *Mindhunter: Inside the FBI's Elite Serial Crime Unit* (1995).

Like thousands of other readers, I found *Mindhunter* intriguing and fascinating.

Instinctively, I knew that to access the super intelligence of a suspect, an investigator must have verbatim communication straight from the suspect's mind. Such communication included police or media interviews, letters, notes, personal journals, emails, etc.

Decoding such statements was identical to the work we do in psychotherapy in which we allow a patient's super-intel to communicate freely and creatively, and the therapist simply stays out of their way. Then the therapist decodes what the patient's magnificent deeper intelligence has revealed. The patient's subconscious mind teaches a therapist how to listen. This was the process I brought to forensic profiling.

This was the method the late psychiatrist Robert Langs, who discovered the super intelligence, came to understand. He saw the extent of unconscious communication by our brilliant deeper mind. I was fortunate to work with him and validate his clinical research over a thirty-year period in a hands-on therapeutic environment. This method is without a doubt the wave of the future in psychotherapy as we continue to gain further understanding of the secrets of the mind.

Langs knew the mind gives up its secrets but does so indirectly, symbolically, between the lines. That's why a criminal perpetrator cannot keep a

---

[118] Let's not fail to credit the pioneer, Freud, for pointing the way to the unconscious and that it spoke in its own symbolic language. Paradigm shifts in knowledge are difficult. That's why the discovery of the super intelligence has not yet reached the public domain. Ironically, Malcolm Gladwell wrote about the "dazzling new…unconscious" in his best-seller, *Blink,* in which he explored the quick-read capabilities of the unconscious mind although he, too, missed the verbal language.

secret. They can lie all they want, but their super-intel will shape their lies to tell the truth symbolically. They will pattern one guilt-ridden message after another.

Simpson, Ramsey, Holloway etc.

I unexpectedly got into forensic profiling when the O.J. Simpson case suddenly became front-page news. Shortly after the slayings of Nicole Brown Simpson and her friend, Ron Goldman, on June 12, 1994, in Los Angeles, numerous communications from O.J. Simpson were available to examine including a recorded interrogation by the LAPD, a suicide note, comments made during the infamous Bronco chase, and a book written in jail from recorded interviews. I uncovered a powerful persuasive confession of guilt in which Simpson unknowingly laid out his motives. He had a painful story to tell which has not been told to this day. Later I ended up presenting my forensic work on the case at an FBI conference at Quantico. One thing led to another and I eventually profiled several major cases all of which involved multiple communications from prime suspects. All the killers had to "put it in writing" to get it off their chest.

Before long, six-year-old JonBenét Ramsey was found dead in her family's Colorado basement and I analyzed the key communication in the case—the alleged ransom note. In that case, I applied the method more thoroughly. I'd been learning from case to case what a perpetrator's super-intel was trying to reveal and how desperately they needed to confess.

The famous Ramsey ransom note was an invaluable document that told the whole story. The chief suspects—the parents—also communicated extensively in public interviews, police interviews and in books. They wrote one book together and John Ramsey wrote one after Patsy died. There was no question the Ramsey's own thoughtprints pointed to them.

In 2005, the BTK serial killer had written several taunting letters and notes to the investigating authorities and others, documents which I was able to study and decode. I determined the killer was on the verge of murdering again for the first time in years. I was the only profiler to predict this fact to which he confessed after his capture a short time later.

That same year teenager Natalee Holloway went missing in Aruba and infant Caylee Anthony was reportedly kidnapped in Florida. After my method was applied to several forensic documents in each case, I knew they'd both been murdered. In the Holloway case, I decoded a lengthy email from one of the suspects and multiple police and public interviews from all three suspects to reveal the circumstances of her death and the location of her body. In 2007 I documented my analysis in a book, *Into the Deep: The Hidden Confession of Natalee's Killer*.

In the case of Caylee Anthony's murder, I published my findings on my website, forensicthoughtprints.com. In addition to numerous text messages prior to her arrest, Caylee's mother, Casey Anthony, wrote 200 letters to a cellmate who saved the letters suspecting they were of value. Between the lines Casey presented a startling confession and several motives. Like Amanda Knox and all the killers mentioned above, they were driven by their super-intel to "put it in writing."

Epitaph for a Genius

As for Robert Langs, the great psychiatrist died on November 8, 2014. He had continually encouraged me to utilize the super intelligence in forensic cases. He embraced my forensic work after assessing several presentations I'd made at professional conferences. Along the way I discussed prominent cases with him privately. In 2010 he specifically suggested that I profile the Amanda Knox case, but at the time I was involved in another project. After studying the case, I eventually presented my findings to him in several professional consultations. Before his death, he reviewed this book and concurred with my conclusions.

Langs was the world's leading expert on emotional trauma. He took us deeper into the human psyche than we had ever imagined possible. Above all he understood that the fundamental secret of the super-intel was that it revealed its traumas in hidden narrative. We could never look our deepest issues in the eye but only through the partially disguised lens of narrative. That's why he eventually called his work "communicative narrative therapy."

His clinical genius showed up again when he specifically wrote to me on June 26, 2014, regarding Amanda Knox and her narrative email, "Have you considered [that she was] **a failed abortion attempt**...[because] there's so much about her feeling actually aborted. I call this a reality/fantasy... it didn't happen, but the patient believes and behaves as if it did." That was one possibility I had not considered. Maybe Amanda Knox had actually survived an abortion.

With that perceptive observation, Dr. Langs had strongly validated Amanda's core trauma, her primary motive for murder. But there was another trauma which he and I also discussed. As Langs put it, deep in her unconscious "the eyes of God" were upon Amanda Knox, and she had a deep need for atonement.

Chapter 18: Amanda Knox, Shakespeare, and the 'Day of Count'

The Amanda Knox spectacle confirms that true-crime stories are the morality plays of our day and age, especially when it comes to first-time murderers. Amanda's saga overflows with tragedies worthy of a Shakespearian script. Her story has all the elements of high drama—sudden murder, first-time killer, innocent appearance, manipulating two co-conspirators, denial, cover-up, a trial, guilt proclaimed, guilt undone, guilt re-established, missing motive, escape from justice, fear of eternal judgment, living in the suffocating prison-of-the-mind, and a secret confession urging a public confession. Will the truth be discovered by the police—and the public?

Underlying this we have a vulnerable young American beauty who opens the door to what I and just a few other forensic detectives have called "the new mind," opening a view into our deeper selves. Amanda demonstrates the surprising capacity of her shadow side, darker than we ever imagined, to suddenly take actions surpassing anyone's immediate comprehension. But simultaneously her deeper mind explains the whole sordid thing with a brilliance beyond that of any detective in history—because she must confess. Must. Above all, she has to clear her conscience. She's a living, breathing Lady Macbeth who lives forever with blood on her hands.

But Amanda's story reminds us of Shakespeare in another important way. The Bard not only wrote passionately about murder to shine a light on the darkest aspects of human existence; he also insisted that awaiting us all is a "day of count" on which everyone must give an account for their lives.

But Shakespeare implied that day of count begins now. That unconsciously, people hold themselves accountable for their actions immediately, especially murder—when they're confronted by their own super-intel, their "inner voice of God."

Having bloodily sent her roommate, Meredith, on to the next world, Amanda continues to be obsessed with it *now*. On her prison wall as she records in her prison diary, Amanda finds the writing, "one leaves, you leave soon—*Liberata* [freed]." She suggests not only her wish for freedom but how she cannot shake her new existential reality. She sent her roommate away permanently, and the same fate awaits her. Murder has produced a death-date for Amanda—in a way, she has died now. Her initial "day of count" is upon her. She hopes for freedom [*liberata*] but suggests it must start with telling the truth and meting out justice to the guilty.

At her trial Amanda thanked the court, *"because they are trying to bring justice to an act that tore a person from this world."* Lady Amanda Macbeth shows up again. She cannot forgive herself for tearing Meredith Kercher's life away from her. Unconsciously Amanda reveals how strongly she desires justice, how desperately she wants to confess.

To go with justice, Amanda shifts to truth. She professes her innocence to a visiting priest in prison who simply tells her, "God is doing what's right." She then introduces the "T-word"—"truth." She writes in her diary after meeting the priest, "I know…will have to believe the truth"—suggesting she will have to believe in the truth enough to tell it, own up to it. Confession, she knows, remains her only true path to freedom.

Amanda Pronounces Own Sentence: 'Convicted Murderer'

Immediately before the Italian Appeal Court's ruling on January 30, 2014, Amanda was asked in an interview what impact "reconviction" would have on her. She responded, "Oh God, it has a practical impact on my well-being and psychology on a very fundamental level. I feel stranded."

Her first thoughtprint, "Oh God," reveals again that immediately after she murdered she ran into a surprising part of herself—a deeper moral compass—which knew intuitively that the "eyes of God" were upon her.

She continues, "convicted again…never going to be OK…some Judge's decision…say I'm a convicted murderer." She adds, "being marked as a criminal…It hurts…It's not OK…like I've just been diagnosed with cancer…nowhere I can go." For the moment she's "much safer here in the U.S., where people still believe in me…being marked as an exoneree."

Still she thinks, "This is damaging all of us…in my mind that feeling of being imprisoned…all of a sudden you could empathize with people who thought about taking their own life…they're just…trapped."[119]

Her own super-intel's secret verdict as the secret judge reveals her overwhelming guilt, "convicted murderer…marked as a criminal…never OK…nowhere [you] can go…trapped…imprisoned."

Still out of jail, she remains behind bars in the prison of her mind—"…in my mind that feeling of being imprisoned." The cancer of guilt is eating her up inside, continually "damaging" her. Her super-intel refuses to mark her "exoneree."

---

[119] Simon Hattenstone, "Who is Amanda Knox?" February 7, 2014 , http://www.theguardian.com/world/2014/feb/08/who-is-amanda-knox-interview .

Her own solution for her day of count: "taking [my] own life," suicide—a murder for a murder. Damage to the one who damaged Meredith. Amanda's pierced flesh for Meredith's flesh which she herself pierced. *Blood atonement.*

If Amanda were a jury member, she's voting for capital punishment. By refusing to confess, she implies a slow suicide—self-atonement.

Jail for Justice's Sake

At points in her memoir Amanda writes about how well she adjusted to prison. Her first day in her prison cell, she describes singing a favorite Beatles' song, "Let It Be," for comfort—suggesting jail was just what she needed. She might not *like* prison, but deep inside she knows that it would start her down the road to peace and freedom.

Amanda has also attempted to meet with her victim's family, but the Kerchers have refused to see her. Still she suggests her real need: not to meet with them to continue her lie—but to look them in the face and admit what she's done, to start by saying she's sorry.

She alone holds the key to begin moving herself from "convicted" to "exoneree," lifting the phenomenal weight of guilt that chokes her. She's stranded until she herself announces her verdict, "guilty as charged." Such a confession would have a fundamental impact on her mental state. She would lessen her secret attack on herself—her cancerous guilt eating away at her—and instead serve out her sentence in the name of justice, fairness for what she had done.

Until Amanda Knox tells the truth she may be out of jail, but she's not free. Nor will she be emotionally free in an Italian prison perchance she ends up there—unless she owns up to Meredith's blood on her hands. Until that moment she remains fixated in her role as Lady Amanda Macbeth, struggling secretly in the dark, trying to wash the blood from her permanently-stained hands. It only comes off in the light.

'The Day,' a Built-In Knowing

Amanda knows, however, that ultimately she'll face "The Day of Count." She can see the next world from here, looking through the window of her super-intel. She's a creature and she must answer to her Creator; therefore she knows "where she's going"—to the Father of super-intel moral compasses, who gave Amanda's hers—a moral compass just like his own. Amanda knows that she bit Meredith Kercher, one of the apples of God's eye. She intuitively knows her murderous deed demands justice.

Repeatedly her thoughtprints point to God. In her memoir Amanda wrote, "I'm not religious. I don't believe in miracles. I'm not sure what I think about God." Reading through her repeated denials, we see that deep down she's quite certain about God. And she *does* hope for a miracle, the miracle not just of another world but of absolution.

On the heels of these three denials, Amanda recalls the powerful impact the priest and a nun had on her soon after she was arrested. Her interactions with these two "God representatives" reveal that her super-intel is looking dead-on at the day of accountability. The priest tells her a story about a bird flying into the room of a wise man, fluttering around before leaving through another window—reflecting two questions: "Where are we from? Where are we going?"

The priest clearly symbolizes God the Father. Unconsciously Amanda's wise super intelligence immediately recognizes the truth of her existence implied in the story. Again she sees herself as intentionally created by another-world God—to live in this world and then to go on to the next world where God resides. Over and over Amanda has insisted she exists, her life is special.

The priest tells her, "God is doing what's right," and she knows she has done wrong. The nun then tells her, "God knows everything and he will help you find the answer." Amanda suggests her super-intel knows all about God and knows she's in deep water because God demands justice. She needs God's help to find the answer to her dilemma.

Bigger Problem than Destroying Roommate

Amanda can see her own blood won't nearly cover her sins. On the day of count there "Meredith awaits" who wants justice for what happened to her—how her life was shortened. If Amanda did not satisfy justice in her earthly life then Meredith's proxy voice will naturally ask for it to be satisfied then. Amanda also has a bigger problem: she "murdered" far more people than her roommate, Meredith.

Does she know how much she has stressed all of Meredith Kercher's family and continues to do so—stolen years and enjoyment from their lives, besides their dear Meredith? Will the Kerchers ever recover in this world from the murder of their daughter and sister?

She manipulated Raffele Sollecito and Rudy Guede—two wounded doves—into carrying out the murder with her. She got them all jail sentences. She robbed Raffaele of a career and ruined the lives of his father and sister. Will the Sollecitos ever get over Raffaele's trial and the fact that he was declared a murderer? Will Raffaele ever recover?

Does Amanda Knox have any idea how much she hurt her former boss, Patrick Lumumba—falsely accusing him of the murder, causing his unrelenting terror for two solid weeks in jail? She selfishly accused Patrick to the point that he feared for his own life as he faced possible lifelong imprisonment for something he did not do. It's an experience he'll never forget. To boot, Amanda terrorized Meredith's friends by committing the bloody murder. One of them was so traumatized she dropped out of school, left her year-abroad program to scurry home, unable to cope with Perugia. Amanda's self-centered crime of passion has produced a life of misery, of suffering for too many; she has destroyed too many lives besides her roommate's.

On top of this she assaulted the truth and justice itself. Amanda flaunted her lies under oath, carried on in court, played much of the American media like a drum with her innocent "U.S. victim abroad" routine, and—instead of returning to Italy for her retrial—she arrogantly sent the appeal court judge an email from Seattle as her testimony. She further declared she will fight extradition with every fiber of her being, dismissively spitting in the face of the Italian justice system and the Kerchers. From her public stage, she asks the world to believe a lie.

Shining the Light on Others

Amanda is not alone. For their part, each of her co-conspirators enabled her. Not only did they bring about their own destruction, they indirectly encouraged her violence. In a sense, she couldn't have done it without them.

Of course we know Amanda's parents have never really considered all the hurtful things they put Amanda through. How deeply they wounded her.

And what about her dyed-in-the-wool supporters—media or no—who are so certain Amanda could not possibly have done it? They're so certain they know precisely what she did in Italy 6,000 miles away on November 1, 2007. So positive Amanda is innocent, they're arrogantly certain they grasp all the details of the investigation.[120]

As a side note her own attorneys—who had to defend her nevertheless—revealed they picked up on the truth deep down. Their super-intel revealed that they were blatantly mistaken.

How about one of her attorneys, whose denial that she was "not Amanda the Ripper," told us precisely what she was—a murderer who mutilated the body of her victim. And another who insisted that Amanda was so innocent he considered her like his own daughter. On top of that, after an impassioned defense speech to the jury, he declared, "And that was no act." His denial informed us exactly what it was—nothing more than a dramatic defense lacking substance—and unconsciously he knew it.

All these folks have no idea that they are contributing to the Kercher family's inability to experience "justice closure" in addition to denying justice itself. The last thing friends, family and certain "experts" put first is justice as they rush to their "sacred opinion" and to Amanda's defense. (Families who never experience "justice closure" remind me of other family victims of murder who never find the body. This is why, for example, Tim Miller of Texas EquuSearch worked so hard in Aruba to help Natalee Holloway's parents gain closure by locating her missing body. Tim knew all about it first-hand, having formed his search organization after going 18 months before authorities found

---

[120] Lacking knowledge and training, Amanda's truth-telling super-intel mind exists and must confess. She is consciously unaware that her super-intel has produced immutable fixed-in-time forensic documents in her casual writings which could be examined 100 years from now and still shout out her guilt.

his own missing daughter's body after a serial killer took her life. I discussed this with Tim extensively in Aruba when I was there as a forensic profiler doing my own research on the Holloway case; I saw his passion up close and personal.)

The Only Way Out

Unconsciously Amanda's behavior provides the solution for "The Day" awaiting her. In prison she attends Mass, plays her guitar in the service and, for three straight years, portrays Mary in the Christmas play. Mass at its very heart points to "communion"—the body and blood of Jesus—an atonement for Amanda's body and blood her crime requires. It's the same atonement which the priest and the nun represent by their very presence, forgiveness through Christ. Her only hope. A body for a body. His blood for Meredith's blood. A murder for a murder. Blood atonement is the only possible path to becoming free, "*Liberata.*"

Her wish to get a tattoo reading "Let It Be," echoes the message. She thinks her own flesh should be permanently pierced in 'scarlet letters' as payment in kind for her awful deed.

How ironic the crucifixion of Christ fits with her deepest needs. How his pierced flesh fits the murder Amanda carried out. Could it be true? A real offer from the next-world Father and his son? A cosmic atonement meeting the needs of vastly imperfect human beings?

Entrapped by justice, she writes, "I might become a more spiritual person because somebody had to help me" implying again she needs God's help—forgiveness through atonement.

She describes people who write to her advising her to believe in God—again suggesting messages from her own super-intel. Immediately after the nun's visit she wrote, "I know I will have to believe." She believes in justice and hopes for mercy—that the miracle of atonement occurred at the crucifixion.

She's desperately looking for someone—for God, the appeal court judge—to mark her "exoneree" instead of "criminal." Suddenly the crucifixion takes on "a practical effect on [her] well-being and psychology on a very fundamental level." Amanda's super-intel suggests powerfully an eternal no-nonsense solution to her dilemma whereby she cries out "Oh God, mark me as exoneree." Grace.

There's only one way in her super-intel justice system—she must have help from someone else brutally pierced for her. Only someone qualified as innocent to serve justice, willing to give his life for hers, a miracle scapegoat who would appear on the scene.

She points the way to the "Big Swap." The pain of unbearable shame for the pain of Christ's crucifixion. Both the believer and Jesus the Christ—each in enormous pain.

No cheap grace, no cheap forgiveness. None of the currently popular pablum of pop psychology, 'Just be your own best friend and forgive yourself.' No—Amanda's story brings us to the end of pride, the end of innocence, the end of denial. A person and a personal God must suffer in their own way for truth to prevail.

The destroyer must own her destructiveness—claim it as her own and plead for grace. Having the faith that makes "amazing grace" come alive. Faith in her super-intel revelation, faith in Christ's revelation.

Exactly as Augustine counseled: without faith, you will not understand. Exactly what therapists and patients (as well as forensic profilers) must have to utilize the super intelligence. They must believe it's there. Just a few do at this point in time.

Destroys Myth of 'all nice people'

The super-intel's clear moral compass destroys the central myth surrounding Amanda's case to which she appealed, i.e., the myth of the "nice person who couldn't have done this." And she, the accused, is clearly (if subconsciously) following that compass, seeking the absolution for her sins that it demands. This is the same myth to which O.J. Simpson initially appealed. JonBenet Ramsey's parents also followed this strategy: How could a parent kill a child? Amanda herself is a living testimony to that possibility, as we have seen from the echoes of her near-abortion. And a more recent case, in which a mother did indeed kill her daughter (in my opinion, though a jury acquitted her), is Casey Anthony.

> Amanda Knox's saga highlights the denial of our shadow side. She brings blood atonement front-and-center in a world that increasingly lives in denial of such. Ironically, only a guilty murderer such as Amanda reveals how atonement actually is absolutely practical.

Amanda's dogged obedience to her super-intel's guilty verdict shines the light on what's really in the human heart—the same heart Shakespeare referenced when he implied that, under the right circumstances, anyone could become a killer.

Jesus said the same thing, "For out of the heart come evil thoughts, murder, adultery, sexual immorality, theft, false testimony, slander. These are what make a man 'unclean'...."[121]

Jesus never let human beings off easily. He insisted that the shadow side of man was the problem. It was the central problem he had come to take care of with his own blood, sacrificing his own life—declaring that nobody took it, he

---

[121] Matthew 15:19-20, New International Version.

gave it. He added, "There is none good but one,"[122] implying he was the perfect atonement for imperfect people all. Then and only then he offered "communion" to everyone personally.

Amanda Knox's saga highlights the denial of our shadow side—the biggest lie of our times. She brings blood atonement front-and-center in a world that increasingly lives in denial of such, insisting atonement is passé—unsophisticated, primitive. Ironically, only a guilty murderer such as Amanda reveals how absolutely practical atonement actually is.

She takes us back to where it all began—the Garden of Eden. It was no accident in the biblical account that the first sin was when Adam and Eve inflicted death on the human race followed by their son, Cain, who killed his brother, Abel. The "murder" sin of the first family has haunted us ever since. Death has been passed down from generation to generation. Don't be so quick to label these biblical characters simply "metaphorical types." Their character is too close to Amanda Knox's.

For good measure in a prison diary Amanda reminds us of her character and her horrific deed as she reflects on the moment of Meredith's death. Amanda wrote: "I can only imagine what she felt in those moments frightened, injured, raped. But I imagine more what she went through when the blood went out of her. What did she feel? And the mother? Desperation? Did she have the time to find peace or in the end did she have only terror?"[123]

In familiar denials she again confesses to the brutal details of her assault on Meredith as she watched the blood pouring out of her victim. Specific sins fixated in her mind. She is Cain who has just killed Abel. Secretly Amanda reveals her own dilemma—only everlasting terror or some way of finding peace.

The Two Destinations—Amanda Wants 'Back in the House'—Upstairs

Deep down Amanda perceives she will go on living in the next world. God the Creator will never ultimately take a life. Of all human beings Amanda Knox knows this better than anyone. She sees two possibilities. She will live "downstairs" apart from God. She will reside with the vampires who refuse to own their destructiveness. She will join the living dead in a hell all their own. But she wants to—hope against hope—*"come back into the house,"* God's house.

Unconsciously, she again suggests the answer for 'the day of count'—the way of the cross. A way, in Shakespeare's terms, to turn this tragedy into a comedy, to find a place where it's "much safer...where people still believe in me...being marked as an exoneree." There's only one place to turn apart from her enablers to find someone who still believes something good can come out of

---

[122] Mark 10:18, King James Version.
[123] http://truejustice.org/ee/index.php?/tjmk/comments/does_her_leaked_prison_diary_talk_to_knoxs_mental_c ondition/.

Amanda, the vicious vampire murderer.

But even though she remains a long way from the truth, from consciously believing in confession and getting God's help for her own soul, she continues to believe in justice. Indeed Amanda knew that the appeal court would find her guilty as they did. Her case is now before the Italian Supreme Court on one final appeal to be ruled on in early 2015.

The compelling drama continues. Will Amanda ever hear her super-intel moral compass—fully reflecting the title of her memoir *"Waiting to Be Heard?"* Or will she remain in prison—whether in or out of jail?

Does her drama touch on the universal drama?

Was William Shakespeare, the seer, right about the 'day of count?' Can Amanda Knox's super-intel—the super-seer—see it from here?

Surely she echoes the words of the great criminologist Vernon Geberth who said, "Death investigation constitutes a heavy responsibility . . . let no person deter you from the truth and your own personal commitment to see that justice is done . . . and remember you're working for God."[124]

Secretly Amanda agrees with Geberth. Like all people, her super-intel is working for her Creator. She has been investigating her roommate's murder since day one, and her own incisive super-intel investigator never gives up trying to persuade her to set her own soul free. She must start by telling the truth, and continue serving her sentence. The judges were right—that's justice. Sadly her enablers, who advise her to avoid jail at all costs, want to keep locked her in the prison of her mind.

And if she really wants mercy she can begin by showing some to the Kerchers—admitting she killed their daughter and asking for their forgiveness.

But at the deepest level of her mind and soul Amanda needs to embrace her desperate need for atonement forgiveness. As C.S. Lewis said, it takes a good man to repent and we are all bad men. Deep down she knows Jesus' offer of communion—the body and the blood—is the true way to God.

Yet she needs God's help to own up—the miracle of faith. She cries out, "'Oh God'—I can't tell the truth, 'Oh God' I can't do right." She's afraid the truth, and God himself, will destroy her. Her post-traumatic fixation that she's on the verge of destruction continues. And all that shame and the pride that goes with it refuses to exonerate her.

She needs God's help to believe in grace for her precious soul. "Oh God" indeed.

---

[124] Vernon J. Geberth, *Practical Homicide Investigation*, CRC Press, 1998.

Postscript: The Last Witness

Note: My comments in this postscript continue to reflect my professional opinion based on sound principles of decoding unconscious communication. Here I have examined the unconscious communication of a journalist as regards her opinion about the Amanda Knox case and about important unconscious values regarding the basic framework of social life.

Accountability Journalism

The more we explore the Amanda Knox spectacle, the more we see this story has a life all its own. Its tributaries lead us into deep waters which wash over Italy, America and the world.

Her story would be incomplete without examining the last of the three major investigative players after the prosecutors/courts and the outside law-enforcement experts—namely the media. Knox's story brings the media front and center now under the new microscope of the super intelligence.

The question becomes to which mind are journalists accountable—exclusively the conscious, or also the unconscious, the super-intel? And which mind best sees reality?

In this case, one investigative reporter who has commanded significant attention atop the media heap is Nina Burleigh, author of: *The Fatal Gift of Beauty: The Trials of Amanda Knox*. A gifted writer, Burleigh vehemently declared in her book that Knox was innocent. Because Amanda was a sexually active young woman, Burleigh maintained, Italian authorities were pre-disposed to find the American girl guilty.

Burleigh has written extensively on feminism, issues of human trafficking, domestic violence, and double standards for violence against women. Her view of the Kercher murder, then, is colored by her belief that "In our PC world, misogyny…is in fact the last allowable taboo."[125]

Like all good writers, Burleigh inherently knows the power of narrative. *The Fatal Gift of Beauty* is chock full of stories illustrated with vivid imagery,

---

[125] http://www.huffingtonpost.com/nina-burleigh/the-last-allowable-taboo_b_846549.html

much of which tells far more than Burleigh had intended.

What Burleigh didn't count on was her own super intelligence reading Amanda's hidden messages. She had no idea her unconscious super-intel was simultaneously researching the same material (interviews, writings, background, jail writings, court testimony) a thousand times faster and deeper than her conscious mind. It's as if she's conducting two levels of research—"first grade and Ph.D." Burleigh simply did not know the super intelligence existed—neither Amanda's nor hers.

Imagine someone who can't see well at all—only blurred images. She can't pass a driver's test but manages to get one anyway. She often mistakes one object for another. But she's used to it and certain she can see well enough to drive and does so—often causing car wrecks. Then one day the person gets eyeglasses and she sees clearly for the first time. She sees a thousand times better—and a whole new world opens up to her. By analogy that's the difference between blurred conscious-mind perception and super-intel perception with its all-seeing glasses.

Conscious-Mind Journalism vs. Super-Intel Journalism

Six key words generally define journalism: "Who, What, When, Where, Why and How." Answer those questions and you have a story. But journalists now have a major problem: they can't tell you *why.* They don't understand deeper motives. Only the super-intel can see deeply into the unconscious mind.

In criminal cases they often can't tell you who did it if they don't know why. That's exactly as Burleigh claimed: she saw no motive, and so she proclaimed Amanda innocent.

The new super-intel psychology exposes limitations in traditional journalism. We have the psychology of the conscious mind and the psychology of the unconscious mind. Two levels on which the mind simultaneously thinks—and a world apart.

If the mind is 10 percent conscious and 90 percent unconscious (and it's even more), a reporter limited only to the conscious mind of a subject and only their own conscious read is a limited journalist, and frequently a biased journalist.

We have two possibilities: a limited 10 percent journalism and a vastly more accurate other 90 percent of the mind journalism. Overtly Burleigh's modus operandi is strictly that of a conscious-mind thinker. And she pays a big price.

Boldly, unequivocally, Burleigh not only asserts Amanda's innocence, but she also asserts her own ability to determine the absolute truth. She can spot injustice and take you deep into the minds and motivations of Amanda's persecutors. She finds the Italian criminal justice system inherently prejudiced against females and foreigners.

Essentially she limits her reporting to what she thinks on a superficial conscious level and what Amanda consciously reports. Rather than looking deeper, Burleigh simply reinforces Amanda's viewpoint, various denials and overt lies.

By now we're aware unconsciously Amanda has repeatedly confessed and pleaded to be brought to justice. In so doing, she provides a lens by which to see Burleigh. By how much did Burleigh then miss the real story? How wrong was Burleigh about the Italian justice system? Whose story—Knox's or hers—is more accurate, more powerful, more truthful, more thought provoking, and touches on universal truth?

Instead of exploring the terrifying reality which overwhelms Amanda, Burleigh offers us the fluff version of the truth. Amanda Knox was just a typical college girl feeling her oats, innocent of anything as unseemly as rape and murder. But what Burleigh's conscious mind misses her super intelligence reveals in spades. In a real way she becomes the last witness.

PART 1: BURLEIGH PROFILES AMANDA KNOX
Key to Case: Decode Subconscious

Now we can see how Nina Burleigh unconsciously picked up an entirely different story about Amanda Knox than the one perceived by the writer's limited conscious mind.

The experienced investigative reporter specifically described how Amanda had given us "a glimpse into the inner working, maybe the subconscious [of her mind]" (see Chapter Three).

Burleigh's super-intel knows full well that Amanda has largely exposed her unconscious mind and her part in the crime. All Burleigh's super-intel needed was a brief glimpse into the mind of Amanda Knox, and she spent months in it. In short, Burleigh knows the entire story.

She first mentions beneath the 'sunny girl' surface, Amanda's mind was "not at all pretty." The reporter then specifically underscores Amanda's violent writings about "rapes, self-cutting, voyeurism and domestic violence"—precisely what occurred during the murder. Burleigh adds that Amanda thus exposed strikingly "an intense detailed description of the physical sensation of *suppressed* rage."[126]

The writer's super-intel has summarized the entire crime in exact order (rape, a knife, voyeurism, and blatant violence) and pointed to the fundamental issue in the murder—Amanda's hidden rage which suddenly surfaced after smoldering in her unconscious for years. Burleigh specifically suggests Amanda used a knife to cut and stab.

Unknowingly Burleigh identifies Amanda's unconscious as the key to the

---

[126] Burleigh, p. 60.

entire case. She intuitively knows Amanda's stories **and her jail-related writings** are of enormous importance.

Still Burleigh displays her basic problem as a reporter: practically speaking, she's in total denial of the unconscious—Amanda's and her own. She lacks insight into the human mind, the vast difference between the conscious and the unconscious. *Two distinct levels of thinking and communicating—not an easy concept to grasp initially.*

Suppression Versus Total Denial Repression

Burleigh's misunderstanding of basic psychology leads her to confuse Amanda's "suppression" of rage with her "repression" of rage. Suppressed rage means rage of which Amanda was consciously aware—and there wasn't any. She just wrote about violence. Repressed rage means total denial of her fury buried in the unconscious behind massive mental walls impenetrable to the conscious mind. It's the difference between "firecracker anger" such as slamming a door, and surprising "TNT rage" that erupts into uncontrollable violence. Amanda's brutal creative stories revealed her walled-off fury.

Burleigh Points to Motive for murder

The author's super-intel confirms she has picked up on Amanda's confession with a classic denial of her own, "Like everything else she [Knox] posted, no one knows why she chose those stories." But deep down Burleigh knows *exactly* why Amanda selected those stories. The super-intel speaks primarily in narratives and rich imagery. Amanda's stories spoke volumes. Unconsciously, Burleigh grasps that Amanda Knox—because of the enormity of her deeply hidden repressed rage—murdered her roommate when that fury erupted. So she answers the big "Why" part of the story.

And Burleigh, as we will later see, also knows why she herself refused to see the real story and had to bury it unconsciously. Make no mistake, we have a two-for-one confession: she sees Amanda's hidden confession but also makes one of her own.

Like Amanda, Nina Burleigh had no idea that she possessed a secret undercover reporter.

Unbeknown to her conscious mind, Burleigh's own dazzling unconscious quick-reads all of Amanda's multiple confessions—heard every one. She followed all her embedded thoughtprints. Burleigh ended up confessing that she really knew the truth after all.

Her profile of Knox continues in her other comments. Take the dedication Burleigh wrote for her book, *The Fatal Gift of Beauty*:

"in memoriam: female victims of sexual violence"

254

First we have one of the worst murders on recent record—but instead she first has to specifically mention "sexual violence." Burleigh's super-intel suggests something crucial about Burleigh and sexual violence which we will keep in mind.

Her central premise is that Amanda Knox was a victim of judicial injustice in a foreign country.

Burleigh couches this in an elaborate feminism steeped in Italy's deep-seated traditional inability to deal with powerful women—now the epitome of the modern woman. Italians historically categorized women as either "madonnas" or "whores." Sexually liberated Amanda would then be "a whore." The author suggests that makes her a victim of sexual violence. Her book title, *The Fatal Gift of Beauty*, itself implies that sexuality, her feminine beauty, was Amanda's only crime which ultimately proved fatal to her in the Italian courts.

Burleigh also believes a man killed Meredith. She portrays the crime as an inadvertent robbery-gone-bad during which Meredith returned home early on her last night. Burleigh fingers Rudy Guede, declaring the evidence points only to him. He was a known robber, she writes. How convenient—the perfect scapegoat. End of story.

Burleigh's sophisticated surface cleverness is no match for the real power of Amanda's story, which Burleigh's super-intel inevitably uncovers.

In the dedication/memoriam and then in her book, Burleigh unconsciously points to her deeper read on the murder with her images of sexual violence and violence in relation to female victims.

First she knows Meredith was a "female victim of sexual violence"— sexually attacked before the murder, just as Knox confessed in her story themes and repeated denials. On the heels of the sexual assault, Kercher was then a "female victim of violence"—murdered by Knox and gang. Looking only slightly deeper, it was an exact fit with Burleigh's dedication.

Motive: Violence Done to Amanda—Unwanted Child

Deeper still Burleigh's ever perceptive super-intel journalist then answers the "why" question —the motive—in her dedication.

Amanda did it because she herself was first a female victim of sexual violence—especially because a sexual act on her parents' part led to them not wanting her. A casual fling by both and suddenly consequences—Amanda's on the way, newly minted in her mother's womb.

Burleigh implies at that point Knox was a female victim of violence—by both parents. They almost got rid of her.

All these levels of meaning in Burleigh's memoriam show us the brilliant capability of the super-intel to send multi-level messages in one communication—all about the murder. First she describes violence done to the victim Meredith, then the violence done to the victim Amanda.

Her super-intel, like Amanda's, always discloses the truth and the specific details of the murder. She continually pictures Amanda's near-abortion trauma. Briefly she mentions the crucial matter of Amanda being an unwanted pregnancy. She describes both parents as *"party animals"* and how mother got pregnant "right away," defining the very tenuous relationship and a casual fling.

Burleigh follows with a plethora of near-abortion images. She described the pregnancy when the parents "hit the real-life wall much too soon in the 1980s, that was the end." She implies they nearly hit Amanda's real-life wall in the womb room far too early leading to the end of her life. Burleigh relates how that pregnancy was "actually the beginning of everything else." This is where Amanda's problems really started leaving her a keg of dynamite inside, a keg which could explode at any time. In the back of her mind, Nina Burleigh knows how Amanda's near-end-of-life trauma shaped her entire life and eventually lead to her murdering her roommate.

Quickly she goes on to more violent images. She describes Amanda's parents fighting an ugly battle. She tells how Amanda's grandmother, Oma, lost her own mother at age eight in an Allied bombing raid. Here she pictures a death at a very early age, the permanent separation of a mother and child in a sudden violent attack—a bomb suggesting utter disintegration.

Next Burleigh mentions the only book Amanda's father ever read: *The Swarm*, a novel about killer bees, suggesting that both he and Amanda's mother together considered the abortion.

While Burleigh goes on to minimize the unplanned pregnancy writing that Edda said in 2009, "Both of the girls were unplanned, but that was fine with me. I wanted a family," she then suggests the real truth. She wrote, "...time and fresh disaster having blurred the edges off the early crisis" implying a near disaster in which Amanda's fresh life was almost obliterated. [127]

Unplanned suggests unwanted, as close as Edda will get to confessing openly. But follow her words—"unplanned—but." Forget the "but." If she had wanted to get pregnant she could have done so long before. Edda gives us an idea of just one way Amanda herself picked up on the real story. If Edda was that open with a reporter who she really didn't know, we can imagine she was that casual with Amanda.

Burleigh Repeats Abortion Narratives—'The Fatal Gift of Life'

A few pages later again in the section on Knox's "suppressed rage," Burleigh focuses on a short story entitled, "The Model" that Amanda had written and posted on her Myspace page just before leaving for Italy in 2007. The story focused on a young girl involved in a triangle with her mother and the mother's disturbed ex- boyfriend who stalks them and may have raped the young girl. [128] Right off Amanda suggests this key narrative was "the model"

---

[127] Burleigh, p. 29.
[128] Ibid, p. 61.

which would explain her crime in Perugia—and Burleigh heard it.

The reporter Burleigh sets the stage identifying Amanda's powerful "unconscious mind-set"—a model of her near-abortion ever fixated in her mind—as she headed for Italy.

Then she notes "Amanda wrote line after line trying to describe the physical manifestation of hidden rage: 'Feelings that left me hollow in my chest like my insides had been poured out of my mouth' and a feeling 'hard and strange, almost like a wounded animal, which had been clawing at your insides, had finally found its way out, and the empty feeling of the space it had left bubbled up inside, and then disintegrated.'"

Burleigh's overwhelming imagery informs us what was eating away at Amanda deep inside, constantly clawing away at her life— pictures how she was a time-bomb set to claw away at her ultimate victim, Meredith.

Amanda's multiple images horrifically depict an abortion/near abortion, the physical attack—"left me hollow, clawing at your insides…poured out, empty space, disintegrated." Burleigh presents intense narrative images of abortion but cannot mention the word "abortion," only millimeters away in her unconscious. She suggests a blind spot, brutality she cannot take in.

Unknowingly, Burleigh confirmed she had picked up on Amanda's core abortion trauma and her ensuing rage. She emphasizes the physical manifestation of rage—the near-abortion attack on Amanda and Amanda's physical attack on her roommate. Burleigh suggests Amanda murdered Meredith in a fit of rage.

Burleigh further implies the real translation of her book title, *The Fatal Gift of Beauty,* was "The Fatal Gift of Life." Amanda's real beauty under attack was her very life in the womb threatened from day one. Surely it's a cruel fatality beyond words to receive the gift of life and then have it immediately taken away—too young to even speak or battle for your life. The victim of all victims. And who's more beautiful than a newborn baby?

Unconsciously, the very title Burleigh chose—another multi-level message— confirmed the key motive in the case.

Secretly it told Meredith Kercher's story, too. In the end her problem was that she existed. She was Amanda's target.

Burleigh's super intelligence reminds us life is a gift. How easily people can forget that about their neighbor and themselves, fail to appreciate how every relationship is also a gift—just as Amanda Knox forgot her roommate was a gift to her. Many who knew Meredith described her in exactly that way—a gift. Later the journalist will reveal how she, too, had been a forgotten gift.

Even Burleigh's subtitle, *The Trials of Amanda Knox,* fits perfectly the revelation that Amanda's trials started from the very day she received her fatal gift —life. Day after day her life was on trial early on fixating the trauma: every moment she about to be a fatality. She was a living PTSD fatality.

With her suggested title and matching sub-title in all its poignancy, Burleigh confesses she saw the true story about Amanda's life—and must passionately tell it.

Burleigh Confession: 'Amanda Hyde' Kills British Victim

For good measure the journalist underscores the matter with a denial confession, "To the press, the stories' sinister images and themes confirmed the presence of a Mr. Hyde buried inside the *smiling girl who never got angry*, and who, even after her arrest kept a prison diary filled with pop song platitudes, doodles of peace signs.... schoolgirl ruminations on faith versus atheism, and plans for a coming home party in Seattle."

But Ms. Burleigh is "the press," as her vivid unconscious message marker highlights. Her super intelligence again sees straight through Amanda's denial spotting her "buried" pain that led to homicidal rage. She even labels her a vicious murderer like Mr. Hyde whose victims were British, a specific detail/thoughtprint testifying how well she know the real story. She further suggests the name "Amanda Hyde"—an extension of her attorney's moniker "Amanda the Ripper," also implying a murder victim who was British.

Burleigh continues to confirm her denial of Amanda's rage when next she describes how Amanda's father denies his daughter's anger. She writes, "Curt had no idea where Amanda had gotten her literary bent...He reckoned it was her way of coping. 'Amanda, since she was this high (gesturing to his thigh)...wouldn't say she was angry. She doesn't confront. She writes down her emotions. She wants to be nice. Helpful.'"

In protective denial of Amanda, Burleigh consciously avoids Amanda's all-consuming anger. She doesn't realize that her own helpful literary skills have again gotten the real story, that Amanda was deeply wounded and furious, wounded by her father and, by implication, her mother.

Immediately Burleigh quotes Curt again. During his visits to Italy while Amanda was in jail

Curt secretly installed GPS-tracking devices on the phones of the two daughters back in Seattle. He didn't trust their dates, commenting, "Boys are bad for girls," suggesting Curt's own confession that he had been bad for Amanda at a crucial time in her life. He'd been distrustful, he couldn't be trusted with her life. He almost terminated her existence.[129] His reference to "GPS," a picture of the super-intel operating in the background, suggests deep down he was tracking how he might have contributed to Amanda's crime. At the same time Burleigh borrows the rich image to explain how her own super-intel GPS is tracking the whole story as an undercover reporter.

Time and time again Burleigh alludes to Amanda's wrath and how she failed to express her anger. She points to how Amanda has deeply buried

---

[129] Burleigh, p. 62.

explosive emotions of an intense nature suggesting a trauma of remarkable magnitude. Amanda underscores that she is a wounded animal—immediately before she heads to Perugia.

Burleigh consciously misses the clue: the most dangerous animal is a wounded animal. Severely wounded people tend to take it out on others—and whoever killed Meredith Kercher was a wild, severely wounded animal. But Burleigh's narrative tells us again that deep down she knew the whole story. She explains why she overlooked Amanda's major passive-aggressive red flags just before her trip: the staged break-in of her house and her wild going-away party.

Burleigh also reported several jocular comments Amanda made in jail. In denial, Burleigh shows no awareness that such things said in jest can have great unconscious import. Only two months before her conviction in 2009, Amanda wrote a male journalist making light of a "catalystic [sic] love triangle." This perfectly matches Rudy Guede's image that the murder involved "an explosive mix."

A year prior, Amanda had sent a friend a cartoon she had created of herself portrayed crying in prison stripes and the caption, "Jail Barbie" along with the balloon reflection, "Why, oh God, why?"[130] Though still puzzled as to why she lost control and murdered Meredith, Amanda knows she deserves jail and pleads her case before God. Amanda will often mention God in a light-hearted fashion to confess that he is perpetually on her mind in her vast unconscious.

Burleigh the Cherry-Picker

The writer moves from one denial to another. Burleigh declared, "Nothing in either students' prior behavior indicted a predisposition to aggression."[131] Burleigh shows no understanding of passive-aggressive behavior which Amanda continually demonstrated.

Burleigh then accuses prosecutors of cherry picking incidents from the lives of Amanda and Raffaele to support their misguided view the two have violent tendencies. But unconsciously, Burleigh's talking about herself. She confesses as a journalist that she cherry picks her observations to support Amanda's innocence—and that includes cherry picking another denial at will. Unconsciously she has repeatedly told us of their violence.

Her super-intel repeatedly says to her, "Thank you very much for your image describing a key dynamic in a denial or in a projection. Log in your eye, remember."

For the record she ignores several first-time murderers who had no prior history of violence (e.g. noted cases including Susan Smith, Scott Peterson, and Casey Anthony along with the killers of JonBenét Ramsey and Natalee Holloway).

---

[130] Ibid, p. 288.
[131] Burleigh, p. 297.

Schoolgirl Instruction, Suspending Disbelief, and Creating False Scenes

Speaking of being on the cutting-edge of knowledge, Burleigh needs to go back to school—recall her reference to Amanda's "schoolgirl" faith. In that striking image, Burleigh's super-intel reads her lack of knowledge and faith in her subconscious mind instructing her to get more education about it—read "go back and look at what your unconscious mind is telling you, even about God." Her super-intel informs her that her absolute faith in her conscious all-knowing mind is schoolgirl.

Her lengthy book contains one attempt after another by her super-intel to teach her about Amanda and then about herself.

Even her image, "cherry picking," contains rich symbolic messages pointing toward Amanda's crucial traumas. It suggests the loss of virginity, uterine bleeding and a fantasy that her father "picked her mother's cherry"—shed her mother's blood.

No wonder in her short story "Baby Brother," Amanda named the rapist Kyle (who "has to show chicks what they really want")—the name of the guy to whom she lost her virginity.[132] Amanda suggests another fantasy that her father actually raped her mother to reveal how violent she saw the undesired pregnancy which resulted. In her mind she was conceived in violence. She further suggests an attempt to preserve a positive image of her mother as simply a victim. This comes into play as Amanda suggests that the near-abortion was picking her cherry—taking her most precious thing, her life.

Burleigh's limited vision and distorted lens affected her take on the forensic evidence at the trials. She wrote how,

"One has to suspend disbelief to buy the [prosecution's] theory that Amanda Knox and Raffaele Sollecito murdered Meredith Kercher without leaving a trace of themselves in the bloody room and spent the night putting up a false scene in the burgled room. There was no believable material proof they did either."[133]

Her statement jam-packed with a secret confession also attempts to guide herself and readers to the truth with invaluable imagery. The super intelligence typically saves powerful messages for the end, like an attorney making a close, and Burleigh's super-intel makes this statement ten pages before the end of her book.

Burleigh's super-intel confesses that she suspended her disbelief, bought the defense team's attack on the forensic evidence, while entirely ignoring forensic evidence in the rest of the house, and showed a remarkable ignorance of the blatant crime-scene staging by two of the perpetrators. She has totally suspended her disbelief that Amanda and Raffaele could possibly be guilty and

---

[132] This in no way implies Amanda's former boyfriend raped or assaulted her when she lost her virginity—but more broadly Amanda's symbolic revelation surrounding the powerful issue of virginity itself.
[133] Ibid, p. 296.

simply presented a theory that holds no water.

To continue with her cherry-picking confession, Burleigh adds another theme song: she suspends disbelief. She sees what she wants to and never looks below the surface. She confesses unconsciously that she spent her entire lengthy book creating one false take/narrative after another about the dual killers' innocence.

And why—because her conscious mind didn't believe she could overlook evidence. It all comes down to what she believes, to her faith. She underscores how a journalist's faith in her conscious mind colored everything—when she had personal blind spots triggered by Amanda's trial.

Her blatant denial confession, "no believable proof they did either," tells us that there was plenty of evidence that both Amanda and Raffaele murdered Meredith and specifically created the "false scenes" both described. In particular they staged the crime scene.

Pay close attention she highlights "believable proof" which her super-intel clearly witnessed. Burleigh refers here to their thoughtprint evidence contained in the very words they uttered or wrote after the crime, evidence right up her alley. A writer intimately familiar with the symbolic language of narrative Burleigh clues us in that her super-intel heard it all.

Deep down she was totally convinced that it was evidence and that she picked up on one subliminal confession after another. In the distinct "material evidence"—recorded or written words—were hidden the secret confessions.

Trace Evidence

Above all we must not miss her key unconscious instruction— hidden in her crucial denial—that we indeed can trace these words to the bloody room. Reading through her blatant denials we have, "leaving a trace of themselves in the bloody room… believable material proof they did [it]."

Burleigh, the narrative expert, suggests that we trace the images and themes—the thoughtprints—in Amanda's epistle of an email written 48 hours after the crime, the first written material evidence.

Those thoughtprints take you right back to the bloody crime Amanda just left, the crime she simply cannot get off her mind. She was there and shows us. Here we find powerful thoughtprint evidence in all its gore, evidence from the mind of a murderer—a startling unconscious confession. She compulsively mentions "blood" at the crime scene over and over. Here are just a few examples:

"[Meredith] emerged from her room with the blood of…vampire still dripping down her chin;" "i stepped out of the shower and… noticed the blood…on the mat…drops of blood in the sink. at first i thought the blood might have come from my ears which i had pierced extrensively…but then immediately i know it wasnt mine… the stains… were too big;"

"i touched the blood in the sink it was caked on already. there was also bloodsmeered on the faucet…it was strange…my roommates and i are very clean…we wouldnt leave blood;"

"apparently her body was laying under a sheet…her foot sticking out…there was a lot of blood."

Thus Burleigh validates a new forensic method of tracing evidence: tracing a murderer's mind, frozen in time, which depicts the murder all over again in one hidden narrative story after another.

It's amazing but hidden between the lines of Burleigh's best seller was another book. That story will become a treatise for how an investigative reporter picks up the truth to which she's oblivious. But then again it took a person like Burleigh—a writer with the gift of imagination and the ability to seamlessly weave images—who identifies the communication model for forensic science as she identifies a suspect speaking in code.

Secretly Burleigh offers more testimony between the lines. In non-stop denial, Burleigh adds that after the murder Knox and Sollecito "did not behave like guilty people."[134] In fact, both repeatedly behaved strangely and in a guilty fashion well documented by multiple people who were there—and in Amanda's unconscious confessions in her writings.

But Burleigh sees what her cherry-picking conscious mind wants to see. She remains oblivious to how her rich imagery describes the cover-up right in front of her and how she participates in it.

Burleigh's blatant denial continues as she proceeds to identify multiple actions reflecting guilt. Staying in Perugia and not calling lawyers reflected Amanda's and Raffaele's unconscious wish to be caught driven by enormous repressed guilt. By getting high before they were interrogated on November 5, 2007, they lowered their impulse-control. The drugs made them more prone to confess, which they did. Amanda insisted on going to the police station with Raffaele when she didn't have to go that night. Raffaele also brought a penknife in his pocket to the police station when he was questioned. Read his behavioral message symbolically, "See I carried a knife when I committed this crime."

Above all she missed the enormous compulsion Amanda felt a mere 48 hours after the murder to put her hidden confession down in writing filled with key details. Burleigh failed to notice how easily Amanda broke on several occasions.

Amanda's Jealousy

Importantly Burleigh claimed special insight into Amanda's relationship with Meredith. She thought Amanda—driven by overwhelming insecurity and jealousy—was going through a self-centered, intensely competitive period with other young women. The author described it as a typical stage of deep envy

---

[134] Ibid, p. 297.

which young women pass through on the way to wholeness. Burleigh implies she speaks from experience.

At one key point Burleigh described how Amanda envied the more sophisticated Meredith but argued that, by itself, it was not a powerful enough motive for murder. Yet on the surface it was powerful enough to serve as an immediate trigger. It was a flaming match, but the dynamite was way down deep in Amanda's psyche.

Unknowingly Burleigh guided herself to delve deeper for a far more violent motive which she avoided. Yet again her super-intel picked up on exactly what it was.

'No Psychic Darkness' – but Trace the Leaks

Burleigh had to comment further on Knox's writings, "Apart from three short stories…nothing Amanda Knox wrote—that the world saw anyway—leaked the slightest trace of psychic darkness. On the contrary, her prison diary and her letters from prison to me, other journalists, and friends were breezy and cheerful…peace signs, smiley faces and hearts."[135]

Again note her keyword—"trace" as in trace the psychic evidence—thoughtprints.

The journalist draws our attention to Amanda's valuable writings surrounding the case symbolized by her diary and her letters from jail to the police, all of which contained valuable confessions. She insists, "nothing Amanda Knox wrote—that the word saw anyway" revealed anything other than cheerfulness. The journalist confesses to her denial that she couldn't see Amanda's deeper messages.

Burleigh's denial confession tells us, "everything Knox wrote," around her imprisonment "leaked" the truth and revealed her psychic darkness. Her reference to Amanda's "letters from prison to me' suggest Burleigh unconsciously had personally reviewed all the jail writings and seen the confessions.

So Burleigh's super-intel issued this instruction: "read everything Knox wrote" after she was jailed or around it. She suggests that is we decode all of Knox's major written communications—the crucial email, signed verbal confessions, hand-written memoriales and her diary—then we'll find darkness almost beyond comprehension.

Burleigh follows up with a matching specific suggestion when she mentions Amanda's hand-written Nov 6th memoriale, "her most important…writing ever, her gift to the cops." (The memoriale reveals a powerful hidden confession—see Chapter Ten.) Burleigh links it to the prosecution's unfulfilled wish for a psychological evaluation. Unconsciously she knows a psychologist trained in decoding thoughtprints could spot the secret

---

[135] Ibid, p. 288

confession, a true gift to the police—the real psychological profile they wanted and needed.

She characterizes Amanda's writings as reflecting only one thing: her "absence of gravitas." But in an almost conscious breakthrough Burleigh's super-intel presents a conundrum, "Was [Amanda] naive to an almost other worldly level? Or was she...*masking evil* behind a screen of pink hearts and flowers?"[136]

No question Amanda was evil—Burleigh's super-intel saw it plainly, using the "e-word." But consciously the reporter saw only hearts and flowers in Amanda and continued to proclaim her innocence.

Tracing Burleigh's reporting thoughtprints, she immediately confirms her denial. She depicts the façade, "Amanda's reflexive passivity in the face of conflict" suggesting passive-aggressive anger and conflict. Then she quotes Amanda's friend, "she doesn't have the skills to fight back" suggesting denial of her fighting. She went on to describe how Amanda thanked the court for doing its job and for trying to bring justice to someone whose life had been taken from this world—a hidden confession she was the one and should be found guilty if the court really did its job. The reporter unconsciously knew there had been a fight that led to murder. But Burleigh saw and reported only the hearts and flowers of gratitude.

Burleigh's super-intel presents its big secret: Pay attention to how I leak information past the conscious mind—and how Amanda did. It comes only in slight traces. You have to look closely to see it, but isn't that the way of science? What Burleigh missed consciously she saw unconsciously.

Burleigh on Her Book: 'Absence of Gravitas'

Recall Burleigh also commented further on Amanda's creative stories, "Taken together, the writings confirmed one thing only: the girl's absence of gravitas." Speaking of cherry picking an image, her super-intel summarizes Burleigh's own book in one grand sweep: an absence of gravitas. Understand these were Burleigh's own words.

They confirm she missed the gravitas of Amanda's unconscious confessions and that truth was wholly neglected in her book. For unconscious powerful reasons of her own, Burleigh reported a fictional story on the crime. She knows her book lacked gravitas, but who could face such a reality?

Of course on a deeper level her book is of enormous importance. It reveals a journalist who has released a super-intel treatise on her blind spots and how she missed a huge story.

She provides one more sterling example in Amanda's own words of how she leaked the truth to the journalist this time in a special email to Burleigh personally on December 17, 2009.

---

[136] Ibid, p. 289.

Trace the Thoughtprints to 'The Email'

Surely Burleigh has seen Amanda's email of November 4, 2007, written right after the murder—and her super-intel would have decoded it for the immediate confession that it was. Unconsciously she points us to that valuable email—the most complete story of the crime. She's shouting, "Think email. Think November 4, 2007 email not far from the December 17, 2009 email I mention now." Burleigh takes us to Amanda's deep time-bomb motive in this later email which perfectly matches the earlier email.

We could predict Amanda's super-intel messages between the lines would contain another important confession—gravitas. Consciously Amanda thinks Burleigh's a friend, unconsciously she must personally confess to her so Burleigh will tell the world.

She writes, *"How young women experience the world and how the world experiences young women...It's an age-old question isn't it?"* Right off Amanda deep down points to the central question in her life since day one: how she as a very young female in the womb experienced that uncertain world and how that womb (i.e. her mother) experienced her.

She continues, *"One [question] that doesn't quite mutate but had peaked* [sic] *it's head out from beneath its shroud to grow and blossom under the direct light of sun.* Strikingly, Amanda presents a head-first partial birth image—coming out into the light to grow and blossom alluding to the peak experience in her life deep down. Note the birth has not been completed, only Amanda's head peeks out of her shroud-womb. The question never goes away in her mind. Did she really make it out of the womb into the world? Is she really alive? Amanda declares that from the get-go she was "The Question." Was her mother pregnant with her—yes she was. Was Amanda, who didn't have a name yet, going to mutate into a false pregnancy? Were they going to keep her? Who knows? Stay with her imagery—the womb was a burial shroud.

Amanda went on in the email, *"I guess any young woman can become a story."*

Read it this way: "Maybe I was going to become a young person and one day a young woman outside the womb and maybe I wasn't—one big constant guess. That's my story."

Amanda continues, *"...I'm not really special other than having to experience a rather exceptional range of experiences the world has felt coming full circle not only regarding me, but also Meredith. It's like we're both in this together...baffled how something so big and exceptional could have happened to both of us, how different our lives became, how horribly hers ended all of a sudden, without us seeing it coming. It's so big and so sad."*

Amanda's super-intel summarizes her deep down story, "It's so big and sad—get it." She was not special from day one. She was an unwanted child. She was nearly aborted. She then brought her pain full circle and took it out on Meredith. Amanda saw it coming for a long time.

In her mind she had to destroy Meredith to survive. Only one of them could live—the stronger of the two, just as Amanda had once been the weak one whom the strong nearly destroyed.

Amanda is shouting at Burleigh, "You want motive? You want darkness? Big deep abiding darkness, utter terror? Big sad terror? So big I could claw and stab the insides of another person until it came out her mouth? It was so big, I could commit a crime you can't handle. Front-page murder. Hear me—so much in pain, so driven that I slaughtered my roommate, stabbed her so badly it was like she had a new mouth. And you want to wash your hands of the story."

Burleigh hears the story and makes sure she gets it in her book first hand with memorable literary skill. She knows it's a huge, tragic story, so big the reporter cannot take it all in—consciously.

Understand Amanda's super-intel knows it's a far bigger story than anyone else realizes. She's uncovering universal truth with specific details. Specifically the meaning of abortion to all concerned. And, in agreement, Burleigh's super-intel repeats Amanda's poignant stories in her own narrative pointing to the same meaning.

Yet can we imagine Burleigh, the ardent feminist, ever owning up to her smarter self, her wiser self, her true self? Owning up to the fact her super-intel is a vastly superior journalist in comparison to her conscious mind? The reporter has the scoop of a lifetime, maybe of the century, and she's unconsciously reporting it.

PART 2: BURLEIGH PROFILES HERSELF

As she turns her all-seeing super intelligence lens on herself, Burleigh again reveals a startling fact—subconscious thinking. She's operating on an entirely separate and vastly higher level of consciousness and intelligence. As we know, it speaks in secret narratives. In reality we experience two separate Nina Burleighs, two separate narratives. Her higher intelligence offers her a chance to meet her better, smarter, truer self.

But she reveals just how difficult the journey to truthfulness can be. She becomes wracked with the worst pain she has ever faced when she discovers that key people in her life are not at all who she thought they were. Her world, as Burleigh knows it, is turned upside down.

Burleigh's unpredictable confrontational personality specializes in shocking others, but now she's faced with the shock of a lifetime. Can she handle her own mind doing to herself what she does to others?

The journalist reveals a full-bodied narrative—a completely unexpected story unless you grasp the pattern: the super-intel *always* surprises.

Telling Own Story: Denial, Anger, and Violence

In reporting on Knox's email, *"I guess any young woman can become a story,"* Burleigh's also revealing her own story between the lines. Just as Amanda provided a glimpse into her subconscious—Burleigh presents a stunning look at her deep unconscious also pointing us to when she was "young." She reveals her extensive blind spots.

Repeatedly Burleigh exposes the omnipresent denial that colors her life and her journalism. Read through her denials and stay with her imagery and we see that she shines the brightest light imaginable on her true self. Unconsciously, she's looking in the mirror for the first time.

Over and over in denial, Burleigh refers to Amanda's rage and how she fails to express her anger. In fact, the forcefulness of the denials makes it clear that Burleigh herself is controlled by secret repressed, not suppressed, anger. Passive-aggressive anger precisely like Amanda's—anger and rage at the heart of Burleigh's primal identity. Her own words provide thoughtprint evidence as she will continue to demonstrate.

She sets the stage—somebody deeply wounded her which led to her fury. We await her secret.

Passive-Aggressive Violence

Consider Burleigh's book dedication: "In memoriam: female victims of sexual violence." First read the dedication more broadly, "In memoriam: victims of…violence." Victims and violence are heavy on her mind. Her super-intel suggests another projection: her book does violence to the truth leaving a lot of victims in her wake.

Consider her memoriam as a warning from deep down: "to readers, potential victims of my secret violence, this book does harm."

Burleigh has worked tirelessly to enable the vicious murderer, Amanda, to go free. She labored long and hard to create an image of Amanda as an innocent victim of injustice.

Was Burleigh trying to tell us she, too, had been an innocent female victim of injustice—way back when? Now read Burleigh's memoriam more specifically, (to) "female victims of… violence." suggesting that she herself has particularly harmed women.

No doubt Burleigh has unconsciously assaulted Amanda Knox. She constantly undermines Amanda's secret wish for freedom: to confess and escape the prison-of-the-mind guilt. The journalist whispers in Knox's ear that it's best to lie about horrifically murdering your roommate. Deep down she wants Amanda to bury her true self.

Above all we must not overlook the violence Burleigh does to Meredith Kercher's family who stand in her place seeking justice, the very justice the reporter would deny them. It's an angry thing to do—overthrow justice, but Burleigh's doing it.

But we wonder, as we decode her super-intel messages, did someone do violence to Burleigh by lying and encouraging her to deny her true self?

Burleigh Encourages Promiscuity/Sexual Addiction

We reflect now on Burleigh's complete memoriam (to) "female victims of sexual violence." Her super-intel suggests that secretly she has done "sexual violence" to women. Sanctioning promiscuity for women is one way she does that. In classic denial, Burleigh insists Amanda Knox was never promiscuous. She steadfastly refuses to see violence in Amanda's promiscuity.[137]

Incredibly, Amanda's documented behavior fails to meet Burleigh's promiscuity criteria. That in spite of the fact that Amanda impulsively had sex with a virtual stranger in a restroom on a train on her way into Italy, took on at least one new sexual partner a week, and spent the entire week before the murder having non-stop intercourse with Raffaele while daring to cheat on him. While Amanda shouts, "I'm addicted to sex," Burleigh puts her hands over her ears. The writer remains in complete denial of how Amanda's promiscuity led to the sexual attack on Meredith which got out of hand resulting in murder.

But Burleigh has already publicly exposed her own indifferently promiscuous mind-set. She once declared—in a notoriously flippant comment about meeting then-President Bill Clinton on Air Force One—"I'd be happy to give him [oral sex] just to thank him for keeping abortion legal."[138] Beneath the jocularity Burleigh's trademark shocking comment suggests total sexual submission to a powerful man in order to avoid a dangerous assault.

Her key idea "keep abortion legal" implies her counter-phobic avoidance mechanism of a deeper unconscious fear— of "an illegal abortion and not being kept."

Burleigh suggests a secret—somebody hurt her terribly as if she had been aborted. Like Amanda, she sexualizes her trauma—converts her vulnerability into sexually aggressive bravado where she's in charge, at least temporarily.

Consciously Burleigh rationalizes promiscuous behavior. Unconsciously she confronts it. She exposed her confusing promiscuous mindset in her counter-phobic in-your-face reporting of playing cards with Clinton when she was a journalist traveling with the press.[139] Burleigh described Clinton's powerful control over her, confessing that she was more than willing to visit his hotel room later if he had only asked. His powerful authority role and also the loneliness she sensed in him made her Clinton's puppet. Burleigh stated a strong, pure woman would have been able to resist—reflecting her healthier

---

[137] In psychotherapy people tell me either blatantly or unconsciously how promiscuity is essentially self-sabotaging, and this fact is often revealed at the same time they are bringing their actions into conscious awareness.

[138] http://newsbusters.org/blogs/paul-bremmer/2013/09/25/msnbc-guest-attacks-boehner-and-cantor-during-segment-amanda-knox

[139] http://www.ninaburleigh.com/journalism/king-of-hearts.html

super-intel moral compass.

Burleigh suggests her own sexual conflicts that she sees in Italian culture. She reports Italians can't handle sexuality, the sexual woman. She notes how they unconsciously split women into either madonnas or whores, and cannot envision a complete woman. Precisely as she just demonstrated with Clinton, she cannot be the self-controlled woman but instead is under a man's control. She speaks of other women who fell under Clinton's spell as "all too willing."

In short Burleigh cannot consistently be the "complete woman"—the faithful wife who enjoys sex with her husband and produces children within the strong boundaries of marriage. She implies a fear of commitments and a fundamental trauma that she had been deeply abandoned.

She moves ever closer to her secret.

Uncovering Abortion Violence

Then we have abortion. What does Burleigh, the self-declared modern feminist, do with her undercover super-intel reporting on that delicate matter?

Unconsciously she reported in courageous fashion on abortion from her unexpected up-close and personal encounter with Amanda Knox. With the vivid descriptions of Amanda's near-abortion trauma, Burleigh's super-intel underscores this fundamental assault on Amanda.

Could the reporter ever endorse inflicting such violence as clawing someone's insides out or attacking someone to the point of total disintegration of a human being if she saw it for what it was? Burleigh's super-intel suggests that endorsing abortion on demand secretly makes her an anti-feminist who attacks women and their womb-mates (just as Amanda had been) making them victims of her violence.

Violence to Truth, Justice, and Knowledge

Straightaway Burleigh has assaulted truth, justice, and in particular the Italian justice system. She portrays the prosecutors and the courts blind to evidence of innocence and disdainful of Amanda's liberated femininity. Burleigh even accused prosecutors of creating the myth that Amanda and Raffaele had "violent tendencies." That's Burleigh's way of unconsciously confessing to her *own* violent tendencies and false narrative.

In an all-knowing fashion filled with intellectual pride and a sophisticated modern science viewpoint, she also attacks true insight and deeper knowledge— her own super-intel's vital feedback.

Anger at God

From the beginning to the end of her book Burleigh makes repeated references to belief and faith. Recall her blatant denial "no believable proof" that Amanda and Raffaele had murdered Meredith and covered it up. But drop the denial and we have "believable proof." Unconsciously she has repeatedly told us this deeper truth: they did, in fact, commit murder.

In another denial she links belief and proof to God. She insists there is no God but her unconscious will tell us the opposite. Burleigh is a proud to be a fifth-generation atheist.

Consider that her atheism reflects a denial confession—God's not there, but my super-intel's fully aware he exists. Burleigh goes on to confirm her atheism represents massive hidden anger.

In the context of Amanda's violent images in her short stories, Burleigh writes,

"To the press, the stories' sinister images…confirmed the presence of a Mr. Hyde buried inside the *smiling girl who never got angry…*who, even after her arrest kept a prison diary filled with…doodles of peace signs…*schoolgirl ruminations on faith versus atheism.*"

First Burleigh attacks God by condescendingly declaring he doesn't exist and is of no concern, just a silly schoolgirl issue. But alluding to Amanda's denial of anger, she's describing herself unconsciously. Behind Burleigh's "schoolgirl" smile she hides a ton of "Mr. Hyde" rage toward God.

Her atheism reflects her attempt to murder God. For some deep reason she's furious with God and has just "murdered him." But her image of "schoolgirl faith" again reveals her immature faith in her conscious mind. At the same time the message marker "schoolgirl" suggests, "Learn about the authority figure who wasn't there for you, the powerful reason behind your rage."

Burleigh presents the mask of "smiles and no anger." Consciously she's certain God's not there. Unconsciously Burleigh has introduced her personal powder-keg issue—something about God and authority figures certainly stirs up her fury.

Mocking God, Paganism, and Evil

Burleigh continues her same thoughtprint confession about God and her disguised anger at him. Consciously God's a trivial, light-hearted matter. Mocking God, she describes Amanda drawing cartoons in jail downplaying her sentence, "Why, oh God, why?" Unconsciously Burleigh confesses her own cavalier belittling of God the overseer.

While she's at it, Burleigh "exposes" Italian Catholicism as a thin veneer of Christianity overlying a "pagan core." Secretly she's confessing to God again about her own iniquities—specifically that she's a hypocritical pagan wearing her veneer of a mask: atheism. Yet somehow she connects herself unconsciously with Christians.

Burleigh's super-intel continues to get to the bottom of her atheism and Amanda's. She writes,

"Was [Amanda] naïve to an almost otherworldly level? Or was

she…*masking evil* behind a screen of pink hearts and flowers?"[140] Read the unconscious message: Burleigh describes herself perfectly. She was naïve to the other world where God reigns—in classic atheistic denial, masking her evil for pronouncing he was nothing, non-existent

And she enabled Amanda's core darkness, denying she murdered. Unconsciously the journalist was in on a conspiracy with Amanda of "masking evil" including Burleigh's denial of the "other-world" God of justice. She sees Amanda in the same boat as a fellow atheist.

Taking her deeper and deeper into her psyche, Burleigh's super-intel calls her "evil" and implies she's secretly overwhelmed with guilt for her dark-side assaults on God—her creator—and for inviting others to join.

Think back to Burleigh's image of how Amanda had "leaked not a trace of psychic darkness." Tracing the journalist's images, her super-intel has just leaked the secret of Burleigh's malevolent atheism and staying in the darkness about God.

More Escapes from God

Unknowingly Burleigh explains her major escapes from God—her masks. Those facades include her atheism, her closed-minded modern scientific views and her fantasies of a parallel universe(s)—an amorphous, undefined world whose existence remains unsupported by any scientific evidence. The writer wants no accountability to God. But decode the message from her super-intel: God is an unseen parallel universe unto himself side-by-side her, unimaginably attuned to her every action. Soon she will tell us just how close God actually is.

Burleigh's Deep Trauma Surfaces

Suddenly in a dramatic turn Burleigh's great secret begins to unfold. In her preoccupation with injustice and innocence regarding Amanda, the journalist explains she was an innocent victim herself.

We see Burleigh deep down repeating the assault on others that her atheistic parents inflicted upon her. It's the deep secret she revealed in comments about "schoolgirl" concerns on "faith versus atheism" and about masks covering rage.

She implies that, when she was a sunny, vulnerable young schoolgirl full of naïveté and trust, her parents imposed the same pain and hopelessness on her which they had received at a similar age. They destroyed her innocent hope and intuitive awareness that there was a God and that life had meaning.

She suggests that when her parents shattered those natural beliefs they wore the mask of a smile to hide their sabotage: "Honey, God's not really there. It's just a childhood wish you'll get over like Santa Claus. Look around. You can't see God. We believe in science, and you will too one day." Her parents forced

---

[140] Ibid, p. 289.

her into atheism, cramming it down her throat, secretly destroying as much hope as possible.

Burleigh confirms how accurately her Knox book's thoughtprints hinted at the secret. In her other writings she tells the story of how her parents imposed their atheism on her,

Burleigh suggests her atheistic parents' destruction of her natural faith in God as a sunny schoolgirl was experienced as a symbolic abortion—emotionally as real as a biological one. Step by step Burleigh indicates she's an *"abortion of faith" survivor.*

"The stateside Burleighs [arriving from Ireland] didn't just have no religion. They actively rejected institutional religion... My grandfather actively despised churches. By the 1970s when I was growing up, the fourth-generation Burleigh was telling the fifth-generation Burleighs [including Nina] that they were free to decide for themselves whether God existed when they were 'old enough' to go to church on their own."[141]

Implying that early on she had a clear sense of self and of God, she was only free to decide about God later. Read her parents' message: "You can seek God on your own after we've programmed you." And, as an adult, that's exactly what Burleigh did and it was a subject she often addressed in her writing. "Churches were anthropological curiosities," she once wrote. "I can count on my fingers the number of times I actually sat in a pew during my childhood." But the reporter's determination to return to church and God would show up later. Unconsciously she was still curious.

Burleigh provides one more clue about her parents' assault on her intuitive young faith. "I often wonder whether this trait [rejecting religion] didn't originate with the man who fled a country [Ireland] where people still blow each other up over theological dogma," she wrote.[142]

Hear her deeper question, "When did her atheism start?" She implies it began as a young girl when it was dangerous for her to believe in God.

Unconsciously she reveals how all-encompassing was the terror she felt if she should violate their atheistic instructions. She might be destroyed—quite literally—for her theological belief in God. Her vivid imagery confirms the picture, "No baptism, no family Bible recording the births, deaths and marriages."

They had, in her mind, destroyed her faith in God—he had died and so had she. But the parents' attack never registered in their conscious minds or hers.

But deep down Burleigh wondered also "why did the family atheism start?" Adeptly, her super-intel declares the trait started with the first atheist fleeing

---

[141] http://www.huffingtonpost.com/nina-burleigh/god-and-christmas-part-tw_b_12773.html
[142] Ibid.

Ireland who linked belief in God (theological dogma) with death and utter destruction. Unconsciously this had triggered the two deepest fears in the human psyche "first death and then the judgment."[143] The terror of death and then the day of count or Judgment Day—giving accountability to God. Deep down every imperfect human being operates on a hidden equation: meeting God equals destruction.

As a result the forefather of atheism in Burleigh's family developed the distorted and protective belief God is imaginary. Better God not exist than to face him became the secret family code. No wonder Burleigh's parents wouldn't let her sit in a church pew—it was too close to sitting down and being enclosed with God. No wonder she reported the longstanding family tradition, "No baptism, no family Bible recording the births, deaths and marriages." The Bible was too close to birth followed by death. A person was in deep trouble with God unless he or she had been baptized—washed clean in atonement forgiveness. So no Bible meant no death really and certainly no judgment. Atheism became the perfect mask.

In turn the family assaulted God with fury at every opportunity. They despised anything that represented God. Then they attacked with their own dogma—"understand, you simple man, God is not there." When Burleigh tells us "my grandfather actively despised churches," she actively perceived the full force of the family wrath.

Burleigh continues this counter-phobic attacking behavior. Once again it's better to be the one with power. Secretly she's still incensed over her parents' assault but buries it and passes it on. She goes on to adopt the same passive-aggressive posture toward people of faith.

Burleigh shows us how, as a journalist, she enacted her parents' anger by behaving just like them. Consciously, from their pedestal of parental omnipotence, they declared there was no God. In her wild reckless reporting subtly disguised as intellectual snobbery, Burleigh declared Amanda innocent. *So smart she couldn't possibly have murdered and Burleigh equally as smart couldn't be anything but an honest peace-loving atheist reporter.* But Burleigh reveals they both possessed a much smarter super intelligence exposing their mutual extraordinary destructiveness.

Her misreporting was an unconscious confession—to demonstrate how wrong her reporting is and just how wrongly she was treated by her parents who reported the false news to her about creation. *Erudite parents certain of their knowledge who couldn't possibly have harmed her greatly*—but they did.

Unconsciously she suggests that her conscious belief in abortion reflected a reenactment of an attack on her as a vulnerable developing youngster. The

---

[143] http://en.wikipedia.org/wiki/Robert_Langs Dr. Langs' extensive clinical work detailed the powerful role of death anxiety deep in the unconscious and a strikingly consistent unconscious moral compass. Scripture extends his thinking, "… it is appointed unto men once to die, but after this the Judgement." Hebrews 9: 27

womb symbolizes the home in which she grew up. *She suggests her parents' destruction of her natural faith in God then was experienced as a symbolic abortion—emotionally as real as a biological one.*

'Abortion of Faith' Survivor

As a young mother herself, Burleigh tells of taking her son to church to expose him to the spiritual life—unconsciously to undo her own trauma. Her son was instantly enthralled—beautiful arches of the church interior were "all I had imagined." Sun streaming through the stained-glass windows—light in her son's life. But when Burleigh spotted the pamphlets in the church vestibule which urged "parishioners to contact their lawmakers about fetal rights," she described how, "The hair on the back of my neck stood up." She grabbed the toddler and bolted.

Instantaneously Burleigh suggests the experience took her back to *her powerful spiritual abortion from God* and her deeply embedded belief that her parents would indeed abort/destroy her if she persisted in her intuitive relationship with God. It was a PTSD flashback. She linked abortion to faith and why she runs from God. She again noted that her young son was duly impressed by the building's majesty: "He was fascinated by the place and didn't want to leave." Burleigh strongly reaffirmed her faith in God even though it had been taken from her as a young child. She did not willingly give it up.

She continued, "Evangelical Christians reading this may be mopping their eyes at the image of that tiny lost soul, snatched away just inches from salvation." Burleigh's super-intel vividly portrays the exact moment her sophisticated parents crudely tore her away from the arms of God. She knew then she was a tiny lost soul snatched away from God—as vivid a picture of a spiritual abortion the gifted and intuitive writer Burleigh could depict. She reflects her deepest self-image: "a tiny lost soul."

She's remains deeply grieved—God is dead, but she knows deep down he's not. Jesus' admonition comes alive, to enter the Kingdom of God one must receive it like a little child.[144] He implies both humility and innate knowledge. Burleigh's images—the rich language of her super intelligence requiring a mature faith—reveal a deep secret of the soul that God is only "inches away."

Surprisingly her super-intel suggests she's not far from embracing God. Don't discount her mention of "salvation. " Like Amanda, she will return to the matter of atonement forgiveness, the only offer on the world's table of religions. Burleigh suggests her super-intel is trying with all its might to break the destructive family cycle of atheism.

Considering again Burleigh's hidden book title, "The Fatal Gift of a Beautiful Life," it indeed fits her perfectly. Her parents had given her life but then suddenly informed her she was now just an accident of atheistic evolution

---

[144] See Luke 18:17.

devoid of purpose. She existed on this earth by pure chance as they did. Now her beautiful gift of life was just an illusion. Nature had just ripped her soul out. The theory of atheistic evolution had claimed another fatality.

But unconsciously Burleigh saw it for what it was—a fatal lie. Deep down she still thought she was a beautiful creation.

At the same time Burleigh has never individuated from her parents, programmed to believe she was evil if she broke the family code of no faith in God. Imagine leaving your parents behind in their fixation on "evil nothingness." The pull to join them in suffering would be off the charts.

Again she followed her parents' instruction and married another trained atheist whose father "a committed atheist...actually threatened his son with a spanking for stepping into a church once." Once more she links physical harm with the slightest belief in God. Burleigh added, "things don't look good for our children's spiritual training." As she was growing up, spirituality was bad news in the Burleigh household.

She further alluded to the deep danger of rejecting atheism. Offended by Christians' "offensive politics" against abortion, she notes they "made it impossible" for her to remain a cultural Christian like her parents. Clearly she links belief to abortion and her parents. Secretly she suggests they made a spiritual life impossible because she would then be destroyed.

As a result she embraced the family faith and substitute religion of politics—here pro-abortion.

Her parents worshipped what their own minds determined was good—ultimately self-worship. Years later this leads Burleigh to declare herself the final word on justice: what her conscious mind shaped by her fear tells her. Then she easily excuses the guilty Knox.

Step by step Burleigh suggests she's an "abortion of faith" survivor. She reflects a deeper PTSD survivor syndrome complete with anger and the subsequent need to re-inflict the fury on someone else. It's the same narrative that came down to her.

Origins of Feminism—Trauma

Uniquely she experienced that trauma as a young girl, a female. Recalling her comment that "any young woman can become a story"— she points to when her central narrative began. Preoccupied lifelong with female victims Burleigh suggests her unconscious conclusion: her faith was aborted early on because she was a meaningless girl.

When she labels "misogyny the last allowable taboo" Burleigh implies the ultimate taboo was an extremely personal violation linked to her eternal destiny. She suggests her deepest question, "How could you allow that, do that to me?"

Still she references her true "daylight seeking" side. She remembers Mennonite neighbors routinely proselytizing her family and sneaking in Advent calendars at Christmastime. In other words, her super-intel snuck in a shining light amidst her darkness attempting to show her the way. All in all, Burleigh has provided a rare glimpse into the battle in the soul between good and evil.

Burleigh's secret takes her deeper and deeper.

Faith and Rage

Indeed Burleigh's super-intel show us all about the eyes of faith as it guides her into deeper unexplored regions of her mind. Declaring a major secret that the unconscious mind contains the pure soul and that the super-intel is really in the business of rescuing souls.[145] She suggests a part of God that indwells us, that seeks to help us find ourselves—a brilliant mind/soul made in the image of God.

Burleigh's super intelligence, with its new eyes, unveils the reality of faith—including the faith needed to decode its messages. It's more real than we thought, more destructive when it's undermined. Her super-intel provides a secret forensic profile of the mind of an atheist.

Burleigh's deep wound left her in a blind rage. She took it out on Christians and God, her parents' preferred target. She once praised fellow atheist Sam Harris' book, *The End of Faith*. She, too, wanted to radically secularize our society and get "God out of Christmas." Burleigh wanted to destroy Christmas for everyone.

Going a step further she embraced the idea of a "Days of Rage" campaign against "pious moralizers"—that is, Christians—where the "Rage-ers would beat the shit out of the offender then hop in their cars and move onto the next town."[146] She also described assaulting a Christian's intimate relationship with God, belittling it as a myth.

Even worse, she calls to mind the first atheist in her family, a man who referred to blowing people up with bombs over "theological dogma." Unconsciously she was murderously furious in her anti-theological "no God" dogma as was her first atheistic relative who "left behind...a long history of bloody religious strife." Similarly, Burleigh leaves the blood of believers scattered about. No Bible, no God, no faith—she wanted the Christian religion decimated.

Burleigh then alluded to words as weapons. Words were her parents' preferred weapons and now hers. Don't think words can't destroy. Simply consider what her parents' words did to her and what her words now do to justice, truth and God. For good or evil, words can conquer the world.

But Burleigh's imagery tells the real story of her parents' very intimate attack on her when, in their own secret "days of rage," they declared "that's the end of your faith"— figuratively beating the crap out of her. It was as if they had bombed her into oblivion over her innate belief in God.

---

[145] The word "psyche" comes from the Greek translated "soul."
[146] http://www.huffingtonpost.com/nina-burleigh/god-and-christmas-part-tw_b_12773.html

Burleigh's Peak Confession: 'I know so little'

Near the end of her book Burleigh makes a startling confession. In its wisdom, her super-intel chose a quote from Shakespeare that best summarizes her blind spots. At this point she's focused on how Italian investigators and the courts ignored forensic evidence at the trial: "It is easy to say that the jury, the judge, and maybe even Mignini were wrong to ignore modern science, but they had their reasons for doing so, reasons that may in fact be as valid as our own faith in it. As Hamlet reminded the rationalist Horatio, 'There are more things in heaven and earth, Horatio, than are dreamt of in your philosophy.'"[147]

Unconsciously she confesses how little her conscious mind really knows, compared to the vast knowledge her super-intel has about earthly matters and heaven itself, the other world.

Intuitively she knows about the earthly matter of Amanda's guilt before the court. She understands a higher science of the mind exists that supported the court's verdict ("reasons…as valid as our own").

Mentioning dreams, Burleigh suggests unconsciously she encodes messages that explain the new forensic scientific method. She links this science to valid reasons for faith. One must believe that this super mind is there or you won't see it. [148] Deeper knowledge, deeper faith.

Burleigh's super-intel also declares that it possesses far more knowledge about subliminal communication between "heaven"—God—and human beings. Deep down she was reading God every moment of her life, and he was reading her. God was the central trigger in the back of everyone's mind—however deeply that terrifying fact gets buried.

Unconsciously Burleigh's fully aware that God had left her a super-intel guide inside, a deeper moral compass exactly like his, compelling her to tell the truth. Her super-intel shouts at Burleigh: "Hear yourself—two separate worlds—earth and heaven."

Stealing Heaven

But like her parents she's passed the destruction along. Deep down Burleigh knows she has hurt thousands of innocent people who are searching for hope, vulnerable victims trying to cling to faith seeking to dispel the despairing assumption that life was a fatal gift. Instead Burleigh endowed them with the fatal gift of lies beginning with her denial of God's existence.

Do not discount Burleigh's (or Shakespeare's) image—heaven. It represents her deepest desire and our deepest narrative. Notice Burleigh's continued references to the "other world." In our far-seeing unconscious

---

[147] Burleigh, p. 304.
[148] Research scientist and scientific philosopher Michael Polanyi underscored how scientific discovery depended upon faith in basic assumptions about human nature. See Polanyi's book, *Personal Knowledge*, University of Chicago Press, 1958.

"heaven" is a very distinct place. The super mind can see from here to there. While we cannot imagine the mockery with which Burleigh the atheist consciously views "heaven," it's simply another mask. If heaven has more knowledge than she does, it's an instantaneous threat. Perchance God knows something about her she doesn't know about herself. Deep in her psyche she wishes for heaven but asks the universal question, "Do I qualify?"

And her great new unconscious has a message for her—look out for your hidden self and your secret fears. Be careful what you mock. Heaven symbolizes Burleigh's greatest fear.

In her soul, Burleigh suggests the biggest crime of all—taking a life permanently in the next world, eternal life. Stealing the gift of heaven from someone.

Tiny Souls

Not only has Burleigh damaged thousands of spiritual souls, in her radical feminism she has enabled horrific abortions which, as a near-victim, Amanda described so vividly. As a crusader for abortion, Burleigh has innocent blood on her hands.

Burleigh heard all of Amanda's powerful super-intel pleadings as the proxy voice for abortion victims.

Recall Burleigh's message of "Christians…mopping their eyes at the image of that tiny lost soul, snatched away just inches from salvation." She also implies an abortion snatches a tiny lost soul literally just inches away from survival outside the womb. Burleigh weeps profusely over their demise.

She thinks all should be saved. These tiny beings possess a tiny soul— making them above all soul mates in the womb. She answers the question of when life begins—the moment you're "tiny." The instant you become a tiny soul, at conception. It's the same way Amanda Knox saw herself from day one in the womb as a living soul.

Burleigh and Knox, with their super intelligence voices, stand as striking witnesses to two destructive abortions: physical and spiritual. They represent *a watershed moment for civilization with the new super-intel lens that shows us ourselves and reveals how the voice of the soul speaks*—and in a high-profile murder case, no less.

Should we be surprised that true-crime stories take us to other overlooked crimes and unsolved murders?

Atonement

All along, Burleigh the journalist has insisted on justice for the innocent and punishment for the guilty. She has punished prosecutors in the Knox case unmercifully, and she has been equally unmerciful toward those who believe in God.

So what does Burleigh secretly imply she deserves on the scales of justice?

She has already told us. Her own inner scales of justice declare self-atonement: an eye for an eye; she deserves to have the crap beaten out of her for beating life and hope out of others; she deserves total obliteration for bombing others out of existence spiritually and physically. She was the terrorist bomber in a religious war—brutally imposing her faith of atheism.

In a kinder moment, Burleigh rules that she should be held in jail permanently. In 2013 she explained that Amanda—guilty, as Burleigh knows—should not return to Italy for her appeal trial " because their system is such that they can put them into jail again right away and hold them...why would you go back?" So here Burleigh implies her own fear of being imprisoned forever for the crimes she has committed.

She even suggests an unconscious awareness of hell—separation from life, from God, from the non-destroyers. Not death but a living death. Such an awareness of a separate other world fits with her vast unconscious knowledge of God, heaven, and justice.

No wonder Burleigh must cling to her mask of atheism. Her unconscious terror of Justice Himself would now be off the charts. She has no answer. But somewhere in her mind she remembers a God of grace. She heard about it long ago in the Christmas carols her atheist parents sang and from her Mennonite missionary neighbors. As she told us, she "knew the story about the baby Jesus."

Now Nina Burleigh's back where Amanda was just as Shakespeare underscored—facing the day of count with only one hope.

But Burleigh has the same two problems with the grace of God as Amanda did. She believes the ultimate authority figure, God—no matter what he says—will destroy her exactly as her parents destroyed her after avowing their perfect love for her and then unknowingly attacking her by passing down their own fathers' sins.

And she now attacks herself—a self-atonement—for punishing others and passing along the same pain.

Burleigh's super-intel instructs her that she must be deprogrammed. Previously she wrote of "religious people (on the right)" who must be deprogrammed with "infinite loving patience."[149]

She suggests that missionary teenagers, for instance, could "In the interest of the future...go door to door in the ghetto" to "at least help us learn to speak their language." Read she needs to learn the language of her super intelligence (and God) now informing her once more how she was a programmed atheist who needs to face her own "ghetto rage." Then, "who knows maybe some conversions will result—to our side." She ends by identifying her old faith, "religious institutions have always known, we can only win one soul at a time," the soul that was given to her alone, no one else. And it can still be won for

---

[149] http://www.huffingtonpost.com/nina-burleigh/god-and-christmas-part-tw_b_12773.html

truth's sake.

Burleigh now must relearn the language of trust, and then she can attain grace.

Final Thoughts

The reporter Burleigh points to the great mystery Amanda alluded to in jail, "Where am I from, and where am I going?" Burleigh heard it and in effect said, "I heard your story, now hear mine. Yes, you were nearly killed, and in return you became a murderer, but look at what I've been doing, sending tiny innocent souls to their graves before they ever made it into the world. Worse yet, I'm also destroying adult souls forever by leading them astray eternally."

In the twist of twists Burleigh admits another huge secret. She writes about guilty Amanda to lessen her own guilt and in an attempt to understand her own abuse. Instinctively she knew enormous buried pain drove Amanda and she sought out the case to find out what it was. Unknowingly her quick-study unconscious sees the whole story of Amanda's near-abortion that haunted her and led to Amanda becoming a vicious murderer.

Suddenly Burleigh then realizes that, as a feminist, she would have likely encouraged Amanda's parents to abort her. *She would have joined them in the utter destruction of the very subject of her book.* She would have taken Amanda's life from her—and carried out the fatal gift of aborting a beautiful life. No wonder Burleigh's tome would center on attacking the great injustice carried out by Italian prosecutors. She was talking about herself.

Beyond Amanda's life, the journalist suggests she would have perhaps advised Mary, the mother of Jesus, to abort her first child. After all Mary was a young pregnant unmarried mother who would face unbearable ridicule from a strict religious community that would never buy such a preposterous idea as a virgin birth. For sure Burleigh doesn't buy it, so why not simply tell Mary "just own up to your sin and spare yourself a lot of suffering? You have your entire life ahead of you." We can almost hear her words now. Of course Burleigh entertains no conscious belief that Jesus was in any real way special.

Nina Burleigh suggests her deepest secret. She went all the way to Italy to investigate and write about a trial unconsciously seeking one man, the one man who could atone for her knowing deep down she was on trial herself for all her injustices. The man whose abortion she could have so easily encouraged while in his mother's womb. All along Burleigh hid that story between the lines, unknowingly searching for her true self, searching for the "baby Jesus." It was just as Burleigh's unconscious told her. She "knew the story."

Atonement Need

Atonement is not a religion but a need. The need may be met by an "otherworldly figure" because of the enormity of the need but it's as real as flesh and blood in this life. It's a need for someone whose sacrificial blood was shed in this world, a cosmic atoner who addresses universal human dilemmas. That's the story Burleigh secretly pursues—the archetype that lies deep in the human psyche. Intuitively she knows the answer lies in one grand narrative. No wonder "religion" is so ridiculed by the intelligentsia like Burleigh. True religion—the person of Jesus—takes them to their own house of horrors, their very human failures in all their shame.

Do we think God—The Super Intelligence himself—is incapable of arranging such a scene in the Amanda Knox murder trial while giving each of the criminals a choice as to whether or not they killed? Bringing together the entire scene sends an increasingly destructive world a message: yes, there are consequences but love has made a way.

As Jesus once said, only the sick need a doctor. The true-crime version is only murderers need forgiveness. When Jesus declared what lurked deep in the hidden heart of man, the first sin he pointed to after evil thoughts was murder.[150]

With one inconceivable twist after another, Burleigh never envisioned that her story and self-profile would take her to these depths. She's a lost angry soul who tells the world how wrong she was and why. Though she's consciously an ardent atheist, unconsciously she's a person of faith which was stolen from her as a youth, and she's secretly trying to find her way back.

---

[150] Matthew 15:19.

Italian Supreme Court: Final Ruling

Amanda's Final Verdict: 'Lucky'

On March 27, 2015, the Italian Supreme Court shocked the world when it ruled in favor of Amanda Knox and Raffaele Sollecito after they filed the final appeals of their murder convictions. They had *twice* been found guilty of murdering Meredith Kercher, once at the original trial in 2009 and again in an appeal court trial in 2014. The Supreme Court's final decision was yet another unexpected twist in this sad saga.

Facing the press in Seattle, Amanda Knox reacted immediately to the March 27 verdict:

"I want to say...I am incredibly grateful for what has happened, for the justice I've received, for the support that I've had from everyone, from my family, from my friends, to strangers, to people like you. You saved my life."[151] "...so grateful...so grateful to have my life back." "All I can say...Right now I'm still absorbing what all of this means. What comes to mind is my gratitude for the life that's been given to me.

Asked what the future held, she said: "I don't know. I'm still absorbing the present moment, which is full of joy."

Asked what she would say to the Kercher family, Amanda said:

"Meredith was my friend...She deserved so much in this life. I'm the lucky one. Thank you."

In a statement earlier in the day, Knox said that knowing she was innocent gave her "strength in the darkest times of this ordeal."

Consciously Amanda is relieved, although she knows she has escaped justice. Unconsciously her super-intel reacts to the verdict revealing what it looks like when a murderer gets off. We pay attention to every word and key phrases.

Revisiting Her Trauma

First, her message marker "I want to say" announces important deeper meanings. Her keyword "gratitude" immediately stands out, "I am incredibly grateful...You saved my life...so grateful...so grateful to have my life back." Amanda was on the verge of death and her life was saved, she has it back. Her

---

[151] http://www.aol.com/article/2015/03/28/amanda-knox-grateful-to-have-my-life-back-after-court-saga/21158865/?icid=maing-grid7%7Chtmlws-main-bb%7Cdl2%7Csec1_lnk3%26pLid%3D635128

super-intel again points to her near-abortion, a pre-birth brush with death which created in her mind a constantly approaching near-death experience.

Indirectly she links this event to her parents, "so incredibly grateful for the support…from my family to strangers…You saved my life." She suggests that her parents, who supported her in Italy, earlier had been strangers to her deep psyche when they'd seriously contemplated taking her life at conception.

She confirms the idea with two message markers, ""All I can say…Right now I'm still absorbing what all of this means." Read it this way: "I'm telling you again the deepest meaning behind this murder—it was driven by my deep unbelievable pain of near-death." Quickly she again provided the deep time-bomb motive in the case. She reminds the world that prosecutors had the missing motive if they had only absorbed her hidden confessions.

Her super-intel then repeats the thoughtprint/image of a life-saving act in even stronger terms, "my gratitude for the life that's been given to me." She declares her parents had wanted to take the life that had been given to her by God.

But now with their heroic efforts to rescue her from 28 more years in an Italian prison, in her mind her parents have finally given her back the life they took from her—but unfortunately it's after the fact of the trauma. Still in a strange way ("for the justice I've received…from parents…strangers") she has "received justice" for all their injustice by unconsciously exposing the true story of her childhood.

The Giver of Life and Justice

Her message marker "still absorbing what all this means" suggests there's more than one meaning to the Supreme Court verdict. There's more to absorb, more to her mind. Her thoughtprints point to God—the giver of life.

Amanda took the life that was given to Meredith alone. Unconsciously she suggests that the God of justice actually exists, and Meredith has not received justice. Amanda can't absorb the meaning of freedom because she's not free.

Amanda Knows the Future

When asked what the future held for her, Amanda's super-intel speaks through a denial confession, "I don't know," meaning sure as the sun comes up "I know deep down." She emphasizes the "present moment…full of joy" but even that she's "still absorbing."

In the back of her mind she knows there's much more to her life beyond this moment. Unconsciously she links joy to Meredith whose friends always described her as a joyful person—but Meredith has no joy now nor does her family.

When asked what she would now say to the Kerchers (and to Meredith), Amanda replied, "Meredith was my friend." She's fully aware she took the life of a friend.

How grateful Meredith would now be if only she had her life back, if only

Amanda had saved her life. Amanda's regret is palpable—but not enough to confess.

Pausing, Amanda added, "She [Meredith] deserved so much in this life. I'm the lucky one." Thank you."

Read it as yet another confession. Meredith "deserved so much...life" she didn't get because Amanda Knox ended it. She further implies that she deserved justice, and Amanda denied her that as well.

Between the lines, Amanda suggests her own verdict, that she herself "deserved life"—a life sentence, so much more than she got. Instead she got lucky, and to the judges she says, "thank you." They administered luck but not justice. Amanda admits they really didn't look closely at the evidence.

But notice two other key words, "this life," was where Meredith deserved more. The next life remains heavily on Amanda's unconscious mind. Meredith didn't get justice in this life, but Amanda knows luck runs out in the next life where reality rules. She's the "lucky one" and Meredith the unlucky one only for now.

Repeating the key word "absorb," she also implies how surprised she was by the verdict. Importantly "absorb" also takes Amanda back to the crime scene where Meredith absorbed physical blows and a brutal stabbing. Afterwards Amanda then spent the night absorbing all the blood up with towels. Day after day in her mind she continually sees the murder and the blood.

Amanda's Mother Confirms Motive

Unknowingly Amanda's mother, Edda Mellas, suggested the secret story of her daughter's time-bomb motive. At the same public press conference staged outside her home following the Italian court's verdict, Mellas briefly announced that the family "was so thankful everything is finally right." With those words, Mellas implies that long ago—many years before Meredith's murder—something in the family wasn't right for Amanda.

Her unconscious mind divulges the dark secret she could never admit to herself consciously. Ever so briefly Mellas takes us back to "right and wrong." And, like everyone who chooses between right and wrong, Amanda must answer for her own choices and behavior.

Darkest Times Ahead

In an earlier public statement the day of the verdict, Amanda said that knowing she was innocent gave her "strength in the darkest times of this ordeal." But unconsciously she points to the true story. Knowing she's guilty affords her no comfort, no inner strength whatsoever. In a real way she now faces the darkest of times, an ordeal unlike any she's been through. Symbolically her unconscious mind speaks about the present.

Knox confesses she has just entered the prison of the mind and heard the cell doors slam behind her. No more court battles, no more fear of justice from law enforcement, but now she must live with her own inner judge deep in her soul holding her forever accountable.

Deep inside she now sees ongoing perpetual darkness—the murky world of the lies that will always haunt her. Again Amanda perceives the world of heavy consequences and heavier justice, and already she can comprehend the final verdict awaiting her there.

Remember, she asked where was she going in the next world—her idea. She got it from a priest, but her unconscious owned it and used it. Remember, too, her declaration that "God is telling the truth." Amanda Knox had a moment of God-realization but continued to lie—to the very deity who gave her life, the God to whom she truly owes her gratitude.

After her post-verdict press conference, Amanda called her co-conspirator, Raffaele Sollecito, to wish him luck. She hints his luck will run out as well.

'Bleeding' Still Haunts Raffaele Sollecito

Shortly after the Supreme Court ruling, Raffaele again followed in Amanda's footsteps by making his own public statements in Italy. Surrounded by his attorneys and his family, he admitted that the shocking verdict had been just a "glimmer of hope...the remotest of chances..." with the "best-case scenario" being a retrial. Quickly he corrects the court's mistaken verdict, hinting that he still deserves to be tried again—and he knows it.

He then eerily describes his family's reaction, "our entire family has gathered...frenzy of...shouts, screams....I was so overwhelmed that I had a moment that I did not realize where I actually was."[152]

At that powerful moment he has dissociated and unconsciously arrives back at the frenzied crime scene as the Manson-like family of three killers took Meredith's life even as she screamed for mercy. His super intelligence—completely taking over—also declares in his dissociative reaction that he deserves to be somewhere else now, in jail. Finally Raffaele comprehends he has been freed in a stroke of luck.

Yet he continues to confess unconsciously as his images harken back to the crime scene, "My heart and soul will be marked for life. This wound will never stop bleeding, it will never heal." [153]

As he marked Meredith permanently, Raffaele can still see the blood flowing ever out of her, her twin stab wounds never healing, leaving his soul permanently stained. In fact, he says, it will never be healed apart from the "remotest of chances." Raffaele's going down with the ship of lies.

With three rapid-fire denial confessions he assigns his own personal sentence:

---

[152] http://www.people.com/article/raffaele-sollecito-speaks-amanda-knox-verdict
[153] http://www.dailymail.co.uk/news/article-3017776/Former-murder-suspect-Raffaele-Sollecito-says-heart-soul-marked-life-despite-judges-clearing-killing-Meredith-Kercher.html

"But now it is time to move on. I no longer want this tragedy to tie us together." "I no longer want to be known as 'Amanda Knox's former Italian boyfriend.' "I want to be known for something else than being connected by the prosecutors to a gruesome murder in which I had no part."

Unconsciously he wants to be forever tied to Amanda, identified as nothing more than her former boyfriend still controlled by her lies. His internal prosecutor will continually punish him for the gruesome murder—his denial making plain he played a major role in the killing. Now he'll live a tragic life as a result of the tragedy he carried out. Consciously he thinks he's free but instead of moving on, he's moving deeper into the prison of the mind.

More Prison of the Mind

Raffaele continues to describe the inside of his new jail asserting deep down he will never be free. "At times, I realize that I do not yet feel a complete sense of freedom," he says. "I was trapped in this for so long that now I won't be able to switch back to how my life was before. Part of me will never be the same. Part of me is destroyed." Just as he entrapped and destroyed Meredith, took her freedom completely away, so will he privately and personally inflict upon himself. He can attempt to bury that voice but the verdict will stand and he will linger in the prison he chooses.

He speaks further about enduring seven years in jail as "a kind of pain without an end" unaware he's unconsciously talking about his new incarceration. Raffaele hints that he has just begun his incredibly lengthy secret prison sentence, one that will never end.

To hammer himself even harder he will never allow another smile deep inside. "I still have a hard time in doing even the most basic things, like smiling. I have to remind myself of how to even smile," he says. "People will say to me: 'Hey! Cheer up! It's all over! Smile!' But for me it hasn't really sunken in."

On the surface he may continue to appear happy but he gives his true intentions away in another striking image. He has plans to be a game developer. In other words, his whole life will still center around playing games with the public, the law and—most of all—himself. He'll live the constantly fearful hermit-life of a player, always hiding. Constantly on the defense, forever fearing that the world might see him for who he actually is.

Raffaele's super-intel guide offered him one way out of his perpetual self-punishment. He recalled "the most beautiful moment without a doubt" was the post-verdict call from his sister informing him of "total acquittal from the High Court."

The door to his mental cell opens only when he approaches the ultimate High Court, publicly owning up to his deed and his lies, seeking the ultimate acquittal—atonement forgiveness drenched in the blood of Jesus the object of

Sollecito's supposed Catholic faith (and coincidentally of Edda Mellas' faith). For those who grieve the lack of justice, they can take comfort in the knowledge that Raffaele Sollecito remains in a metaphoric but nevertheless profoundly punishing prison.

Acknowledgements

In 2012 Dan Dupont, a true-crime reader in California who had studied my earlier book *A Mother Gone Bad* on the JonBenet Ramsey Case, spontaneously wrote me urging me to profile the Amanda Knox case. He was convinced by my "thoughtprint decoding" forensic profiling method as applied to the Ramsey case. For several years he had followed the Knox case and thought her multiple communications were ripe to be decoded. Since I was involved in other projects at the time, I put him off but Dan persisted by sending me several books on the Kercher killing.

Earlier my esteemed psychiatric colleague, the late psychoanalyst Dr. Robert Langs—whose clinical work inspired my method—had also recommended that I profile the Knox case.

One thing led to another and I eventually reviewed the case, but without Dan Dupont this book would never have been written. In September 2014, Dupont passed away after a short illness. While he lived, however, his instincts were spot on about what happened in the murder of Meredith Kercher and that Knox's communications were revealing.

I also owe much gratitude to two fine editors, Russ Tarby and Duncan Jaenicke. The encouragement and feedback of many professionals and friends also sustained me in the difficult task of looking deeply into the brutality that humans can inflict on one another and why. Day by day my respect grows for those on the front lines in law enforcement and the military who attempt to protect us all by containing such impulses in others. At the same time, I'm also uplifted by the reality that every single person possesses an internal moral compass of justice which guides them to unconsciously confess their crimes in various ways often verbally.

About the Author

ANDREW G. HODGES, M.D., is a psychiatrist in private practice. He previously served as an assistant clinical professor of psychiatry at the University of Alabama at Birmingham School of Medicine. Dr. Hodges has helped pioneer a breakthrough to the brilliant unconscious mind, which he explained in his 1994 groundbreaking book *The Deeper Intelligence* (which he now calls the "super intelligence"). The newly discovered unconscious operates hundreds of times faster than the conscious mind. It sees the whole truth including consciously overlooked motives.

A noted forensic profiler, Hodges developed his "thoughtprint decoding" technique by uniquely accessing unconscious super intelligence messages of suspects during criminal investigations. He bases his analyses on forensic documents—verbatim testimony, transcripts of police interrogations, letters and emails created by the suspects.

Dr. Hodges discovered a deeper moral compass which prompts people to invariably tell the truth—between the lines—in the special symbolic "thoughtprint" language of the subconscious. Tracing repeat matching "thoughtprints" —unique in each case— verifies the message. His work has added an entirely new dimension to the science of psycholinguistics.

Law-enforcement authorities nationwide, including the FBI, have consulted him. Criminal investigators and journalists have sought Hodges' expertise on cases ranging from the murder of JonBenét Ramsey in 1996 to the high-profile disappearance of Natalee Holloway in 2005. In the Ramsey case he applied his technique to the infamous ransom note then wrote two highly acclaimed books on the case, *A Mother Gone Bad* and *Who Will Speak for JonBenét?* (Village House, 1998 and 2000).

He also collaborated with the former police chief of the Wichita Police Department in 2005, just weeks before the apprehension of the "BTK killer." Hodges was the only expert to accurately predict that BTK would kill again after 20 years of dormancy, as the perpetrator later confessed.

In the Natalee Holloway case, Hodges described the exact scenario to which Joran van der Sloot confessed in conversations secretly videotaped months after Hodges' prediction. The FBI consulted with Hodges at the request of Aruban authorities who read his profile. His book, *Into the Deep: The Hidden Confession of Natalee's Killer* (Village House, 2007), told the whole story.

He also has written for a major FBI publication and presented his cutting-edge technique at a law-enforcement conference at the FBI training facility in Quantico, Virginia.

In other writings he has shown how super-intel communication helps in understanding leaders and in providing a deeper moral compass to address social issues. He utilized decoding techniques to explore the human personality of Jesus Christ in his book, *Jesus: An Interview Across Time—A Psychiatrist Looks at His Humanity* (Bantam, 1988), which religion columnist Mike McManus called "the most important book I've read besides the Bible." Also Hodges' forthcoming book tells the courageous story of his father's lifesaving WW II exploits, *Behind Nazi Lines: My Father's Heroic Quest to Save 149 World War II POWs* (release August 2015, Berkley Books).

The author has been interviewed extensively in the media with appearances on Fox News, *Geraldo at Large, Hannity*, CNN's *Anderson Cooper 360*, ABC's *The View*, and Court TV.

More Feedback Regarding Dr. Hodges Work:

Dr. Hodges has successfully applied a sound and validated method of decoding the unconscious mind to the world of criminal investigation. This exciting work demands serious consideration.

M. Mark McKee, Psy.D.
Associate Professor of Psychology
Illinois School of Professional Psychology

A remarkable application of a new psychological technique.

Marc Lubin, Ph.D.
Professor of Psychology (retired)
Illinois School of Professional Psychology
Chicago, Illinois

Following this well-validated new forensic method of psycholinguistic decoding sometimes feels like Dr. Watson hurtling behind Hodges' Sherlock Holmes.

Arthur R. Jacobs, MD
Clinical Instructor in Psychiatry
Albert Einstein College of Medicine
Bronx, New York

Regarding the Natalee Holloway Case[154]

In his book on the Natalee Holloway case, Dr. Hodges steps 'out of the box' of conventional law enforcement forensic techniques and shares a remarkable method that reveals one's truth – truth that is thought to be safely locked away. What a powerful tool – law enforcement should wrap their arms around this!

Janice Windham
Supervisory Special Agent, FBI (retired)

154
  Into the Deep: Hidden Confessions of Natalee's Killer (Village House Publishers; 2007)

Andrew Hodges is the ultimate "mindhunter." In this book he retells the Natalee Holloway story from inside the mind of a major suspect. Dr. Hodges has been the courageous reader of the mind from the JonBenet Ramsey ransom note to the search for BTK. Several times I have been along for the ride, listening to him think about forensic cases. Hodges is a practicing psychiatrist who knows how to read the forensic roadmaps to the unconscious.

Patrick J Callahan, PhD, FAPA, ABPS
Fellow, American College of Forensic Examiners

Dr Hodges advances forensic psychiatry and forensic profiling—both lacking new tools particularly in solving puzzling cases. With "thoughtprint decoding" Hodges offers a solid way of getting at crucial overlooked clues. Based on clinical and mathematical work, "thoughtprints" is completely consistent with the notion that every criminal leaves behind clues about their crime. In this gem, Hodges deals with little known workings of the mind that reveal vital information in a disguised form. For the reader who wants the best look imaginable at the criminal mind, this will be a fascinating read.

Harold S. Schaus, Jr., M.S., DAPA Past President
The Society for Communicative Psychoanalysis and Psychotherapy

34992623R00166

Printed in Great Britain
by Amazon